WINE
WESTERN AUSTRALIA

WINE

WESTERN AUSTRALIA

MICHAEL ZEKULICH

The BankWest
CENTENARY
WINE BOOK

ST GEORGE BOOKS

BankWest

Published by St George Books, 219 St Georges Terrace, Perth, Western Australia 6000
— a division of West Australian Newspapers Limited

First published as *Wines and Wineries of the West* 1990; reprinted 1990, 1991

First published as *Wine Western Australia* 1994

© Mike Zekulich 1994

Fully set up on Macintosh computer by P. J. & T. L. Wells Typesetters

Printed and bound by Singapore National Printers Ltd

Edited by Ross Haig

National Library of Australia cataloguing-in-publication data:

Zekulich, Michael.
    Wine Western Australia.

    Bibliography.
    Includes index.
    ISBN 0 86778 055 X.

    1. Wineries – Western Australia. 2. Wine industry – Western Australia. 3. Wine and winemaking – Western Australia.
    I. Title.

338.76632009941

Foreword

WHEN Mike Zekulich produced his original book *Wines and Wineries of the West* it was hailed as a landmark. It was the first time that the long and colourful history of the West Australian wine industry had been so meticulously chronicled from the very first years to the current period.

The success of that first book was testimony to Mike's diligence, perseverance and energy in researching and documenting more than 160 years of our rich wine history.

The result was an outstanding monument to this dedication.

But in the four years since *Wines and Wineries of the West* was published the wine industry in this State has continued to go from strength to strength as established areas expand and new areas come on to the wine map.

In many ways the West Australian wine industry is entering its most exciting period. The State's reputation as a producer of quality, and not quantity, continues to be enhanced as the premium areas at Margaret River and the Great Southern add their considerable weight and influence to traditional wine areas such as the Swan Valley.

Now we are seeing the emergence of other exciting new southern areas such as Pemberton and Manjimup which are sure to add a new dimension to our industry as they develop.

The wine industry in Western Australia has never been healthier. Demand for West Australian wine is strong both within Australia and overseas where, despite intense competition from other countries, our winemakers have been successful in finding niche markets for our limited production premium products.

All this has meant that it is both appropriate and timely for Mike to produce a follow-up book, and BankWest is again delighted to be associated with Mike in this venture, particularly as it coincides with the Bank's own centenary celebrations.

As with his first book, Mike's rapport and empathy with people shine through as he brings the West Australian wine industry to life with his words.

And there is no one better placed to document the industry in this State. Mike was weaned on wine in the Swan Valley where he lived with his parents for many years, and as a journalist on Perth's morning daily *The West Australian* has written about the subject for nearly 30 years.

Mike writes about wine and about people, and that's what this book is all about.

It is also appropriate that BankWest continues its association with the wine industry through Mike's book. We have been keen supporters of the West Australian wine industry and have a comprehensive cellar of West Australian wine. I take great delight in being able to allow our guests the opportunity to appreciate the quality of wine this State can produce.

I congratulate Mike and all those associated with the production of *Wine Western Australia* which I know will be every bit as successful as its predecessor.

I trust you will appreciate and enjoy this book as much as I do.

Good health!

WARWICK G. KENT
Managing Director
BankWest

Your money couldn't be in a better state.

BankWest

Bank of Western Australia Ltd. ACN 050 494 454

Contents

Preface

THERE IS a saying that a week can be a long time in politics. Let me tell you that four years has made a huge difference to the West Australian wine industry. Since St George Books first published my original book, *Wines and Wineries of the West*, in October 1990, the industry has burgeoned. Dozens more vineyards have come into production, from Esperance to Forest Grove (south of Margaret River) and from the Porongurup Range to Gingin. At the same time the number of labels has almost doubled with the State's crush boosted to record levels, and set to continue to rise. Despite a despised Federal Government increase in the tax on wine (1993), export successes have opened up tremendous opportunities for the national industry, including Western Australia. Sales of $1 billion by the turn of the century have been forecast, representing a fourfold increase in the last six years of the decade for the country's winemen, if achieved.

Such was the situation in 1994 that grapegrowers around the nation were being urged to plant more vines to meet the demand, with one national producer restricting exports to some countries to maintain a regular supply to customers in major overseas markets.

The bullish situation did not mean that the industry was growing dollars on vines. Indeed, the competition for sales remains fierce while unseasonable climatic conditions, like heavy rain and hail, and problems with disease, insects and birds remain a constant worry.

No doubt some of the less soundly based producers will fall by the wayside. Nonetheless, it has been stimulating to see the enthusiasm of the newcomers, keen to learn and to do well. I wish them every success and can only hope if there is another edition of this publication in four years' time, they will all be prospering.

For some years in my journalistic career, including many writing about wine, I had considered a book of this nature. The appropriate opportunity, however, seemed never to present itself. Then a combination of circumstances, including the urging of colleagues John Hamilton and Peter Kennedy, renewed my zest to take up the challenge.

There were several other important factors as well, including the support of my employer, West Australian Newspapers Limited, for whom I have worked for 30 years; the sponsorship of BankWest; the help of Ross Haig, manager of St George Books; and the ready acceptance and co-operation of the wine industry.

As with the initial project,too many people have contributed to this renamed, revised and greatly enlarged sequel to list individually. However, I would like to express my gratitude for their assistance to Bill Jamieson and my parents, Joe and Rose Zekulich, who between them have been part of the industry for more than a hundred years.

Most of all, however, I would like to acknowledge the tremendous support of my wife Elka for her outstanding help often under pressure with new technological equipment, my son Wayne for helping us through difficult computer times, and old friend Tony Devitt. This unassuming man with such great knowledge of the industry and its people once again gave me the benefit of his wisdom to proofread my material throughout the intensive three-month writing and research period, the most gruelling of my life. Without the contribution of this trio, the preparation of the material would not have been possible.

At times, when I despaired of ever finishing, my wife kept up her unstinting encouragement while Tony gave up valuable private time, including some of his holidays, to help check details. Bless you both.

Pictures play an important part in this book, and I salute the efforts of West Australian Newspapers Limited photographic colleagues and other commercial photographers for their work (see Acknowledgements) and WAN cartoonist Dean Alston. I would also like to thank Jean Elezovich, whose painting of Swanville Winery, Upper Swan, appears on page 33. The Battye Library too has provided invaluable service.

Another old friend, long-time wine educator and cartographer Rod Properjohn, also played a key role, helping me assess many of the wines submitted for the publication.

To you, the interested consumer, may I wish you enjoyable reading and happier, more knowledgeable drinking from our efforts.

May I take this opportunity for a bit of personal indulgence and dedicate this book to our first granddaughter, Isabelle Rose. May she and her brother, Thomas Cameron Zekulich (our first grandchild) enjoy the wines of Western Australia, and the people involved, as much as I have.

Finally, I hope this contribution will be of significant benefit to the West Australian wine industry, helping to consolidate its long and colourful history for continued healthy expansion into the next century.

MICHAEL ZEKULICH

Introduction

IT IS A WONDER I still have a love of wine, for I hated the stuff as a youngster.

That came about through the chores on the family vineyard in the Swan Valley. One was rather simple, and yet the most hateful of all. It involved filling the family carafe for our mealtime supplies from one of the storage barrels in our small cellar.

I would dip one end of a thin, pale red hose into the wine and take a huge suck at the other end. If I was in good form, a flow of our dry red made from grenache and shiraz grapes would reach the container held below the bottom of the barrel. If not, another suck would be needed, and another . . .

Sure enough, about one in four times the gush of red wine would end up in my mouth, often as I was about to take another suck, thinking I had not drawn the wine. Spluttering and gasping, I would spit the darned stuff out as fast as possible while dashing to a nearby tap for a long drink of lovely fresh water, trying to rid myself of that nasty taste.

Why, I would wonder, couldn't those darned barrels hold my favourite soft drink just for a change!

My father, a 1924 economic migrant to Australia, had brought with him the Dalmatian (Croatia, part of the former Yugoslavia) custom of adding water to wine. I cannot recall him imbibing without eating, except on a stinking hot summer's day while picking grapes. He had found that pouring a bottle of our red over half a billycan of iceblocks was one of the best thirst-quenchers you could have.

I usually stuck to the water bag and certainly did not worry at all about adding any wine to my water at mealtimes, because of my cellar experiences.

We made about 4000 litres a year, for our own use and for certain of Dad's mates who had also migrated to Australia. Some had settled in the eastern goldfields and others in the vegetable-growing areas of Spearwood and Osborne Park, near Perth. In exchange, we would get bags of potatoes and onions or whatever crops were in season, but alas, never gold.

Our other duties included just about everything necessary in running a mixed vineyard operation. For besides wine grapes, we produced table grapes for the local and Asian markets, as well as dried fruit, which was also exported through the local co-operative packing shed, usually to Europe.

Another job I had difficulty with was helping my brother Tony harness our horses. We had two Clydesdales, Mitzy and Ginger, before the blessing of technology and a bank overdraft saw a shiny new Ferguson tractor delivered to our yard.

The size of the horses to a small schoolboy seemed enormous. I would look at their big hooves and feel I could be stamped into oblivion as I moved under their bellies to secure a harness buckle.

Mitzy was the first I recall and when she went to her Heaven for horses, Ginger, a more aggressive fellow, came along. Even though I was bigger by this stage, I was always very wary of him.

Our job was to bring the horses and whatever equipment our father wanted to a spot in the vineyard. They never went willingly and we always had to urge them along. But boy, there were no problems going home. They would almost break into a trot, knowing there was a feed of chaff to come. I can still hear those big munching teeth, making paste of their food.

At winemaking time, until we were strong enough, father would pour the boxes of grapes into a small hand-operated crusher set over a concrete tank. My sister Anne and I would turn the handle while the fruit inside jumped, tumbled and twisted on the revolving crusher spindles, hoping, it seemed, to avoid an inevitable fate. Finally, the grapes would be caught and crushed, disappearing into the vat below, a mixture of juice and berry residue (known as the must).

The stalks were caught in a wire mesh under the crusher and dumped among the vines from where they had come. After fermentation, the wine would be put into wooden barrels with the skins bucketed into an adjacent press, turned by hand with the help of an extension pipe over the steel press lever in order to extract every last drop of wine.

It wasn't very scientific, I suppose, and yet I have often reflected while travelling the world of wines how many people enjoyed drinking a jar or three with my father, yarning about industry affairs and problems while sitting on boxes and sharing some bread and cheese.

Often I would carry the food from the kitchen wondering about the world's first winemakers, recalling a school lesson which informed us that no one knew who they were, but that the Egyptians learnt how to make wine early in their civilisation. Then wine had a more practical reason than drinking for pleasure. Ancient people had little pure water and had found that alcohol formed by fermentation helped to prevent fruit juice from spoiling. Those drinking the fermented juice, it was said, did not get as sick as often as those drinking impure water.

I would also wonder at the cellar door, passing over the plate of cheese and bread, why adults did not get sick drinking, as I observed, more than the odd glass.

Closing my eyes, I can still see the inside of the old cellar, its only window made up of squares of tin, the glass broken too many times by cricket balls to be replaced. The barrels were set in two lines on a dusty concrete floor, smelling as only old barrels in a cellar can. There was certainly nothing glamorous about our operation, no romance or mystique like television or glossy magazine advertisements might have one believe.

In the less busy times, however, as infrequent as they seemed, we kids had our share of fun. Indeed, our existence, though poor in financial terms, was rich in life. With the Swan River so close, it was something of a Huckleberry Finn existence, swimming in the long, deep pool called The Lookout. Roaming to and fro on our bicycles, we could always find an orange or mandarin to plunder, perhaps a watermelon or a bunch of early ripening grapes before one grew heartily sick of them. There was fishing in the river, gilgies (freshwater crustaceans like a yabby) in the Majstrovich creek or in my grandmother's flooded cellar where we had brought small ones to grow, and in season, mushrooms. During World War II, these became a lucrative source of income for me. I would stand by the Great Northern Highway in front of our home, holding up a billyful to show passing convoys of military personnel. Very quickly, a vehicle would slow down and someone would jump off. It was always more lucrative if it was an American, for they had no idea of our pounds, shillings and pence system. Often they would say: 'Hey kid, is this enough?', pouring coins into my hand, two and three shillings, a fortune at the time for a small boy.

Sometimes, joyously, there would be a bonus of a rarely seen chocolate bar or some chewing gum, reward for information on where to buy wine.

I would often recall such incidents as a teenager to take my mind from the tedious task of picking grapes and making wine. To us, vintage was just plain, old-fashioned hard work, especially without mechanical aids. I can still feel my aching back from bending over low vines, cutting off bunch after bunch, the sun burning from above, and the sand from below.

Oh, then, how I would envy my Midland schoolmates, knowing they would be down at Scarborough or City Beach, enjoying the cool refreshing waters of the Indian Ocean, sharing their time with all those lovely girls.

Then I would mutter: 'Damn the grapes, damn the grapes . . .'

Industry in Review

THE VALUABLE West Australian wine industry has a rich and long history. From humble beginnings when inexperienced English settlers planted the first vines, the State's vineyards have produced some of the finest wines in the world, recognised at international competitions against the best from major producing nations.

Today throughout the southern half of Western Australia vineyards flourish with many new and exciting projects set to maintain, and indeed enhance the sound reputation won over the years.

But while vine plantings date back to the settlement of the Swan River Colony, the industry, in premium table wine terms, is really barely 30 years old. For it was not until the 1960s that Western Australia (and Australia generally) began to realise that the future lay in table wines as opposed to fortifieds, no matter how good these wines were. Indeed, up until then many people were not interested in wine, seeing the product as part of the none-too-savoury wine saloons which dotted Perth and other centres, attracting customers not associated with good food and wine, rather the consumption of alcohol.

Margaret River pioneer Dr Tom Cullity told me that as a boy before World War II, his parents would take him to up-market places like Perth's elegant Palace Hotel for a meal. 'You would never see wine on the table', he said, 'only whisky and beer. And if you had not finished eating by about seven-thirty, too bad. The waitresses would just go ahead and clear the table anyway. You did not have much choice. There were not the restaurants around as alternatives like there are today.'

I remember inviting a school friend from Midland home in 1950 for the weekend. The red wine on our kitchen table was a shock to him.

Despite living a few kilometres from the centre of West Australian viticulture, he had never seen wine drunk with a meal, while the garlic in the roast lamb was a stench to him, such that he screwed up his nose in disgust.

I have often since wondered how general was his lack of understanding of another culture. Friends at school had told me that his impression of my father was something of a drunk. Nothing, of course, could be further from the truth. Like many Europeans, my father would sometimes have a 20-minute siesta after lunch, a rest before resuming work, for he was often up as early as 5 a.m. It was certainly nothing to do with having a glass of wine and water with his midday meal.

How much this situation has changed. Now, those who do not partake of garlic-flavoured dishes and wine are the minority; Australians across the board enjoy the delights of good multicultural food enhanced by the product of the processed grape.

An important transition to serious wines for many during this period were products like Barossa Pearl, Rhinegold and Woodley's Est. A night out in the '50s involved a couple of bottles of such fun products which were winners, especially with the ladies. Those wines, however, would not have been in the minds of the pioneers who found that vine establishment was no easy task.

The story of viticulture in Western Australia began before the official founding of the Colony, and before the first settlers arrived on Garden Island. Records show that Captain Fremantle, who had been instructed to prepare a camp for the newcomers, set to clearing and digging the land for a garden, near the mouth of the Swan River, just south of Arthur's Head. In a diary entry for 8 May 1829, he wrote: 'I thought it advisable to plant the cuttings of the grapevines I had brought from the Cape of Good Hope in the best of the earth near the tents on the beach'. To the modern day vine grower, that would hardly seem the right place, and it is almost certain that none of the cuttings survived.

Then professional horticulturist James Drummond, having brought rooted vines with him on the *Parmelia* from England, proceeded to plant them on Garden Island. But again, there is no record of their survival. Botanist Thomas Waters, who arrived three months later, brought cuttings and rooted vines from the Cape to provide the beginnings for Olive Farm at South Guildford, still in existence today. He had gathered stock at the historic Constantia vineyard near Cape Town, whose wines Napoleon Bonaparte had lauded. When he was imprisoned by the British on the island of St Helena, one of the privileges given was that he should be able to eat and drink in the style to which he had been accustomed as Emperor. He chose for his prison table champagne and claret from France along with wine from Constantia.

According to the Department of Agriculture's publication *Agriculture in Western Australia 1829-1979*, produced for the State's 150th celebrations, it is generally accepted that Charles McFaull was responsible for the first successful introduction of grapevines into the Colony. In 1830 at Hamilton Hill he planted 300 cuttings which he had obtained from the Cape. But the soils at the site were considered unsuitable, and the cuttings were lifted and taken to a nursery location at the foot of Mount Eliza (Kings Park) apart from several which were presented to Governor Stirling. These were planted in what is today Supreme Court gardens in Perth.

Another reference identified the grape variety as royal muscadine. By 1833 the canes were reported to be some ten metres long with many settlers placing orders for cuttings. At that time, the wine-producing prospects were considered promising, and the foothills of the Darling Ranges were compared favourably with the wine districts of France, Spain and Italy.

The *Perth Gazette* of 16 February 1833 reported: 'The vines in the Botanic Gardens are flourishing most luxuriantly, and the rapid progress the vine has made in the Colony wherever properly attended to has established beyond a doubt that both the soil and the climate are admirably adapted for its cultivation. We have not the slightest doubt that a peculiarly rich flavour would be imparted to the grape.'

Two years later interest in the grape was reported as lively with a meeting of Agricultural Society directors in September 1841 canvassing the possibility of introducing European labour because of the lack of skills in winemaking and grapegrowing among English settlers. Eventually, a motion was proposed to introduce Moravians into the Colony. It was also decided to offer a prize of £2 10s for the best example of not less than five pounds of raisins with a similar prize for a gallon of wine made from locally grown grapes.

George Fletcher Moore, who became the Colony's first Advocate General in 1834, also brought rooted grapevine cuttings from Cape Town. He is credited with being the first to plant grapevines in the Swan Valley, destined to become the heart of the industry in the State, producing millions of dollars worth of fresh table grapes for local and export markets, dried fruit and wine, a complete range from fortifieds to dry whites and red, and sweet styles, in bulk and bottles.

The spread of early plantings continued along the reaches of the Swan, Helena and Canning rivers, and within 15 years of settlement vines were planted to the south of Perth at Australind, near Bunbury, and at Toodyay in the Darling Ranges to the east. Other early vineyard areas were at Katanning, Glen Forrest, Bakers Hill, Armadale, Vasse and New Norcia.

Two big early land grants on the Swan, still enjoying major industry positions, were those which became Sandalford and Houghton. The former was made to the Colony's first Surveyor General, John Septimus Roe, while Houghton had more diverse beginnings.

Originally assigned to Revett Henry Bland, the estate became a legal entity on 1 November 1836 with the transfer of deeds through the purchase by a syndicate of British Army officers serving in India — Lieutenant Ninian Lowis, Lieutenant Colonel Richmond Houghton and the retired Thomas Newte Yule. The property was named after the Colonel as he was the senior ranking officer, but he never set foot on the prime site. Yule did, to manage the estate and to become an important member of the small community.

Prior to this, however, he was arrested for murder when he was involved in the only duel to have occurred in the Colony. In 1832 he acted as a second for merchant George French Johnson who fought solicitor William Nairne Clark at Fremantle. Johnson was fatally wounded with Clark, his second and Yule all being arrested and charged with murder.

Fortunately for them they were acquitted. Noted historian Rica Erickson, in a paper called 'A Gentleman of Misfortune', described Yule as a man fond of good company,

Thomas Yule, one of a syndicate which acquired Houghton estate in 1836

good food and drink. She wrote: 'There were many dinners given and since Yule was a noted wit, every party that he attended was expected to be a merry affair'.

Botanist Thomas Waters, who established Olive Farm, is acknowledged as having made Western Australia's first wine in 1834. Other attempts were made on a limited scale in 1838 with one of the earliest, credited to John Septimus Roe in 1840, revealing commercial promise.

Closer to Perth, on the South Perth foreshore, the quality of grapes grown in the 1840s was described as superb. Produced from vines planted by French-born settler Charles Tondut, their sweetness attracted praise from the Governor of the day, Charles Fitzgerald, who would gallop his favourite hack to the vineyard each Sunday afternoon to enjoy a chat and a glass of wine. Tondut, or 'Pappa' as he became known, was the first to be granted a licence to sell wine to the public. A colourful character, he had jumped ship, a French whaler, in Albany to walk to Perth with a crewmate to establish a new life.

A report of a meeting in October 1845 of the Vineyard Society by its president, Mr. R. W. Nash, referred to vineyard plans of three acres by a Mr Duffield three kilometres from Fremantle, made up of 5700 plants 'all thriving extremely well'. The report commented that the 'success attended upon this trial was considered the more praise-worthy and remarkable from the fact of the soil being about the worst known in the whole district'.

Mr Nash went on to record samples of wines exhibited, both dry and sweet, as being too numerous to specify individually. 'Altogether, the samples sent afforded excellent proof of the progress in this manufacture and were highly encouraging of the success to be obtained from future and more mature operations.'

About this time the society also recorded that the use of hawks in gardens kept small birds away, a move adopted at Margaret River some 125 years later without success.

In August 1861 a Mr W. Burges wrote in the *Perth Gazette* that samples of wine had been highly approved in England. Three casks were drunk at the United Services Club and much liked, with more asked for. He had made arrangements to visit principal vineyards in the south of France and Germany to learn 'by actual experience the art of winemaking'. He said: 'The Duke of Newcastle has agreed to give free passage to all practical winemakers and their families that I can induce to go out to the Colony. All in the Colony, who wish to cultivate the vine on a large scale and make a good wine fit for export, ought to write to me at once and say they will give permanent employment to such men. This opportunity should not be lost.'

Mr Burges received strong support a few months later when a leading article in the same newspaper urged settlers not to leave their money in the bank, but to invest in vine production. 'The cultivation of the vine in all the sister Colonies is being pushed with the greatest vigour', the paper noted, adding some more advice:

'This supineness on the part of the settlers is not owing to the vine being an unprofitable culture, as on the contrary, we know of many instances in which no other crop could have produced so large a return for the capital and labour invested. We believe the production of wine by careful selection of soil, the right sort of vine and careful manufacture, though requiring a greater amount of capital than for dried fruit production, might be made equally if not more profitable and there is little fear of the market offering for any quantity or even quality we can produce as shipments to England of some of our poorest have found ready purchasers.'

Such words must have inspired Dr John Ferguson, the Colonial Surgeon who had purchased Houghton in 1859 for £350. Like many other medicos, Dr Ferguson believed in the health-giving qualities of wine and his purchase of the property was to prove significant in the developing history of the industry in the State. This was mainly through the energy and enterprise of his son Charles who spent 50 dedicated years living and working on the property to ensure its progress.

Charles wrote once of a bizarre incident at the winery relating to the recapture of the elusive bushranger 'Moondyne Joe' whose real name was John Bolitho Johns. The eyewitness account had been left among some personal effects and discovered by his son Don for whom my brother-in-law Len Radalj had worked for many years. An excited Len had telephoned *The West Australian* to tell me of the find which was duly passed on.

Moondyne, who had eluded a manhunt for almost two years after a daring escape from Fremantle gaol, had chosen the evening of 26 February 1869 to raid the Houghton cellars. It was to prove a serious mistake.

The previous day, Mr Ferguson had received a message that a man had drowned in the river at Upper Swan. He notified the police in Guildford and two mounted troopers, with a dozen other men, found the body about one o'clock the next morning. The searchers, who were all wet and cold, were invited to the wine cellars for a drink. Unbeknown to them, Johns had picked that night to break into the cellars to steal wine.

Moondyne was well over six feet tall and, though spare of build, he was extremely powerful and an experienced bushman and horserider. He knew every inch of the country between the Helena River, the head of the Swan and Chittering Brook. When caught, his hair was growing in long plaits over his shoulders and he had a long beard. He was carrying two empty kegs in a sack and his boots were covered with sheepskins to disguise his tracks. In a small canvas bag round his neck were six skeleton keys, a brass tap, a lantern and a club.

Unfortunately for Johns, he arrived at the cellars only a short time before the search party. When Mr Ferguson put his key in the lock of the cellar door he found it was unlocked. He thought it strange but concluded that it had not been locked when work was finished for the day. He lit a candle and started to walk along the cellar, between the rows of wine barrels. The spluttering flame lit only a few feet in front of him. A man was behind him carrying an empty jug. They had gone only a few feet when there was an unearthly yell and the tall figure of a long-haired man sprang out of the darkness. He struck at Mr Ferguson with his club, lunged at the man carrying the jug and dashed towards the door straight into the arms of the two troopers.

It was some time before the weird figure was recognised as Moondyne Joe, a catch indeed. Johns coolly asked for a drink because he said he did not have time to get one before he heard voices.

If Moondyne was alive today, he would find a vastly different Houghton with a most modern winery, perhaps as good as any in the land. Yet it was very different in those early days. Don Ferguson told me his father had also written that 'The grapes were all trodden with bare feet in a long trough with a false bottom'.

According to the *Inquirer* of 11 December 1878, the Colony's first international medal was awarded to Richard W. Hardey of the Peninsula in Maylands, for Colonial wine at the Paris Exhibition. Pleased Perth and Fremantle agents Ferguson and Mumme advertised large quantities of old red and white wines on hand, including those which took the prize.

Once again the *Inquirer* took up the cudgels for industry action with a leading article in June 1881. It said the moment for vignerons of the Colony to stir themselves had arrived. In the eastern colonies, prejudice against local wines had died out such that wines of Australia found as ready a sale as those of Europe. Winemakers were urged with 'might and main' to improve on their efforts. 'Let us hope that the people of Western Australia are convinced that the prejudice against Colonial wines has passed away among them', exhorted the article.

About this time vine growers round the world had become concerned about phylloxera, a plant louse that had ravaged European vineyards earlier in the century and which had spread rapidly. It reached Victoria in 1876, and ten years later was discovered at Cape Town. Fortunately for Western Australia, keen horticulturists such as Harper, Waylen and Ferguson, who were alive to the dangers of allowing the louse into the Colony, pressed for a ban on the importation of any vine material except from South Australia, which was known to be free of the pest. To this day, phylloxera has not affected the vineyards of the State, testimony to those responsible for the good health of the industry.

By 1895 vine growing was still small scale with only 240 hectares planted to wine grapes producing 225,000 litres of wine, the main centres being the Swan Valley, Toodyay and York, and the areas around Guildford and Fremantle. No large areas had been planted because there were not enough consumers. The discovery of gold, however, boosted the population enormously with a dramatic upsurge in wine production, almost fourfold to 837,000 litres by 1905.

The situation had led to a number of vine and fruit grower associations being formed, which were extremely active. Among other things they pressed for quarantine measures to protect their industries, and they sought the appointment of a travelling viticultural expert. By the turn of the century most of their requests had been acceded to, including the appointment of Adrian Jean Despeissis whose authoritative textbook *The Handbook of Horticulture and Viticulture of Western Australia* is still a bible to some.

In his introduction he asserted that the awakening of Western Australia as a fruit-producing area dated only from the beginning of the goldrush days. Prior to this the

For the princely sum of £350, Colonial Surgeon Dr John Ferguson bought Houghton in 1859. For half a century his son Charles (below) strove to improve the property

Colony had proved it could produce grapes and fruit of great excellence, but gardens were few in number and far apart.

One of them was St Leonards at West Swan, established by Edward Pomeroy Barrett-Lennard, a pioneering settler. A relative later wrote about a large dinner party of VIPs, including the Governor and his wife, invited to enjoy some of the fare of the property. 'People were talking happily away when the cook appeared with eyes rolling heavenwards, extremely agitated and quite incoherent. It appeared, after he had been calmed down, that one of the kangaroo dogs had burst through the kitchen door and seized the large roast suckling pig resting on the oven door ready to be taken to the dining room, and made off with it, dragging it over the floor and through the dirt outside.'

The family went on to establish Belhus at Upper Swan, one of the finest table grape-producing vineyards in the country.

I can recall watching the pickers and packers at work as a small boy soon after World War II, preparing thousands of cases of prime fresh fruit for export to South East Asia in granulated cork. A few years earlier, 22,000 cases were exported to London in one season, fetching £5 a case at a time when wages were £4 a week.

Recognition of the quality of the fruit (and wine) came early in the property's history. For example, certificates of merit and gold and silver medals were won at the French Exposition Universelle in 1900, the Glasgow International Exhibition in 1901, the Franco-British Exhibition in 1908, and the Malay Borneo Exhibition in 1922.

Edward Pomeroy, the fifth son of Sir Thomas Barrett-Lennard and grandson of Lord Dacre of Belhus in County Essex, arrived in the Colony on the *Marquis of Angelsea* on 23 August 1829 to take up St Leonards for the purpose of running stock and growing crops. In 1896 grandson George purchased Belhus and using indentured Chinese labour set about its development, planting vines for wine and fresh fruit. He also had a profitable sideline; lucerne for export to India, for British army polo ponies.

St Aubyn (more popularly known as Norm) and his brother Trevor carried on with the property, tending some 60 hectares of vines, including a trellis so large that tourist buses could drive under it. The property was subsequently subdivided, providing for small vineyards and other developments. Descendant John Barrett-Lennard, a former winemaker who ran Sveta Maria winery in the Perth suburb of Bassendean for 12 years (since redeveloped into units), still grows grapes on part of the original estate, where many vines continue to flourish.

Then again, vines do very well in many parts of the planet. I recall on a visit to a vine and wine museum in San Francisco being told that the grapevine often seems to be the pampered darling of nature. It thrives in all but the most inhospitable climates, nestles its roots in gravelly soils and yields fruit without a great deal of tending. Given sun, water and loving care, a vine, no matter how grizzled, can be a prodigious producer.

Through the ages, though, growers have sought yet another aid, that of divine providence, often through pious devotion to various saints. In the 12th century, for example, Saint Genevieve, Patron Saint of Paris, was credited with rewarding the labourers for their zeal by supplying them with wine from a bottomless well. In German-speaking wine-growing areas, an important patron saint is Saint Urban. Farmers once believed that sunshine on 25 May, his feast day, promised a good grape crop. Rain meant a poor crop in the offing and the farmers sometimes showed their displeasure by upending the statue of the saint in a watering trough.

In my journalistic career I have found no evidence of superstitions or practices based on mythical beliefs in the West Australian industry. But a shocking incident in the Perth Hills in February 1903, however, could have led to stories of a ghost among the vines.

It involved the bizarre murder of Swiss wineman Charles Lauffer who set up the Helena River Nursery in 1897 with Jacob Hawter. The drama began when a party of French picnickers, five men and three prostitutes from a Fremantle brothel, arrived on the 9.10 a.m. train on Wednesday 4 February for an outing in the hills. They proceeded initially to the Glen Hardey cellars at Smith's Mill, now Glen Forrest, where they purchased a cask of wine for delivery to the nearby railway station. They also bought six bottles of wine (local vendors could not sell less than this number at a time) to drink with their lunch in a nearby shed. The party carried a revolver, from which shots were fired during the time at Glen Hardey, and a small shotgun. About noon, they headed off in high spirits, and at Lauffer's they asked for a bottle of wine. An argument erupted apparently when the winemaker explained that by law he could not sell less than six bottles, and a fight developed. Two quick shots were fired and Lauffer crumpled and fell.

The police at Mundaring were advised by telegraph and the French party returned to Glen Hardey. According to a witness one of them, Frederic Maillat, was wearing Lauffer's hat when arrested.

On the arrival of a Constable Gannon, the whole group was chained to a tree in front of Smith's Mill station while waiting for a train to take them to the security of the Guildford lockup. All eight were later charged with murder with six found guilty. Eventually, an appeal acquitted all except Maillat who was hanged on 21 April 1903.

I visited the Glen Hardey winery before a distressing fire prevented the historic building from being restored. Built in 1896, it was a superb example of the craftsmanship of the period. At the time it was constructed, it contained the most modern features of Australia's best wineries and was the finest in the Colony. The builders had skilfully used the side of a hill so that the wine was gravitated during the winemaking process, to avoid the use of pumps. A similar technique was used at the Coorinja winery at Toodyay owned by the Wood family, who at one stage owned Glen Hardey. Present day members of the family say that Thornton Wood, in his first vintage in 1919, made 54,000 litres of wine on his own, while still a teenager. At the turn of the century, more than 100,000 litres of wine a year were produced at Smith's Mill, of which more than 60 per cent was made at Glen Hardey.

I talked about the winery to another owner, a Mr A. Summers, whose home was a few hundred metres away, across a picturesque and peaceful valley. Recalling the time he entered the old cellars for the first time, he said he noticed a strong smell which initially seemed a bit of a mystery. 'Then we looked around and found that all the port in a ten-gallon cask, the last left in the place, had spilt on to the ground. The cask was the only one in the place that had a cork bung. A rat had taken to it, and eaten enough of the cork to let out all the wine.'

I recall a report of a visit in 1902 to the winery by a representative of the *Swan Express*. He wrote that the building up the hillside had sliding doors at one end with a platform the height of a cart outside. Here, at vintage time, carts laden with grapes in small barrels were brought and placed in trolleys which ran along an overhead tramway to the crushing machine, which was mounted on wheels, and could be moved along to the required position.

The grapes were tipped from the barrel into the crusher which was turned by manpower. The skins, juice and seeds which escaped the separating processing then dropped to a huge vat beneath. A number of these were arranged in a line below and served the dual purpose of fermentation and storage vats.

When the juice of the grapes was sufficiently matured it was drawn from the vats by means of a siphon and run into casks in the next building, the floor of which was several feet lower.

The crushed berries left in the vat were then placed in a circular cage of heavy

The ravages of fire, the elements and neglect took their toll on the historic Glen Hardey establishment. The disused cellars continued to decay after this picture was taken

wooden strips and a heavy pressure placed upon it to press out what juice remained.

The process of clearing and purifying the wine was accomplished by drawing it through siphons from one cask to another, the settlings being cleansed from each cask as soon as it was empty.

Richard Watson Hardey began clearing the land and planting the vines in the early 1880s, for the establishment of Glen Hardey.

It was a daunting task, given the terracing of the slopes required on Chittawarra Brook that are still visible today. Eventually, 14 hectares of vines graced what was a clearing in the forest, ten hectares of red and the rest white. Until the winery was built, grapes were packed into baskets, taken to Smith's Mill siding by horse and cart and then by train to Maylands where Mr Hardey's father had set up a vineyard and winery.

The last winemaker at Glen Hardey was Walter James, son of a former West Australian Premier, Sir Walter James. Walter the son was recognised as the doyen of Australian wine writers in his day and a number of his books are still widely used as references in the industry.

The push of the railway into the hills was significant for those would-be orchardists and vignerons who sought out the fertile valleys close to the new line. Enthusiasts believed vines would do well because the gravelly ironstone soils of the slopes resembled those of Graves in the Bordeaux region of France.

One of the successful applicants for land was Dr Alfred Waylen who established the Darlington vineyard, the cellars of which were later to become part of the local hall. He married a cousin of Richard Hardey (of Glen Hardey) and also owned the Garden Hill vineyard at Guildford. Of this property, Government Viticulturist Adrian Despeissis wrote in 1900: 'The vineyard is planted on a heavy loam rise overlooking the left bank of the Swan. The soil, as was the practice in the early days of vinegrowing in Australia, was trenched by hand labour with the result that some of the more retentive red clay subsoil was brought up to the surface and rendered cultivation rather heavy. The vines are mostly aramon, locally called fontainebleau, and morastel, known in Western Australia as burgundy. Unlike the aramon in the south of France which is somewhat thin and poor in colour, that grape produces here a more robust wine to which body and colour is further added by the admixture of morastel.'

On 31 March 1886 a long advertisement appeared in *The West Australian*. It read in part: 'Darlington Vineyard. The well-known property belonging to A. R. Waylen Esq., M.D., consists of 150 acres freehold, being amongst one of the first sections of the Eastern Railway line and especially selected for vine growing by the owner.

'Improvements consisting of 24 acres planted with choice vines, 3-roomed cottage, stable and 30-acre paddock fenced with sheep-proof fence of which 4 acres are cleared. The vineyard has been thoroughly cleared and is fenced with wire netting, barbed wires and mahogany posts. The vines comprise burgundy, fontainebleau and shiraz for red wine, sweetwaters, pedro and riesling for white wine. The supply of permanent water is from three wells and any quantity can be obtained by shallow sinking. The greater portion of the Darlington soil is suitable for fruit growing. The present plant consists of horse, cart, scarifier and all necessary tools. At the suggestion of one or two friends, Dr. Waylen has decided, in order to increase the present area under vines and extend operations, to open a share list upon the following terms. Present capital to be 20 shares of one hundred and fifty pounds each, of which Dr. Waylen receives (fully paid up) 10 shares to recompense him for his outlay (about twelve hundred pounds) and for supervision and goodwill to date, say three hundred pounds or 2 shares. There are therefore only 20 shares to dispose of and upon the amount of these shares (fifteen hundred pounds) having been expended in increasing the area of planted vines, wages and other improvements. Dr. Waylen is prepared, if necessary, either to go halves in future expenditure, or concur in a further issue of shares and so increasing the concern.'

Further east were two other significant developments, at Mundaring and Bakers Hill.

Peter Anthony Gugeri was the first to acquire freehold land at Mundaring. Educated on the Continent with wine industry experience in Italy, he came to Western Australia in 1871, renting 6.5 hectares at Houghton on the Swan River. For three years he built up a stock of wine to go in to business as a wine merchant in Hay Street, Perth, opposite the Town Hall. The business was successful and he continued to buy grapes and make wine when in 1882 he took up land in the hills to establish an extensive vineyard and orchard called St Barnard. By 1888 he was handling about a third of the whole wine and spirit trade of the State.

He quit the property in 1893, with the collapse of the Kimberley goldfields adversely affecting his business. As well, exceptional frost made the vineyard unprofitable.

However, this did not appear to daunt purchasing brothers Mathieson and Frederick Jacoby, and father Daniel, who was proprietor of the Café de Paris in Murray Street, Perth. About ten hectares were under vines at the time, including aramon, shiraz, morastel, cabernet, purple morocco, muscat gordo blanco and sweetwater.

Despite late frosts, always a danger in the locality, it is recorded that the vineyard was one of the most successful in the hills. The business was later registered as the Mundaring Vineyard Company (derived from an Aboriginal word meaning 'high place on a high place') with eventually Gugeri's siding being renamed Mundaring.

Railway contractor Edward Keane took up property at Mount Baker (Bakers Hill) in 1884 for a vineyard, the land being given as part payment for the building of the railway from Chidlow to Spencers Brook. The cost of the vineyard and 20-room house is believed to have been £8800. Apparently, when things were quiet in the railway business, workers were sent to plant vines and build the cellars and home. The vines were irrigated from a large dam at the eastern end of the property supplied by miles of pipe, with an engine used to pump water to two large tanks on top of a hill behind the cellars.

But the big house burnt down in a bushfire and the family left, their departure speeded by misfortunes in the contracting business. The property was taken over by the Wood family, strong supporters of vineyards in the hills with their ownership of Glen Hardey and still today, Coorinja at Toodyay.

The Hooper family were the next owners, buying the 400-hectare property with its 60 hectares of vines in 1911 for £1200. They made extensive improvements, elevating the property to reflect status with fine lawns, gardens and sporting facilities including a cricket pitch, tennis courts and even a golf course.

I recall a tasting in 1985 with descendant Ross Hooper of some aged wines which had been stored in two old pine boxes. He believed they were the best ever made in Western Australia, which was reasonable, considering the winemaker was his father Glen.

As he poured the first wine, a 23-year-old port, I remembered Government Viticulturist Bill Jamieson telling me on his retirement that a port made from shiraz by the Hoopers was the best he had ever tasted.

When the property was sold in 1974, members of the family selected some of the rare wines left in the cellar. They were in flagons and did not look much, the white ants having made a mess of the labels. I expected the aged port to be deep black. Instead it was a light, see-through, tawny colour with a palate that was smooth and velvety, swamping the mouth with flavour. The home-made spirit was in excellent balance and the acid ensured no stickiness.

Most of the production was fortified, sold in bulk to farmers and miners in the goldfields. Some was bought by Houghton and Valencia for blending with their own wines. The wines won a number of prizes at shows in Perth, Melbourne and Sydney.

The family was self taught, and there were some hard times. The vineyard had been let go to such an extent that Ross's grandfather Richard had to prune at night by the light of a hurricane lamp to try to catch up. At its peak the winery produced more than 100,000 litres a year, with some storage in elaborately carved casks. The family also made sparkling wine for their own use.

Later Evans and Tate established a small vineyard in the district. Principal John Tate considered the quality superb, but the yields were low.

Now the Brockmans keep the flag flying in the district with their Reinscourt label from a small holding of cabernet sauvignon and semillon. The closely spaced vines were planted in 1980 and produced three tonnes of fruit in 1994, a year the area was to be doubled.

Not far away at Toodyay, viticulture had become a prosperous industry during the booming gold years. The most successful vignerons were Bull and Stevens who were well established before the discovery of gold. They bought more land in 1885 and planted 16 hectares of vines by 1891, a year in which they produced more than 20,000 litres of wine, or in the old terminology, 5000 gallons at four shillings and sixpence a gallon. In 1892 they planted a further six hectares of vines, building a new cellar and storeroom, 18 metres by 6.7 metres, for a cost of £600. The property, using the label Avondale, became a district showpiece, producing other fruit including raisins for which the demand far exceeded supply.

The desire for land suitable for viticulture in the district resulted in the Road Board agreeing to the sale of the old Toodyay Commonage between 1893 and 1898, in lots of up to 80 hectares. The Avon Valley between Deepdale and Toodyay was described in those times as a picture of prosperity, with many cottages and vineyards lining its banks. Several of the vine growers established their own cellars and made wine which, according to the local correspondent of the *Western Mail*, was remarkable because 'we can boast of being one of the most temperate towns in the Colony'.

However, a split was to appear in the ranks of the producers over a move to establish a co-operative winery in the district with Bull and Stevens seceding from the local vine and fruitgrowers' association over the issue. Instead, they offered to buy all the grapes from the small growers around, expecting to make about 45,000 litres of wine.

Another major West Australian producer about this time was a winery established by Frederick Piesse at Katanning. An indication of the determination of the man can be gained from an incident in 1872. With his brother and another man he travelled to Shark Bay, there to have a marked input into the establishment of a pearling industry. After two years the men decided to return to Perth, making the journey on foot. It is said that Frederick was unable to purchase a suitable pair of shoes and covered the distance of 900 kilometres barefoot.

Obviously, the journey would have broadened his knowledge of part of the territory of which he was to become acting Premier and Leader of the Opposition.

Initially in the Katanning operation about 30,000 litres of wine a year were made at a winery built just before the turn of the century under a flour mill in the town, also operated by the family. Despite the unlikely location, the chance to work there must have had widespread appeal. For when Frederick's brother Arnold, who was in charge at Katanning, put an advertisement for a winemaker in an Adelaide newspaper while on a holiday visit, the response was overwhelming. When he awoke in the morning, at the given private address, the front fence and garden had been trampled down by hordes of enthusiastic winemakers anxious to try their luck in Western Australia.

Dignity prevailed amid the chaos, however. A gentleman standing quietly with his wife on the footpath was the first interviewed, and was successful.

He was German Carl Joseph Bungert whose family had been connected with vineyards and winemaking for three centuries. He had come to Australia as winemaker for Penfolds and worked at Magill where his efforts earned promotion to New South Wales. Despite selling furniture and house in preparation for the transfer, his plans were thwarted — his employer had a change of mind, deciding he was still needed in South Australia. This was the last straw for Bungert, who decided instead to look to the west.

Such was his influence that wines he made won the C. W. Ferguson Challenge Cup in 1904 and 1907. International honours followed in 1908 with a gold medal awarded to wine in the Franco British Exhibition in London. Similar success was achieved in Paris.

According to a story held by the Katanning Historical Society, these awards appear to have been the crowning glory of the wine venture in the Great Southern.

An indication of the lack of knowledge about the industry at the time was shown when Bungert introduced the making of fortified wine. The move required an excise officer to travel to Katanning to supervise the use of the fortifying spirit and gather the taxes. When a customs officer was not available, the local medical officer attended. It is recorded that he was 'shocked beyond belief' on the first occasion when he discovered that pure spirit was used for the fortification!

Originally, the spirit was purchased in Adelaide and sent by ship to Albany and railed to Katanning. As production increased and grapes became available for distillation, Western Australia's largest still was made in Adelaide for F.H. Piesse and Sons and installed in Katanning in 1904.

On the prime property was to rise the stately Kobeelya homestead, resplendent with the beautiful things of a gracious period, including an underground cellar. It was completed when the family returned to Katanning at the end of Frederick's Cabinet duties.

The beautiful two-storey home, named from the Aboriginal for 'a place to rest', was a magnet for all important visitors to the region, including viceregal dignitaries, valets as well.

On important occasions, such as for dinners and banquets, food was prepared at kitchens 2.5 kilometres away and brought to the house by horse and cart. The table fare produced on the property included meat, poultry, bread, butter, fruit and, of course, the wine.

But after Frederick Piesse passed away on 29 June 1912, his family showed little interest in the conduct of the vineyard or winery, and all trace of its former glory had disappeared by 1920. The vineyards are now neat rows of houses and the home became a church college for young ladies until it was closed in 1986.

In more recent times, former Katanning baker Ted Bride tried his luck with a six-hectare vineyard on the edge of the town and a winery with a colourful background. In its lifetime, it had been a butter factory, ice works, a rental machinery headquarters, wool store and an Islamic mosque. The label chosen for the brief renaissance was Pinwernying, the original name of the Katanning subdivision.

Not far away at Boyanup, another vineyard that flourished for many years, and is no more, was established by Englishman John Duce. Now cows roam the banks of the Preston River where the vines once flourished.

The first wines from extensive plantings were made in 1907 and sold throughout Western Australia, and even exported to London in the 1930s. A family descendant told me on a visit to the property that up to 30 people were employed to run the operation at times.

I recall a 1959 claret made from shiraz from the property taking the limelight when the winemaking team from Thomas Hardy and Sons came to Western Australia to hold their first post-vintage seminar in Perth. Other wines were lauded by former State Government Viticulturist Bill Jamieson. He was well qualified to make such assessments, having been a judge at the Perth Wine Show for a quarter of a century.

According to the Royal Agricultural Society, which hosts the Perth Wine Show as part of the Royal Show (the industry's main judging event of the year), the first cash prizes were made available in 1865. In that year the prize of £3 for the best red was won by Mr de Burgh and the best white, worth the same amount, by Mr Chidlow.

At a meeting in June Messrs Padbury, Brockman, Waylen, Gull and Hardey 'signified their intention of subscribing one pound each for the purpose of offering a special prize for Colonial wines'.

The Perth Show is important to producers as a gauge of quality, and can have significant marketing benefits. As well, it gives producers the chance of tasting wines entered by their competitors, an extremely useful yardstick. Other events like the Sheraton Perth awards, the SGIO WA Winemakers Exhibition and the Mount Barker Wine Show are also important in this regard with some valuable and prestigious prizes available. Some producers, however, have their reservations about such events and do not enter, preferring their wines to be assessed by consumers.

Judges use the shows to point out basic winemaking faults and to help lift standards — aims of the original promoters, no doubt. Take, for example, notes by Mr Despeissis published in April 1886 of 'the recent wine show at Guildford':

'The purpose and object of a wine competition is obviously an opportunity offered to growers of tasting the comparative degree of excellence of their wines, and a mere enumeration of the order of merit in which the several competitors stand in respect to one another conveys little information unless either supplemented by actual sampling on the part of those interested or by commentatory notes bearing on the question of the part of the judge entrusted with duties of pronouncing on the merits of the wines shown.'

That is a mouthful and a half, but it showed the way, for previously wine competitions in the Colony were 'conducted in rather an arbitrary manner as regards the classification of the wine on the judging itself, and the growers as well as the public were left in blessed ignorance respecting the qualities or the defect of the wine shown'.

In modern day judging, samples are provided in glasses based on classes, the wine being poured by stewards hidden from the assessment area. In his day Mr Despeissis warned exhibitors that they should carefully refrain from bottling their wine for show purposes in fancy bottles or flagons of any particular shape. Furthermore, they should not use branded corks, capsules, sealing wax, labels or anything which might from the outward appearance of the vessel and its general get-up lead to the identification of wines coming from any particular cellar. 'I have noticed that at both the last Toodyay and Guildford shows, that sufficient attention had not been paid to this point by exhibitors, thereby putting the judges at the inconvenience of having to leave the room whenever the wine was being poured out in the glasses', he said.

At Guildford he had the use of a well-lit and well-ventilated room, free from penetrating smells of paint or other matters, but heat was a disadvantage. 'The old and well-known European practice of warming red wines before serving them on the table does not hold good in a climate like ours', he went on.

Of 68 samples judged he recorded only four as being absolutely unsound and three slightly pricked, a marked improvement on previous shows. Among the exhibitors were Houghton, Darlington, Mount Baker, Coorinja, Bindaring, Garden Hill, Mr Logue's Upper Swan, and the Helena Nursery and Vineyard Company.

In his concluding comments he said: 'I shall be much mistaken in my appreciation of the West Australian wine made and reared with care and produced from the choicer grape-vines that are now being extensively grown in this country, if it does not, the other conditions being alike, compare favourably, in years to come, with the best wines the Eastern colonies can produce, and, placed on the export market under suitable conditions, be regarded there with the same amount of favour, as some of the choicer growth of France have won for themselves'.

Bill Jamieson had for many years been a regular visitor to our family vineyard where my father had given over a section of the block for experiments with vine rootstocks. Invariably, he and my father would end up in our shed that served as a cellar, sipping our dry red while I had the task of carrying from the kitchen supplies of cheese and bread. Bill later praised the efforts of the Yugoslav and Italian migrants who took up land on the Swan Valley, considering them outstanding vignerons, spot on in areas such as disease control and pruning. 'They got the best possible result from the land', he once told me.

Immediately after World War I, many of the large estates in the valley were subdivided into smaller holdings, either for soldier settlement or to satisfy the demands for vineyard land by Yugoslav miners and timber workers who had brought their families from Europe and wanted to settle on the land. It was a natural move, for along with market gardening, grape production and winemaking were skills these immigrants, mainly from the Dalmatian coast, really understood.

My grandfather, Ante Beus, with his wife Antica and Ivan Nizich were among the first to come to the Swan, in March 1916, having previously bought land in Millendon.

An early panoramic view of the Swan Valley area taken from Houghton vineyards

At the same time Ivan Kukura with his wife Perica also arrived from Kalgoorlie to take up an adjoining block, to run with his brother Paul. These, and others that followed them, were hard-working people with wives and children contributing towards economic survival as well as introducing new dimensions in the appreciation of food and wine.

But times were difficult. My grandfather, for example, would walk as far as Belmont to prune vines while developing his property. In winter, to protect his feet, he would stand in kerosene tins because there were no gumboots available.

My father arrived on the Swan in 1925 to work for my grandfather, not long before his death. Disaster struck soon after when the cellar burnt, including the barrels full of wine. Work began immediately on a new and bigger facility, using horses to dig out an area of 15.5 metres by nine metres by four metres deep. It was to cater for a substantial production of mainly dry red table wines, about 50,000 litres a year, with fruit bought in from other growers supplementing their own 4.5-hectare vineyard production. But fate was to take a hand again in winter the following year when the cellar was flooded, as a big drain behind the structure linked to the nearby Swan River broke its banks following three weeks of continuous rain.

My father went on to work for the Derrynasura Vineyard Ltd at Armadale which was established by an English baronet, Sir Arthur Stepney. Derrynasura — Irish for valley of the vines — no longer exists though terraces where the vineyard once flourished can still be seen among the houses.

In 1896 Sir Arthur had purchased a share of a vineyard planted two years earlier. A cellar was built to accommodate the 1898 vintage of about 800 gallons. An extract from J. S. Battye's *Cyclopedia of Western Australia* describes the scene:

'The hillside has been excavated for the construction of cellars specially designed for

How it was for some in the early 1920s when few lorries were in service — muscle power, and faithful Clydesdales

coolness and ventilation. They are very substantial structures and present the appearance of a terraced erection of four storeys, one lying behind the other and following the slope of the hill. They are all well ventilated from the roofs and side on the up-to-date principle of double doors, by which means a cool, even temperature is maintained even in the hottest days of summer, the dark-claret cellar never registering higher than 68 degrees. Into the top storey of the series is received the new season's yield of grapes, which are passed through a Mabille Brothers' crusher and stemmer, the winepress working on a tram which serves the fermenting vats wherein the must is left for the requisite period. As a preventive of deleterious microbes all the vats, presses and machinery are treated with a coat of paraffin.'

Sir Arthur assumed full control in 1899, extending the original 26 hectares of vines to more than 50 hectares. He died in the United States in 1909, and under later management output rose to some 20,000 gallons. In the period 1927-29 Derrynasura ports were awarded first prize each year at the Royal Agricultural Society Show. When my father left the property, he returned to the Swan Valley and eventually his own block.

Once, when we were picking grapes on either side of a row of vines, he told me how he got the fright of his life, fearing he had been caught for illegally distilling grape spirit called rakija, the Yugoslav equivalent of the Italian grappa. The high-powered drink is enjoyed regularly on cold nights, and even used to rub on rheumatic joints. In their own countries such production was freely allowed, and the new settlers found it hard to

For a bigger operator like Valencia, transport was a little quicker, even if space on the tray was at a premium

The imposing old stone winery at Wyening was built by Benedictine monks to last. Austrian winemaker Gustaf Schwarzbach had been there nearly a quarter of a century when, in 1973, the last of the wine was drawn to signal the end of an era

understand the restrictions which prevented them from making a bottle or so for their own pleasure.

My father had made a small still and had it working on the stove for the first time on a night in 1931 when car lights appeared in the driveway. He knew of no one with a vehicle who would be visiting, and thinking the worst he moved swiftly to dump the gear outside, only to find that it was in fact a Swan Valley friend out to show off a newly purchased vehicle.

'He said later he had smelt the spirit and was disappointed not to have been offered a drink', my father recounted. 'The few drops I had made were with the still thrown under a passionfruit vine. It was the first, and last time for me.'

For much of his life Mel Jarvis, formerly Senior Inspector of Excise, had the job of supervising the operation of legal stills such as at Houghton, Valencia, Coorinja, Bakers Hill, Swanville, Luisini (Wanneroo), Duce's (Boyanup) and at the Roma Vineyard, Flat Rocks, between Kojonup and Broomehill.

He also monitored the use of spirit at various vineyards, many of which have now gone, or been sold off to others. Among them were Richon, established in the foothills just south of Armadale, Welby's Wines of North Lake Road, Kardinya, Waldeck Wines and Glenalwyn in the Swan Valley, Parri Wines at Wanneroo, Derrynasura and for the Benedictines at New Norcia who operated a vineyard and winery at Wyening, near Bolgart.

Built from granite collected from surrounding paddocks, this latter winery was 12 metres tall with the walls more than half a metre thick. Said Mel: 'It was a beautiful place, cut into the side of a hill. The monks would travel down to Valencia for their spirit and I would go back with them, returning to Perth the next day by bus.'

Two bottles in his cellar labelled Muscatelle, Benedictine Abbey New Norcia were a reminder of a vineyard which once covered more than 30 hectares. It had a colourful winemaker, Austrian Gustaf Schwarzbach, who prided himself on the wines and especially the altar wines which had to be made entirely without chemicals.

At its peak the vineyard produced about 65,000 litres of wine. After nearly three-quarters of a century it gradually became uneconomic, ending a history of the monks having their own wine that began with cuttings brought from Spain about 1865 by the monastery founder, Bishop Salvado.

Other vineyards established for winemaking which mostly produced their last drop years ago were in wheatbelt centres such as Merredin, Williams and Kellerberrin, and in the South West at Dardanup, Kirup, Donnybrook and Bridgetown. Generally, these were the work of Italian migrants who sought to make wines for themselves, or for sale in bulk.

As well, Mel Jarvis watched out for the moonshiners who made spirit for sale. 'On one occasion in the early 1950s we got 16 stills in three months', he told me at his Perth home. 'The fines ranged from £25 to £125 — a lot of money in those days. We paid for information, and there was no limit to it. I paid out £300 in one month, with the average payment about £70 to £80. We had to stop the illegal activities. It was a moral issue with concern about spirit being sold through milk bars to young people in the Eastern States. If we lost £1000 in revenue, that was regarded as chicken feed compared to losing one girl to vice and prostitution.'

Mel was once described by a television commentator as Western Australia's Elliott Ness. He recalled an operation where one man was followed for about 1500 kilometres around the Perth metropolitan area till he was caught. He had operated two stills in a house in Victoria Park and had sold spirit at 30 shillings a bottle. In another case, a gallon bottle of spirit was found under a bed at a West Swan property. The person charged consistently maintained it was not his, and that the bottle had been planted. After being convicted and fined in the Midland Court, he approached Mel and asked if he could have the bottle back, for it had cost him three shillings.

One of the most surprising convictions in the industry occurred in 1933 when Wyndham Hill Smith, then manager for Yalumba Wines in Western Australia, was fined £5 for giving a trophy for the York races. Sitting in an armchair in his Barossa Valley home, he explained that in those days wineries were not allowed by retailers to sell stock privately, or to promote business by giving trophies. 'Wine and Spirit Association representatives would go around spying', he said. 'They would even go to parties and count the bottles to make sure people were toeing the line. If they felt you deserved it, publicans would blackball you.'

Wyndham, or Windy as he became affectionately known, came to the State in 1931 to set up Yalumba's Fremantle office. He became so keen on Western Australia, indeed 'fanatically secessionist', that he talked the company into establishing a winery at Middle Swan on the corner of Great Northern Highway and Toodyay Road. It is now a Telecom depot but it operated for many years, crushing about 200 tonnes annually, supplied by many small growers, including my father.

'Under the liquor controls of those days', Wyndham went on, 'we were allowed to sell West Australian wines cheaper in South Australia than we could our own home-based products. The main production was fortified wines, ports, muscats and sherries which were sent to South Australia. No wines were ever bottled, but the quality was good, despite the relatively primitive equipment.'

He recalled that the hardest work at the winery was emptying the individual boxes of fruit that came from some growers on to a small weighbridge, to be individually weighed. Such time-consuming effort added to costs, and this finally led to the winery's closure. 'Wine in those days did not have much credibility', Wyndham said. 'We did not have the technique of manufacture or the variety of fruit. Looking back, I regret that we did not take up an attractive State Government offer of 800 hectares in the Mount Barker area. I liked the climate and the region.' Fifty years after he left the State, the company of which his son Robert is now head took a share in a new vineyard development on the outskirts of Mount Barker, since purchased by Houghton.

Despite the effects of the Depression and the over-production of grapes in the Eastern States, there was continued vineyard expansion in Western Australia. By 1948 the area under vines exceeded 4000 hectares. Much of this was table grapes for Perth and export markets, and for dried fruit, especially currants and sultanas.

But wine production was also increasing though imports, particularly from South Australia, were growing at alarming proportions. This was due to the public taste for sweet fortified wines which could be produced cheaply in the irrigated areas of South Australia.

The move into the 1950s saw the price of wool soar to unprecedented levels, and those few farmers in the Great Southern and South West who had vineyards abandoned the vines for sheep. In the Swan Valley vines on the badly drained, poorer soil types were gradually grubbed, particularly affecting the area under currant vines.

About this time people like Jack Mann of Houghton were questioning the emphasis on fortified wine production and looking to table wines as the new direction. This was

A scene in the Swan Valley in the 1950s when the table grape market was an important and stable one for many growers

to see attention swing to new cooler producing regions in the south of the State, such as at Margaret River, Mount Barker-Frankland and, more recently, Pemberton-Manjimup, resulting in a viticultural dream becoming a reality in just a few years.

Certainly that would have pleased people like Hunter Valley industry leader Maurice O'Shea who never visited Western Australia but pinpointed Albany as a place for premium wine from a study of its climate and soils. It would have also pleased the pioneering producers. I have already referred to some. Others include the Bussell family, who planted vines in the 1830s, Ephraim Clarke, who operated at Bunbury about the turn of the century, and Sam Moleri, who grew grapes and made wine, selling door-to-door at Margaret River in the 1930s.

Another would have been University of California expert Professor Harold Olmo, who had been brought to the State in 1955 by the Vine Fruit Research Trust in association with the Fulbright Foundation to investigate the premature decline of vineyards in the Swan Valley. His report, 'A Survey of the Grape Industry of Western Australia', also included the highlighting of cooler southern areas of the State for premium table wine production, specifying Mount Barker-Frankland, though he did not visit Margaret River.

He also noted at the time that the Australian palate favoured sweetness. Even so, he reported that the Swan Valley wines of the day made for table use were much too heavy for the average palate; they were high in extract, often too sweet and had the unmistakable marks of being made from grapes that were overripe. They had an oxidised flavour and considerable residual sugar that led to a rapid build-up of volatile acid when exposed to air. He recommended a number of technological improvements to assist local producers in making better wines.

I had come to know the professor during this time from visits to our property where my father was heavily involved in rootstock grafting. Years later I met him again, at the Davis campus of the University of California where he recalled with great pleasure his time in Western Australia.

But little was done on his southern recommendations until 1963 when Bill Jamieson (State Government Viticulturist) was asked by Les Slade, the then assistant to the Minister for Industrial Development, Charles Court (later Sir Charles) to suggest methods of helping the flagging grape industry in the Swan Valley, and decentralising. In 1964 the Grape Industry Committee was formed, and it eventually recommended a small experimental planting be undertaken in the Mount Barker area.

Initially, a site was considered at the Mount Barker Senior High School but rejected by the Department of Education. Then the Perrilup prison farm was suggested and also rejected, no doubt to the dismay of the inmates.

Finally, Bill Jamieson and Dorham Mann looked across the Pearse family farm from a nearby hill and decided this was the place for the experiment. Arrangements were duly concluded, but it was nearly all over before it had really begun, as the initial planting failed dismally, due to waterlogging. Considerable political pressure against the proposal then followed.

'People became sceptical, some regarded it as ridiculous and there were strong moves to have it dumped', Bill said. 'Even some Department of Agriculture officers believed losses should have been cut.'

Fortunately, Government Minister Jim Craig, whose electorate included the Swan Valley, threw in his support and it was agreed to try again with Charles Court in overall charge. 'It was make or break for me, and a real relief when the vines began to thrive', Bill said. 'It had been a worrying five years, not knowing whether frosts would be a killer or birds an enormous problem.'

The favourable recommendations alluding to the production of high-quality table wines in the area inspired former Adelaide Lord Mayor John Roche into planting vines on a sheep and cattle grazing property he had purchased at Frankland River. I once had breakfast with him in Perth and was surprised to find he would never drink any of the millions of bottles produced from the development. An acknowledged teetotaller, he told me he had reached this state not for religious, medical or moral reasons, but rather because he had a very sweet palate. 'Things like wine and beer taste terribly sour to me', he explained. 'I have tasted the wines from Frankland grapes just to see how they are coming along. But all wines taste like old boots to me.'

The Frankland property was bought in 1956 when the family was looking for bigger tracts of land. Now the vineyard is leased by Houghton and it provides an important part of their production.

The other major pioneer in the district was Plantagenet Wines, headed by former Englishman Tony Smith. Its wines have done much to boost the area's image while Tony himself has taken a strong hand in industry affairs.

Meanwhile, activity was mounting in the Margaret River area following the highlighting of the district by scientist Dr John Gladstones. In a report in December 1965 in the journal of the Australian Institute of Agricultural Science, he concluded that an examination of the soils and climate of south-western Australia revealed several regions where natural conditions were highly favourable for viticulture. 'For light, dry table wines very good conditions appear to exist in the cooler southern part of the State, especially around Mount Barker and Rocky Gully, and perhaps, even more, in the area north and north-east of Margaret River', he wrote. This was followed by a more detailed account of the Margaret River area, pinpointing Capel, Vasse, Cowaramup, Bramley and Witchcliffe-Forest Grove for their soils.

Dr Gladstones, an academic who had lectured in agronomy, horticulture and climatology before joining the Department of Agriculture to develop an international reputation for his expertise with lupins, knew the Margaret River area well from many holiday visits.

During these times he would explore the region, concluding that it was less prone to the extremes, like spring frosts, high temperatures in summer, and to rain or hail during the ripening period. 'In many respects it seemed ideal for the production of quality grapes for wine production and looked better than Bordeaux', he later told me.

As he spoke I recalled an old German proverb which says the grapevine is a child of the sun. It loves the hills and hates the winds. And winds have been a problem at Margaret River, but Dr Gladstones argued they were a two-edged sword. 'While they can be harmful, they provide equability of temperature', he said. 'With winds mainly from the ocean, you do not get the temperature fluctuations.'

He also argued that ripening of the fruit would proceed more steadily at Margaret River than at Mount Barker, and be more reliable. 'The only disadvantage relative to Mount Barker would be a higher winter rainfall which would necessitate closer attention to problems of soil drainage', he said.

No doubt the idea of a wine industry at Margaret River came as a surprise to the more traditional farmer, but it sparked a lot of interest with a well-attended public meeting held in Busselton in July 1966.

It was later claimed that the meeting had been given an exaggerated estimate of the profits to be made from wine grape growing. State Government Viticulturist Bill Jamieson was also reported as saying the grape growing for the sale of wine grapes in the Busselton-Margaret River area was not an immediate practical possibility, nor would it be highly profitable. He said that although the climate and some soils appeared promising, the area was unproven in regard to the quality of the table wines that could be produced. 'At present, there was no possibility of a commercial winery being established to process grapes', he said.

However, Dr Tom Cullity, who began planting Vasse Felix in August 1967, praised Bill Jamieson for his help. In a review of winemaking in the district written 20 years later,

Dr Cullity said: 'When it was departmentally inconvenient to foster at this time another gestating wine region, he [Jamieson] supported this amateur venture in the South West and was generous in giving advice. I remember him spending a dreary weekend helping me clean up after one of the managers had left.'

It was hard going in those early days in an area bereft of expertise and sceptical of such bold moves as grape growing and winemaking. But Tom Cullity persisted and he was soon joined by fellow doctors Pannell and Cullen and then others like the Hohnens, Sandalford, Wrights and Horgans (Leeuwin Estate). Certainly the State owes such people a great debt of gratitude. For they could easily have spent their money on other things, and their time in other more relaxing ways. The latest Department of Agriculture survey at the time of writing shows there are now 105 wine grape growers in the Margaret River area with 45 in the Mount Barker-Frankland region and 35 in Warren-Blackwood.

Even so, the Western Australian industry is small in national terms, producing less than two per cent of Australia's wine. But it is a case of small is beautiful with most of the production based on premium 750ml bottled wines, a much higher proportion than in other states. In 1994 West Australian earnings from wine was estimated at $70 million and with exports were forecast to rise rapidly. Predictions for the important United Kingdom market, for example, indicated per capita consumption would more than double by the turn of the century, to two billion bottles a year!

In 1994 West Australian wines were being shipped to more than 25 countries and were valued at $12 million.

The industry's focus is now firmly fixed on product quality, diversity and value. It would be almost impossible to compete on price with Eastern States production from irrigated areas which have the advantage of high yields, mass production methods and closeness to major markets.

A lot of early Swan Valley wines were condemned as bombo or plonk, but they were often misunderstood. They were made specifically for a southern European market by people without formal training, under primitive conditions, with lesser grape varieties and old wood. In the last 30 years there has been a revolution with significant winery investment, modern processing techniques and the introduction of classic varieties. Men like John Kosovich, for example, can hold their heads high with the quality of some of the best wines in the State — soft, full, flavoursome, and extremely drinkable. Even so, it is hard to see a forecast made in February 1900 by Despeissis, likening the Swan to the Margaux, being fulfilled. This is despite the success in 1974 at an international wine judging in London when Jack Mann's 1971 Houghton cabernet sauvignon was acclaimed one of the world's best 11 dry red wines from 700 entries. It was described as being of outstanding excellence and astonishing elegance. At the time in Perth it was selling for less then $2 a bottle!

That certainly brought home strongly the point made the following year by (the then) South Australian Minister for Agriculture Brian Chatterton. On a visit to Western Australia, he told me: 'The State's retailers have an inferiority complex about Western Australian wines which is unfounded'. A winemaker who had written two books on wine, he said: 'Retailers and restaurateurs were apologetic about Western Australian wines and they should not have been'. Certainly such criticism could no longer be justified, with many liquor outlets keen supporters of local wines.

Another visitor to stimulate interest was Professor C. S. Ough, Chairman of the Department of Viticulture and Oenology at the University of California. He spoke of egg white, milk powder, casein and isinglass being used in fining (clarifying) wine. Isinglass is the dried bladder of the sturgeon, not cheap, but highly valued for top quality dry white and red table wines.

I watched winemaker Bill Crappsley once separate four eggs into a container, and beat the whites into a froth. He poured the egg whites into a bucket of red wine, stirring gently during the process, then poured the whole mixture into a cask of wine.

It is an old method used in many parts of the world in which basically the albumen of the egg whites picks up suspended impurities from the wine as it settles in the cask, leaving the wine brilliantly clear. It is a very gentle fining and it has a softening and mellowing effect on the wine. But it is messy and certainly not for winemaking in big quantities. It would need an associated custard-making business to handle the leftover egg yolks!

Fred Noack, whose father established Swanville Wines at Upper Swan, told me that egg whites and gelatine were the main methods of fining in the 1920s.

At one stage in its 57-year history, Swanville had some 60 hectares of wine grapes, including a major holding at Bullsbrook. Peter Andreas William Noack, a ship's carpenter who was born in Copenhagen, Denmark, had travelled the world before settling in Bayswater. Then he worked in the South West building Group Settlement houses before buying the Swan property on the banks of the river in 1919.

Swanville boasted its own still and at its peak in the early 1960s produced 850,000 litres of wine, selling throughout Australia and winning numerous show awards around the nation. An associated part of its business was the ownership of seven wine saloons and liquor stores, including one at Geraldton which Fred claimed as the first to be given a licence to sell single bottles, as opposed to the old gallon or six bottle sale system.

Swanville was sold in 1976 and has subsequently been subdivided and sold in smaller parcels.

Another grand old name to go by the wayside is that of Valencia at Caversham. The first vines on the property were planted in the 1890s by an eminent trio, John Leighton Nanson, Associate Editor of *The West Australian*, American-born Lancelot Lindley-Cowan, Secretary of the Western Australian Department of Agriculture, and Despeissis. Nanson

The equipment may have changed since this picture was taken, but the basic techniques remain constant. This picture of the Valencia laboratory dates back to the 1950s

had purchased 44.5 hectares of land from his editor, Charles Harper, naming it Carlisle after his birthplace in Cumberland, England. Soon after, when Nanson retired, Sir John Northmore joined the partnership which was then formed into a limited company, called the Santa Rosa Wine Co. Ltd.

R. George Mann joined the company in 1906 as winemaker, a move by the former South Australian sparrow-shooting champion that was to see the Mann family have a powerful influence on the Western Australian industry that still exists today.

In 1925 Sir John, later to become the Chief Justice of the Supreme Court of Western Australia, and mining engineer and financier George Ridgeway had taken over, renaming the company Valencia Vineyards Pty Ltd. Cellars and distillery were constructed and the varieties grown and the wines they made included semillon (sauterne), malbec (claret), shiraz (claret, burgundy and port), pedro (sherry), grenache (sweet sherry, port), doradillo (sweet sherry) and cabernet (claret).

The Emu Wine Co. Ltd of London, which had Australian headquarters in Adelaide, purchased Valencia in 1945 and acquired Houghton in 1950.

It was not a particularly bright start for the new owners, for in April 1946 a disastrous fire destroyed the distillery and the bond store, with part of the fermenting cellar plant damaged. An excise officer, Mr C. Bottrill, who was the only person at the distillery when the fire broke out, was a victim of the tragedy.

Charles Kelly, who had been transferred from South Australia as manager and winemaker after the purchase, recalled that the fire brigade had to pump water from the mains at the front gate, some 250 metres away, to try to fight the flames. 'There was not much pressure when the water arrived and the distillery and bond store burnt to the ground', he said.

Mr Kelly, grandson of Dr A. C. Kelly — founder of Tintara in South Australia — had come to Western Australia for 12 months but stayed until his retirement in 1977. He told me that when the merger came with Houghton, the two wineries operated as separate organisations. 'We made a complete range of wines and were more the commercial side of the business, while Jack Mann was more the specialist. We handled about 1000 to 1200 tonnes of fruit a year with fortifieds our strength, sold mainly in flagons.'

Another fire which caused concern though not a death occurred in Perth in the old Musgroves building in Murray Street. During the fire a wall of the building collapsed on the adjoining Rural and Industries Bank (renamed BankWest in 1994). Water aimed at the blaze flooded the bank basement. Besides general damage, it soaked the labels from the bank's wine collection used for entertaining local, interstate and overseas visitors.

'It was fairly clear to which bottles some labels belonged', bank cellar master Ian Archibald later recalled. 'But we had to take pot luck with some.'

He told me the story when we were in another of the bank's cellars, in the basement of a St Georges Terrace branch. Deep in the cool location, it was a place any wine lover would drool over, especially in the heat of a Perth summer when it is vital to try to keep wine temperatures down.

For a period in the early 1990s emotional temperatures in Western Australia ran hot at proposals to cut up big areas of the Swan Valley for major roads and urbanisation. A strong protest movement finally led to State Government agreement for protection through an Act of Parliament.

The 1990s have also seen many more West Australian wines to choose from. More than half a million cuttings were planted in 1989, for example. Official forecasts indicate a doubling of production to 17,000 tonnes by 1995.

Some of the new labels may fall by the wayside, others will prove exciting, with those from Manjimup and Pemberton adding an extra dimension of special interest.

Though wine is reported to have been made at Middlesex in the midst of the region in the 1930s, the modern history began on 5 May 1977 when Agriculture Department officers John Cripps and Tony Devitt proposed a wine grape trial to the State Government's horticultural research committee. Initially, it met with a hostile reception because general fruit production in the area was considered more important. At the same time Margaret River and Mount Barker producers argued it was unnecessary to consider another area when they could supply the market. After much pontification and conjecture by many people over the area's suitability, work began later in 1977 at the department's research station (later sold) half way between Pemberton and Manjimup.

In all, 15 varieties were planted, six red, seven white and two specially for juicing. The premier sparkling wine varieties of pinot noir, chardonnay and pinot meunier did best, thriving in what was obviously a happy environment. The first and only field day to show the results was held in February 1987, attracting a big crowd including many from Margaret River and the Swan Valley. Many other viticulturists also visited the site, and were impressed with the strong growth of the vines. The department made experimental wines from grapes produced in the vineyard, surprising a number of winemakers with their quality. A sparkling style was also made.

I recall travelling to the region in 1993 with a party of British Masters of Wine who tried the first chardonnay and pinot noir from fruit grown at Smith Brook. They were impressed, especially with the pinot. Said one over a tasty lunch: 'If they can do this with their first crop [not usually associated with the best of wine from a vineyard] what will they do as the vines mature?'

In climatic terms Dr Gladstones has described the Manjimup area as one of great viticultural potential, fully comparable with the lower Great Southern and Margaret River. 'Wines produced from appropriate grape varieties should be very much in the mainstream of Bordeaux styles', he said.

Between Manjimup and Pemberton the soils change from gravelly redgum to mainly karri loam and marks what appears to be a fairly major environmental change with lower temperatures, lower sunshine hours and higher rainfall and relative humidity. The karri soils are also less warm, leading Dr Gladstones to caution against planting late-ripening varieties like cabernet sauvignon. Instead, early maturing grapes like chardonnay are favoured.

While many small vineyards are being established, there are some sizeable operations as well. For example, 37.5 hectares of premium variety wine grapes are part of the Fonty's Pool Farm on former rich apple and cattle grazing country seven kilometres south of Manjimup. It is expected to produce 450-500 tonnes at full production with early sales of chardonnay and pinot noir made to major Victorian sparkling winemaker Domaine Chandon. Houghton parent BRL Hardy has purchased half a major development in undulating karri country near Pemberton, acknowledging its confidence in the region. The 77-hectare planting is to be doubled, leaving 40 hectares of karri in the rest of the block.

But good areas of themselves do not make good wines, despite their special qualities. I recall a comment of wineman Dr.G. Hamilon Mowbray: 'The naked truth is that growing grapes for the making of superior wine is not a game for amateurs or dilettantes. It requires a concentration of effort and expertise that is not found in the growing of other fruits.' As well, huge investment is required for land, vineyard development, wineries and equipment.

Erl Happ of Margaret River once told me: 'The French say it takes three generations to develop a vineyard of world reputation. We should not be impatient. There is a tendency for people here to want their first wines to be a world-beater.'

In the rash of Western Australian plantings, other new producers have come from more obscure places like Esperance, Wandering, Gidgegannup, Cuballing and Williams.

In the latter district Blaz Kralevich established a vineyard in the early 1930s, producing about 1000 gallons a year mainly for sale to migrant families working on the railways in the area. After 35 years the property, which also produced stone fruit and tobacco, was sold and the vineyard abandoned. Some 30 years later, however, the surviving old vines are being rejuvenated by David and Susan Geerlings as part of a new vineyard venture.

In the rural hamlet of Cuballing, 180 kilometres south-east of Perth, can be found Stratherne Vale Estate, planted initially in 1980 by the Suckling family to meet their own wine grape needs. A decade on, they began having wine bottled under their own label.

In the foothills of the picturesque Ferguson Valley not far from Bunbury, senior high school principal Brian Wansborough, wife Jan and daughter Kristen have planted six hectares on their property, about 300 metres above sea level. In 1992 the first significant vintage produced 10,000 bottles.

Another schoolteacher development is Lauren Brook at Bridgetown. Stephen Bullied and wife Laurie planted a small area in 1992. With extra plantings and purchased fruit, they are looking for a crush of 20 tonnes in 1997. Up the road a bit to Kirup is Emerald Park, sold to overseas investors in 1994. Some old bush vines tell of another era but during his ownership Darryl Harris expanded the vineyard to 12 hectares, selling most of the fruit to Cape Mentelle at Margaret River.

Then there is Saint Allourn Vineyard being established at Margaret River by Perth identities Dr Peter Tannock, Fred Chaney and Ron Hawkins, Cape Bouvard at Lake Clifton, Golden Rise run by the Cocking family at Denmark, Bolganup Wines, an original label from the Porongurups, Florabunda Wines, Perillup, the Lennox vineyard (nine hectares grown by Ian and Kris Carter mainly for Houghton) at Marybrook, Driftwood Estate, Willyabrup, and Wolfsburg of Rosa Glen. Principal Wolfgang Schubert, a Perth-based commercial chairmaker, has plans to expand the existing 1.4 hectares of cabernet sauvignon on the property to a production level of 50,000-60,000 bottles. With exports a key part of the chair operation, it was no surprise that early sales were quickly made to Germany and Switzerland.

Then in the Perth Hills, there are a number of small, budding producers like Lawnbrook Estate, Cosham Vineyard, Excalibur, Chidlow Brook, Ashley Park, Scarp Valley, Brookside and Stoney Brook. In the more traditional areas — the Swan Valley, Wanneroo and suburban Perth — there are many older names like Lakeville Vineyards, Maddington, Riverside Vineyard, Bassendean, Long Valley Wines, Vindara Cellars, Visnica Wines, Vino Italia, Benara Wines (Swan Valley), and Faranda Wines, Ioppolo Wines and Bonavigna Wines from Wanneroo.

The explosion of new labels seems to go on and on. I thought I had heard of them all until I met a long-time friend, Dick Old, a former State Government Minister for

Agriculture, in a Perth restaurant. He bought to our table a bottle of 1991 Ridge View Estate Margaret River cabernet sauvignon, the production of a Perth neighbour. 'Try it', he said. 'I would like to know what you think.' The four-hectare vineyard on Caves Road, Willyabrup, is owned by Ray and Elsa Todd and was planted in 1986 with the first vintage in 1990. Their intention is to settle on the property in 1995 and get serious about the business.

Such a profusion of wine opportunities in Western Australia reminded me of a meeting with British Master of Wine Robin Day. 'Nothing is more conducive to gastronomic boredom than drinking the same wine, day in day out, however good that wine may be', he said. 'The world can provide so much variety that it is a pity to get into a rut over one's wine drinking, whether it is a claret rut, a burgundy rut (you have to be rich to do this nowadays), an Australian rut, a grape variety rut or a quality rut. There are so many good wines right throughout the price range and so many different grapes to enjoy that if you do not branch out a bit sometimes, you are missing out.'

One of the most unusual labels in the State and unlikely ever to be seen on export markets, is called Three Virgins. Agriculture scientist and journalist Eric Lawson combined with Perth architects, brothers Gordon and Bob Allan, to buy a small mature vineyard in the Swan Valley, after completing a wine appreciation course.

The vineyard went underwater during winter river flood times but the rich soils produced excellent shiraz and muscat fruit. Most was sold to Westfield with the trio keeping a trailer load of fruit each year, making wine initially in the Lawson Wembley Downs bathroom and laundry. The label took its name from the three small Lawson girls — Juliet, Nicola and Rosalind. Eventually, the block was sold and Eric teamed up with brother John, another well-known West Australian rural journalist, to purchase a small block at Margaret River. So the Three Virgins persist, from a new vineyard and a new generation of granddaughters. But the winemaking has well and truly passed the backyard and bathroom stage. Wines from seven different grape varieties are made with high-tech cool room facilities — backed by the best Department of Agriculture advice of course!

While the Lawson label may be a bit of family fun, the serious producers have made an immense contribution to the development of the State through investments of many millions of dollars, strong promotion, employment and contribution to the tourism industry. Today the industry stands tall, having well and truly gone from 'rough red' status to the production of world-class wines in little more than two and a half decades.

Swan Valley

COBANOV

Stock Road, Herne Hill
Cellar door sales: Wed — Sun 9 a.m. —
5.30 p.m.

Another crate, another smile . . . Tony Cobanov and father Steve enjoy the fruits of their labour during vintage time

'HEY ZEK', colleague Len Findlay once called across *The West Australian* newsroom. 'Have you ever heard of an eight-year-old port made in the Swan Valley? It's very good. We really enjoyed it.'

I recalled the conversation as I sat chatting to Tony Cobanov about the wine and the Swan Valley vineyard his grandfather started in 1937. A migrant from the Dalmatian coast of the former Yugoslavia, he cut sleepers in the South West for 13 years before buying the Swan land. His next step was to bring his two schoolboy sons to Western Australia, one of whom was Tony's father Steve.

On the day of our visit Steve was preparing to make yet another delivery with the family wines. For half a century, he has loaded his vehicle and travelled the sub-

urbs, taking his mainly bulk wines to long-established customers. Even in his early 70s he was on the road, often twice a week, driving up to 200 kilometres.

It was a humble start, however. Initially, only a few hundred gallons were made each vintage with most of the vineyard geared to dried fruit. But the volume soon increased; a few years later an annual production of some 3000 gallons was being achieved. Most was dry table wine with a lot railed to country clients.

Today the father and son team manage 21 hectares on two blocks made up of varieties including chardonnay, chenin blanc, verdelho, sauvignon blanc, pedro, cabernet sauvignon, shiraz, merlot and grenache. For a time, fruit for winemaking was also produced on a Bindoon vineyard that had been purchased, but the emphasis was then switched totally to the Swan.

A boilermaker-welder by trade, Tony Cobanov returned to the valley in the early 1980s, growing watermelons initially on vacant family land next to his father's vineyard. Then he planted a few chenin blanc vines, next some chardonnay. 'It just kept growing and growing from there', he said.

The combined operation produces about 200-250 tonnes, some sold to premium producers like Houghton and the rest processed in the jointly run winery.

About a third goes into bottles (on which Tony has been concentrating) to make wines like the unwooded, dry, fruity and grassy sauvignon blanc, and cabernet-merlot, a soft, round, ripe red, as well as the eight-year-old port and a slightly sweet light tawny.

Fruit for the ports is picked after everything else is finished, usually in April, to achieve maximum ripeness. Sometimes the grapes for the eight-year-old — which are picked last — are slightly raisiny with low juice yield. However, the name (eight-year-old port) suggested by a relative is not the wine's age. It is a blend of four varieties taken from a range of years.

Tony's aim is to make half the production into premium bottled wine with the marketing intention to quit most or all wines made between vintages.

EVANS & TATE WINES

Swan Street, Henley Brook
Cellar door sales 9 a.m. — 5 p.m.
Weekends 10 a.m. — 4 p.m.

THE West Australian wine industry owes a lot to a man, long since dead, who never grew a grape or made wine. His name was Abraham Tate, a Russian who emigrated around 1908, and who for many years was a wine merchant and wine saloon owner in High Street, Fremantle. Like many European migrants who had established themselves in a new land, he proceeded to bring his family to the State. One, a brother, was to become the father of John Tate, principal of Evans and Tate, now firmly established as one of Western Australia's premium producers.

John recalls as a boy that there was always wine on the family table and that his interest in premium wine was sparked as a young man. It led to foundation membership of the Beefsteak and Burgundy Club of Western Australia and partnership in a speciality bottle shop in North Fremantle with Harry Stone and Mark Staniford. It was called the Wine Mine and claimed to be the first of its kind in the State.

During this period John, a trained accountant, was building up a successful paint-making business with partner John Evans. The two families decided to move into grapes and wine after John Tate and his wife Toni returned from a visit to Europe in 1970 which included the premium producing areas of France.

But they made an inauspicious start in an area which had a history in the industry, but was never thought to be of real consequence. This was Bakers Hill, about 75 kilometres east of Perth on the Great Eastern Highway, where John Evans had a farming property and where, with much enthusiasm, two hectares of cabernet were planted in 1971. But a small creek at the bottom of a south-facing slope where the vines were planted flooded, and nearly half had to be replanted the following year.

Today John Tate realises how terribly inexperienced they were; making wine then was like someone trying to cook for the first time, recipe book in one hand and stirring spoon in the other. But he recalls with pride the tremendously rich, deep, dark-coloured wines that resulted, wines of such quality they were still drinking very well ten years later.

At the end of 1972 the partners were to establish their Swan Valley base, with the purchase of the 4.5-hectare Turkich family Gnangara property at West Swan, which they took over after vintage the following year. A tremendous amount of work was needed to fashion a premium wine venture out of one that dealt mostly in bulk wines, fortifieds and table grapes. And yet the Evans and Tate Gnangara shiraz based on Swan Valley fruit is believed to be Western Australia's biggest-selling red table wine and is a vital company foundation stone, despite the top-quality wines like chardonnay, semillon, cabernet and merlot produced at their Margaret River property, Redbrook

It is an unpretentious, well-made, soft, flavoursome dry red that people like to buy, though there was a time, John recalls, when it came in for some heavy flak from ultra-critical Eastern States winemen. They concluded that the Swan Valley was the wrong area, shiraz the wrong variety, the label was the wrong shape and the name was wrong. Despite that view, annual production of 8000-9000 cases has sold easily, and since 1975 the shiraz has won four trophies and 117 medals. If that is the

result of being 'wrong' then John wishes the same fate would befall his other wines as well.

By 1982 the Bakers Hill vineyard had run its race and the partnership arrangements with John Evans were wound up the following year — he to run the paint business and the Tates to concentrate on wine. Prior to this John and Toni had taken a keen interest in the early Margaret River wines, especially those of pioneer Tom Cullity. The Tates moved to share in the new area, buying 25 hectares in 1974 and planting the first vines the following year. That was to include seven hectares of cabernet and nearly two of shiraz. Subsequent plantings included merlot, cabernet franc, chardonnay, semillon and sauvignon blanc for a total of 20 hectares.

Processing is centred on the Swan with the annual crush to rise significantly as a result of a new vineyard development at Jindong, south of Busselton. In the past its red loams and ample water supplies have provided for the growing of prime potatoes and vegetables, but in 1994 they became home to the initial plantings of a 40-hectare vineyard, with ample land for further expansion if required. The project will make Evans and Tate more resource independent, reducing the need for outside fruit purchases. It will also provide quality grapes for its best-selling whites, like the Margaret River Classic, a blend of semillon-sauvignon blanc enhanced with a touch of verdelho — a fruity, slightly sweet wine introduced in 1987 and now selling more than 20,000 cases a year —

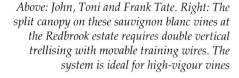

Above: John, Toni and Frank Tate. Right: The split canopy on these sauvignon blanc vines at the Redbrook estate requires double vertical trellising with movable training wires. The system is ideal for high-vigour vines

and the soft, round, popular Two Vine-yards chardonnay, one of my favourites for the price. It is less complex than its big brother from Redbrook but it is a more accessible wine early, with more prominent fruit and less obvious oak. Of the Classic, a friendly wine without a lot of sophistication, I recall Toni's comments: 'It goes like a runaway bus'.

In 1989 mechanical harvesting was successfully introduced at Redbrook for the first time — on the cabernets — a move that will continue and include the new vineyard.

A key factor in the Evans and Tate story was the appointment of winemaker Bill Crappsley in 1978. John realised a skilled professional was essential for his goal of serious wines that demand respect. It proved a happy union, resulting in a range of wines that would do justice to any maker in the nation. Then, in 1993, experienced Eastern States maker Brian Fletcher joined the team which had been previously expanded to include John and Toni's son Frank, later appointed managing partner. In the midst of recession he was to propose a bold move, the winery's own team in Sydney, set to play a vital role in continued expansion plans.

Certainly, they would have had no problems selling what I believe is the pick of the wines to come from Evans and Tate, the 1991 cabernet. Rated by prominent Eastern States critic James Halliday as the best red from Margaret River in some years, it is an outstanding example of superb rich fruit, balance and extreme palate length, a wine to savour, and no doubt a reflection of vineyard improvement and maturity, as well as an outstanding year for cabernets in the district. The buffs may argue that it was about time such a wine was produced, for Evans and Tate was set up to make the best of reds. Market forces, however, see white production occupy almost two-thirds of output with semillon another top performer. For me the 1993 has been the pick, its delicious fruit flavour and soft cleansing acid giving it immediate distinction. At the 1993 SGIO awards, where the wine won a gold medal, I recall being so impressed with the structure and mouth feel. The 1989 vintage grabbed the headlines at the Sheraton Perth awards of that year when it was judged wine of the show, going on to win the best dry white at the Mount Barker show a few months later. Over time, these wines have been found to age gracefully, developing honey characters in the bottle, but as youngsters they are in strong demand at fish restaurants, where they are especially popular with shellfish.

The Evans and Tate Margaret River chardonnay is big, full, rich and refined with lovely toasty oak, at the opposite end of the scale to many made in Australia that John describes as 'blowing you over when first purchased and rigor mortis two years later'. Intensity of flavour and long life are hallmarks with the 1988, a stunning, sophisticated wine and Perth Wine Show trophy winner, having a fragrance described by Eastern States winewriter Huon Hooke of honey, nuts, butter and vanilla.

The early reds from Redbrook were also wines of the highest quality. I recall the first release in 1981 when the 1979 cabernet was the wine of the night at one of my panel tastings. It led former government viticulturist Bill Jamieson to conclude: 'The great thing about Evans and Tate is the ability they have shown to combine lightness with flavour. These wines are showing the way for Western Australia, and indeed the Eastern States.'

But later vintages did not show the depth of flavour such as found in top Coonawarra cabernets, for example. This set up a significant challenge for the vineyard, with special emphasis on soil nutrition as well as trellising.

I have also enjoyed the merlots from the winery, often more French-style than Australian. For me they have been memorable for their rich, plummy flavours and great length.

Exports take up about ten per cent of the Evans and Tate production; there are solid sales to the UK, US, Indonesia, Switzerland, Canada and Germany, with the business expected to expand steadily.

John Tate has always adopted a strong industry profile, being chairman of the wine committee of the Royal Agricultural Society responsible for running the annual Perth Wine Show. He has been awarded the Order of Australia and Jack Mann Memorial medal for his contributions. At the same time his interests have extended beyond the cellar door. For 13 years John was a member of the board of Sir Charles Gairdner Hospital in Perth, and for eight years its chairman.

And though today he may think of himself as a wineman first, his business instincts remain a powerful force. For when asked of the most significant thing that has happened to Evans and Tate, he replied: 'The winning of the West Australian Small Business Award for 1988'. That may well be his view, but mine is totally bound up in the quality of the wines that can be recommended with confidence at any time.

GARBIN WINES

209 Toodyay Road, Middle Swan
Cellar door sales: Mon — Sat 8.30 a.m.
— 5.30 p.m. Sundays, noon — 5.30 p.m.

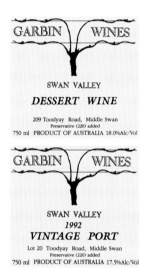

Duje Garbin and son Peter bring a blend of tradition and modern marketing to the family business in the Swan Valley

DUJE GARBIN learnt his winemaking in between fishing on a small island in the Adriatic Sea, just off the Dalmatian coast. It was basic stuff, but ideally suited to the family needs.

As a migrant to Western Australia in 1937, he was soon to continue his craft, after a stint working on his brother's Spearwood market garden. Money saved, he purchased a property at Millendon in the Swan Valley, moving to Middle Swan in 1956.

The Garbin business was built up on bulk wine, some 2000-3000 gallons a year, delivered around the suburbs or purchased by customers visiting the property. It was traditional winemaking and marketing for the times, catering mainly for a keen southern European demand, like other small valley producers.

However, in 1990 son Peter, a design draftsman, decided it was time for a new era of production, and a new marketing direction. This led to the first table wines in 750ml bottles the following year. Committed to a firm improvement policy, he began to invest in equipment new to his father, especially a laboratory. In addition the old varieties on the two-hectare irrigated block have slowly been replanted — to verdelho, chenin blanc, cabernet sauvignon, merlot and shiraz.

At full production by the year 2000 Peter is expecting a crush of 50 tonnes, including 30 purchased from other Swan growers. Backed by a winemaking consultant, he is producing several dry white and red table wines, a vintage port and a sweet fortified white wine. The latter duo are their best-sellers, a reflection on Duje's skills, despite modern developments, and wines of which his son is proud.

Made from pedro ximinez, the white is labelled Dessert Wine. Light and sweet, it could be served chilled as an aperitif style or in place of a sherry, to which there are similarities.

The port is more ruby than vintage. Made from very ripe shiraz grapes, it is smooth, soft and sweet, very good value for people who like such styles. .

Peter, who has studied viticulture and wine quality, has a vision based on being small and good, with wines marketed at modest prices. For example, in 1994 the two best-selling wines were priced at $9.

A major motivation for Peter and wife Katrina continuing with the property was to give their two sons an appreciation of the land, and hard work. 'As well, I find it exciting to see the improvement and the result in the bottle', he said.

HENLEY PARK WINES

Swan Street, Henley Brook
Cellar door sales: Tues — Sun 10 a.m. —
5 p.m. Café style light meals available

THE SMALL Scandinavian country of Denmark does not feature on world wine maps. Yet one of its sons, Claus Petersen, is making his mark in the West Australian industry despite an unconventional entry into the business.

His father, Hans Buchart Petersen, a former Danish politician of ten years and a vice-consul to Western Australia, bought Henley Park Wines at West Swan as an investment in 1986. Established by the Yujnovich family in 1935, it was without doubt one of the best maintained properties in the State, and immediately appealed to Mr Petersen. 'He thought it looked magnificent', Claus recalled. (In early 1994, Mr Petersen sold his interest in Henley Park to a Malaysian businessman but his son retained the major shareholding.)

At the time of the Petersen purchase, Claus had been no stranger to Western Australia, despite his youthful years. He had visited the State three times to help his brother who was running a wheat and sheep farm near Northam. The experience convinced him this was the place to settle, and Henley Park Wines became the vehicle for his new life.

Claus, just 23 at the time, admitted later: 'We did not know anything about viticulture and we thought winemaking was easy'.

So began his 'apprenticeship' lasting until 1994, his eighth vintage, when he finally took full control, with the encouragement and help of wife Lisbeth. During the Petersen reign, the Henley Park crush has doubled, to 100 tonnes. Under vineyard changes, for example, table grapes on the property have been grafted to chardonnay and trellis changes introducing a split canopy have increased yields, as well as quality. In addition, grapes from selected areas such as Margaret River have been purchased though some estate fruit has been sold as well, in the interest of winemaking balance.

Strategic watering to the rich, fertile soils is provided by an artesian bore via a pipe running under West Swan Road, keeping the vines flourishing and helping to meet the winery's aims of providing West Australian wines at reasonable prices.

And consumers in Denmark have shared in the produce. Through Mr Petersen sen. some 20,000 bottles have been exported in a bid to develop a firm

Above: Claus Petersen atop the distinctive wooden-wheeled dray at the Henley Park entrance

market for Henley Park. Some have been stored in the family cellars of their impressive 45-room mansion, once owned by Prince Erik, the uncle of Queen Margrethe, and his wife. The historic building was constructed in 1805 and includes guest quarters especially built for the Prince of Wales, who opened an exhibition in Copenhagen in 1932.

The latest ownership changes will no doubt see exports to Malaysia, and possibly Japan, through associated partnership interests.

The Henley Park business has been built through its history on a sound range of wines including flagons and fortifieds. But Claus has since changed the emphasis firmly to table wines, dropping flagon production in 1994 and restricting fortifieds, though he still produces a tawny port and a drier style from the classic Portuguese varieties grown on the estate.

He explained that the policy was based on economic reality, regardless of the high quality of Swan Valley fortifieds. Stocks of the more luscious sweeter styles from vintages going back to 1977-78-79 and 1982, a legacy of the Yujnovich days, remain in the Henley Park cellars, a 'treasure trove' of old wines slowly declining in quantities as enthusiasts buy them up.

On average Henley Park makes ten wines with the most popular frontignan, a sweet, fruity, late-picked style enjoyed especially by Asian visitors to the cellars. The classic white, an unusual blend of chardonnay and verdelho, also sells well. The latter provides a tropical fruit character that jumps out of the glass, while the chardonnay adds fullness and structure. The wine is made with about 8 grams per litre of residual sugar, while the standard nutty, butterscotch chardonnay, which is completely barrel-fermented and left on yeast lees for about ten months, is dry. A *méthode champenoise* sparkling wine made from shiraz and called Mousse, is generally onion skin in colour, has a soft, fruity palate with the acid adjustment giving it a clean, refreshing finish.

Over the years Henley Park wines have been recognised by retailers in their tastings, and sometimes promoted as wine-of-the-month. But there is no doubt which award Claus prizes above all — the most successful small producer at the Mount Barker Wine Show in 1990. A plaque at the winery marks the success while the name Henley Park is now permanently inscribed on the perpetual silver tray trophy.

About half the production from the 4.5 hectare vineyard is sold at the cellar door with the business plan aimed at consolidation for the rest of the decade. And while the emphasis will be firmly focussed on estate-produced fruit, Claus will keep his buying options open, perhaps even to consider grapes from Denmark — that is Denmark, Western Australia, of course.

HIGHWAY WINES

Great Northern Highway, Herne Hill
Cellar door sales: Mon — Sat 8.30 a.m. — 6 p.m.

QUIETLY nestling in casks and storage tanks in the heart of the Swan Valley are 40,000 litres of fortified wines. That is about the average quantity the Bakranich family of Highway Wines have on hand, maturing away before release. Given the move away from such wines in recent years, it is a remarkable vote of self-confidence in the wines they produce, and in their market. But founder Tony Bakranich and son Velko, with strong family support, have established a sound customer base for fortified wines over the years and they make up most of the family production.

Another feature of Highway Wines is the modest price of their bulk and bottled wines. The dearest is the 1967 Golden Muscat, the oldest in the winery, which sells for $14.50 a bottle at 1994 prices. Its name is taken from a gold medal won at the Perth Show in 1969.

Velko proudly poured me a sample. Made from muscat gordo blanco, it has plenty of luscious sweet fruit character associated with the variety that really blows out the palate, a big mouthful of wine in anyone's language.

When Tony Bakranich migrated to Western Australia in 1930 as a 16-year-old, he first worked on a farm at Waroona. Three years later found him in the Swan Valley employed on various properties and before long, he was buying land to run his own vineyard. The first, in 1936, was a virgin bush block he cleared by hand, the second six years later, an existing vineyard. In 1945 the present property was purchased and on it today are his home and those of his two children, as well as the winery and cellar door sales facility.

Gradually, the two hectares of currants for dried fruit production on the property, were removed and the land planted to wine grapes. The first wines were made in 1954, in a small shed at the back of the existing winery, bulk lines mostly delivered to Perth suburban customers. During these development days Tony supplemented income by working at the Midland railway workshops, and traded the other blocks for better land in the valley, to produce table grapes and citrus fruits as well as wine grapes.

Velko joined the business in 1960, taking over with wife Helen in 1990. They produce about 100 tonnes of fruit for winemaking from some nine hectares of irrigated vineyard, selling fruit surplus to their needs.

Most goes into their fortified range, some 20 different styles in all! Included are six different sherries, muscats, three different ports . . . the list goes on and on. Of the bottled range, the liqueur port — a blend of various vintages, some up to 15 years old — is the most popular. Made from ripe shiraz and cabernet sauvignon, it is big and full bodied — nothing wimpish about this son-of-the-Swan.

All the wines are sold at cellar door, a lot to passing farmers who call in to have containers often of 20 litres filled. The service is provided by Helen, a girl from the suburbs and a former bank officer who admitted to knowing nothing about winemaking before marrying into the family. Now her tasks are considerable and she recalls sore wrists from pruning

and getting bogged in gum boots in the winter-wet vineyard. She also helps in winemaking, a task the trio have learnt over the years through trial and error.

Tony Bakranich and son Velko sample their muscat alongside an old 1000-gallon oak cask

T HREE families have dominated the history of Houghton, Western Australia's most important wine producer. They are the Fergusons, Manns and Hardys who between them have guided its destiny for most of its long life, dating back to the settlement of the Swan River Colony. They have seen it grow from humble times to a position as proud as any national winery.

Situated on the banks of the Swan River in attractive grounds marked by towering pines, the winery is a pleasant 1.5 kilometre drive from Great Northern Highway, 22 kilometres north-east of Perth, in the heart of the traditional centre of West Australian viticulture.

My earliest recollections of Houghton centre on a small man with a big heart and a gladstone bag who spent much of his life at the winery, providing samples to interested visitors in the old tasting area. This was adjacent to the German Passage, so named because of the 500-gallon casks imported from Germany which lined its walls.

I am talking about the late Bert Thomas, in charge of sales at the winery and for some years president of the local Herne Hill Football Club, an Australian rules team in the district which enjoyed great success in the Hills and South Midlands football associations.

I had the privilege of being a team member for some of the time Bert was in charge, and the traditional 'lemons' — the three-quarter time lemon squash break for players — had a significantly different meaning for the Herne Hill players. Bert would come out on the ground, gladstone bag in hand, joining the circle of players. While the coach was busy urging greater effort and victory, the president was busy doing his bit by offering us all a nip of Houghton's sweet sherry. The opposition players would glare at him when he extended the courtesy to the umpires! Certainly his methods must have had some influence, for the team won numerous premierships and remained a powerful force for a number of years.

During this period Jack Mann was at the winemaking helm. He had taken over from his father George in 1930 after having joined the company as an apprentice in 1922, and was to be part of its operations for 51 consecutive vintages. A well-known brandy maker from Chateau Tanunda in South Australia, George Mann had worked for a period in Western Australia at the former Santa Rosa winery and at Glen Hardey, Smith's Mill (now the district of Glen Forrest), before returning to South Australia. But it was not long before he was back again to be employed in 1910 by Houghton, injecting much-

HOUGHTON WINES

Dale Road, Middle Swan
Cellar Door sales: Mon — Sun 10 a.m. —
5 p.m.
Picnic area available
Functions can be arranged

The beautifully restored old Houghton home-stead, built in 1863, is today the company's administration headquarters

needed skill and experience which resulted in a marked improvement in the quality of the wines.

His ability extended beyond the winery — for in 1894 he won a pruning competition in Tanunda against all comers and was awarded a certificate of merit and a gold medal.

George Mann had been employed by Charles William Ferguson, son of Dr John Ferguson, the Colonial Surgeon who had bought the Houghton vineyard for £350 in 1859. The property at that time was mostly virgin bush, with only about two hectares cleared. In that year the first vintage of 25 gallons is recorded. Charles reported that the cask was not full, so his father washed some pebbles and put them in the container. It was the son's job for many days thereafter to drop in more pebbles, to make good the loss from evaporation, and to test the progress of the fermentation by holding a lighted match at the bung hole. Initially, the fumes extinguished the flame quickly, but when half a dozen matches in succession burned right to the fingers, fermentation was deemed to have ceased.

According to Charles Ferguson's grandson, Don Barrett-Lennard, his pioneering ancestor was very much the 'canny Scot', moderate in his ways and a man whose word was his bond. His diminu-

tive stature (only about eight stone, or 50 kilograms) belied his great vigour, for he quickly set about clearing and developing the property with enthusiasm and dedication. Wheat initially was the main crop, and large crops of hay were grown. As well, horses, sheep and pigs were bred and there was even a small dairy.

From the outset there were only a few vines at Houghton, and for a time the emphasis was on fruit production before it was finally resolved to concentrate on vines for wine and raisins.

A résumé of the early plantings revealed them to be just over three hectares and made up of verdelho, gordo blanco and 'Galops Large' verdo (sic), and white sauvignon.

Further plantings included muscat and hermitage, and by about 1880 it was estimated that there were some four hectares under vines.

Soon after the turn of the century the vineyard extended to over 50 hectares and was being added to each year. At that time grape varieties were referred to as carbinet (sic), malbec and red shiraz for the clarets, riesling and white shiraz for the hock and chablis, and grenache, red shiraz, dolcetto, pedro ximines (sic) and doradilla (sic) for the ports and sherries.

Charles Ferguson was proud of the

Contributory trio in the Houghton success story (L to R): The late Jack Mann, doyen of winemakers; present-day senior winemaker Paul Lapsley; state manager Brad Starkie

five large, cool cellars that could hold nearly half a million litres of wine. There was also a lean-to fermenting room and distillery, with all the wine being at least three years old when it was sent to Perth for bottling and distribution. For many years this involved transportation in casks by horse and wagon to Midland where the wine would be railed to Perth, and then again taken by horse and wagon to the Houghton city headquarters, which initially were on the corner of St Georges Terrace and William Street, and later at the corner of Murray and Milligan streets.

Don Barrett-Lennard had lived and worked at Houghton for many years with his uncle Jack Ferguson, who managed the property and was winemaker until the arrival of George Mann. Jack and his brother Don, who looked after the Perth office, were given control of the property by their father Charles in 1911, when he retired.

Don said their policy, and that of their father, was to concentrate on private trading at the Swan cellars and in Perth because they feared being forced to the wall if they tried to compete with big Eastern States companies. 'They could make as much in a day as Houghton could in a year', he said. So they aimed at producing good grapes and bought a lot of small casks, the best they could get from Germany, much to the envy of other winemakers. For many years crushing and pressing was by hand.

But with the property heavily mortgaged, profits were hard to come by as the brothers pursued the development path after World War I. Then like the community in general they had to suffer the disastrous Depression years which saw hungry men take to the roads in droves looking for work, and the brothers battle to meet interest payments.

Even as late as World War II, Don reminded me, it was a struggle to sell 500 gallons of chablis a year.

But the pair worked their way through the problems and gave thousands of hours to their interests — Jack to trotting and Don to local government. Years later at his home by the river at Oakover, adjacent to Houghton, Don Ferguson proudly produced a medal impossible to wear, being the size of a dinner plate. It was awarded to his grandfather, Dr John Ferguson, for Swan Valley raisins shown at an intercolonial exhibition in Victoria in 1866-7.

In 1950 the Emu Wine Company Pty Ltd of London, which had purchased Valencia Vineyards five years previously, bought Houghton. But the sale did not go down well with many, especially Jack Mann, for the commercial approach to winemaking required by Emu was far removed from the Ferguson style of operation. Of greatest disappointment was the directive which saw the blending of top Houghton wines with those of Valencia to a 'commercial standard and quality'.

Early in his reign Jack sought to produce something new in the Houghton range, and in 1937 made the first of the acclaimed white burgundy style. Years later it was described as the company's 'million-plus ambassadors a year', a reflection of its sales success in the Eastern States and overseas.

The blue-striped classic Australian has done more to put Western Australia on the national and international wine map than any other product of the State.

At the time the move was a gamble, for nearly all the wine consumed in Australia was fortified. But the risk proved to be well taken and the wine soon showed its class; it won first prize at the Melbourne Wine Show in its maiden year, and again

MOONDAH BROOK

1993
VERDELHO
WESTERN AUSTRALIA
750 ml PRODUCT OF AUSTRALIA 12.5% ALC/VOL

MOONDAH BROOK

1993
CHENIN BLANC
WESTERN AUSTRALIA
750 ml PRODUCT OF AUSTRALIA 12.5% ALC/VOL

HOUGHTON

1993

WESTERN AUSTRALIA
Semillon
Sauvignon Blanc
750 ml PRODUCT OF AUSTRALIA 12.5% ALC/VOL

in 1938. Leading judge W.W. Senior made special mention of the wine, likening it to the great white burgundies of France — hence the idea for subsequent labelling.

Among its famous devotees were long-serving Prime Minister Sir Robert Menzies and international entertainer Rolf Harris, who was born and raised at Bassendean just a few kilometres from where the wine was made.

The wine really came about when Jack persuaded the Ferguson family to buy a Seitz sterilising filter from Germany, one of the first brought to Australia. Son Dorham felt the equipment provided for stable bottling. 'It gave my father the opportunity to make a white burgundy style confident that the wine would not spoil', he said.

Explaining his technique to me once, the great winemaker said: 'I decided to leave the skins in contact with the pick of the free-run juice for 24 hours before fermentation. I wanted to extract flavour without loss of refinement. I was agreeably surprised, and so were a lot of people around Australia. They had not thought that a warm area like the Swan Valley could produce such a wine.' Indeed, many were astonished by Jack Mann's early success, leading to constant visits to Houghton over the years by prominent Eastern States producers, not to mention those from overseas.

Until the 1950s, when muscadelle was introduced into the blend, Houghton white burgundy was made entirely from chenin blanc. Muscadelle generated an extra flavour and added softness but was also an insurance to production, especially important with the wine increasing in commercial popularity. Muscadelle does not suffer from rain damage like chenin, reducing the risk of lower fruit supplies.

A feature of the wine over the years has been its generosity of flavour and ability to live in the bottle. It has always done well at masked tastings I have conducted over many years. Then I would find myself in total disagreement with one of the 'commandments' of Saint Jack, as he was once dubbed, when he advocated adding water to wine.

A staunch opponent of the nation's brewers, he sought to have wine replace beer as the national drink of Australia.

He saw the way to achieve the goal by making wines with such flavour and character that they would be able to take an equal amount of water, so satisfying the discerning buff and 'reducing the hazards of modern travel' by cutting the alcohol intake. Many an important visitor — fa-

mous musicians, High Court judges, politicians and academics — were introduced to Houghton wines under the estate's big pine trees with a bottle of chablis poured over a jug of iceblocks. As I explained in the Introduction, I was brought up on wine and water but I was never prepared to do that with styles like the white burgundy, preferring to leave it a year or two in the bottle, maturing quietly to allow the wine to develop and show its true breeding.

When Houghton held its 150th celebrations, winemakers who had worked at the property were brought from all over Australia to join the party. They included David McNamara (1971-74), Bob Cartwright (1974-77), Bill Hardy (1977-78), Jon Reynolds (1977-85) and Peter Dawson (1978-93). At a special lunch Jack Mann held pride-of-place at the boardroom table made in 1890 from Australian cedar for the Palace Hotel, and purchased by Houghton when renovating the original Ferguson homestead. Built in 1863 to plans which came from Scotland, this building is today the company's administration headquarters. Originally, it consisted of five rooms in a row surrounded by a narrow verandah with the roof made from hand-cut sheoak shingles grown on the property. Two wings were added separately at later stages while a second building at right angles to the main house contained stables and the original kitchen with an open fireplace and baking oven.

Around the boardroom table were 18 chairs bought in Perth, Scotland, part of the original set made from oak in 1894 for the Royal Burch (borough) of Leith. On this day they accommodated the cream of the nation's wine writers, as well as the winemakers, all enthralled with Jack's recollections of a lifetime in the industry. Some smiled when he spoke of modern thin wines made in wineries 'more like dairies' or 'small oil refineries' — for at times he was a vocal critic of such modern practices as temperature-controlled fermentation which he referred to as the 'cold castration of grape juice'.

To Jack the problem was clear: grapes were being picked before they were fully ripe, from vines often forced to overproduce. As a result the wines just did not have enough flavour.

In the winemaking industry, Jack Mann was certainly something of a sage, and I always enjoyed his little pearls of wisdom, some of which I have recorded over the years:

— If you do not depart from the orthodox, you cannot advance. You have to be different to be better.

— It is wrong and improper to describe any man as a winemaker. Nature makes the wine and man, if he is skilled, gives nature the opportunity to perform to the best advantage.

— In winemaking you have to absorb an enormous amount of knowledge before you realise you know nothing. And when you realise you know nothing you start to learn.

— Cabernet sauvignon (his favourite grape) is the only variety that would be tolerated in heaven.

— I have never picked grapes unless the vines had reached the stage where they would not nourish them any more.

— You can never make perfect wine, but you should strive for it.

— A wine is perfectly balanced when it is glowing with life, blessed with refinement and adorned with flavour.

— If grapes are left on the vine till they are properly ripe, enjoying the generosity of our sunshine, the aroma of the fruit becomes the bouquet of the wine. Nature should be allowed to do its work.

A visit to Houghton or the Manns invariably ended up with something special being brought out, like a 1936 frontignac, a black, treacle-like wine full of rich, ripe, powerful flavours that was velvety on the tongue, a rare tasting experience. Jack recalled that the ripe fruit development involved such a sugar content that fermentation was a problem. Such wines were used for blending, being too concentrated to drink on their own. 'If you could get it into the bottle, you could not get it out without breaking the container', he told me with a laugh.

Besides wine the other Mann family passion is cricket, reflected in a necklace worn by Sally Mann, Dorham's wife. It was won by George Mann for the best bowling average with the Tanunda Cricket Club in 1888, while nearly a century on — and at a vastly different level — Tony Mann (Dorham's brother) has played Test cricket for Australia.

But cricket had come to Houghton long before the Manns. Charles Ferguson laid down a pitch in the vineyard in the 1880s, and for some years it was the only centre for cricket outside the towns and villages of the Colony. When it came to refreshments, visitors were often supplied with grapes from the vines, the wines themselves being kept in the cellars. The locals did not want their inevitable victories attributed to an inebriated opposition!

Jack Mann's cricketing career spanned 40 years and he achieved widespread recognition as probably Western Australia's

most famous underarm bowler. He took more than 2000 wickets playing for the State's oldest cricket club, Middle Swan, near Houghton — a tally that included a 1927-28 seasonal harvest of 81 wickets for 929 runs (average 11.4) and a fine match performance in 1935 of 9/29 in an innings, with all the opposition batsmen being bowled.

In recognition of Jack's prowess the Swan Shire Council named the team's home ground the Jack Mann Oval.

Jack's love of cricket and his unusual eye for work detail often crossed paths. For example, on 21 October 1932 he left a group of workers in the cellar bottling about 1250 litres of the 1931 hermitage while he took the train to Perth. His destination was the Western Australian Cricket Association headquarters, and the occasion was the controversial 'bodyline' tour by the English team led by Douglas Jardine. From his favourite seat in the grandstand, Jack was keen to see fast bowler Harold Larwood in action.

I asked son Dorham how he was able to remember the date so precisely, and he picked up a bottle with a roll of paper inside. It was one of his father's 'filing systems'. On the sheet can still be seen the details he had written of the bottling. The wine was made from shiraz grown on the adjacent Oakover block, and was very ripe at picking. Dorham still has a few bottles and every now and then brings one out of the cellar. This he did for the 1989 panel of judges officiating at the Perth

Magnificent jacaranda trees shade the grassed cellar door sales area where local jazz artists perform each November at the annual Houghton 'Jacaranda Jazz' day

Wine Show. Their conclusion — magnificent.

Another proud possession of Dorham's is the Royal Agricultural Society of Western Australia's silver Challenge Cup donated by C.W. Ferguson for the exhibitor gaining the highest points in the wine section. Jack won it three times, so that it became a family possession, or their 'absolute property' as the description records. Jack's recognition as a winemaker was to go as high as the Queen herself, for he was awarded the MBE in 1964. No less satisfying were his successes in earlier years such as championship first prize at the Melbourne show for 13 consecutive years with the Houghton Oloroso sherry, and the 'Champion of Australia' accolade over four years for sweet wines.

For me the sensational flavours of the great Houghton liqueurs will remain for ever. In travels to winemaking areas round the world, nothing has come close to them. There were five in all — frontignac, muscat (gordo), hermitage (shiraz), tokay (pedro) and port (grenache and shiraz). Sadly, modern day consumption trends and economics have seen these wonderful styles of Houghton fall by the wayside, but perhaps one day they will be back, no doubt watched by Jack Mann in his vineyard in the sky.

He passed away in 1989, to be missed by all, including Peter Dawson who took over the senior winemaking role with the company in 1985.

He brought his own stamp of class to the company wines, but they are still based on ripe fruit flavour with white wines like the white burgundy, verdelho and chenin blanc, for example, developing honeyed fullness and complexity if left to age.

It all came together for Houghton at the 1989 Perth Wine Show when its wines were awarded a record eight trophies, an outstanding performance. It bettered that of Peter's predecessor, Jon Reynolds, with whom he worked for seven years. At the 1980 Perth show wines Jon made won six trophies, yet he had never won one before in five years of winemaking in Western Australia and South Australia. It was a turnaround for the company, bringing them in from the cold (they had not won a show trophy since 1977). At the time Houghton was a classic old winery of character and great potential, but poorly equipped.

The 1980s were to be the start of a new era with millions of dollars invested in new equipment and the latest technology. Included was the first must chiller on the Swan Valley in 1980. The unit's place in the winemaking process is immediately after the grapes are crushed, when the must — the grape juice, skins and seeds — is cooled as it passes through the assembly pipes. The pioneering of the process is credited to former Penfolds giant Max Schubert (of Grange Hermitage fame) who was seeking to overcome problems in Griffith, New South Wales.

He set out to control fermentations in the hot climate that were over in a day, far too quickly. Must chilling takes the heat out of grapes, helping retain flavour and bouquet, with the chemical reactions slowed as the temperature is lowered. Winemaker Bill Hardy, who had proudly shown me the unit, had been transferred to the west from South Australia when Thomas Hardy and Sons purchased Houghton in 1976.

Hardys had been involved in a tough takeover struggle for the purchase of Houghton and Valencia against WA Worsted and Woollen Mills Ltd with bid and counter-bid being put to the British-based owners, Emu Wine Holdings Limited. The battle pushed Hardys to paying $30,000 more than the $4.25 million maximum target the company had set. The defeat for the wool company, then controlled by Robert Holmes à Court, who was on the way to becoming one of the country's richest men, was to delay his entry into the wine business until the late 1980s when he purchased the two historic properties of Vasse Felix (Margaret River) and Forest Hill (Mount Barker).

But while Mr Holmes à Court may have been disappointed with the result, the West Australian wine industry generally welcomed the new owners. For the Hardy family had a long and rich history in the business, and it was dedicated to build on its strong foundations. This meant for Houghton the gradual amalgamation of Valencia and a heavy investment programme for the latest equipment and facilities to modernise the winery, now a glowing jewel in the owner's crown. (Houghton is today part of the BRL Hardy Wine Company. In 1992 Thomas Hardy and Sons merged with Berri Renmano Ltd to form the second biggest wine company in Australia.)

When the Hardy takeover occurred, Houghton production was 14,000 cases a year. Today it is 400,000 of which more than 160,000 is white burgundy, the biggest dry white wine seller in the country.

The company buys in fruit from around the State as well as developing a strong liaison with contract growers, such as in

the emerging Pemberton-Manjimup district. Senior vineyard manager Ron Page, who has played a vital role in helping improve fruit quality from associated vineyards, has the major task of looking after more than 300 hectares around the State.

Two older ventures are important contributors as well. They are the leased Frankland River vineyard belonging to former Adelaide Lord Mayor John Roche, and Moondah Brook at Gingin.

The pioneering move to the north of Perth (to Gingin) came at a time when industry attention was being firmly fixed on the new cooler areas in the south of the State. The development idea was put to Managing Director Ian Smith by the co-ordinator of Agricultural Industries, Mr J.M. Clayton, in 1968 after an Australian company had rejected the idea. The property was considered ideal, mainly because of the availability of water and suitable soil types.

The first vines were planted in 1969, but there were immediate problems: the young vines were sandblasted by strong winds that whipped up the top soil from the newly cultivated areas, and then the grasshoppers moved in. Big numbers of vines were destroyed and had to be re-planted. But persistence was rewarded and today the vineyard is responsible for some of the best value-for-money premium wine produced in the State.

It was at this vineyard that I saw in action the first mechanical harvester to operate in Western Australia. That was 1978, and it cut a strange sight as it straddled the vines.

It was in March 1973 when I first met Ted Holland at the Frankland River development. The Eastern States stockman turned West Australian viticulturist was full of satisfaction as he showed us the healthy young vines. The 7500-hectare sheep and cattle property where the vines had been planted was bought by Roche after its potential was defined by the 1964 Grape Industry Committee which investigated the industry and considered future expansion possibilities.

It recommended the Frankland area, along with others in the South West, for the production of high-quality wine grapes, and in 1968 the first plantings were made, a modest two hectares on a picturesque slope. 'By the end of 1969 we were convinced that grapes would do well', Ted said in that initial visit as we sipped the first wines produced from the vineyard. So plantings were increased each year with the vineyard flourishing, despite the problems of dry years, birds and, later, salinity.

Houghton finalised leasing arrangements for the vineyard in 1981 and today it has an important role in the company's plans.

But Houghton produces more than 60 per cent of its own fruit needs with a long-term commitment to its own vineyards. Moondah Brook, for example, the most prolific major vineyard in Western Australia, produces about 1200 tonnes a year, while the Swan and Frankland River op-

The neatly manicured slopes of Houghton's leased Frankland River vineyard yield some of Australia's finest wines, particularly the acclaimed rhine riesling

erations each provide 900 tonnes in contributing towards 22 different wines in five product ranges — the show reserve (made only in special years), Gold Reserve, Moondah Brook, Houghton line range, and Wildflower Ridge. Looking towards the late 1990s, Houghton plans to increase its crush to 8000 tonnes.

Fruit from the fertile soils of the Swan Valley result in full-bodied dry whites, with the chardonnay, verdelho, chenin blanc and semillon the backbone of the white burgundy. They provide the depth as a young wine and, with the ripe flavours, generate the beautiful complexity that develops with bottle age.

This was evident in the 1982, 84 and 86 show reserve vintages which won best full-bodied dry white table wine trophies at the Royal Adelaide Wine Show in 1989, 90 and 92. Full and rich but with surprising freshness for aged wines, they are undoubtedly among the best ever produced in the State. The 1993 vintage, in which growers rated the base chenin blanc as some of the best fruit ever, should still be drinking well in the year 2000.

The white varieties grown at Moondah Brook — chenin blanc, chardonnay and verdelho — display distinctive varietal character, having the capacity for great richness with time in the bottle. The verdelho from the vineyard in particular has been one of the State's great success stories, regarded by many as a benchmark in Australia because of its depth of flavour, attractive aromatic fruit characters and natural balance. It does not need oak treatment to add complexity, though tasters have been deceived at times in the past. For, with some development, the wine generates a distinctive toasty character.

Chenin blanc showed its class when the 1992 vintage was named joint white wine-of-the-year at a London international judging event, a sensational result given the variety's lowly status compared to many others.

In good years its fruit characters range from passion and tropical fruit to honey.

Cabernet sauvignon from the vineyard is the basis for the outstanding rosé produced by the company, a fresh, lively, stylish wine, well suited to Australian summers. As a youngster (when it should be consumed) it is soft and full with distinctive cabernet aromas and flavour that have also appealed to the show judges. It has been awarded a remarkable number of medals and trophies.

The cuttings for the Moondah verdelho plantings originally came from a single Houghton vine that survived by accident. The variety was grown at the vineyard last century with C.W. Ferguson winning a certificate of merit for a dry verdelho at the World Expo held in Melbourne in 1890-91. But powdery mildew and bird attacks saw the vineyard, called 'four acres' by the workers and running from near the winery to the river, grubbed out and replanted with shiraz. Jack Mann found the surviving vine, and enjoyed many a meal from the fruit.

When it was decided to replant the variety on land near Great Northern Highway, cuttings from the verdelho vine were used. Indeed, most of the plantings in the State can now be sourced to that vine. Today Houghton produces more than half the verdelho grown in Australia and has great faith in its future. A comprehensive tasting for this publication justified the confidence. I have also enjoyed Houghton chardonnays, especially the 1990 show reserve, released in 1994. This is a wine made from the most selective fruit, given the best oak, and a great deal of care. It swamped the palate with flavour, was beautifully balanced and it lingered, and lingered . . .

But the tremendous success enjoyed with its white wines has led many people not to regard the company as a significant red wine producer. This belief, however, began to change in the 1990s with a new direction that has seen all the red varieties removed from Houghton's Swan Valley vineyards in favour of a concentration on supplies from southern areas — Margaret River, Pemberton, Manjimup, Mount Barker and the Frankland River vineyard, where important measures have been taken to overcome salinity problems. The shiraz from Frankland River has already impressed, but Houghton believes the cabernets will eventually prove more elegant and refined than those from Margaret River, and be slower to develop.

Major trophies and gold medals in 1992 supported the company claim of sound improvement. Wines I have enjoyed include the 1992 Gold Reserve shiraz, 1989 and 1990 Gold Reserve cabernet sauvignons, 1992 Wildflower Ridge shiraz and the 1990 Moondah Brook cabernet sauvignon, from Frankland River fruit, part of company policy to select the best full-bodied material from around the State for the label.

But think of Frankland River and the winery's rhine riesling springs to mind. In a relatively short time the area has produced some of the best wines in Australia, deliciously flavoursome, lime-citrusy styles as youngsters with acidity to provide freshness and balance and the base for a decade of development. The 1983 vintage, for example, was delighting judges six years later and for many consumers the style represents a really pleasant alternative to over-oaked chardonnays. The 1986, a favourite of mine, won the chairman's trophy for best wine at the 16th annual Sheraton awards in 1993.

The variety also produces excellent sweet styles like the 1984 Beerenauslese, one of the most successful show wines in the country in recent years.

Chardonnays from the Frankland River vineyard are also set to make their mark, with rich, peachy fruit flavours, certainly restrained and different from so many Australian styles that develop quickly and are big and buttery. This is more the direction of the Moondah Brook chardonnay, which gives Houghton two distinctly different wines from the variety.

The Houghton move to seek contract growers from various viticultural areas ensures a supply of fruit of different characteristics, enormous blending opportunities and spreads the risk of a bad year in a particular district.

Paul Lapsley, who was appointed senior winemaker in 1993 when Peter Dawson was made chief winemaker with parent BRL Hardy, says in-field crushing introduced in 1990 has boosted wine quality. In the process the grapes are picked, crushed, chilled and loaded into a tanker within 20 minutes of being harvested, enhancing freshness, colour and flavour. Houghton also employs wineries in Margaret River and Pemberton for contract crushing.

Back at the winery the solid investment programme has now provided a modern bottling hall to go with the stainless steel tanks, refrigeration, air conditioning, modern laboratory, new wood storage, grape receival and processing facilities. Paul and fellow winemaker John Griffiths smile today at their predecessors who had to look to flooding the concrete upper deck of the cellar as a means of keeping stored wines cool.

The winemakers are looking to the vineyard for future potential. 'That is where the major scope for improvement lies', Paul said. 'We will see what really can be done in Western Australia as young vines and those being planted come into maturity.'

Certainly most of the 80,000 visitors a year to Houghton will drink to that. Its tourist importance was acknowledged in January 1986 and 1992 when Houghton was selected as winner of the Sir David Brand tourism award for the wine industry.

Winemakers Paul Lapsley (left) and John Griffiths assessing juice quality

JANE BROOK ESTATE WINES

Toodyay Road, Middle Swan
Cellar door sales: Mon — Fri 10 a.m. — 5
p.m. Sat, Sun and public holidays: 12
noon — 5 p.m. Light lunches, garden
courtyard

*David Atkinson's strategy stretches from this
cellar to the emerging Japanese wine market*

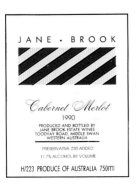

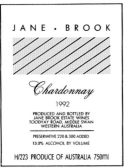

I T TOOK an unscheduled stop at Wubin,
a small wheat-growing centre 270 kilometres north of Perth, for the turning point
to come in the life of a young West Australian who has gone on to make his mark
in the wine business.

David Atkinson, who runs Jane Brook
Estate in partnership with his wife
Beverley, was on his wheatbelt beat as
area marketing manager for a fuel company when he lingered at Wubin for a
cuppa and a snack in the local roadhouse.
There he picked up a book on wine by
prominent Victorian retailer Dan Murphy,
and became absorbed.

'I read it from cover to cover, twice', he
recalled as he sat under the attractive per-
gola adjacent to the winery in Toodyay
Road, Middle Swan, and next to the small
creek from which the operation has taken
its name. Before that, when the Atkinsons
bought the property in partnership with
relatives (former winemaking brother-in-
law John Barrett-Lennard and his wife
Lyn) from the Mateljan family, it was
known as Vignacourt, after a town in
France with which post-World War I
owner Henry Mountjoy had been associated. Shortly before the war started, his
father, Mr David Mountjoy, had originally planted the property with table
grapes for the owner, a Mr Jack Bassett,
who had bought the land from the Church
of England. Unfortunately for the younger

Mountjoy, he had been forced to walk off
the property in the late 1920s, unable to
meet the commitments of the soldier settlement scheme in which returning serv-
icemen were encouraged to go on the land.
He had been hit by low grape prices in a
deteriorating economic climate as the
world moved towards the Great Depression.

For a period the vineyard was worked
by a Mr Morcombe until it came under the
control of the Mateljans. Initially, their
emphasis was on table grapes, but in the
early 1950s they replanted with varieties
suitable for winemaking, with the first
vintage of 450 litres in 1954.

For David, a former West Australian
rugby player and shotput record holder,
decided he wanted to run a business of his
own, and he was considering getting married. Although he knew nothing about
viticulture and winemaking, the seal was
set when the purchase was arranged. Indeed, he later conceded he did not know
how to operate the crusher or the press at
the time of his first vintage. But the move
heralded a new era for the small property
that has seen $2 million invested in winery
and vineyard development to make a
proud Swan Valley label.

If the couple had any fears in the struggle through the early difficult years, an
event in 1980 went a long way to dismiss-
ing them for ever. That was when their

1977 cabernet sauvignon won first prize at a show in Italy, beating 500 other entries. But the Atkinsons never collected the award. When the organisation found out that the wine was not made in Italy, it was disqualified. The couple had not known about the show, or that their wine was entered. That was done by a Sydney customer who travelled regularly to Italy and wanted to see how the West Australian wine would fare.

While a professional winemaker is employed, David directs the operation and Beverley is responsible for marketing. Jane Brook has spread its wings far and wide, including to Japan. The lateral-thinking duo decided against seeking sales in the traditional UK-North American area, but to look to the land of the rising sun. This was because of the country's affluence, its rapid westernisation and low wine consumption levels. So they invested $250,000 in a five-year programme aiming at sales worth $500,000 a year, 40 per cent of production, by 1996. To support such sales, vineyard developments and contract grower arrangements provide for a doubling of the crush to more than 200 tonnes by the year 2000.

In terms of the rich history of the valley and the people with several generations in wine, the Atkinsons are johnny-come-latelys. However, that has not stopped the former fuel seller from being very forthright in his views if he believes they are in the valley's, and the industry's, best interests. For example, his support for Sunday trading put him offside with some other producers.

But exciting wins in the SGIO Winemakers Exhibition in 1985 with the 1984 wood-aged chenin, and trophies at the Sheraton Perth wine awards in 1991, 92 and 93 with rhine riesling in aromatic classes, amid other successes, combined with a continuing flow of visitors to the winery, estimated at up to 35,000 a year, are testimony to the progress the couple have made.

Many of the visitors who are curious to learn of the origin of the name Jane Brook are happily accommodated. Jane Currie was wife of Captain Mark Currie, Fremantle's first Harbour Master. The couple themselves had arrived in the new Colony in 1829, and the brook was so named by Captain James Stirling during an exploration of the upper reaches of the Swan River. Another pioneer, John Septimus Roe, who was the Colony's first Surveyor General and the founder of Sandalford Wines, noted Jane Brook in Exploration Plan 134, dated September-October-November 1829.

Today the emphasis in production at Jane Brook is on white wines, which make up 75 per cent of the output. The main wines are the best selling wood-aged chenin blanc, sauvignon blanc, rhine riesling, chardonnay and cabernet merlot.

A combination of new and used (mainly German) oak is used for the Swan Valley chenin, a dry, soft, fruity wine with a lovely clean finish. The rhine riesling, made from Mount Barker fruit, has a fresh aromatic bouquet with classic limey citrus characters on the palate, and is slightly sweet. It sells at cellar door for $14 a bottle (1994 prices), testimony to its quality.

The chardonnay, from Swan Valley grapes, is a full, buttery, fruity wine, with the wood not at all dominant, a good mouthful of wine like the cabernet merlot. Also made from Swan fruit, it is rich and soft, aided by egg white fining, and with good cellaring potential — five to seven years say the Atkinsons.

In 1993 an unwooded sauvignon blanc was introduced. Made from early picked Swan fruit, it is a slightly sweet fresh style, lighter in tropical fruit flavours than those from southern areas of WA. It is very palate pleasant, with excellent length.

A *méthode champenoise* made from Swan chardonnay and used for the 1994 visit to WA by Prince Charles, is labelled Elizabeth Jane, after the Atkinson's daughter. Son Ben has his place with B.D.R. (Benjamin David Robert) on a sparkling burgundy. It was made with shiraz in 1993 after trials the previous year with cabernet merlot.

One of the most popular wines from Jane Brook is a white port, produced from a Portuguese grape variety that is one of David's secrets. Made as a Swan response to success with such wines by South West producers, it is an excellent aperitif poured over ice with a slice of lemon.

A controversial move by the Atkinsons was to introduce a $2 tasting charge in October 1993, the first in the valley, necessary say the couple to offset higher Federal Government taxes on wine. 'There has been a barrier to such a move by winemakers, a feeling of guilt because free sampling has been a basic part of the industry', David said. 'But we sat down and did an evaluation which showed that our sampling costs were $40,000 a year, and that is based on [1994] wholesale prices.'

Only a few visitors have objected, obviously because of the Atkinson goals — better quality wines at reasonable prices, and to give people a good time so they will come back.

LAMONT WINES

Bisdee Road, Millendon
Cellar door sales: Wed — Sun 10 a.m. —
5 p.m.
Alfresco and à la carte restaurant
Functions by arrangement

Above: A family affair — Mark Warren,
Fiona Lamont-Warren, and Kate, Corin and
Neil Lamont

CONSIDERING they are both committed third-generation Swan Valley vignerons and winemakers, it seemed appropriate that Neil Lamont and Corin Mann, daughter of the late Houghton giant Jack, should establish Lamont Wines.

The summer sun was sinking across the vines as Neil, with whom I went to school, recalled his family history. At the time, we were gazing out over green, healthy vineyard growth to nearby Susannah Brook, sipping a glass of his sparkling cabernet, the making of which follows a Jack Mann tradition. His grandfather Neil had come to the Swan in 1921 as a soldier-settler. A veteran of the Boer War and World War I, he took up blocks in Haddrill Road, between Great Northern Highway and the foothills, to grow grapes and make wine that he sold to the Palace Hotel. But the winery was no palace, though it could perhaps claim to be the only one of its type in the world. It was made from blackboys like a log cabin, with blackboys laid on the floor as well — a technique often used for stable floors on the Swan in those days.

It was no surprise then, given such history and strong family devotion to the Swan Valley, that the Lamonts were at the forefront of battles in the early 1990s to save the area's special rural qualities from intensive urban and major highway development.

Young Neil had a diverse journey into the vine and wine industry. After completing an apprenticeship as a boilermaker welder at the Midland railway workshops, he and his wife Corin, a domestic science teacher, worked at Yampi Sound for four years. They returned to the Swan in 1966 to start a commercial piggery, in association with currant production from the property, bought from Neil's father Len some years earlier.

Then came the turning point — Jack Mann's retirement from Houghton. 'He immediately urged us to convert the vineyard to wine grapes and drew up a sketch plan for a winery based on traditional producing methods', Neil said. 'The idea was not to be commercial, but to make wines the family liked to drink.'

The philosophy was based on ripe grapes, natural yeasts, open waxed-lined concrete fermenters, fruit crushed carefully and slowly, normal fermenting temperatures as opposed to refrigeration, a suitable amount of time for the juice to be on skins whether it be red or white wine, dry wines to be dry and not slightly sweet, and having the generosity of flavour to take water or ice. There was one more thing. All fruit had to go through a butcher's mincer, a technique now being adopted by other Swan producers.

Jack Mann introduced the mincer to Houghton soon after taking over as

winemaker, in the search for more colour and flavour, a softer finish, and more refinement. The berries go through the mincer for shredding after the stalks have been removed to eliminate coarseness in the wine. The shredded berries are fermented with the juice. Jack once told me that the method allowed for the release of the high level of sugar contained in the raisined berries, a result of the Swan's intense sunshine and drying east winds.

Another unusual feature of the Lamont Winery is a huge wooden beam and a 44-gallon drum hung at one end. This is slowly filled with water pulling down the beam gently to press the fruit.

The vineyard conversion took in the varieties verdelho (60 per cent), semillon (20 per cent) and muscadelle (20 per cent) to produce the very best white burgundy style, made famous by Jack at Houghton. Cabernet was also planted and the first vintage was in 1978. It was only about 500 litres, small indeed compared to the massive Houghton vintages which Jack had supervised for so long.

But it was a very exciting moment, Neil recalled, with Jack 'loving the wine to death'. For it had been six years since he had made his last wine at Houghton and he was delighted to be back in harness, and teaching his daughter. The following year was even more exciting with the first white burgundy, and immediately after bottling, a cork was ceremoniously pulled.

Jack remained heavily involved at Lamonts, almost up to the time of his death. 'He used to walk through the vines pulling berries off here and there to chew and spit out, assessing the maturity', Neil said. 'We always joked he had an inbuilt pH meter.'

Jack's traditional winemaking philosophy has been preserved at Lamonts, and built upon with added expertise provided by Neil and Corin's son-in-law Mark Warren (Fiona's husband). A University of Western Australia science graduate, he has done post-graduate studies in wine science through the Charles Sturt University at Wagga.

The Lamont crush is about 85 tonnes a year, of which about 50 tonnes is bought from different growers in the Swan Valley, East Bullsbrook and Bindoon. The rest is produced on the property, the unirrigated vines growing in good gravelly loam soils. Some 17 different wines are made including limited quantities of a flor fino sherry and the *méthode champenoise* (cabernet) as well as a wide range of dry white and red table wines, and other fortified styles. The dry white blend white burgundy makes up about a third of the production. It is big, generous and full flavoured, reflecting the climate and soils of the Swan Valley. No oak is used and it is released about six months after vintage.

Another extremely popular wine produced by Lamonts is a rosé from cabernet, a full-flavoured, crisp style fermented dry, excellent in summer when poured over a glass of ice. It gave the father and daughter winemaking team a special thrill in 1979 when it won their first medal at the Perth Wine Show, a bronze.

I have two favourites in the range, an unwooded cabernet made from fully ripe fruit, and the Navera, a liqueur dessert style. Features of the red are the lovely taste of the berry fruit character and soft tannin finish, though for some it may seem jammy or even porty. The Lamonts were especially pleased when the 1989 vintage was judged top dry red at the 1990 Swan Valley Wine Show. While the style of wine may be unusual in terms of oaked cabernets, the commercial reality is that it sells quickly to a very keen demand. And contrary to what many might think the style has shown its ability to age over at least five years, aided by the tartaric acid added at the crusher, an adjustment made to all the table wines.

As well as the liqueur from the Navera, Corin makes a dry wine and a sauterne style from the variety — which takes its name from one of her mother's and grandmother's christian names. Jack grew a cutting from seed at Houghton; it is from the aromatic muscat family and, initially, the liqueur has a dried apricot character that becomes honey-like with age. Jack chose Navera because he feared it would be condemned if muscat was used, before it was even tried. He had ignored the variety for many years during which it was cut to the ground.

Fortunately, the Lamonts have nearly two hectares growing, ensuring the variety's future regardless of its past. Served chilled it is a special experience, being clean, rich and intense, a legacy of the 50 per cent of raisins used in its production. The fruit for the liqueur is left on the vines till the first rains, the longer the better, according to Neil

Without doubt a special attraction of Lamonts is the restaurant where daughters Kate and Fiona provide top quality but uncomplicated dishes from the freshest of produce, local if possible. Their food philosophy has made a meal there a must for any West Australian or visitors. In 1993 the restaurant was named the best in Australia in the annual Citibank customer-based awards.

LITTLE RIVER WINES

West Swan Road, West Swan
Cellar door sales: Daily 10 a.m. — 5.30
p.m. Country style café meals from 11
a.m. — 5 p.m. Weddings and functions
by arrangement

*For cosmopolitan Count Bruno and Countess
Jan de Tastes, pictured walking their dog
Shooster, Little River represents a challenge
and a chance to rejuvenate*

WHEN Count Bruno de Tastes drove through the Swan Valley in August 1993, little did he realise he was about to bring 800 years of French winemaking tradition to the Swan Valley, historic heartland of WA viticulture. He was on his way to dressage lessons when he spotted an auction sign for the sale of Little River Wines. Keen to get into wine production, and having decided to settle in Perth, he did not wait for the auction, but purchased the property immediately.

The Count's family established winemaking at Chateau de Tastes, a former fortress and now a historical monument, in Bordeaux on the banks of the river

Claremont, before the Little River purchase.

Listening to the international journey to the Swan, I could not help recollecting the story of another journey by a previous owner, and definitely not based on the comfort of a jumbo jet.

It involved the late George Pasalich, riding a bicycle from the vineyard to Midland balancing a barrel of wine on the handlebars. For that was what he used to do in the 1930s, a round trip of about 20 kilometres, in order to get wine railed to customers in the Goldfields.

His son Len told me the story as we discussed the family origins of Glenalwyn,

Garonne in the 12th century. But all their properties were lost in 1789 during the French Revolution, and never returned.

Born in Paris in 1950, the Count studied design and architecture at the Bordeaux School of Fine Arts. While holidaying on the Greek island of Mykonos, he met former Kalgoorlie woman Jan Blackburne, establishing a WA connection, and the couple married in Melbourne. Later, however, they developed a successful wholesale wine business in Hawaii, selling out to beer brewing giant Budweiser after a decade. Now Perth beckoned, and their interest in food and wine led to operating Prideaux's restaurant in

the nine-hectare property his father purchased in 1933, retaining the Welsh name. Mr Pasalich had left his native Dalmatia, part of former Yugoslavia, after phylloxera destroyed the family vineyard, migrating to Australia in 1926 to eventually establish his own vineyard and make wine.

The property was sold some 60 years later but not before its fertile soils produced high-quality fresh table grapes for local and export markets, as well as some outstanding wines.

At the 1981 Perth Show, for example, a Glenalwyn verdelho of that vintage was awarded a gold medal in class 66. Previously, in 1969, the father-and-son Pasalich

team had shown their versatility when they were awarded the trophy for the best small winemaker at the Perth Show, a proud moment indeed. But it came under controversial circumstances, for the trophy had originally been presented to Waldeck Wines. Len had telephoned me at *The West Australian* to say he believed a mistake had been made in tallying the points made by the various medal-winning wines for the prized trophy. A check confirmed his claim and an embarrassed Royal Agricultural Society admitted the mistake. Waldeck Wines had received one gold, three silver and three bronze medals at the show, while Glenalwyn was awarded two gold and three silver medals. On the point system of five, two and one, Glenalwyn polled 16 and Waldeck 14 points.

Another major show success was a silver medal for a 1978 vintage port at the 1980 Bristol International Wine Show, reflecting the winery's strength with such wines. But Len was forced to pull out many of the vines on which his father had built the business, as customer preference moved strongly to table wines, where the focus is firmly fixed today. 'I do not have any affinity with fortified wines', Count Bruno said.

The couple plan to rejuvenate the existing vineyard and extend plantings, buying in fruit from Bindoon and south-ern areas as required for an annual crush of 90-100 tonnes. The main wine styles are chardonnay, chenin blanc, shiraz and cabernet sauvignon.

Swan Valley fruit provides the base for lightly wooded, buttery, full-bodied chardonnays that swamp the mouth with flavour, and are suitable for dishes from raw fish to duck and turkey. A smoky, flinty bouquet is the introduction to the chenin, from Swan Valley fruit. It is a wine of good structure with a clean, fresh, slightly sharp acidity making it ideal for oysters and shellfish.

Cabernet fruit is purchased from the Pemberton-Manjimup area with the Count seeking, naturally enough, a Bordeaux style based on ripe berry fruit and a clean, well-balanced palate. A dash of Swan Valley cabernet franc adds complexity while softening the tannins. The shiraz he is seeking will be very ripe, full bodied, jammy, plummy, a typical Swan Valley style. 'The wine will be a meal in itself, big and chewy', he said. 'I am not interested in spicy or peppery wines.'

Count Bruno regards himself as the guider of the wine styles while wife Jan is the marketing and promotional force behind Little River. For the cellar door visitors, the range includes two sweet wines, particularly enjoyed by Asians calling at the winery.

N
OT MUCH further than a good champagne cork pop from where the Swan River Colony's first Governor, Captain James Stirling, blazed his inaugural trail stands a new winery with a church-like appearance cut into the high bank and commanding panoramic views across the winding river below.

This is Dorham Mann's headquarters for his sparkling wine, labelled simply Mann. It is made from cabernet grown on the four-hectare property, and follows on from a long-held family secret. Father Jack made such a wine at Houghton for many years, producing it only on special occasions like birthdays and Christmas. 'We were not allowed to tell anybody about it', Dorham said. 'It was kept in dump cases behind big casks in the cellar.'

Dorham and his wife Sally, born and bred Swan Valley people, purchased their property in Memorial Avenue, Baskerville, in 1966. Immediately he set to and planted cabernet with the aim of producing his own sparkling wine in batches when required by the family. During this time he was employed as an industry adviser by the Department of Agriculture, calling on knowledge gained through his father and his formal training as a graduate oenologist from the Roseworthy Agricultural College in South Australia.

The work involved guiding Swan Valley producers in the transition from fortified wines to table wines as well as helping select many of the locations for the pioneering vineyards in the South West and Great Southern districts. Then in 1973 he was appointed senior winemaker at Sandalford, a position he held for 14 vintages. In that time many people had come to enjoy his home champagne, posing the question, 'Why don't you make it commercially?'.

It seemed like a logical move, and 1989 saw the first release of 500 cases. But why cabernet instead of pinot noir, traditionally used in France and elsewhere to produce the best sparkling wines? 'When it comes to finesse and sheer inherent quality, I believe that cabernet in our conditions is vastly superior', Dorham said. 'I consider the best champagnes are made from red grapes because of the extra flavour and

MANN

Memorial Avenue, Baskerville
Cellar door sales most days

completeness such fruit generates. Like my father, I believe cabernet provides the best red grape material we could use. And if I did not have cabernet I would use chardonnay, because I feel that in warmer Australian conditions, it too is much better than pinot.'

The purist might argue strongly against this, but Dorham is adamant that pinot does not achieve the finesse and refinement on the finish that cabernet can get. 'We do not have to follow the French', Dorham went on. 'This is a mistake I believe many Australian producers make.'

It is not that Dorham is anti-French and there would be few imbibers of my acquaintance who would enjoy a top French champagne more. Such wines, in fact, have been part of the inspiration for what he is now doing. 'Australian winemakers', he argues, 'should seek to make the best wines from fruit grown in their climatic conditions. They should concentrate on bringing out the best in their material

in the style that it lends to naturally. It is just commonsense to follow nature.'

Over the years Dorham has made many fine wines with Sandalfords, from the Swan and from the new southern areas of the State. They have received their accolades, like the 1975 Forest Hill (Mount Barker) rhine riesling which won nine trophies and 12 gold medals over a seven-year show career. His industry contribution has been such that in 1993 Dorham was awarded an Order of Australia.

But the Mann wine is distinctively their own, one that can be enjoyed equally with or without food, for its dryness makes it acceptable either way. It is not that the cabernet from the Swan Valley is necessarily special, for Dorham says, 'I have seen it growing happily in many different parts of the world, from the warmest to the coolest regions. Invariably, it produces a lovely wine, though the regional characteristics can make it quite different from place to place.'

Bottles, bottles, bottles, soon to grace the public palate with the fruits of Dorham Mann's labours

IF TROPHIES were awarded for enthusiasm and innovation, then the late Ivan Yurisich would have been an early recipient. At the tail end of the 1920s it was his custom to buy two tonnes of grapes a year from the Swan Valley and have them railed in boxes to the Goldfields where, at his Boulder 'winery', he would use a mangle to make wine for himself and a few of the boarders he housed. At first Mr Yurisich used to press the grapes down so that they would catch in the mangle. Then he put chicken wire around the rollers to catch the fruit, and later grooves so that they would mesh.

The resulting wines were very high in alcohol, about twice the dry red table wine levels of today, because sugar was added to the must before fermentation. The wine was consumed with water and there were never any problems with storage, for it was all drunk before the next vintage.

A few years later Mr Yurisich, suffering from dust that is so much a curse of mining areas, left the Goldfields permanently. He purchased the four-hectare Olive Farm property at South Guildford, extending from Great Eastern Highway to the Swan River, to grow grapes and make wine. He has been followed by his son Vince and now grandson Ian.

But the Olive Farm story goes back to early settlement when British botanist Thomas Waters planted vine cuttings and rooted grape vines brought from South Africa in 1829, packed in soil in barrels, on his 20-hectare land grant at Guildford. As well, olive trees were planted along the old Guildford road (now the highway), giving the property its name. The cellar still used today is thought to have been dug by Waters (or under his supervision) in the early 1830s. He was later to sell wine for two shillings a gallon, also using it to barter for stores, boots and newspapers with Guildford storekeeper Abraham Jones in the 1840s.

But by 1933, when Mr Yurisich took over, the cellar was in a state of collapse and neglected vines were overrun by couch grass and scrub. The property was used to graze racehorses and trotters, and only a few fruit trees remained. Immediately, he set about replanting the vineyard to produce dried fruit, table grapes and wine, generating early income by buying in grapes for winemaking, and purchasing a truck to cart logs. Like many other southern European migrants hard work was the basis of his life, and constant struggle, especially in those early days. For example, when he arrived at Fremantle on 26 December 1912 at the age of 18, he had just five shillings in his pocket and had to find

OLIVE FARM

77 Great Eastern Highway, South Guildford
Cellar door sales: Mon — Fri 10 a.m. — 5.30 p.m. Weekends and public holidays 10 a.m. — 3 p.m. Café lunches in the underground cellar Fridays, Sundays and public holidays 11 a.m. — 3 p.m.

Above: Ian Yurisich samples a red on the same site once frequented by colonial British botanist Thomas Waters

his own way to Kalgoorlie. Previously, he had been in New Zealand with his brother, digging for gum.

Years later, when the family were celebrating 50 years at Olive Farm, he offered me a sample of a unique wine — a madeirised fortified that blended material dating back 40 years, and was made by the father, son and grandson.

For years the family business was based on dry red wines and fortifieds. Then in 1960 Vince was given the challenge by his father — either run the place successfully or it would be sold. This was to herald a new era for Olive Farm with State Government adviser of the day Dorham Mann having a vital influence on its future direction. 'He encouraged us all in the Swan to start making table wines and to take an interest in showing them', Vince recalled.

Olive Farm won its first gold medal in 1966 with a dry muscat. This was the first year it had put wine into a 750ml bottle. The following year it won a gold with a chablis, and began steady investment in sophisticated winemaking equipment with the initial purchase of a refrigeration coil for controlled fermentation. A string of show successes followed as the range of wines increased, leading to the golden years of the 1970s when Olive Farm dominated the Perth Show small winemakers section, winning the coveted most successful exhibitor award six years out of seven.

This was the time of hock, made mainly from chenin blanc, and rosé from grenache, which did more to put the winery on the consumer map than any other wines.

Ian became the first member of the family to have any formal training in winemaking, graduating from the Roseworthy Agricultural College to return home and eventually take control in 1983. Today Olive Farm crushes about 120 tonnes of fruit a year, mainly from the new Swan Valley Poplars vineyard which had its first harvest in 1990.

The $l million project — the first significant new development in the valley for many years — is on part of the former Belhus Estate where the rich, loamy soils produced top-quality table grapes over a long period.

Varieties planted in the 13 hectares of irrigated vineyard include chardonnay, chenin blanc, semillon, verdelho, sauvignon blanc, cabernet sauvignon, cabernet franc, pinot noir and merlot.

Ian argues that the Swan's biggest advantage is that it is a reliable producing area which has been overlooked in recent years, with the emphasis on new southern

areas. 'Yet the styles produced on the Swan Valley are the styles people look to', he said. 'I am talking about drinkability year in, year out. These are the wines that have flavour and are pleasant with an inherent softness and refinement.'

Some of the fruit will be used for sparkling wine — a highly successful range which Vince began in 1965. In those days butcher's string and bees wax were vital parts of the production line. Because of the difficulty in getting wire securing cages (muselet) and corks, slots were cut into plastic stoppers and tied down with string as a substitute. The wax ensured that it would not stretch.

It was a slow process and painful, recalled Vince's wife Janet. 'You had to pull the string down tight, leaving cuts in your fingers for weeks', she said.

Today 3000 cases of bubbly a year are made at Olive Farm in three styles, selling to a keen demand.

Included are a pink rosé style made from shiraz, one from chardonnay and a brut from madeleine purchased from an Upper Swan grower. This is a neutral variety that lends itself to secondary fermentation yeast characters.

In all, 15 different wines are made at Olive Farm. Characteristically full bodied, the main white table wines are chenin blanc (formerly the hock), chardonnay and chablis, with Ian looking to get as much flavour into the wines as the fruit can offer to represent the variety grown under Swan conditions.

To meet consumer demand, the level of oak on the chardonnay has been reduced by about half, leaving perhaps melon flavours the most dominant. The crisp, clean chenin is an attractive casual drinking style. Light to medium in body, it is Olive Farm's biggest seller.

There are two main dry red styles that are at opposite ends of the spectrum, a cabernet sauvignon and a cabernet shiraz-merlot blend. The varietal wine is a much lighter style for it does not have the skin contact and extraction is minimised, while the blend is fuller bodied, more traditional — a big, gutsy red wine.

Ian regards the relatively mild 1993 year as the best in his first decade and was chuffed with the Swan Valley show of the year when he won the trophy for the best *méthode champenoise* against seven other competitors.

Cellar door sales represented about 25 per cent of production in 1994 But Ian plans to treble that in his second decade, capitalising on Olive Farm's natural riverside advantages.

A RURAL setting on the edge of suburbia is the location of Pinelli Wines, established by Italian migrant Domenic Pinelli in 1980. The three-hectare vineyard is part of the property of former leading West Australian producer Waldeck Wines which was subdivided and sold. Domenic's block was generally considered to be 'the pick of the place'.

A few years after his arrival in Western Australia in 1955 to join an uncle, Domenic Pinelli began work at Waldecks, developing the skills of viticulture and winemaking. There was rich experience to draw upon.

Mick Waldeck's father Ken began growing grapes on the property in 1908, mainly dried fruit. The wine thrust began in the 1930s with the property gradually converted to wine grapes. Production was boosted from other land in the Swan Valley, and at Bindoon which still is in the family and run by third-generation vigneron Robert Waldeck. At one stage the Waldecks produced 200,000 litres of wine a year, mostly bulk. Before his death in 1993, Mick told me he rated 1968 his blue ribbon year when one of his wines was judged the best West Australian dry red at the Perth Wine Show.

The Pinellis — Domenic having been joined by son Robert, a Roseworthy graduate — produce modestly priced table wines from $5 to $11, the flagship silver-medal winning chardonnay being the most expensive. Like the Waldecks before them, the Pinelli emphasis is firmly fixed on bulk wines, based on cellar door sales, with some deliveries to a number of Perth's fancied restaurants.

The annual crush is about 120 tonnes of which the property supplies about 20, the rest purchased from the Swan Valley and Bindoon. 'We will be looking to put more premium wines into bottles', Robert said, 'but flagons will remain the basis of our business, 75 per cent of our production. We have established a good trade for people who like soft, fruity wines. That is where we aim to stay.' His target also encompasses improved quality while retaining the basic styles.

In all, the son-and-father team produce some 25 different wines including several fortifieds — well-made, easy drinking styles.

The chardonnay, to be consumed in two to four years, is a Swan Valley fruit-driven wine, soft and flavoursome, with only a touch of wood, ideal for people who do not like a heavily oaked style. The chenin, an unwooded wine also from Swan fruit, has impressed in the past. Often

underrated as a variety, its flavours and acid make it extremely versatile as a fresh early drinking wine, able to take oak if required or to develop soft honey characters with graceful ageing. Judges have recognised the quality of Pinelli chenin blanc by awarding the 1991 vintage two bronze medals and then a silver at the 1993 Perth Show, endorsing its improvement with time.

The winery's reds, cabernet sauvignon and shiraz, are for people who like honest, uncomplicated wines with plenty of flavour and palatability. And the price is right at $6 a bottle (1994 prices).

The winery's marketing advantage is that consumers can try whatever they wish in pleasant surroundings at the cellar, with generous serves at that. Some may like to sit under shady grapevines on a high trellis, others to lean on an impressive jarrah bar.

It will cost them $16, however, (1994 prices) if they want to try the top fortified, for me, the best in the range. It was Robert's first, a 1987 vintage port from home-grown cabernet sauvignon. In a sense it was made by chance. The pressure of vintage did not see the crop harvested in time for the making of a dry table wine. It had become too ripe so Robert decided instead to make a port using brandy spirit.

PINELLI WINES

Lot 18 Bennett Street (off Benara Road), Caversham
Cellar Door Sales: Daily 10 a.m. — 5.30 p.m.

Above: Domenic Pinelli with some of the winery's range. Outside the bar is an attractive alfresco area

SANDALFORD WINES

West Swan Road, Caversham
Cellar door sales: Daily, Mon — Sat 10
a.m. — 5 p.m. BBQ facilities available,
functions by arrangement

*Two ends of the Sandalford historical
spectrum: Estate founder John Septimus Roe
(bearded) as he appeared in a painting of the
Colony's first Legislative Council; and
winemaker Bill Crappsley and general
manager Ted Avery enjoying a gourmet
picnic in the grounds*

SANDALFORD
COLLECTION
1992
CLASSIC DRY RED
Mount Barker

SANDALFORD
COLLECTION
1993
CLASSIC DRY WHITE
Margaret River

T O SPEAK of Sandalford at Caversham is to touch on an important part
of West Australian history in which a single
family has featured prominently from the
early days of settlement. In 1840 Queen
Victoria granted 1250 acres on the banks
of the Swan River to John Septimus Roe,
the Colony's first Surveyor General, in
recognition of his services. Turn the clock
forward by a century and you find another Roe — John Frederick (Fred) —
making his first wine, a frontignac, with a
mangle during World War II. Tradition
certainly has a place in this picturesque
estate which remained for so long in the
one family, and which has made such a
solid contribution to West Australian viticulture and winemaking.

Today it is owned by Perth businessmen Peter Prendiville and Paul Naughton,
but in the 1850s it was leased to a former
convict, Malachi Reidy Meagher, an Irish
civil engineer from Limerick who was
transported for forging an order for delivery of goods worth £94. He received his
ticket-of-leave in Perth in October 1860,
and some two years later leased Sandalford

from Mr Roe and engaged a number of
ticketers.

At the time it is recorded that the
vineyard on the property required constant expert attention. In 1865, blessed
with a fine crop, Meagher made application in a letter to the resident magistrate
for the necessary spirit to fortify his wine.
It read:

Sandalford
Mid Swan
30 Aug, 1865
Sir,

I, Malachi R. Meagher of Middle Swan
declare that I am tenant of vineyard situ-
ate at Sandalford, Middle Swan, and that
I have manufactured two thousand one
hundred and sixty gallons of wine from
grapes grown therein this year and I apply
under the 16 Vic. No 3 for seventy gallons
of spirits to be delivered to me from the
Bonded Store at Fremantle duty free, for
the purpose of admixture with such Colonial Wine. Dated this 30th day of August
1865.

M.R. Meagher
The magistrate forwarded on the let-

ter, commenting that he had visited the cellars and believed the request to be a proper one.

Seventy-five years later Fred began his winemaking after a period of dedicated development. For some time he had been employed by the Bank of New South Wales and the Lands Department, but whenever possible he would leave the family home, Glynlee, in Adelaide Terrace, with a swag on his back, catch the train to Guildford and walk the remaining five kilometres to Sandalford. There he would dig wells and work the land.

Eventually, he left the bank and went to live in a simple iron shelter at Sandalford. He later built two dwellings, for himself and for a married couple who helped with the work. In the meantime he cleared the land and planted the first of many varieties of vines, as well as growing Cape gooseberries and other vegetables.

The vineyard prospered, its table grapes and dried fruit proving very successful. Fred was eventually succeeded by sons John and David.

John became the managing director in 1971, a position he held until his retirement in 1988. During this period there were many changes, including the decision to concentrate on premium wines, updating the winery, development of the largest vineyard at Margaret River, and the introduction of outside shareholders.

In 1973 John was joined by Dorham Mann as Sandalford's senior winemaker, a position he was to hold until 1987. In that time there were many fine wines made from Swan Valley fruit and from the new Margaret River development. But of special interest to Dorham was the first fruit from the Department of Agriculture's experimental plantings at Forest Hill. He had helped select the block with Department of Agriculture colleague Bill Jamieson and had been heavily involved with its planting and progress. Without doubt the highlight was that most decorated wine, the 1975 rhine riesling, winner of 12 gold medals and nine trophies.

'There was a lot of excitement about as we processed the fruit from the property, and that of the Roche development at Frankland River', Dorham recalled. 'When they quickly won awards, it vindicated the decision to plant vines.'

On two occasions during his time at Sandalford, the crush exceeded 1000 tonnes. Also an outstanding show record was achieved with Sandalford winning the most successful exhibitor trophy at the Perth Show for five consecutive years.

Dorham moved quickly to introduce varietal wines into the range, beginning with a chenin blanc, believed to have been the first in Australia, and a verdelho. He also introduced the liqueur Sandalera, a rich, luscious dessert wine. That was in 1973 and was from fruit from Oakover, next to Houghton and the same vines his father Jack used for the source for his fine liqueur tokays. Meanwhile, production from the new Margaret River vineyard was building up. Such was the West Australian consumer interest in the district that the 1976 cabernet, of nearly 3000 cases, sold out in a few weeks. The grapes had been left to ripen fully, resulting in a wine of intense colour and herbaceous character with soft, refined tannins.

Another wine from the vineyard to capture the imagination was the outstanding 1977 verdelho, a gold medal winner in Melbourne and Perth.

In 1983-84 the winery made more than $500,000 profit before tax — a particularly pleasing result, according to Dorham.

Meanwhile, the multi-national Inchcape group of London, which had bought a major share of Sandalford in the late 1970s, picked up the remaining 30 per cent in December 1991 to end more than 150 years of financial interest by the Roe family. Less than a year later Sandalford was back in WA hands again with the Prendiville-Naughton purchase, and immediate moves were made for a Sandalford rebirth. Recruited by the new owners as chief executive was Houghton general manager Ted Avery who was joined by Evans and Tate senior winemaker Bill Crappsley. Both men have played key roles in the WA industry, enjoying the respect of all, and their move to Sandalford was a major coup for the new owners.

Wines Bill has made in South Australia and WA over the years, for example, have won hundreds of medals and trophies, so many in fact he would need another cellar to house them!

It was not revealed how much it cost to 'buy-back-the-farm' but the new owners almost immediately launched a major upgrade, $300,000 to boost disappointing yields from the Margaret River vineyard, $200,000 on new equipment and refurbishment of the Swan Valley winery, and $85,000 to improve the Caversham vineyard. Previous production levels of 50,000-60,000 cases a year worth $4 million were to be increased in the years ahead to 150,000 cases worth $13-$15 million. This would by the year 2000 come from a vineyard area of 200 hectares at the Swan Valley headquarters, Margaret River and the

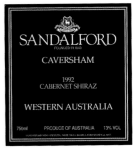

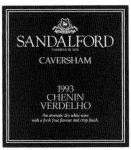

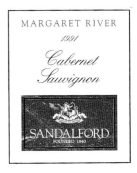

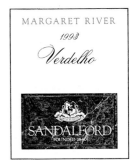

The cultural influence of southern Europe is ever-present in the colourful Swan Valley, and at the annual Sandalford vintage workers of various age groups gather for the picking

leased Landsdale development at Mount Barker, as well as purchased fruit from various parts of the State.

Sandalford produces a variety of wines to meet all palates and pockets. The Caversham range, of two whites and a red, not necessarily from the Swan Valley, includes an unusual blend of chenin and verdelho. Popular in the Eastern States, the unwooded dry wine appeals for its freshness and crispness, and tropical fruit

characters. The chardonnay, from Mount Barker fruit, carries about 15 per cent Swan Valley verdelho, another unusual combination, aimed at enhancing richness and flavour especially in a lighter southern year. The cabernet shiraz is the traditional old style, big flavoured and earthy, mainly from warm area fruit.

Introduced in 1993, the 1840 Collection acknowledged the founders and launched the rebirth of Sandalford. A

Mechanical harvesting has obvious advantages, not least of which is to enable cooler night-picked grapes, with lower oxidation in the must, to be processed. The central beater rods are surprisingly effective in shaking the berries on to the moving base plates

classic white and red, the wines are soft, fruity and easy drinking, meant for early consumption.

A Margaret River premium range provides for the flagship white, verdelho. The wine is unwooded, generates an abundance of tropical fruit flavours, and holds its acid very well, rarely needing adjusting. A popular cellar door line — for it has good early drinking qualities — the wine does particularly well in the Eastern States and the UK. Surprisingly, a 1992 chardonnay was the first released by Sandalford, well after most producers around the nation. The 1993 was the initial full-on, barrel-fermented, lees-stirred wine

— the works, the oak providing a strong backbone for the guava melon intense fruit which included grapes from Pemberton.

Shiraz from Margaret River, with its richness and fullness, is seen as ideal for blending with the pepper and spice of Mount Barker for a premium red alongside cabernet, of which Sandalford has big areas of vines available.

Bill Crappsley sees these wines as having berry, minty characters as opposed to the more herbaceous styles, with a pedigree already in place. At the 1988 SGIO Winemakers Exhibition the 1983 reserve cabernet won top prize of $5000 for being the best wine at the show.

TALIJANCICH WINES

121 Hyem Road, Herne Hill (formerly Millendon)
Cellar door sales: Mon — Fri 9 a.m. — 5 p.m. Sat closed. Sun 11 a.m.— 5 p.m.
Light Mediterranean food available

THE description 'salt of the earth' perhaps fits Swan Valley producer Peter Talijancich better than anyone I know. The big, friendly man with a hearty laugh and a huge handshake has had his feet in the dirt from a very early age, for he inherited the daunting task of looking after a vineyard when still a schoolboy.

Peter was just 13 when his migrant father Jim passed away in 1945, leaving the youngster to help his mother run their former Herne Hill property. That involved getting up early, at cultivating times, har-

nessing the horses, and ploughing a certain number of rows of vines before leaving for school, and doing the same thing again on his return home.

It was not always easy to buckle down, because like any normal young lad Peter liked to play football with some of his neighbouring mates, whereas his mother held a different viewpoint. She knew that Peter, her only son, was the vineyard's manpower; outside labour was just not possible in those days for a family in their situation. Peter recalls clearly her opposition to him wanting to spend leisure time with his friends, and her ultimatum for him 'to finish those rows tonight' as part of the need to shoulder responsibility.

Hard work, however, was very much a family tradition. Peter's late father, having arrived in Western Australia in 1926 from the Dalmatian coast of the former Yugoslavia, where he had been a fisherman, headed for the bush to hand-cut jarrah sleepers in the South West. Later he ran a wood yard in Wellington Street, Perth, carting firewood around the city in baskets. In 1931 he moved to the Swan Valley to concentrate on bulk wine production, supplementing income with various off-farm jobs.

It was a lead Peter was to follow, working as he developed their present property about ten kilometres from Midland.

Mrs Talijancich had decided to move from the previous block because it was much easier land for her young son to work.

In the early days the business was based on dried fruit, table grapes and bulk wines made for general delivery and for a major market in Carnarvon. Slowly, however, the vineyard was converted totally to wine grapes, especially shiraz and grenache, and it was during this period that Peter looked elsewhere to provide a much needed cash flow.

He worked in the fishing industry and in timber — felling, milling, carting and truck driving for a local carrier. At night he would put in time at the winery, sometimes till the early hours of the morning.

These were the days of hand crushing and pressing, with present-day technology a dream away.

Peter and his wife Mary even turned to establish a market garden in Osborne Park, with a relative helping to maintain the Swan operation. 'It was something different and a challenge', Peter told me, 'but after five years I felt the wine industry was the place to be'.

Son Jim joined the family business in 1977, providing new goals with an increase in premium grape varieties for greater table wine production as he moved gradually to take charge of winemaking. It was also to lead to changing the label from 'Peters' to the family name.

While economic factors have inevitably led to a reduction in the winery's fortified range, some of these outstanding wines will be retained, for they have earned the plaudits of many as rich, luscious, classic Australians.

Take, for example, the results of a day-long tasting of such wines by the Eastern States consumer magazine *Winestate*. This saw the 1974 Talijancich tokay unanimously voted top wine from Australia's best by the judges and given the highest rating, five stars.

'There is no question that this tokay would hold up its head with the best from Rutherglen or Hungary for that matter', the reviewer said. 'It begins with that delightful dark, olive green, almost khaki colour which is so intriguing.' The wine was bestowed with a barrage of complimentary remarks such as luscious, perfectly blended, excellent spirit, brilliant rancio, finesse and style. 'Suffice to say', the magazine said, 'it was a very, very good wine'.

Such comments were extremely satisfying to a man with no formal training in the industry, and whose efforts have come from genuine sweat on the brow. When you reflect on one of Peter's favourite Slavic sayings — 'good news travels a long way, but bad news travels even further' — this praise is particularly apt.

The father-and-son team want to make sure there is no bad news and their initial target is to see that every berry picked is of good quality, with trickle irrigation to keep the vines happy.

For a time, prominent South West winemaker Rob Bowen acted as a consultant for the family, and was quick to spot the 'true vigneron' in Peter.

'He has a love and understanding of every individual vine', he told me. 'If anyone deserves to succeed, this family certainly does.'

But success was achieved with the fortifieds well and truly before the *Winestate* review. I recall the release of the 1961 liqueur muscat, 25 years after it was made. Packaged in half bottles, it set new price horizons for a small Swan Valley producer, selling at $25. That may have seemed like a lot, but how many people would be prepared to wait so long for their money after having completed a job?

And consider the pedigree. Five gold medals and three silvers, including one at an international exhibition in London in 1986. It was beaten by a South African wine by 0.5 points for the gold medal with 27 countries competing.

It is hard to believe, but the muscat was sold in flagons when first made for the equivalent of $1.50 each. Peter confessed that about half of the production went this way before he realised the true quality of the wine. So he put the rest in wood and forgot about it.

Regrettably, it was the first and last, the fruit having been bought from a Swan

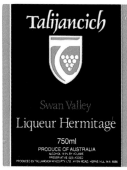
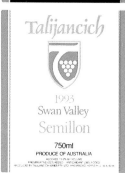

Facing page: Peter Talijancich and son Jim. With assured success in a range of fortifieds, the family business seeks to expand table wine production

Valley producer who had decided there was no more future in the variety.

Imagine Peter's devastation when he visited the property to negotiate further supplies of fruit, only to find the vines ripped out, and stacked in heaps, ready for burning. The wine was still being acclaimed at national tastings 32 years after making. Naturally enough, the old muscat is not included in the Talijancich wines available for tasting, for which a $2 charge applies, refunded on any purchase made.

But all others are, including liqueur tokay and hermitage, both seven-year-old blends, a four-year-old rich ruby port and the full table wine range, including a rosé from grenache, semillon, shiraz and arguably the pick, verdelho for which Jim believes the Swan is special.

'We have tried the finest from around the world and do not believe they compare with the depth, complexity or richness of flavour', he says. 'These are three components we do not hold back on.' Up until 1989 oak was used on the verdelho, and the semillon.

But analysis of tank and barrel samples led Jim to believe the measure was unnecessary for the retention of freshness,

varietal fruit flavours and palate richness

A combination of gross and secondary lees contact for about a year adds complexity to the wines and the impression of oak maturation.

The Talijancich shiraz, soft, rich and often distinctly plummy, is big in alcohol but has the necessary fruit power for balance and life, with the 1989, for example, definitely a big beef wine, still drinking well five years after being vintaged.

The fruit for its fortified 'brother', the liqueur hermitage, is left much later for picking so that it is as ripe as it can possibly be.

Inherent in its make-up are rich, dark chocolate and liquorice characters, the backbone enhanced by nestling in small French brandy barrels. The liqueur tokay brings to mind ripe dried-in-the-sun raisins and splendid nutty flavours, developing in maturity. This wine is matured in English oak adding soft, sweet flavours with subtle and refined tannins.

These wines are extraordinary West Australians, assisted by a Jack Mann technique of using a butcher's mincer to increase intensity of flavours, and will always make a visit to the Talijancich winery something a bit special.

TWIN HILL WINES

Great Northern Highway, Millendon
Cellar door sales: Mon — Sat 8.30 a.m.
— 5 p.m.

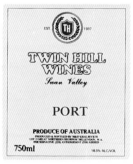

WHEN 18-year-old Dalmatian (former Yugoslav) migrant Steve Kraljevich arrived at Fremantle in August 1926, he certainly had a financial incentive to do well. As he stepped ashore to meet a brother who had arrived a year earlier, he had just four pennies in his pocket.

So, like many of his countrymen the strong young man headed bush, to the State's South West, and the tough life of contract sleeper cutting. His initial aim was to repay, as quickly as possible, the £35 borrowed for the fare from a moneylender, at 40 per cent interest.

After about a year he turned to farm clearing at Bindi Bindi, 150 kilometres north of Perth. It was the only job he could find while waiting for the grapes to ripen and picking to start on a relative's property in the Swan Valley, the Kosovichs, of Great Northern Highway, now known as Westfield Wines. Steve was to manage the vineyard for six years, beginning a connection with the West Australian industry that lasted more than half a century, to his death, and seen sons Mark and Eddie carrying on the family involvement.

Production in that early period centred on dried fruit, clarets, ports and muscats.

But the will of independence, to be his

own boss, was too strong, resulting in the purchase of a 12-hectare property in the Perth foothills called Twin Hills. Interestingly enough, the name is not derived from a geographical feature; rather a local midwife called the area 'twin hill' in recognition of the multiple births on neighbouring properties.

It was hardly a prime location as far as the valley was concerned, but wine production began immediately and enthusiastic customers drove long distances to make their purchases. The main market was formed of other Yugoslav migrants who enjoyed the big, soft table wine — so similar to those in their native land.

Wine production expanded with fruit purchased from other growers. Dried fruit production also increased. But the low-yielding vineyard was struggling economically, and in 1955 the family moved to a much more fertile block on the Great Northern Highway, to become neighbours of Kosovichs.

The brothers took over in 1974, with Mark and his wife Dorothy assuming full control in 1991. They crush about 50 tonnes a year as well as producing dried fruit and fresh table grapes. The varieties grown for table and fortified wines include shiraz, grenache, cabernet sauvignon, chenin blanc, verdelho, riesling, semillon, pedro ximinez and muscat.

In the Swan Valley tradition the grapes are picked when very ripe with the wines full in body and abounding in character. As well, they are high in alcohol (though not as high as they once were) so that consumers can readily add a quantity of water, or ice. 'People like to identify the variety immediately they sample the wine', Mark said.

Made to be drunk when sold, the wines are mostly packaged in flagons and containers up to 50 litres. Only if he considers there will be a demand, or when seasonal conditions are favourable, does Mark put wine into 750ml bottles.

Another Swan tradition he follows is to deliver each week to individual customers in the metropolitan area. But the business is also established on word of mouth, and old-established buyers regularly visit the winery to take advantage of its sound, honest wines selling (in 1994) at the modest price of $4 to $8.50 a flagon.

There they find a winery where some of the stainless steel trappings of modern-day establishments stand among fixtures of the past, such as concrete fermenting vats. In the vineyard, though, horses have long since gone. Steve once estimated that at ploughing times he would walk 25 kilometres a day, up and down rows of vines, controlling a single-furrow plough pulled by two horses. In those days the vineyard men of the Swan kept their blocks meticulously cultivated. It was a matter of pride and the accepted way of controlling weeds to ensure the best from the vines. Today neatness and intense cultivation is

secondary to soil care and management.

The Kraljevichs have not had any formal training in winemaking. Their knowledge has been built up through long years of experience. But Steve acknowledged help from the late Jack Mann at Houghton, especially with acid balancing.

In their lifetimes, the two men had plenty in common, especially in their love of the Swan and in their criticism of some modern day wines. 'A lot of them are just acid and water to me', Steve once told me.

With picking imminent, Mark and Dorothy Kraljevich inspect their ripening cabernet sauvignon grapes

MOONSHINE and Jungle Juice are hardly labels associated with fine wines. Yet Charlie Zannino who marketed the products — wine-based fruit juice and soft drink mixes like coolers introduced by big companies years later — at the Swan Valley wine festival held at Caversham's Lilac Hill park during the 1970s, believes they made a significant contribution to the industry. 'People liked drinking them', he said. 'They were pleasant and fun. I believe they introduced many to serious premium wine consumption.'

Charlie, friends and relatives dressed as 'hillbillies', in bags and weird old hats and wigs, introduced a very different attraction to the festival with their stall. Dry ice was added to their Moonshine and Jungle Juice, allowing the brews to bubble and smoke. Copper tubing fitted to a bar-

rel on the back of an old Model T Ford under which a mock fire burnt, created the impression of an illegal still, while around the stall hung rabbit traps, a crosscut saw or two and corrugated iron.

But it was controversial. Opponents argued it created the wrong image and drew attention away from quality table wines on which the festival was based. It was a significant factor in the demise of the event but years later, Charlie Zannino was unrepentant. 'We gave people something different', he said. 'That is marketing. And the critics must remember that wine was the basis of all our mixes.'

Valley Wines had its origins with the migration of Charlie's father Antonio from southern Italy in 1950. Initially, he worked near Kalgoorlie cutting timber in the area known as the woodline, an important

VALLEY WINES

Lennard Street, Herne Hill
Cellar door sales: Most days, 10 a.m. — 5 p.m.

Antonio and Charlie Zannino take a break during vintage time at Valley Wines

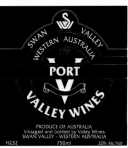

source of fuel for power generation in the gold mining industry. Many a migrant, including my own father, made a start this way in their adopted land. Three years later Antonio was joined by his wife Mariangela and young family of three children, including Charlie. (Two more were later born in Western Australia.) After about a year they moved to the Swan, where an eight-hectare property had been purchased. It was a natural progression, for like so many southern Europeans before him, the land and its products, especially grapes and wine, was what they knew best.

He worked the property in every spare moment, while earning a cash flow for family living needs through a job at the Midland railway workshops. It was a situation that lasted some 15 years. Again like other women of migrant families who settled on the Swan, Antonio's wife was a vital labour source, helping out in the vineyard at every opportunity. In those early days, he cultivated with a horse and plough, the latter still to be found on the place. Slowly, winemaking was introduced, at first for the family's own consumption, with the vineyard production based at the time of purchase on dried fruit and table grapes. As friends and relatives sought supplies, an old cellar was rebuilt. During this period, schoolboy Charlie was helping his father in many ways, the beginning of his training to eventually take over. An extra eight hectares of vineyard was purchased to expand activities, and fruit from surrounding growers was being bought to meet an increasing demand. Of course, production was in bulk, but the wines suited the European palate.

Today Valley Wines have introduced classic varieties into their vineyard such as chardonnay, semillon and chenin blanc, supplementing old Swan stalwarts like shiraz and grenache. The unirrigated vineyard on sandy gravel produces 50-70 tonnes of fruit a year. This provides for three dry reds, one from grenache, one from shiraz, and one a blend of the two, as well as two whites, a chenin blanc and a chardonnay-chenin blend. The shiraz, which sells out quickly, is a big, full-bodied, high alcohol Swan style made from very ripe fruit. The chenin-chardonnay is also made from ripe grapes, producing another full-bodied and fruity style, able to fulfil the Jack Mann philosophy of adding half water.

Most are still sold in bulk, in containers of up to 200 litres, often brought in by customers and filled in a big, modern winery which has long since replaced Antonio's old facility. And later land purchases aim to expand premium wine production and include cabernet sauvignon.

'We want to become a small boutique winery selling good quality wines at modest prices, under $10 (1994 prices)', Charlie said. But the bulk side remains important with many other customers now as well as the southern Europeans of the past. One is a former resident of the Bronx in New York.

Charlie has been joined in Valley Wines by wife Sally Monti, an active worker for the annual well-established Spring in the Valley festival. An American, she was working in the Swan Shire council as a research officer when she met Charlie, who was president for two years.

Other popular Valley Wines products are the fortifieds, ports, sherries, vermouth and marsala. Made from shiraz, the ports are the biggest seller—big, rich and sweet, plenty to fill any palate.

THERE IS an old broad axe pinned to a massive seven-metre wooden beam in the Swan Valley cellars of Westfield Wines which has special significance for principal John Kosovich. It was used by his late father, Lilo, to cut down a gum tree in the foothills of the nearby Darling Ranges, and then to hew the beam that is still today an important part of the building once used as the family residence and in which John was born. I remember it well, for we were regular visitors, being neighbours for many years.

The late Mr Kosovich came to Western Australia in December 1911, disembarking at Fremantle on his 24th birthday. Like many other Yugoslav migrants he turned initially to the gold industry for work, and then to sleeper cutting amid the tall jarrah trees in the South West. By this time he had bought land on the Swan with brothers Nick and Matt and left them to establish the vineyard while he provided the vital cash flow to keep them all. By the mid-1930s he had assumed full control, producing mainly dried fruit and a little wine. John left school at 15 and by the time he was 18 he was responsible for winemaking, strongly supported by his mother, with Mr Kosovich in deteriorating health. Certainly few Australian winemakers could claim to have been involved with 36 vintages by the time they had reached 50.

John quickly became convinced that, for the Australian climate, table wines were the way to go, rather than fortifieds, no matter how good they might be. He argued, for example, that while a sherry might be ideal before lunch in England, it certainly did not fit the bill over much of sunburnt Australia.

So in the early 1960s he planted rhine riesling, finding there were few premium varieties available in those days, and with not much known about them. For this was the time when any white wine was called riesling, and any red, claret.

But the riesling met Westfield's needs for many years and was in fact a bread-and-butter line for the winery till other varieties became available. Today the flagships are chardonnay, verdelho and cabernet.

John believes that the Swan Valley is an excellent location to grow chardonnay. 'You only have to eat the grape and it tells the story', he said. 'It is fantastic, with lovely flavour and acid, and it holds its colour well. It is still green and gold when very ripe. In comparison, other varieties do not have the life.' Others agree with the 1988, for example, one of my favourite wines from Westfield for its sheer inherent qualities. It won the trophy at the 1993 Perth Wine Show for best WA chardonnay, a marvellous achievement, given the international qualities of some entries from the south. It also won the 1993 SGIO top Swan white award, bringing in the double with a Westfield 1991 cabernet judged best of the Valley reds.

'I would have to say that 1988 has been the best vintage of my time', John went on. 'If anyone asked me which year would I like repeated, I would say 1988, thank you very much. The rainfall was just right and it never got hot, allowing for beautiful even ripening for all varieties with no pressure for urgent picking due to rapidly rising ripeness from excessive heat.' The 1991 vintage on the Swan was also memorable, but for red wines.

A feature of the Westfield chardonnays is their ability to live long, ageing stylishly. A tasting of ten vintages from 1983 revealed that wines of a decade ago to be drinking beautifully, development in the bottle adding dimensions to the fruit and subtle French oak quality to reward the cellaring.

Wines from Westfield have a common theme, being flavoursome, balanced and soft, very drinkable as young wines without the harsh tannins and biting acids sometimes found in wines made from the same varieties in other parts of Australia. A key factor in my tasting is whether I look forward to a second glass, and the Westfield wines certainly pass that test. Produced from moderate crops of quality fruit, they have earned a respected position for John in the local industry, cemented with other outstanding Perth Show results, including most successful exhibitor on two occasions.

In one year, 1979, 14 entries were awarded seven gold and five silver medals. It must be remembered that this is from a very small production base, only about 50 tonnes from eight hectares of vines — a thimbleful compared with some bigger competing wineries. But it is to be expanded, by about 30 tonnes, as a result of a new vineyard being developed at Middlesex, in the Pemberton region. The move south surprised me for John's Swan roots are so deep. But a visit to the 1988 Mount Barker Wine Show resulted in him returning home through the Pemberton area.

'I had never been there before and it immediately appealed', he recalled. 'There was so much lovely land, so much water, so much green grass, so many fat cattle, there had to be potential.' A prolonged

WESTFIELD WINES

Cnr Great Northern Highway and Memorial Avenue, Baskerville
Cellar door sales : Mon — Sat 8.30 a.m. — 5.30 p.m.

search and many trips to the area finally led to the purchase of a well-drained 36-hectare block of loam and deep gravel some 10 kilometres south of Manjimup. A big area is suitable for viticulture with nearly five hectares planted initially to chardonnay, merlot, cabernet sauvignon, verdelho and shiraz for the first vintage in 1995. The wines are to be marketed under a new label with about four to five wines in the range. John believes they will be elegant, clean wines, a little lighter than those of Margaret River but with plenty of

Flavour, balance and softness — three hallmarks sought by John Kosovich from the Westfield vintage

It must be remembered that the Swan is the State's oldest producing area, and it has suffered at times from being old hat and unfashionable. Yet it is really no older than the new areas of the State with the best wine-grape varieties. 'I know there might have been some ordinary wines made here in the past, but they were different times, without the benefit of modern day knowledge and equipment, and without the classic varieties', John said.

John's problem — if he has any — is that unlike so many other winemakers

intensity and class.

For me Westfield's verdelho takes some beating. It is a very floral, aromatic style with rich flavours that are mouth filling. While the chardonnay needs wood treatment, the verdelho has the characteristics to stand on its own. John believes that wood treatment would rob the wine of some of its pleasant flavours.

The cabernets have soft, velvet-like tannins and flavours that easily pass the winemaker's ultimate test, to drink and enjoy. The quality at times has been such that some have wondered whether the fruit had come from cooler producing areas.

who push and promote their products, he would rather be tending his vines. Customer contact he leaves to wife Mary, the vital and important marketing arm of Westfield Wines.

On a visit, fortified enthusiasts should seek a sip of the Westfield liqueur muscat — rich, sweet and raisiny with an average age (in 1994) of 16 years. Sold only at the cellar door and priced at $35 (1994) it surely should be regarded as outstanding value, given its age and its drinkability over a period, compared with a youthful chardonnay for example, priced at $18 and consumed over a meal.

Darling Range & environs

AVALON

1605 Bailey Road, Glen Forrest
Cellar door sales: By appointment

Above: Glen Forrest vignerons David and Catherine Brown tend their vines, watched by labradors Pharaoh and Tosca

A T TIMES, when he has completed work on the Magistrate's bench, big, hearty David Brown will step into his other world, that of wine. Samples in hand, he will head off to some of Perth's best liquor outlets and fanciest eating houses, to convince owners they should buy his wines. It is not that tough a task, for his annual production is relatively small and the wines have spoken for themselves, by quickly winning medals and trophies, but it is certainly a different role for the legal man.

David and wife Catherine have established Avalon in the Perth Hills, after initially considering cherries. But when Agriculture Department research indicated the eight-hectare property surrounded by bush to be suitable for vines, they decided to go ahead.

Born in England, David joined the Colonial service to work in Kenya (where he first met Henry Wright who has established Wrights at Margaret River with wife Maureen), later moving from administration to wildlife and eventually becoming the country's chief game warden. Subsequently, he worked for the United Nations in Zambia, again in the wildlife service, before returning to England to complete legal studies and work in a Norfolk practice. Three years later, however, he was globe-trotting again, being

appointed resident magistrate in Fiji before coming to WA in 1978, to take up a similar position at Narrogin, and then finally Midland.

'We felt we wanted some land, and having bought it, decided we should grow something', David said.

Planting began in 1986 but it proved disastrous, the vines all dying from the lack of water, despite a full dam nearby. By the time of replanting the following year, the irrigation network had been completed and the vineyard was away. About two hectares are involved, mainly chardonnay, semillon and cabernet sauvignon, with the first vintage in 1990. A production of 15 tonnes is achieved, depending on birds, disease, weather and insect problems which have affected the vineyard from time to time.

The wines are made at Jane Brook with the 1991 semillon winning the Perth Hills best white wine trophy at the SGIO Winemakers Exhibition. The same trophy was won the following year, this time the semillon blended with sauvignon blanc. This was necessary because of unseasonal rain damage to the semillon while the sauvignon blanc, planted on the edge of the vineyard for birds to feast upon, provided enough fruit for the blend. 'That year the birds chose to ignore the sauvignon blanc, though they ate the chardonnay', David said.

The vigneron-magistrate is looking to increased ripeness in his barrel-fermented chardonnay for more fullness in the style. So far the young vines have produced a lighter style which may also have been due to the fruit picked a little early, to counter birds. 'But we won't be falling into the trap of over-wooding', he said. 'I want the wine to be fruit-driven.'

Normally dry, the herbaceous, unwooded fruity wine, the most popular at cellar door, changed in 1993 when fermentation problems led to a sweeter than planned wine. While its popularity was unaffected, it will not be a style pursued.

New American oak is used on the cabernet, softening the tannins and smoothing out the wine. Initially earthy, it is now more inclined to berry fruit characters.

David says his wife Catherine, a nurse, is the family 'green fingers', keeping the vineyard flourishing on the mainly gravelly redgum loam soils. 'I don't know how many other vineyards are tended by qualified nurses', he said with a laugh.

FROM Merseyside to Mount Helena has been a tough and fascinating journey for former Liverpudlians Jim and Carole Elson, modest producers of the West Australian industry. They have chosen the small eastern hills settlement some 38 kilometres from Perth for their Carosa vineyard development, hoping it will become a full-time occupation. Their faith undoubtedly gets some support from the whims of geography — near to their property is scenic Lake Leschenaultia, a popular tourist attraction, while only two kilometres away is the Great Eastern Highway, Western Australia's major link with the Eastern States, which again provides ready access for potential customers.

The Elsons' journey into the wine world began in South Australia, after their emigration from the United Kingdom and initially a job on the State's roads. Then Jim, an industrial chemist, became 'bored with bitumen' and took a job at Seppeltsfield, the stately old Seppelts winery in the Barossa Valley, marked by a long entrance of graceful palms. That was in 1970, and he soon came to the conclusion that it was much more pleasant to make wine than to analyse it. So when he was transferred to Rutherglen and asked to make small experimental batches of wine, he jumped at the chance. Those early efforts were not a total success, but some-

body must have seen some talent for two years later he was appointed winemaker at Chateau Tanunda, being responsible for a crush of 10,000 tonnes of fruit a year — almost twice the total West Australian production of the time.

Four years later the Elsons were on the move again, this time to Great Western in Victoria where Jim was senior winemaker — a change that brought him in contact with sparkling wine. 'We love these styles and have decided to base half our production on them', he said. The first is due for release at Christmas 1994, when the property is fully developed.

The first vines were planted in 1984, three years after the couple came to Western Australia (Jim had then decided to take up a position as manager at Swanville in the Swan Valley). When that winery was sold they decided to try their luck themselves, and chose the name Carosa from the first two letters of their daughters' names — Catherine, Rosemarie and Sarah. The main planting was chardonnay along with cabernet, merlot, pinot and rhine riesling, for they were anxious to establish what would do best on the sandy loam soils with a clay underlay, unirrigated in the first decade.

Like so many other new vignerons however, the Elsons quickly came to realise how attractive their new crops were to neighbouring birds. In 1989, for example, the silvereyes devastated the fruit, while in the previous year crows were the problem. Such damage is especially disappointing when the vineyard is small and low yielding.

The Carosa plan involves the buying of fruit from other growers in the hills to supplement their own as needed and their sparkling wine — 'as near to the French as possible'. The wines will have a minimum of three years on lees to show plenty of yeast character with delicate fruit and complexity of flavours.

Besides the bubbly, other wines made include a chardonnay, semillon — dry and late-picked — pinot noir and cabernet merlot, mostly sold at cellar door. The chardonnay is lightly wooded in line with the style and usually shows peachy characters, while the cabernet merlot, medium to full bodied and given new French oak for a year, generally reflects blackcurrant flavours. The well-made 1990 was a good example, perhaps showing more plummy characters.

Jim's general policy will be to provide whites with little or no oak. Woody wines, especially chardonnay, have little charm for him.

CAROSA

Houston Street, Mount Helena
Cellar door sales: Weekends and public holidays 10 a.m. — 5 p.m, and by appointment. Light lunches served

Jim Elson during crushing operations at his Mount Helena vineyard

CHITTERING ESTATE

Chittering Valley Road, Chittering
Cellar door sales and Le Chardonnay
restaurant: Sunday noon — 5 p.m.

*Above: Steven Schapera with French
winemaker Francois Jacquard*

CHARDONNAY

WESTERN AUSTRALIA

THE picturesque mixed farming Chittering Valley, an hour's drive north of Perth, is the area chosen for one of Western Australia's most innovative vineyard and winery developments, Chittering Estate. Boasting a striking colonial-style winery in an attractive garden setting, its lofty location provides panoramic views across vines and fruit trees in the valley below that would delight any visitor, wine lover or not.

The development differs markedly to others in the State, especially in the availability of investment dollars to provide for the best in winemaking and packaging. For the market target at Chittering Estate is in exports with 85 per cent of sales in 1994 to consumers mainly in Japan and the United Kingdom.

The project's proprietors seem an unlikely combination — Perth fish merchant George Theo Kailis and a South African migrant from Cape Town, Steven Schapera. On an earlier holiday visit to Western Australia, Steven had suggested that they extend the family friendship developed over many years, through business interests in fish and food, and try something different.

So an agreement was reached, and Steven — a mechanical engineer and wine enthusiast — called in leading South Australian viticulturist Di Davidson to help find a suitable site. The decision to go to Chittering might have raised a few eyebrows, but Steven had no misgivings. Altitude was a key factor; the vines are 330

metres above sea level, among the highest in the State. 'We may have hot days here, but the nights are very cool, and that is what we were looking for', Steven said.

Plantings began in 1982 and by 1990 contracts were in place to supply overseas markets with about 5000 cases a year. The first vintage was in 1987, and despite being a trained winemaker (he studied oenology at the University of Davis in California), Steven turned abroad to bring in experienced Californian Steve Dooley to help with the first vintage. And the policy has continued with another Californian, Joe Martin, brought to Chittering Estate in 1988, followed by Frenchman Francois Jacquard who was appointed to the position in 1992.

'Our intention', said Steven, 'was to have the benefit of their skills in special areas of expertise. These include barrel fermentation and the right type of wood for our white wines, and extended maceration with the reds — skin contact with the wine for four weeks after fermentation, unheard of in Western Australia at the time.'

The initial crush of 36 tonnes in 1987 has reached the target of 200 from the 28 hectares of vineyard, less than four kilograms of fruit on average per vine. The vineyard is made up of chardonnay, cabernet sauvignon, sauvignon blanc and semillon, with small amounts of merlot and pinot noir. It is trickle-fed and fertilised with no cultivation; instead weeds are mowed and mulched.

The soils range from lateritic gravel on an ironstone base to a combination of loam and clay over a clay base, with some vines on steep slopes.

The estate philosophy is based on sound vineyard management, backed by a winery with the best equipment money can buy, to produce wine that will complement fine food.

The two main wines under the Chittering Estate label are chardonnay and cabernet merlot with other styles sold under Brockman River Estate introduced nationally in 1993 and involving wine bought from anywhere in Australia, and blended to a style.

The estate chardonnay includes a reserve, the 1992 vintage being the first. Francois says structure, length and finesse are his main goals with complex and full-flavoured wines but lower in alcohol. Fruit from 'snake gully', an elevated block of pea gravel where the vines really struggle, is used exclusively for the reserve because of its clean and pure qualities. 'I would describe the flavours as leaner, livelier and muscular rather than flabby and flat', Steven said. 'The crop is about half as much as that from the better soils.'

Experimentation has also been undertaken with wild yeasts, with a preferred strain isolated and cultivated for use. 'I am not trying to make French wines', Francois said, 'but wines that are different and so more interesting.' By 1994 about a third of the reserve chardonnay was being fermented using the wild yeast.

I recall at my initial visit the attraction of cloves, spice and lemony characters in the chardonnay bouquet with a long very dry aftertaste, more austere than buttery. In the past alcohol levels have varied from about 13 per cent by volume in the whites to about 14 per cent in the reds.

The best cabernet merlot is the 1993, according to Steven and Francois. Dense in colour with blackcurrant and raspberry flavours, it will take years to develop in the bottle. I enjoyed the previous vintage for its fruit generosity and oak integration, a wine with plenty of cellaring life as well.

Marketing strategies in 1993 saw the reserve wines selling for about $20, estate labels for $15, and Brockman River about $10.

The presentation of special wines has been stunning. A specialty gift pack included a straw-lined wooden box, thick cartridge paper, dried wildflowers and rough-torn labels, hand made from recycled vine leaves. 'If you want to be a competitor in the export business, stylish presentation is vital', Steven said. 'You cannot put good wines in plastic jugs.'

By 1994 export sales were worth $750,000 with a rosé made from cabernet produced under a private label for a chain of 107 restaurants throughout Japan.

Chittering Estate does not enter wine shows. 'We make our wines to please people not judges', Steven said. 'They do not have shows for carrots or steak, so why wine?'

The picturesque Chittering hills form a pleasing backdrop to the neatly kept slopes of the estate

CHITTERING VALLEY WINES

Lot 12 Great Northern Highway,
Chittering
Cellar door sales: By appointment

THE Chittering Valley vineyard story began with an 18-year-old youth from Calabria in southern Italy. Antonio Nesci migrated to Western Australia and began planting the first vines in 1948, convinced that the area and its soils would produce quality fruit for a range of wines. He and his wife cleared the heavily timbered country by hand, setting the scene for consolidation by their only son Kevin many years later.

Previously, Antonio's father Kosmo had pioneered the family's journey to WA and purchased land in Chittering, later bringing out his three sons. Vince still runs Neroni Wines which his father established six kilometres south of Chittering Valley Estate, on Great Northern Highway. The other son, Frank, has also been heavily involved in the wine business.

Winemaker Kevin Nesci oversees more than a dozen grape varieties at Chittering Valley Wines

Today Kevin's holding of 200 hectares has 24 planted to vines. More than a dozen varieties flourish on the property, irrigated from a dam which stores the waters of a natural spring that runs through the vineyard. The vines yield an annual capacity of 120,000 litres, with about three-quarters sold off as grapes or juice mainly to southern Europeans for their own wine needs.

About half the remainder is processed into bottled wine while the balance goes into bulk and fortifieds. However, Kevin, who learnt his skills from his father like his father did before him, hopes by the year 2000 to produce only bottled premium wines.

The best-selling Nesci wine surprisingly is a liqueur port made from currants. Normally, this variety is used to produce dried fruit but Kevin argues its small seedless berries concentrate the flavours and the very high natural sugar levels from late-picked fruit produce a distinctly different, rich, luscious dessert wine selling for $14 (1994 prices). Something else also very different is the 1992 Nesci auslese muscat, a heavy sweet wine that swamps the mouth with flavour. Rich, full and ripe, this well-made wine (perhaps needing a little acid lift on the finish) is almost worth the journey up the highway itself for people who enjoy such styles.

Among the table wines are an unwooded tropical fruit full-bodied chardonnay, a classic dry white made from semillon and sauvignon blanc, an aromatic sweet frontignac, the most popular after the liqueur port, a light red and several full-bodied styles based on cabernet sauvignon, merlot and shiraz.

The Nesci philosophy is based on very ripe fruit with big, soft and smooth flavours. Among the latest varieties to be harvested are chardonnay, semillon, cabernet sauvignon and merlot — the latter two often in April. The merlot, which is the only estate red to have oak maturation, usually shows strong plummy characters and is a big wine, high in alcohol.

To avoid confusion with Chittering Estate about six kilometres away, Kevin sells his premium wines under a second label, Nesci. And when asked about image problems because of summer heat, especially when compared with cooler southern parts of the State, he replies: 'We get excellent fruit. You need warmth to achieve ripeness and also fruit flavour.' Certainly, the parrots, crows, foxes and kangaroos which live in the nearby bush must agree for their share of annual production is about 15-20 tonnes.

| 13.5% ALC / VOL | Chardonnay MCMXCII | 750 ml |

| 12.5% ALC / VOL | Auslese Muscat MCMXCII | 375 ml |

| 13.0% ALC / VOL | Merlot MCMXCII | 750 ml |

A VISIT to Coorinja at Toodyay, 85 kilometres east of Perth, is far more than a wine experience. It embraces history going well back into the last century, and mystery. Just who did plant the first vines and when, and who built the original winery? The present owners, the Wood family, do not know and Mrs Rica Erickson, of Nedlands, was unable to find out either during her research on the history of Toodyay. 'But I do know that the first pruning competition in the Colony was held on the property', she told me once. 'About 60 people were there in June 1894. The early camel trains on their way to the Goldfields would branch off at Coorinja because they were not allowed to go through the town.' No doubt they called at Coorinja, or one of the other vineyards which once flourished in the area, to pick up supplies for the trip, and to sell in the booming Goldfields.

Today Coorinja stands as a solitary survivor of that era, and there has been little change since additions were made to the historic hillside stone cellar in 1893.

The land was first taken up in 1858 by James Poole who had arrived in the Colony some ten years earlier, employing ticket-of-leave men until 1874. Over the years the property changed hands on numerous occasions, with C.W. Ferguson of Houghton a brief owner in 1916, when barrels and wine were transferred to the Swan Valley.

In September 1897 the Governor, Sir Gerard Smith, visited the Toodyay district and a special correspondent for *The West Australian* reported that Coorinja, on Harper's Creek about six kilometres from Newcastle (as Toodyay was then called) had been tastefully prepared for the occasion. The party was received by a Mr H. Serisier and Mr B. H. Woodward, one of the largest shareholders of the property and who in 1893 was made president of the first Vine and Fruitgrowers' Association in the district. It was recorded that as estate superintendent, Mr Serisier — the son of a vigneron who had trained in France — had made many improvements in the four years since he had taken over, including the planting of new vines and the erection of extensive new stone cellars capable of storing 16,000 gallons of wine. 'The cellars were replete with the latest and most approved appliances for making high class wine, for which Coorinja has an excellent reputation, the demand far exceeding the supply, which amounts to 5000 gallons a year', the report said. 'The wine is of only two kinds, Coorinja red and white.'

His Excellency, replying to the toast of his health, highly praised the wines he had tasted, particularly the white, adding that he had not believed such a good vintage was available in the Colony.

At the time, there were about 30 hectares under vines. Some years later there were 12,000 gallons stored in the cellars from the 1898 to 1901 vintages, with the management securing two awards at the National Show in Perth, and showing three classes of wine at the Glasgow Exhibition.

This century, however, ownership of the property has been dominated by the Wood family. A plaque on the winery wall marking more than 70 years of family winemaking reveals that Horace Wood moved to the property from the Glen Hardey winery at Glen Forrest, which the family owned, in February 1919. Even then it was obvious from the rotting jam-tree strainers in the front vineyard that the vines were possibly 50 to 60 years old.

Today the family owns about 650 hectares of land, running some 2500 sheep in association with the vineyard which has been reduced to about 17 hectares with shiraz and grenache the main red varieties, and muscat and chenin blanc the main whites. The vineyard is not irrigated and is low yielding with a crush of about 60 tonnes, producing bigger, robust wines with plenty of flavour. A planting of three hectares of shiraz and chenin blanc in 1991 will produce full-bodied wines with lots of berry flavours and exceptional colours. The vineyard is on York gum red clay country over the ridge from the winery from which vines were removed some 50 years ago.

The family have passed their skills down the line, but basically winemaking techniques have not changed much. The fruit is picked in wooden boxes and stacked into a roofed but open-sided vintage shed so that cool breezes blow through at night, acting as a Coolgardie safe to bring down the temperature of the grapes. 'It is very effective', said present-day winemaker Michael Wood. 'Your hands can get quite cold handling the fruit the next day.'

In the past wagons of fruit were backed up a ramp by horse to the third-floor level and dropped into a crusher for gravity to move the wine — the system used at Glen Hardey. Although Michael now uses wax-lined fermenting tanks, century-old basket presses are still part of the process along with natural yeasts.

In 1950 Coorinja received its biggest-ever order for wine, about 13,500 litres of sweet sherry for the Eastern States. It was poured into 60 casks, each of 225 litres.

COORINJA WINES

Toodyay Road, Toodyay
Cellar door sales: 8 a.m. — 5 p.m. daily
except Sunday

Winemaking is very much a family tradition for the Woods of Coorinja, each generation passing on the skills from the past. Pictured are Hector Wood and son Michael

Black smoke marks around the cellar are a reminder of the wood-fired still once operated at Coorinja for grape spirit, requiring a customs officer in residence to supervise the bond store while an old four-wheeled horse-drawn wagon stored in the cellars was a key transporter for the winery. Michael's father Hector told me how cut saplings used to be jammed into the wheels so that the laden wagon would skid slowly down steep slopes and not run out of control.

He also told me about the hungry night predator, the cutworm. Because there were no control sprays, men searched the vineyard looking for tell-tale small mounds of dirt near the base of vines, then digging them up. 'It was no good stamping on them because in the soft dirt you would not kill them', Hector said. 'So we put them in small tins, into which we had placed some gravel stones. We would then give them a good shake, and they would be killed.'

Declining yields at Coorinja have seen much of the vineyard area let go. The vines grow on very shallow soils varying from red clay to sandy loam over gravel, and are subject to stress in late summer.

About 80 per cent of the production is fortifieds, mainly ports, but also sherries and muscats. Given the decline in the fortified market in recent years and the number of producers cutting production and stock, this may surprise. But Michael says Coorinja sells all it makes — about half at cellar door and the rest to Perth retail outlets.

'The key to our wines is flavour', Michael said. 'We get it in the grapes on the vines and that is the same for citrus grown in this area. Mincing [adopted from the Jack Mann technique] of the fruit helps bring out the flavour, and you get a much cleaner wine as well.'

The Woods set modest prices for their wine, to encourage people to make the pleasant drive from Perth.

The combined winery, cellar door sales area and restaurant above is in an attractive bush setting

DUTCH names certainly do not feature prominently in the world of wine. It is not in their blood, say Balt and Francesca van der Meer (pictured left). But this has not stopped them making a success of their unique Darlington Estate development in the Perth Hills. Just 25 kilometres from the city the couple have established vines on the steep slopes of catchment country, surrounded by state forest. The vineyard is terraced with the vines closely planted, enhancing the picturesque valley, a pleasing perspective from the couple's modern home on the hillside. The location is near the site of the original Darlington Vineyard which flourished in the area from the 1880s to the 1920s.

Helped by trickle irrigation the vineyard has thrived, despite the foxes and rabbits, and especially the kangaroos. 'Kangaroos love grapes', says Francesca, 'and like the rabbits they have found new young shoots a treat. They have devastated some rows several times and initially, we had to do a lot of replanting.' Unfortunately for the van der Meers, the kangaroos have persisted, with feasting forays of the succulent green growth increasing as the surrounding bush dries out in summer.

Such problems are a world away from their previous lives. For Balt's career in fashion clothing took him into a business founded by his great grandfather. From Europe the couple moved to Hong Kong, base for extensive travelling throughout the Far East. When it was time for a break they visited Balt's sister in Perth. With the

DARLINGTON ESTATE

Lot 39, Nelson Road, Darlington
Cellar door sales: Wed — Sun and public holidays, noon — 5 p.m; Thurs — Sun café style lunches; à la carte dining Fri, Sat evenings. Weddings and functions by arrangement

Balt van der Meer draws a sample of red for further tests during maceration

DARLINGTON
ESTATE

1991

*Cabernet
Sauvignon*

door demand, while Minuet, or Blanc de Noir made from cabernet, is a touch sweeter. An easy drinking wine which is pink in colour, it is very popular served chilled at lunchtime, having plenty of flavour, even going well with curries.

Other wines include a semillon-sauvignon blanc blend, the 20 per cent sauvignon blanc which is wooded, adding complexity and increasing the flavour of the drier, chablis style semillon; chardonnay, the flagship white with the 1993 vintage, the biggest so far, in a range that is generally rich and full flavoured; an unwooded tropical fruit sauvignon blanc introduced in 1993; a Darlington Estate cabernet including a dash of cabernet franc and merlot, a big, full, soft style with strong blackberry fruit characters; a more tannic, dusty, chocolate cassis-like cabernet from Parkerville which needs time in the bottle; a full, soft, peppery shiraz with spiciness on the late palate; an early drinking light soft red including 20 per cent gamay labelled Vin Primeur; and a ruby port. This is a clean, fresh, early drinking, sweeter style fortified redolent of blackberry and violets.

Winemakers always tell me their first major show success is one they never forget, and that is also true for the van der Meers, with the trophies for the best white and best red from the Perth Hills at the 1989 SGIO Winemakers Exhibition. The wines of Darlington Estate reflect the gravelly soils and climate with the vineyard slopes allowing an air movement to produce an important cooling effect in summer.

Son Caspar, who has completed a science degree at the University of Western Australia and has turned to post-graduate studies of oenology, will no doubt take over winemaking duties from his father in the years ahead.

But even specialised knowledge is no insurance against natural disasters such as February rains in 1992, for example, which devastated the chenin blanc, semillon and sauvignon blanc plantings. Then there are the birds. Sometimes the nearby forest residents have taken up to a third of the expected harvest, a bitter blow. Early picking of chardonnay to prevent such damage will provide fruit for a sparkling wine base.

A trip to the winery now means much more than just wine sampling. There is relaxed dining based on well-presented, fresh home-style cooking, the opportunity for bushwalks (especially appealing at wildflower times), or for winter visitors, the temptation to linger around a log fireplace in congenial surroundings.

open spaces appealing immediately, they emigrated in 1981. After a stint in suburbia the couple headed for the hills to purchase a 16-hectare block, initially with an orchard in mind because they wanted to work with the land. But the appeal of the vine and wine industry quickly took hold.

Subsequent plantings included cabernet sauvignon, merlot, chardonnay, semillon, sauvignon blanc and gamay, the famous Beaujolais grape, making Darling Estate one of the first vineyards in Australia to grow the variety. Later shiraz was added for total plantings of 15,000 vines with a crush of 50 tonnes at full production, including fruit from the leased Parkerville (Woodthorpe) property, producing about 40,000 bottles in all. A range of wines is made in an attractive rustic winery built from stone found on the property and timber from an old wool store demolished at Fremantle.

The culture-loving couple turned to music to name some of their wines. Symphony, a blend of chenin blanc and (purchased) colombard was the first, joined later by Sonata and Minuet. The Sonata is a blend of 60 per cent sauvignon blanc and 40 per cent chenin blanc, a slightly sweet (7-8 grams per litre of residual sugar) style specially made for an increasing cellar

PETER and Helen Fimmel of Hainault Wines at Bickley, in the Perth Hills about 40 minutes drive from the city, knew exactly what they wanted when searching for land for their vineyard. Most importantly it had to be a gentle sloping valley running east and west, and as high above sea level as possible, for climate moderation in the growing and ripening season.

Armed with maps they identified the area and set about finding property for sale, their old Land Rover bouncing over many a bush track. At one spot they came through a clearing to surprise an old Italian orchardist who asked what they were doing. 'Looking for land' they told him, yet he gave no hint that the very property would be up for sale a few months later. The Fimmels snapped it up. 'You only need that sort of luck once in a lifetime', Peter said, gazing out over his thriving vines which have replaced most of the apple trees, pears and stone fruit that previously dominated the seven-hectare property.

There was never any doubt in their minds that the prime orchard should give way to vines. Peter was convinced of the area's potential through his involvement with a group of academic friends includ-

ing near neighbour and surgeon Alan Bray at Woodhenge, later to be renamed Piesse Brook. 'He persuaded me to help with their plantings and I liked it so much, I decided to go into my own venture', Peter said.

So the former biologist who worked in cancer research became a man of the land, planting vines as the orchard gradually was grubbed out, and building a small winery. Anxious to get producing, he bought fruit from Frankland River in 1980 and 1981 to make the first wines under the Hainault label. This was the name of the family farm at Harvey, a small town in Essex not far from where his wife had lived, and the name of an old Kalgoorlie goldmine in which a great uncle once worked.

Today the Fimmels have 17,700 vines planted in a vineyard designed far from the state and national viticultural norm. Vines are planted in narrow rows at four times the usual density. Peter's reasoning is based on reducing the ground available to each vine, to restrict growth in the search for better quality fruit.

'Man has learnt a lot about viticulture over the centuries', he explained, 'and we are still learning. I believe properly se-

HAINAULT VINEYARD

Walnut Road, Bickley
Cellar door sales: Thurs — Sun and public holidays, 10 a.m. — 5 p.m. Other times by appointment

Above: Peter Fimmel uses his own adapted version of the European broquette de vigneron to burn cuttings after pruning

lected pockets of land in the hills can support such intense practices.'

The varieties at Hainault include chardonnay, semillon, traminer, pinot noir, cabernet sauvignon, merlot and cabernet franc, with an expected peak production of 3000 cases.

Peter believes that successful horticulture in the area over the past century is proof enough that vines will flourish. This is despite occasional severe frosts which have covered the landscape in white, killing fruit trees in the most susceptible valley areas.

Birds have not been serious problems, at least in most years, while nature is being looked to as an ally in the fight against pests and diseases. Peter says this is possible as insect numbers are allowed to build up with no synthetic chemical insecticides being used.

There are six wines produced by Hainault, three whites and three reds, with the emphasis very definitely aimed at consumption with meals, where Peter believes they will be enjoyed most. His target is broader, mouth-filling styles, but with strict limitations on the use of oak. 'We are not looking to a mouthful of toothpicks or pencil shavings', he said. 'Too much oak can lead to aggression in reds and whites.'

The primary and secondary characters in his wines are matters for some complexity, and Peter talks of initial responses based on fruit sensations such as apple and pear blossom in chardonnay, and mushrooms, truffles and moss in pinot noir. Outsiders may think he has a vivid creative imagination, but Peter is quick to point out that this is a real reaction by people who have tasted his wines over the years. Certainly a peak came when an Eastern States reviewer referred to a Hainault pinot as having 'marvellous damp forest' overtones.

A reserve pinot has been added to the range because, Peter says, it is different. Richer and more elegant, the fruit is from vines growing in an old (drained) swamp, on gravelly loam over peat, half to three metres deep.

Chardonnay has been top dog at the winery in the 1980s but personally I have preferred the pinots from tastings, with the 1988 a pace setter. I confess to not being able to detect the rotten oranges on the nose, which Peter claimed was a hallmark of the great French Burgundy chateaux.

'Time will show just how well the valleys of Bickley are suited to pinot', he predicts. 'The wines produced have been very Burgundian, not the fruity little numbers that are pretty common in Australia. We will be striving for complexity in all our wines so that a bottle consumed over a prolonged meal will generate different flavours with each glass, almost as if a new wine is being poured every time.'

Exports by the end of 1994 are expected to reach 15 per cent of production, mainly to the United Kingdom.

In this year too the Fimmels put the property (but not the labels) up for sale. Peter planned to continued making wine at a nearby location, concentrating on pinot noir from purchased fruit.

HOTHAM VALLEY ESTATE

North Bannister — Pingelly Road, Wandering
Cellar door sales: By appointment

THE TINY rural town of Wandering, 120 kilometres south-east of Perth, is reputed to be the coldest spot in WA in winter. It is certainly not known as a place of vines and fine wines.

Jim Pennington at Hotham Valley Wines plans to change that, and he will no doubt regard 1993 as the turning point in the pioneering development. For the year saw the hillside vineyard win its first trophy, with the 1993 semillon being judged the outstanding white wine in the Perth Hills region at the annual SGIO awards.

Previously, the semillon had won a bronze medal at the 1993 Perth Wine Show, along with the 1992 chardonnay. Yet two years earlier, disaster struck the vineyard, leaving Jim to wonder about its future.

The worst attack by locusts in living memory, part of a huge state-wide invasion, wiped out the crop. Not a berry was picked, not a leaf left. Jim thought the vines were finished, but miraculously they recovered to flourish, producing the grapes to make award-winning wines. As Jim escorted me around his new winery prior to the 1994 vintage, I recalled the words of Andrew Mountford of Mountford Wines at Pemberton. A trained horticulturist, he said of the grapevine: 'It is one of the most forgiving plants I have ever worked with'.

The Hotham Valley vineyard has been established on a 1800-hectare mixed cereal and fine wool producing property that has been in the Pennington family for 70 years. But Jim Pennington's early direction in life was away from the land. He became a science teacher and taught at Scotch College, the school he attended as a pupil.

On exchange in England, he visited French vineyard areas, beginning a passion for wine that was to lead to the establishment of Hotham Valley. Returning to WA, he decided he wanted to get back to the land, initially to develop a vineyard in a new area, like Manjimup or Pemberton. An investigation of the reports by Dr John Gladstones revealed that Wandering was similar to the premium Clare Valley area of South Australia. But there was concern about the severity of frosts and the dryness of summer.

'My father's crop growing experience with frosts indicated that as long as we planted on the hillside where there was good air drainage, there would not be a frost problem', Jim said. 'And all we needed was an adequate water supply for the dry summer stress period.'

A one-hectare trial planted in 1985 proved successful and, backed by Perth investors Evan Cross, John Saleeba, Jeremy Shervington, Robert Bird, Shane Atwell Richard Saleeba and Aaron Constantine, Jim quit his job to become a full-time vigneron, and then to take up the ultimate challenge, to make wine. A 65-hectare selection of the property's best land was subdivided to become the basis for Hotham Valley Estate, representing an investment of more than $1 million, including the winery.

In 1988 and 1989 the main vineyard, 12 hectares in all, was planted to chardonnay, chenin blanc, rhine riesling, semillon, cabernet sauvignon, cabernet franc, merlot and zinfandel. Four tonnes was picked in 1990 with a full production target put at 130-150 tonnes. The initial wines were made at Killerby Wines with Jim completing a bachelor of applied science in wine science at the Charles Sturt University, as an external student.

The vines grow on gravelly loam over clay, and Jim claims the bitter Wandering winters to be an asset. 'It puts the vines into an early precise dormancy', he said. 'The vines lose their leaves together and burst into bud and flower evenly.'

But the overall warm climate, Jim says, will develop rich traditional Australian wines, shown in the early releases. While the chardonnay may be the Hotham wine with the most potential, the unwooded 1993 semillon was the pick of the early releases, a refined style of delicious fruit, without the grassiness of some South West wines, and blessed with lovely balancing acid.

On many summer nights, the 'Albany doctor' is a welcome arrival, dropping hot daytime temperatures. 'Aboriginal elders

have told me they called the spot timber ridge and it was the coolest place in the district, a good place to sit', Jim said. 'The altitude here, 360 metres above sea level, also helps modify temperatures '

The Hotham Valley plan is to make four whites, a chenin blanc and a classic dry white besides the semillon and chardonnay, and two reds, a soft early drinking wine and a full-bodied dry, Bordeaux style.

'Our philosophy is full-flavoured wines at modest prices', Jim said. 'We will blend fruit from other WA regions, to make the best possible wines in a consistent style.'

Chilly Wandering? Not a problem, says local vigneron Jim Pennington

JADRAN WINES

Reservoir Road, Orange Grove
Cellar door sales: Mon — Sat 9.30 a.m.
— 8.30 p.m. Sundays 11 a.m. — 5.30
p.m.

*For Stephen and Paul Radojkovich the recipe
for success is sound wines at modest prices*

I N 1975 the domination by Olive Farm of the Perth Wine Show's most successful small winemaker trophy was halted. It was not, however, one of the more fancied West Australian producers who was presented with the award, but Jadran Wines of Orange Grove. In all, the winery's entries received eight gold and two silver medals, an impressive performance for a producer who had only begun showing two years previously. For years afterwards Jadran did not show again. 'We felt we had made our point about the quality of the wines we can produce', winemaker and principal Stephen Radojkovich told me. 'We decided to concentrate on making wines our customers wanted, rather than putting effort into show wines.'

His father Wally established the Jadran vineyard in 1927 and the winery in 1929. But his story of migration to a new land was different from many of his former countrymen. While most were young men, he was just a schoolboy. Wally Radojkovich was 13 years old when sent from the family village on the Adriatic Sea

of Dalmatia to live and find employment in Western Australia's Swan Valley. He worked hard and saved every penny he could with one aim in mind — to buy his own land and to grow grapes. In just two years he had accumulated enough to buy, with a partner, four hectares of virgin land at Orange Grove on sloping land less than a kilometre from the foothills, 20 kilometres south-east of Perth.

He had been attracted to the area by a cousin living in nearby Maddington, and other fellow migrants who had planted orchards and vines in the district. The pattern of hard work continued with clearing by hand at weekends, and before and after other jobs. By 1932 he was able to buy out his partner and produce his own wine.

Over the years, the emphasis of production at Jadran has been on bulk table wines, and fortifieds. Today the fortified range has been reduced with more emphasis on table wines. Bottled premium wine makes up about a third of the production, but Jadran remains the only producer in Western Australia to market bag-in-the-box wines.

Slowly, the nine-hectare vineyard has been replanted to varieties like chenin blanc and verdelho. But change is a delicate matter, for over its 60 years Jadran has established a following for sound quality wines at modest prices.

The wines are sold mainly through the cellar door sales area adjacent to the winery and shaded by four magnificent flame trees. There visitors can enjoy tasting the range during opening hours that are the longest of any winery in the State — well into the evenings six days a week, in the face of competition from local liquor stores.

Among the wines is the premium Grove range, with the 1993 chardonnay from Swan Valley fruit being the first. It is also the first chardonnay from the winery. Others, depending on the year, include a cabernet and rhine riesling, a variety in which Stephen has retained his faith, despite a market trend away from the variety.

The vineyard is not a big producer, yielding only about six tonnes to the hectare from the sandy loam soils over clay. Its location also makes the vines prone to strong, battering easterly winds.

The production means that most of the fruit for the crush is purchased from other districts, especially the Swan Valley and Great Southern. I recall a very good rhine riesling from fruit purchased from the Roche Frankland River vineyard before it was leased by Houghton, with other wines from Boyup Brook and Margaret River fruit.

The fact that six of the eight gold medals awarded to Jadran in 1975 were for fortified wines reflects the quality of such styles.

'There is still a very good market for port despite the decline in popularity of fortifieds', Stephen said. 'We introduced a white port as a gimmick and it has been very successful, winning us a lot of customers.'

He took over from his father in 1974 with son Paul employed in the business. One of the lesser-known varieties they handle is sercial, also known as ondenc, and Irvine's white, grown mostly in South Australia and Victoria where it has been particularly successful in the Great Western area for sparkling wine production.

Jadran also has a bubbly in its range, a spumante, plus marsala, muscat, vermouth and sherries to meet all tastes. 'Our aim is to cater for every visitor making the trip to Orange Grove', Stephen said.

LENNARDS BROOK ESTATE

Lennards Road, Gingin
Cellar door sales: By appointment

Barbara Potter uses a pipette to draw a keg sample for testing

BARBARA Potter began her working life as a nurse, tending patients at Fremantle Hospital. Now she tends vines with her son-in-law Ian Atkinson on a picturesque property at Gingin, 100 kilometres north of Perth.

It takes its name from the permanent brook which flows by, providing valuable fresh water for the vines, first planted in 1985.

Initially, Barbara and Gerry Chrystal purchased the 40-hectare property in 1979 as an investment. Later, however, they sought to generate income from the land, trying watermelons. Inspired by the success of the nearby Moondah Estate, they moved to vines, at first growing chardonnay and verdelho under contract to Houghton from a six-hectare development. In 1993, however, the decision was made to establish their own label with some of the production, and Lennards Brook Estate was born.

Three wines are made, a dry chardonnay and verdelho, and a sweet wine from the latter variety. Some 40 tonnes are produced from the vineyard, with about two-thirds sold off as fruit and the rest made into wine in the Swan Valley. Eventually, Barbara aims for half the fruit to be part of the Lennards Brook range.

Apart from pruning, she has come to enjoy the lifestyle. That is not surprising, for she is a woman of the land. Her parents farmed at Toodyay, east of Perth.

From nursing she progressed to running a boutique fashion shop in the ritzy Perth suburb of Peppermint Grove. Now she makes the drive regularly from the property to Perth, to sell wines instead, and to persuade customers that not being part of the more fancied cooler southern regions of the State is hardly a problem.

Certainly, her 'public debut' at the 1993 Spring in the Valley and the SGIO Winemakers Exhibition in the same year did much to introduce the new label.

A surprise was that the sweet wine drew most favoured attention. That was understandable, following a tasting of the range. While the two dry wines were sound and well made, very good first-up efforts, the other was a style of some quality. Tropical fruit flavours spilled out of the glass when poured, leading to a sweet palate full of abundant flavour. The feature was the balance, the skilful use of acid leaving the mouth fresh and clean. Served chilled, such a style would please many palates.

PIESSE BROOK

Aldersyde Road South, Bickley
Cellar door sales: 10 a.m. — 8 p.m.
Sundays

ONE OF Western Australia's smallest vineyards, Piesse Brook in the Perth Hills, had its origins in the heart of the academic world — the University of Western Australia. There, four wine-loving mates who enjoyed sharing and comparing and who launched the University Wine Society, decided to go that big step further, to make their own. The foursome included statistician Brian Murphy, microbiologists Peter Fimmel and John Finlay-Jones, and medico Alan Bray.

Alan lived on a property in the Bickley Valley, half way between Kalamunda and Mundaring Weir, and reasoned that as it had been a premium orchard area for 80 years, it should grow grapes well. This meant that some of the old uneconomic plums and lemons had to go, though property owner and long-time tenderer of the orchard, the late Mick Boyanich, would hardly have approved of the noisy buzz of chain saws.

Today in their place on the gravelly slopes and on the deep, fertile soils of the valley floor, healthy shiraz and cabernet planted in 1974 certainly testify to that early faith in vines.

The property was originally labelled Woodhenge, coined by a visitor when he saw the group erecting solid two-metre long jarrah logs as vineyard strainer posts. 'Stonehenge in wood' was the observation, and the name is still part of the business, though the present label acknowledges a small brook which flows through the bottom of one block. The original property has since been divided in two and is owned by Ray Boyanich, a former champion Perth and Melbourne Australian Rules footballer, and his sister Di Bray.

For a long time Brian Murphy continued as winemaker, retaining an interest as the remaining member of the original quartet. Since 1992, however, he has been involved as a consultant.

Brian learnt some of the skills in the business in a very unlikely winemaking location, England, and with very unlikely materials, dried berries in tins from Russia and Poland. During a seven-year stint as a lecturer at the University of London, he turned to making his own wines because French wines had become so expensive, and that involved sweating over 20-gallon plastic rubbish bins as boiling water was poured over the berries, and sugar added.

But it was not easy, getting a new operation off the ground — and there was real pain when Piesse Brook flowed red

from the dumping of the 1980 vintage, as if the property was bleeding. But 1986 proved a significant turning point when the winery's 1985 cabernet shiraz won the SGIO Winemakers Exhibition trophy for the best dry red from the Swan Valley-Darling Ranges, then combined together as a single producing area. While the result might have made the Swan boys smart, it was a big boost for the Bickley hopefuls. For the first time it meant that Piesse Brook was a serious contender in the business and not a fun, hobby operation. Beating the best from the Swan had been a real tonic for all. More good results followed when the 1986 cabernet shiraz won the award in 1987 and again the following year, this time however, the competition was against the best from the hills.

In 1993, Piesse Brook repeated the success, with the 1990 vintage — like the other wines, another big block-busting blend of cabernet and shiraz.

Piesse Brook has also done particularly well with its shiraz, gaining a four-star rating (out of five) with the 1989 vin-

tage in a national wine magazine's assessment of Western Australian wines. Ray says impressive vintages in 1991 and 1992 convinces him that the vineyard is a happy place for the variety, which could become its flagship.

Subsequent plantings have including chardonnay — with the first vintage in 1993 — on rich loamy soils that have extended the vineyard to 3.25 hectares and provided greater challenges than the production of a single red blend.

This will show conclusively that the vineyard, despite climatic fluctuations from bitter winter cold to extreme summer heat, with a lot of mild weather thrown in, can produce quality fruit from which various styles can be made.

Production of the big, full, gutsy reds of the 1980s, catering for a select band of red wine lovers, certainly not weaklings, has continued in the 1990s. But styles are now also made to provide for other tastes, a medium style dry red from cabernet-merlot with a touch of wood, and Cabernova, a light summer red to be drunk chilled.

Another crate of cabernet for lovers of the big, full red styles — and ex-footballer Ray Boyanich has every reason to smile

REDHILL ESTATE

North Wandering Road, Wandering
(To be renamed Wandering Brook in
1995)
Cellar door sales: Weekends 9.30 a.m. —
6 p.m. Restaurant set menu lunches, also
weekends

*A 100-tonne annual crop is the target for
Laurie and Margaret White*

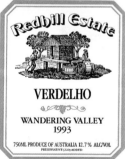

YOU could not blame Laurie and Margaret White for thinking they had done something seriously wrong when they made the decision to join the wine industry. For one disaster seemed to follow another. In two years locusts devastated their young vines; hail, heavy rain and flooding did further damage, oddly enough when local people were fighting bushfires; white ants destroyed their packaging material; and a cockeyed bob hit their home.

The couple might well have been advised to revert to the family's 130-year-old farming tradition in WA of hay, grain cropping and sheep grazing. Not Laurie White, though he confessed to distinct ageing at the time! In fact, it just made him more determined than ever to produce quality.

Amazingly, the Whites had no knowledge of the industry before taking the bold step — they had not even drunk a bottle of premium wine. Imagine, then, the pride they felt when four years after planting their first vine, their chardonnay was selling for $24 a bottle in classy places like the Swan Valley Vines Resort, and the Esplanade Hotel in Fremantle.

The White story began because of dry summers. Laurie was keen to see green in his paddocks and inspired by the Hotham Valley vineyard development just down the road, decided to take up the vine growing challenge.

The Whites, whose family farm is called Redhill (after the heavy red soils of the hillsides), began planting in September 1989. Two blocks now nurture just over ten hectares of vines on a variety of well-drained soils, from the heavy red to gravel and coarse rock — all on top of clay. The varieties include verdelho, cabernet sauvignon, merlot, a few rows of mixed Portuguese port varieties, and the chardonnay.

The first vintage was a modest 3.5 tonnes in 1992 with the early wines made at Goundreys. From 1994, however, the Whites turned to the newly built Hotham Valley winery for their processing. At full production, with further plantings planned, they are aiming for a 100 tonne-a-year crop.

The early wines include a verdelho, wooded and unwooded chardonnay, a light soft, slightly sweet red, and a cabernet. And while winning a bronze medal in a show is certainly no big deal, it is all the more special when it is your first ever. At the Mount Barker show in 1993, the Redhill (oaked) chardonnay picked up the gong. I gave it a similar rating, enjoying the wine for its balance and fresh, clean, slightly citrus and lemon fruit qualities. The uncomplicated 1993 cabernet proved another sound wine in the range, enjoyable as well for its softness and pleasant fruit quality.

To help the Whites in their new venture, friends and neighbours have rallied to pick the fruit on a voluntary basis, enjoying for their labours a vintage party held, appropriately, under one of Redhill's distinctive redgum trees.

South West Coastal

AQUILA ESTATE

85 Carabooda Road, Carabooda
No cellar door sales

THE USUAL start in the wine industry is a vineyard with a winery development down the track. At Aquila Estate, Elaine Washer is doing it the other way round.

In 1993, the first production year, Elaine organised the purchase of 30 tonnes of fruit to make into wine in a corner of the family packing shed, part of their major avocado operation run by her mother Nola. A year later her buying brief had extended to 98 tonnes with plans for a 500-tonne crush by the turn of the century, making the estate a significant West Australian producer. By that time some of the fruit will be their own, from four-hectare plantings at Carabooda and an investment in a Margaret River development.

The Aquila story began with Elaine, a science graduate from the University of

be able to create the grape with a certain taste. For example, if fig or melon characters were wanted in chardonnay, they would be able to programme a grape to produce a protein to create the flavours.'

Her father Malcolm, a lover of wine, suggested that she try winemaking as a career. With a financial interest in the new label, he becomes another West Australian general practitioner to become involved in the wine industry.

Elaine got her initial winemaking tutelage from Margaret River consultant Mike Davies, and the first Aquila Estate vintage included a chardonnay, sauvignon blanc, semillon-sauvignon blanc blend and a cabernet sauvignon. Later vintages are to include a semillon, shiraz and light soft red. Long-term contracts have been ar-

Can science genetically manipulate the grape? Elaine Washer sees a new dimension in winemaking

Western Australia with a double major in biochemistry and microbiology who then went on to complete a genetic engineering honours degree at Murdoch University. After this protracted study, she wondered what to do with her life, but with such qualifications there was no doubt the choice would be wide.

In her honours year, she had wondered about genetic research in viticulture and the possibility of seeking out special fruit qualities in grapes for programmed vineyard production. 'I believe the day will come when scientists will be able to organise crops of desired flavours, aromas and colours in grapes', she said. 'They will

ranged with four Margaret River grape growers.

Elaine says the estate emphasis will be on exports as production increases, though a concentrated effort will seek a firm niche in the domestic market.

So far the fruity, slightly sweet semillon-sauvignon blanc blend has proved the biggest seller, though I preferred the full, ripe, unwooded sauvignon blanc, a good food wine. Generally, chardonnays will be in the lighter styles with a gentle touch of oak. With the cabernet, Elaine is looking to a medium-bodied style with ripe berry fruit character.

A T FIRST glance Serpentine is not the
sort of place to attract attention when
it comes to establishing a vineyard and
winery — particularly with such a favoured emphasis on the cool southern
areas of the State. Indeed, at a superficial
level the hungry grey sands of Baldivis
Estate would tend to confirm this view.
But there's a lot more to any new venture
than meets the eye; and unquestionably
Baldivis is a project of substance, as are the
people behind it.

For example, Peter George Kailis is a
successful Perth businessman and investor
whose brother Theo is involved in the establishment of Chittering Estate north of
Perth. Consultant Di Davidson of South
Australia enjoys a national reputation for
her skill while bearded winemaker John
Smith has earned broad respect for his ability.

The Baldivis vineyard is part of a 120-
hectare $5.5 million 'fruit salad' project,
designed to produce round the year supplies for domestic and export markets. Included are 10,000 avocado trees, 450 man-
goes, 1000 limes and a hectare of table grapes.

The estate and other wide-ranging
business interests are a far cry indeed
from the time Peter's father George walked
door to door around Perth, selling fish
from a basket. But his labours, and those
of wife Evangelia — who arrived in WA
during World War I from the tiny Greek
island of Kastellorizo — provided the basis for a major national seafood business,
ultimately allowing Peter to realise his

dream of producing a premium table wine.

Planting of the eight-hectare vineyard
began in 1982, the first commercial release
occurred five years later, under the Lake
Kathryn label, and Baldivis Estate made
its debut the following year. Today
chardonnay is 'queen' of the vineyard with
three hectares planted. Other varieties include semillon, sauvignon blanc, cabernet
sauvignon and merlot.

The vines are on higher ground of the
property, to avoid the wetter, lower land.
The soils are boosted by mulching and
'fertigation' — the consistent supply of
weak solutions of fertiliser with regular
watering throughout the day in summer.
This seeks to maintain healthy growth
and control vigour. The vines have re-
sponded well; the Kailis aim is to crush
about 100 tonnes.

The main wine styles produced are a
chardonnay, cabernet merlot, and a
sauvignon blanc-semillon blend. In exceptional years a straight semillon and
merlot is also made while the Lake Kathryn
label provides for two wines, SBS, a blend
of sauvignon blanc and semillon, and Mt
Solus, an unwooded cabernet, styles especially for export markets but also available at times domestically.

I recall early wine tastings from the
estate being light in body, but as the vines
have matured concentrations of flavours
have built up, such as in the 1993 vintage.
This was a much lower yielding year than
the previous season, mainly due to a spring

BALDIVIS ESTATE

River Road, Baldivis
Cellar door sales: Weekends and public
holidays 10 a.m. — 4 p.m. Weekdays by
appointment. Outside alfresco functions
by arrangement

*A happy moment for Peter Kailis (above),
pictured against a backdrop of Baldivis vines
and lime trees*

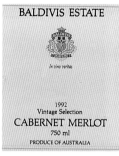

frost which hit the chardonnay especially, cutting expectations by nearly half. But cooling summer sea breezes help create a micro-climate for the wines, which are enjoyable for their freshness and brightness.

The label's progress stands out clearly; for example, first class passengers flying across Australia have been offered various vintages of Baldivis chardonnay, and the 1991 vintage rated second among Australian small winemakers at the 1992 Sydney top 100 International Winemakers Competition. Then in 1993 the Baldivis 1990 cabernet merlot was judged best from the south-west coastal area in the SGIO Winemakers Exhibition. I especially enjoyed the wine at the judging, impressed with the bright vibrant red colours, and the softness and velvety merlot characters filling out the more

austere and astringent cabernet berry-like backbone.

When Peter's son Mark joined the business in 1987 he soon impressed with his marketing and promotional efforts. And he made a broader contribution as well, by becoming president of the WA Wine Industry Association's fine wine marketing committee. In the period exports have climbed to 25 per cent of production with sales to the United States, United Kingdom, Sweden and other European countries, resulting in the Kailis conglomerate looking south to Pemberton and Mount Barker for extra fruit supplies, and perhaps another vineyard development, as part of a five-year plan.

Baldivis wines are priced in the mid-range of West Australian wines, reflecting Peter's philosophy to 'give people more than they pay for'.

CAPEL VALE

Capel North West Road, Capel
Cellar door sales: Daily 10 a.m. — 4 p.m.

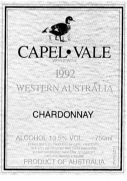

WHEN Dr Peter Pratten and wife Elizabeth reflect on their Capel Vale development they will recall many highlights. None, however, is likely to be sweeter than their success at the 1986 Adelaide Show — the prized trophy of champion dry white wine, entered in a year when the event was at national championship level.

What made it specially memorable was that the Capel Vale wine was a rhine riesling (1986 vintage), and it beat the best of the trendy chardonnays, sauvignon blancs and semillons as well as other high-flying rieslings from the more fashionable Clare and Eden Valley areas. It also must be remembered that South Australia is easily the Goliath of the Australia wine industry, so a small, then little-known WA producer winning a trophy in Adelaide was especially notable.

The Capel Vale wine was also voted the best white at the Sydney Smallmakers Competition.

There have been other big show days for the winery, such as when it won four prizes at the Sheraton Perth wine awards the previous year. These included the most successful exhibitor and the Chairman's Trophy for the best wine of the show.

A visitor to Capel Vale, however, will find no trophy cabinet or special stand to feature these and other prizes. Instead, they are stored discreetly in a back shed. While Peter and Elizabeth enjoy the success, they put more emphasis on their wines winning medals — a sign of consistent quality. Every wine shown since 1984 has done so, including, in 1993, gold

medals awarded to the 1992 chardonnay and 1993 rhine riesling.

The couple's wine journey to Capel, two kilometres from the coast between Bunbury and Busselton, had its origins in Connecticut. Then a professor, Peter was lecturing in radiology at Yale University when they decided there was more to life than the American academic rat race. They returned to Australia, Peter taking up a temporary medical position in Bunbury. Liking the area, they decided to buy a property on the Capel River. Thus was formed the basis for their entry into the wine industry.

'Medicine is basically a service industry', Peter observed on my first visit to the winery as he prepared to crush fruit. 'It is not creative like growing grapes and making wine. This is why I believe so many doctors have entered the field.'

Peter graduated as a general practitioner at Sydney University, later specialising in internal disorders before concentrating on radiology, an area in which he is still actively engaged as a means of supporting Capel Vale vine and wine developments.

Planting at Capel Vale began with cabernet sauvignon and shiraz in 1975 on the rich, deep soils of the nine-hectare river frontage block, once a big producer of quality stone fruit. (Old timers in the district, whose guilt has long since vanished, fondly remember raiding the area in their younger days to feast on the fruit.) But there were early problems establishing the vines because of the wind, and old tyres were used as a protective device.

A satisfied Peter Pratten displays seven of Capel Vale's best

Ironically, the problem later became reversed as unusually vigorous growth had to be controlled.

Subsequent plantings included a number of varieties with the grafter's skill later employed, converting vines to other varieties in the search for an optimum result. For example, shiraz now produces chardonnay; rhine riesling, merlot; cabernet, semillon; and traminer, chardonnay, sauvignon blanc and semillon.

The first commercial vintage (for red wines) was in 1980, with whites out the following year. Peter's aims remain the major motivation today, to make wines that people find interesting, enjoy drinking and that taste like the berry from which they have come.

Helping him to achieve these goals, Peter believes, are the overcast skies so often a part of Capel climate. A constant band of cloud in the area meant a longer, slower ripening period for the fruit, improving the flavour and acid balance.

However, his horizons were far from limited to Capel. In 1983 he began buying fruit from elsewhere in the State, making the wines separately to see what charac-

ters were desirable and what were not, to seek better overall wines through blending. For example, Peter looks to Mount Barker rhine riesling for greater early floral aroma, delicacy and finesse while the Capel fruit, which has an apple, spicy character, provides mid-palate strength. A 70-30 blend results in a fuller, more complex and longer living wine.

Peter believes the combination of these characters brought about the Adelaide success where the blend was just right. 'Our theory is that no area is necessarily the best on its own for a particular style', he said. 'We are prepared to blend across regions and across varieties to make the wines we seek.' The 1993 and 1994 sauvignon blanc-semillon blends, for example, are made of fruit from Mount Barker, Pemberton and Margaret River. The result is a delicious combination of gooseberry fruit salad flavours and soft grassiness.

But the Prattens are now looking to more estate grown-fruit where possible, with major plantings at their Mount Barker Whispering Hill property and at their Wellington and Stirling vineyards at Capel. This has seen some eight hectares

of mature vines taken out by front end loaders and transferred to other locations, in vineyard restructuring.

In all, Capel Vale has 40 hectares of its own irrigated vineyards producing 500 tonnes of fruit. A five-year plan aims to export about half with Peter taking the unusual step for a moderate-size West Australian producer of employing a Boston-based American to promote and sell Capel Vale in the region.

The winemaking team is led by highly respected former Plantagenet maker Rob Bowen and includes Krista and Candy Jonsson and South African Mark Ravenscroft.

Six whites and six reds are made in a diverse range which aims to provide for all consumers, from moderate to higher priced wines. Included is an excellent CV range, five fruit driven styles made for early drinking.

The pick for me is the special reserve chardonnay — big, rich, full and complex, with melon and fig characters and made with all new oak. It is high in alcohol and will reward long cellaring. The duck label or standard chardonnay is the winery's best seller, similar to the reserve but a little less of everything, and priced accordingly. But it has the potential to age gracefully, if not for so long, generating complex lime, nutmeg and honey flavours.

Of the reds, the Baudin, a blend of merlot and cabernet, has been the flagship. An elegant, intensely flavoured wine that is soft and approachable early, it is destined, however, to be overtaken by a 'big red' from the best of the Capel Vale fruit and made with all new oak. I have long been a fan of shiraz from the winery, a combination of Mount Barker and Capel Vale fruit since 1985. On its own, the Capel shiraz produces spicy blackberry characters, soft and forgiving with a long taste. Great Southern fruit adds a peak in the mid palate with its aggressive, more peppery characters which are softened in the blend. It is a wine that sells itself. 'We wanted to get away from the cordial styles to a more-ish, pleasant-drinking food wine', Peter said. A sparkling wine, *méthode traditionnel* from chardonnay and pinot noir, is also made by Capel Vale, with plans in the latter half of the 1990s to expand the small production.

The Capel Vale label carries a mountain or shell duck as its logo, acknowledging the wildlife sanctuary on the Capel River from the town to the mouth. In the early years, a brace of ducks would nest near the winery, a source of pleasure to all, softening the damage caused by such hungry invaders as parrots and wattle birds. They would cut off whole bunches, dropping them to the ground.

CARABOODA ESTATE WINES

297 Carabooda Road, Carabooda
Cellar door sales: Daily 10 a.m. — 6 p.m.

THERE IS a strong international flavour to Carabooda Estate, 40 kilometres north of Perth. Principal Terry Ord hails from Newcastle-upon-Tyne while wife Simonne is from Jersey in the Channel Islands. His appetite for wine grew out of a holiday trip in Europe where he was impressed especially with the wines and lifestyles of small family operations in Spain and Italy. Further fine impressions of the wine industry resulted from visits with Simonne to the impressive Stellenbosch and Paarl regions of South Africa's Cape Province.

Once settled in Western Australia, the couple purchased 16 hectares of land in 1974, initially to set up a horse stud and agistment centre. But the call of wine was strong, and a cellar was built in 1981, the concrete top providing the base for the stables. This was to provide for wines that Terry had already started to make, not from grapes from their own vines, but from fruit purchased locally. In 1979, using the crushing equipment of a neighbour, Terry made his first wine from a tonne of grenache. The processing vat he had purchased stood in the open paddock!

The policy of buying in fruit has continued with Terry gaining valuable hands-on winemaking experience, helped by friends Alan and Karen Powley. In latter years the emphasis was switched to shiraz.

The couple planted a small area of the variety in 1981, expanding it to three hectares in 1989. Other varieties include chardonnay, sauvignon blanc and cabernet sauvignon. The first major vintage of 6.5 tonnes was in 1994, and this is expected to reach 40 tonnes by the year 2000 from further plantings.

Carabooda made its initial public release in mid-1994. The wines involved were the 1990-91-92 vintages of shiraz processed from purchased fruit topped up by their own.

Terry says he is looking to medium to full-bodied wines made from shiraz with plenty of skin contact for the maximum extraction of flavour and colour. The fruit is picked ripe, to achieve alcohol levels of 13 to 13.5 per cent for pleasant palate weight.

A similar approach is to be taken with

The verdict (straight from the horse's mouth) is that Terry Ord's Carabooda shiraz is not a bad drop. But what else would you expect from 20-year-old Standard-bred gelding, and family pet, Sam?

Carabooda
Estate Wines

Shiraz
1992

Made from a blend of premium Carabooda and Swan Valley Shiraz grapes vintaged in small oak casks to produce an intense varietal wine. This wine is showing peppery fruit and dusky oak integration with a typical soft tannin finish. Enjoy now or cellar for four to six years for additional flavour dimensions.
Carabooda Estate Wines
297 Carabooda Road Carabooda W.A.

T & SM ORD — Preservative 220 added
12.7% Alc Vol PRODUCT OF AUSTRALIA 750ml

Carabooda
Estate Wines

Sauvignon Blanc
1994

Made from estate grown Sauvignon Blanc grapes vintaged late in the season to intensify the fruit characters of this premium variety. This wine is showing a tropical fruit / gooseberry bouquet with a full palate, typical of unwooded styles, which is balanced by a clean acid finish. Recommended for early consumption or short term cellaring.
Carabooda Estate Wines
297 Carabooda Road Carabooda W.A.

T & SM ORD — Preservatives 220,300 added
15.0% Alc Vol PRODUCT OF AUSTRALIA 750ml

cabernet, the early samples of which revealed strong ribena characters and plenty of tannin. The sauvignon blanc, the first white, showed gooseberry flavours in juice samples.

While parrots and crows have inflicted their share of damage to the ripening fruit of the trickle-irrigated Carabooda vineyard, the couple are undaunted. Their aim is to produce quality wines based on traditional vineyard and winemaking methods using hand picking, open concrete fermenting vats and a basket press. 'I believe too much emphasis has been placed on making wines to a formula', Terry said.

Family involvement includes daughters Michelle, Nicole and Rachael and any willing friends. But there has been a lot more hard work that Terry thought. For example, he told his wife the pressing of the 1994 cabernet would only take an hour or so one evening. 'At 2.30 a.m. we watched a meteorite light up the eastern night sky in a dazzling display. But I was able to say, see what you would have missed', he concluded with a grin.

A DRAUGHT horse called Mary has special memories for Wanneroo producer Paul Conti. For years she was a vital part of the family enterprise, the power base for a variety of vineyard chores, including pulling a scoop to dig out the original cellars under the family house in 1948. As a young man in the 1950s Paul spent many hours behind a single furrow plough pulled by Mary, plodding for countless miles up and down the rows of vines. For these were still primitive times in the West Australian wine industry.

For example, the cooling down of a hot fermenting tank would mean a trip to Perth for a load of ice to be added to the warm bubbling mixture, while problems getting a fermentation started could also mean another journey. But this would involve usually only a visit to a neighbouring winery to gather a bucket or two of their fermenting material to trigger the troublesome Conti juice which the wild yeasts had failed to activate.

Today the operation is based on mod-

CONTI WINES

529 Wanneroo Road, Wanneroo
Cellar door sales: Mon — Sat. 9.30 a.m. — 5.30 p.m. À la carte restaurant: Wed — Sat 6.30 p.m., Sun 12 noon

ern methods and equipment with refrigeration for controlled fermentation temperatures in stainless steel storage, new American and French oak and cultured yeasts. This has resulted in the winery developing into an important premium producer in the State, but one that still maintains some ties with the past through bulk wines at the request of old, loyal customers.

It was in fact on bulk wines that the operation began, though initially Paul's father, Sicilian immigrant Carmelo Conti, bought the 12-hectare property 20 kilometres north of Perth in 1927 to grow vegetables for the city market on its black, swampy soils. In those days Wanneroo Road was a track with jarrah blocks used to provide a base in bad areas.

Mr Conti began planting vines in the early 1940s, inspired by other vineyard developments in the area, especially nearby Luisini which for a long period was the biggest privately owned winery in Western Australia. (It was established in 1929 but the vines today have given way to housing and an industrial complex, though the old winery has been classified by the National Trust.) Mr Conti planted about five hectares of vines, mainly grenache and muscat of Alexandria, producing table wines in demijohns and five and ten-gallon casks for the southern European migrants who had also settled in Western Australia. Subsequent purchases of land a few kilometres to the north, at Mariginiup and Carabooda, have increased the area under vines to 17 hectares and now include varieties like chardonnay and shiraz.

At its peak in the 1980s, when the Conti winery was involved in making wines from the then Pearse family property, Forest Hill at Mount Barker, the crush reached about 200 tonnes. Since that arrangement ended, however, it has stabilised to about 150 tonnes, at which level Paul intends to consolidate.

His initial commercial vintage was in 1968 — the first time the family had bottled a wine. Despite a lack of formal training — he left school at 14 to work with his father on the land — Paul need never have doubted his winemaking ability. Some friends even nicknamed him Romoni — a reference to the Prince of Conti who was associated with the famous Burgundian vineyard, Romanee-Conti. And the young winemaker did not have long to wait for show successes with regular medal-winning wines, culminating in the trophy at the 1977 Perth Show for the most successful Western Australian pro-

ducer making less than 135,000 litres. His ten entries won three gold and four bronze medals.

The Conti properties are only six kilometres from the coast so that they immediately benefit from any sea breezes. The soils are sandy, limestone based, some in lighter tuart and jarrah country (Mariginiup) and others in slightly heavier tuart and redgum land (Carabooda), creating a different environment to that of the nearby more fertile Swan Valley, but akin to other coastal plain vineyard properties stretching southwards.

The Conti flagship wines are chardonnay (from Carabooda), shiraz (Mariginiup), frontignac (Mariginiup, and known fondly as Conti fronti), and chenin blanc made from fruit grown at Carabooda and in the Swan Valley. Perhaps the most popular is the frontignac, a light, fresh, aromatic sweet wine in which the powerful characters of the fruit, more popular as a table grape, have been restrained.

In his first year as winemaker Paul produced a dry style, but ten years later fate took a sweeter hand. A sluggish yeast failed to ferment all the sugar, leaving

Paul Conti and son Jason amid oak barrels in the winery's below-ground cellar

residual sweetness in the wine, and the consumer response was immediate. With the wine served chilled the balancing acid leaves the palate clean and crisp, yet with a distinctive fruit flavour strongly supporting the Conti 'PP' philosophy — palate pleasantness.

The Conti chardonnay is a full-bodied, flavoursome wine picked ripe to ensure a fairly high alcohol level, a package that is usually complemented by about three months in oak. My favourite Conti wine, though, is the Mariginiup hermitage from the vineyard opposite the old Mariginiup townsite gazetted in March 1904. It produces a fine-textured wine with a soft palate. 'We leave the juice on the skins for as long as we can and still do not get excessive tannins', Paul said. 'People like the wine for its delicate fragrance. They are quite high in alcohol but are not big, heavy wines, and I put that down to the soils.'

The combination gives the wines plenty of cellaring life; a tasting of the early vintages put paid to the belief that soft wines do not keep. Not one had deteriorated to the point of being tired and

over the hill. They were surprisingly fresh and reflected the fruit and acid balance in the years they were made.

A cabernet from young Carabooda vines, where further plantings of shiraz were made in 1994, is the first from the winery for about 20 years, and is due for release in 1995. Paul also makes a reserve port, a blend of new wines with those aged in oak for an average of four years. Made from shiraz, they fit into the port spectrum between a tawny and ruby style, lighter and more elegant than such wines from vineyards of heavier soils.

Paul's son Jason joined the business in 1992 after graduating from Roseworthy Agricultural College in marketing. He is keen to introduce one of his favourite wines, sparkling burgundy, to the Conti range, following successful trials using shiraz from Mariginiup.

Certainly, Paul's wines are very different from those his father produced, especially the big extracted reds made under hot fermentation. No doubt Jason, when he completes winemaking studies and gains experience, will be different again.

KILLERBY VINEYARDS

Off Lakes Road, Stratham
Cellar door sales: Daily 10 a.m.— 5 p.m.

Matt Aldridge with wife Anna Killerby and their daughter Grace

I N THE year 2011, when Grace Aldridge celebrates her 18th birthday, a chardonnay of the same age will be opened. It was made in March 1993 by winemaking father Matt at Killerby Vineyards, in the month of her birth. Matt later told me: 'This is our best yet. It will last for years.'

Despite his brimming confidence, it was a bold claim. For Killerbys and Leschenault (as it was previously known) in the Capel shire, 180 kilometres south of Perth, have made some outstanding wines from the variety over the years. Take the trophy-winning 1991 and 1992, for example, made by Matt and his wife Anna Killerby, superb stylish elegant wines

Ian Smith trophy for the best 1989 Australian red wine. It went on to win a further two trophies at the Mount Barker Show later in the year to make the total 14 for all wines, in four years.

Barry Killerby, who passed away in 1991, was another of Western Australia's medical profession to turn to the wine industry as an alternative interest in life. He and Betty set out to establish Leschenault in 1973, putting their faith in the tuart soils of the coastal plain. His research had shown that such soils had the capacity, with the right management, to produce first class horticultural crops.

A bonus at the property was the plen-

backed by the skilful use of oak, benchmarks in their own way. But it was the 1989 I recall best, if not as much for the wine itself, though another trophy winner, as for what it meant — a turning point in the medium-size producer's history.

How well I recall the joy on the faces of founders Barry and Betty Killerby when the chardonnay was announced as best West Australian wine of the variety at the Perth Show of 1989. It was 15 September and their glass of pleasure brimmed over when they were then awarded a second prestigious trophy, best small West Australian winemaker of the show. It was the hard working couple's first major show success, a tremendous boost and a fitting reward for 16 years of pioneering dedication to their area.

Another stunning wine was to help cement the authority of the vineyard. It was the 1989 cabernet sauvignon, arguably one of the best wines to come out of WA. It won a record four trophies at the 1991 Perth Show including the pinnacle

tiful supply of good water beneath limestone, while large tuart trees provided protection from most strong winds off the sea, about a kilometre away. Similar maritime climates had shown their worth in other vineyard areas of the world.

Four hectares of shiraz were planted in the first year, but it was an unhappy start. The trickle irrigation system, without which the vines could not exist, was not in place and most were lost. Undaunted, the couple replanted the following year, and put in four hectares of cabernet as well, this time with a 90 per cent success rate. Today there are 16 hectares of vines planted at Killerby with varietal wines semillon and shiraz besides the high profile cabernet and chardonnay. There are also two blended wines, the April Classic Red and the April Classic White. The pair are unwooded, bottled in the month of April and designed for immediate enjoyment.

The winery's first vintage was in 1978, and it immediately brought success with a

gold medal for a cabernet-shiraz. Other wines, including ports, have won medals from Melbourne to Mount Barker over the years.

Barry's hopes that daughter Anna, a Roseworthy graduate, would return home to run the operation were realised in 1991. With her came husband-to-be Matt Aldridge, another Roseworthy-trained winemaker. The couple brought with them an extra dimension of knowledge, for they had gained valuable experience working at respected Upper Hunter producer Rosemount Estate with internationally awarded winemaker Phillip Shaw, and in France, Matt at Joseph Drouhin in Burgundy and Anna at the famous Chateau Petrus. Her brother Ben has since given up law and joined the family operation to manage its affairs. To acknowledge the effort of their parents, Leschenault was changed in favour of the family name.

Matt's winemaking philosophy is based on consistency and complexity to add interest, with the wines approachable when young to complement a range of foods with plenty of cellaring potential.

Semillons from Killerbys are generally full bodied with soft ripe fruit, well balanced oak adding spicy, vanillin characters, and a clean crisp acid finish.

It is a style I have come to enjoy along with the rich fig and nutty aromas of chardonnay, usually wines of elegant fruit and toasty oak on the palate with smooth and creamy flavours that follow through to a long finish.

While much has already been said about the quality of cabernets from Killerby, delightful for their full-flavoured spicy berry fruit, the shiraz, generally harvested at full ripeness and once known for its plumminess, should not be overlooked by any red wine lover. The 1992, for example, showed rich and dense fruit flavours, the aroma lifted by minty eucalypt characters with hints of chocolate and spice. The supple texture is supported by cedary oak with a smooth, soft, tannin finish rounding off the wine.

The winery at Killerby is modern and well equipped. Attached is a pleasant tasting area set in lawns and gardens. In such relaxed surroundings on a warm spring day, for example, typical vineyard problems such as winds and frosts and birds seem a long way away. In one of the early years at Killerby, parrots took five tonnes of chardonnay and five tonnes of pinot noir, a serious setback at the time. Now, however, Anna says such problems are greatly diminished.

PEEL ESTATE

Fletcher Road, Baldivis
Cellar door sales: Daily 10 a.m. — 5 p.m.
BBQ available

W HEN Will Nairn, principal of Peel Estate at Baldivis, 50 kilometres south of Perth and just off the Mandurah road, switched on the press at his new winery in 1980 it was the first time he had seen one work. 'I was so green it was unbelievable', he said. Yet he was quickly to achieve a rare double with shiraz and cabernet wines, being judged the best West Australian dry reds at their initial showing.

I remember the shiraz, a 1979 vintage, very well. It scored 18.8 points out of a possible 20 in winning the gold medal, enabling it to be in the trophy taste-off. This was the first show Will had ever entered, and what the judges did not know was that the wine had been put into new oak casks and rolled into the property's shearing shed for 12 months, because Peel Estate did not have a winery at the time.

Paul Conti of Wanneroo had made the first three vintages, starting with 1.5 tonnes in 1977. Planting had begun in 1974, encouraged by former State Government Viticulturist Bill Jamieson and supported by old friends, the Gardiner family of England, who regularly visited Western Australia.

For Will it meant renewing a family contact with wine. His grandfather, Mr W.R. Nairn, was manager of Penfolds and McWilliams in Western Australia and Victoria, and in 1933 he set up agencies for Penfolds in Canada. With Bill Jamieson he started the Wine and Food Society of Western Australia.

Today grandson Will is confident of his place in the industry, backed by several years of show judging experience, but retains vivid memories of his first vintage. 'The press we had sent across from New South Wales, while we were waiting for our new one from America, broke down on the first day, along with a pump', he recalled. 'We had grapes everywhere, so it was not a particularly bright start. We really live wine during vintage. For four weeks or so, it is a 16-hour day commitment.'

The 16-hectare Peel Estate vineyard grows on sandy, coastal tuart soils, the roots drawing water from beneath limestone, like the famous South Australian premium area of Coonawarra. For much of its life it has been tended by former Swan Valley vigneron Matt Banovich, in his day a national and international darts

*The Peel Estate winery and tasting area
has an attractive rustic appeal.
Below: winemaker Will Nairn*

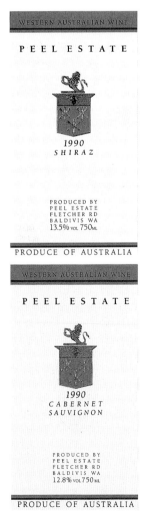

champion who is as meticulous in vineyard management and maintenance as when scoring treble 20s on the dartboard against the world's best. In 1991 Will was joined by winemaking son Mark, a Roseworthy graduate who has had vintage experience in France and, of all places, at a major co-operative in Czechoslovakia, a rare experience for an Australian winemaker indeed!

Originally, the Peel Estate property had been bought to graze sheep and stud cattle and to grow lucerne. But Paul Conti's success with wine on similar country at Wanneroo sparked the new interest, and a partnership was formed with the Gardiners.

The main varieties grown at Peel Estate include chenin blanc, four hectares, chardonnay, 3.25 hectares, and shiraz, three hectares. Others include semillon, verdelho, cabernet sauvignon, cabernet franc, merlot and zinfandel, with a few rows of the Portuguese port varieties touriga, tinta cao, tinta amarella and souzao.

The crush in 1989 was 90 tonnes. By 1994 it had reached 120. Besides the ready availability of water just a few metres below the surface, other vital factors contributing to the wine styles of Peel Estate are the soils, which generate good acid levels and low pH, bringing out the fruit characters, and proximity to the ocean. Just three kilometres away, it has a cooling influence on the vines, reducing stress conditions on hot summer days.

Along with the soft, fruity, slightly peppery and sometimes spicy shiraz styles from the estate, my other favourite wine is the wood-aged chenin blanc. A unique West Australian, it is rich and complex, a

real mouthful of wine, ideal with food. The 1991, winner of the best dry white award at the 1993 SGIO Winemakers Exhibition, was a particularly good example, especially impressive for its balance and lingering, harmonious after-taste.

The vineyard conditions allow for full ripeness to be achieved to intensify depth of flavour for oak maturation, without becoming fat or flabby, so often the case with very ripe fruit. The estate chardonnay is another fine white. Previously, it was fermented in stainless steel and matured in oak like the chenin, but winery changes led to barrel fermentation with the wine left on lees for nine months, adding complexity with lovely toasty characters from the new French oak.

Red tradition sees two years in oak

and two years in the bottle before release, generating soft tannins, richness and roundness.

A feature of the 1986 shiraz, one of my estate favourites, was its brilliant jewel-bright colours. Other shiraz wines to show up exceptionally well at tastings include the 1988, 1984, 1983 and the first, the 1977 which filled just one used American barrel.

However, the skilful use of oak at Peel Estate reminded me of a Will Nairn story told at a retrospective tasting. A visiting expert Frenchman warned him of the dangers of economy in reaming out casks for further use. 'When an old man gets into a shower, no matter how much he scrubs and scrubs, he still comes out an old man', he said. Immediately, Will dumped any ideas of saving money on oak with new imported quality material a cornerstone of the many fine reds produced at the estate.

Will describes himself as a university drop-out, but he has benefited from his studies in medicine and economics. 'The chemistry has been very helpful in winemaking and the economics in setting up and running the business', he said. 'It has taken 20 years to break even, so we are not in it for the money. It is a lifestyle that becomes an obsession. You get a tremendous amount of satisfaction in making a good wine, creating something people really enjoy. It is exciting too, because of the high risks. In 1988, for example, we lost 30 per cent of our chardonnay due to frost. In October 1982 and again in 1983 severe frost cost us all our chardonnay and half the chenin.' In 1992, 175mm of rain in February cost two-thirds of the chenin with a frost later in the year wiping out 75 per cent of the chardonnay. Then there are the birds, with parrots and silvereyes creating havoc to vines and fruit at times.

Located in a pleasant rural bush setting, Peel Estate has an attractive winery cut into a hillside. This provides functional facilities for production and storage and a relaxed atmosphere for visitors out to sample an excellent range of wines.

IT WOULD be hard to imagine any setback affecting the sense of humour of jovial Bunbury chemist Gill Thomas. For despite a series of unfortunate events in his vineyard that might have seen lesser men throw in the crusher, he still manages a hearty laugh.

Take, for example, a cyclone devastating the vineyard, ripping off all the leaves just as it was starting to produce; and then the following year, a black frost of such intensity that not a berry was picked. The trunks of the vines burst open under the pressure, and many had to be cut off at ground level, with new growth retrained to the wire.

Then a few years later, in 1989, despite costly protective netting, birds destroyed about five tonnes of fruit, a significant slice of what promised to be one of the winery's best vintages.

In 1973 two events occurred that helped shape future directions: John Hanley, a prominent West Australian wine show judge, was transferred to work in Bunbury, and Dr Bill Pannell of Moss Wood at Margaret River asked Gill's wife, Dr Janet Pearson, to do a locum for him while he looked after the vintage. 'John taught me how to appreciate wines, and Bill how to make them', Gill said. When Dr Pearson was asked the following year to do another locum during the Moss Wood vintage, Gill decided to take a stand, agreeing only if he was allowed to participate. For nearly a decade thereafter he lived in a caravan during vintage at Moss Wood, taking his annual holidays to make wine.

Gill, a third generation Bunbury pharmacist, had purchased in 1969 a 4.5 hectare block at Gelorup, ten kilometres south of Bunbury, as an escape from town. While the hungry grey sands and often strong winds made it an unlikely place for a vineyard, he was determined to proceed, inspired by his experiences at Moss Wood, choosing a contrary variety — pinot noir. He wanted to do something different, and in 1979 planted his first vines. 'I had not tasted a good Australian pinot when I planted them', he explained, considering they might do well in the hard conditions on his block.

The first commercial crop was in 1983 — something of a miracle to the family, given the cyclone and frost disasters. And it is fair to say that those early wines did not set the world celebrating. But the happy spirit was undiminished and the target remained, a pinot unlike anything else made in the country.

Early trophies under the Thomas label were an inspiration. First came a 1978 cabernet sauvignon, deemed the best West Australian dry red in open classes at the 1981 Perth Show, produced from grapes grown and made into wine at Moss Wood. The same award was duplicated the fol-

THOMAS WINES

Crowd Road, Gelorup
Cellar door sales: By appointment

Chemist-cum-vigneron Gill Thomas sees pinot noir as the ultimate test, but a variety well worth the effort

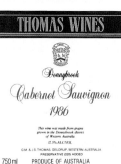

lowing year. This was again made with grapes grown at Moss Wood but vintaged at the Thomas winery. Then the pinnacle — trophies for his own wine from his own fruit, for the 1984 and 1985 pinots at the Lord Forrest Hotel competition in Bunbury, and at the SGIO Winemakers Exhibition.

Convinced about his wines with such successes, Gill has not shown since.

While basic winemaking may not be difficult, to Gill the same cannot be said for good winemaking. 'The microbiology of making wine is quite complicated', he said. 'You have to be good at remembering the mistakes of the past and applying these lessons subsequently.'

Armed with the benefits of past experience, Gill pins his faith on two hectares of mature vines, boosting the soil with lupins for nitrogen along with intensive application of fertiliser and trace elements, adequate watering, sprinkler control for frosts, and general vine management to minimise the effect of strong winds.

He describes pinot as a brute of a grape, a shy, thin-skinned producer that tests the winemaker out all the time.

'Some say pinot has to smell like very dirty socks at some stage of the process', he said. 'Otherwise it will not be any good. I prefer to call it a real earthy character. It is a difficult wine to clean up, leaving a fine sediment which is very hard to get rid of. Unfortunately, Australians regard that as a fault in our wines, whereas it is some-

thing to be admired in French wines.'

The pinot is marketed under the Briar Holme label, taken from the name of his grandparent's property in Kalamunda, with cabernet bought occasionally from Donnybrook going under the Thomas name.

In 1994 Gill released the 1986 pinot. 'My wines need that sort of time before release', he said. 'I am not making beaujolais styles. I believe bottle age is essential and I do not want the oak and the acid to be too obvious.'

Processing involves a slower, longer fermentation for 'oomph' with so many whole berries left, and for soft tannin extraction. The result usually is tremendous concentrations of flavours and early colour, more akin to a young cabernet. Only half is given oak treatment for freshness of the final blend.

Despite the fact that the vineyard is only two kilometres from the ocean, it can get very hot in the summer with the burning sand no place for bare feet. But Gill says that early, cool sea breezes modify the effect of the heat, to generate the required flavours and acid balance.

Early wines tended to be tannic, resulting in a change to gentler winemaking techniques and culminating perhaps in the most old-fashioned way of all — bare foot stomping and plunging. For a week during vintage, Gill can be found two-three times a day up to his knees, resulting he says in the blackest toenails around!

Margaret River

ABBEY-VALE VINEYARD

Wildwood Road, Yallingup
Cellar door sales: Daily 10.30 a.m. — 5 p.m. Lunchtime restaurant facilities available. Functions by arrangement

Above: Mist rises over the lake, creating a special magic at Abbey-Vale. During scheduled concerts, guests sit on the grassy banks to enjoy a distinctive Margaret River ambience

FORMER Irishman Bill McKay sits on the verandah of the family restaurant feeling at peace. Across the water — a small lake created by a dam — the estate vineyard flourishes, and about him is the picturesque progress of a new life. Indeed, Abbey-Vale represents a dramatic transformation for Bill and Pam McKay in a career journey that has taken them round the globe.

Initially Bill, a graduate in electrical engineering from Queens University in Belfast, and Pam went to Uganda to work, an assignment which was to last seven years. Their travels then took them to the UK, Canada and California before Australia beckoned as a desirable place to settle.

An electrical business was established in Perth and on trips to the South West the couple decided that land was a good investment, especially when prices were compared to those of North America. By this time son Kevin, who had been considering wheat and sheep farming, decided instead on vines and wine, following employment at neighbouring Amberley Estate.

And so the family decision was made to develop a farm they had previously purchased. But ironically, the initial claim to fame was on a rival brew — beer, or more precisely 'Moonshine'. Bill and Pam had decided to fund the vineyard development with the amber fluid they would make, despite a complete lack of experience in the field. Undaunted, however, and with the knowledge gained in a Californian crash course in 1990, they produced their first beers, a pale ale and a bitter. It was immediately successful, fulfilling their most ambitious hopes. 'It captured the imagination', Bill said. Now, however, the focus is fixed firmly on wine, the family having sold the brewery operation, though retaining the name.

Abbey-Vale (originally called Kidepo after a national park in Uganda, but changed because people could not pronounce it) has 32 hectares of irrigated vineyard growing on a wide range of soil types. The first vines were planted in 1987 in what is a warm and well-protected environment resulting in early ripening. More than 100 tonnes were harvested in 1994 and, at full production, by 1998, 350 tonnes are expected.

The McKays intend producing a full range of wines to please as many visiting palates as possible. Included is the estate's best-seller, Festival White, a slightly sweet, fruity blend of semillon and sauvignon blanc. Verdelho, a classy ripe varietal, is not quite as sweet with the tropical fruit flavours of the 1993 vintage powerful and persistent. The excellent use of balancing acid left the palate clean and fresh, a great inducement for a second glass! Sunburst, also made from verdelho, is the sweetest of all, ideal with spicy Thai food, Kevin says.

In the dry wines, there is a floral sauvignon blanc, a big oaked semillon which is a real mouthful of wine, and a cabernet sauvignon. The 1990 which included 10 per cent merlot, is a stylish wine. Intense rich blackberry flavours combined with herbaceousness to fill out the palate with smooth, sweet fruit from beginning to end. An excellent wine with roast lamb, I mused, noting the long aftertaste.

Reflection on the wines, however, suggests that Abbey-Vale may become best known for its opulent verdelho, used as a varietal dry style, in the sweet range or as part of a blend such as with semillon. The two varieties make up more than half the vineyard area with cabernet sauvignon and merlot each about 20 per cent.

It may also establish a reputation for concerts, as Leeuwin Estate has done. In early 1994 visitors on the grassed sloping banks of the lake were entertained by the Budapest Symphony Orchestra, arranged

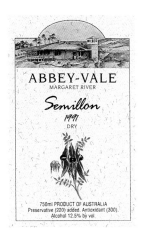  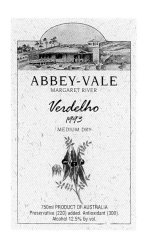

with the Festival of Perth.

In a small section of bush destined to remain uncleared, Abbey-Vale has its own style of grape pickers and processors — kangaroos. Says Bill: 'We have learnt to co-exist', but he hastens to add that, as a winery is not among the McKays' plans, the marsupials won't ever get the bonus of pawing through winemaking residue.

A VISIT TO the dentist was anything but painful for South African immigrant Albert Haak. In fact it was to lead to the start of a new life in Western Australia with the development of a vineyard and winery at the northern end of the Margaret River wine producing strip.

His interest in the State as a possible place to settle had initially been stimulated by leading South African oenologist Helmie Wagener who had tasted some of the early wines from the area during a visit to Australia for an industry congress in 1978. When the two were on a tour of winemaking areas of America, France and Italy some five years later, he told Albert: 'If I was a young man I would go to Margaret River and set up my own operation'. He had been fascinated, Albert recalled, by the exceptional integrity of flavours he had seen in the cabernets from the area, rating them the best outside Bordeaux.

Subsequently, Albert's mind was made up when his accountant, brother-in-law Mark Turner, who was working in Bunbury, made an inspection of the area and wrote in glowing terms of its potential.

'That was all I needed', Albert said. 'We sold up and in November 1985 headed for Western Australia.' As an agricultural engineer in his native country, he had been involved with various rural projects that had developed land to produce, proc-

ess and market commodities like sugar, fruit juice and wine.

Immediately on arrival he set about searching for land in the area from Augusta almost to Dunsborough. For two fruitless months he looked at every available farm on the market, applying his shopping list of requirements — suitable soil reflected in big stands of redgums and water availability.

Then one day he and an agent stopped on the side of a gravel road. 'This is just what I want', Albert said, looking across a gently sloping block full of big trees. But it was not for sale. Undaunted, Albert put his feasibility plan under his arm and visited the property owner, Rockingham dentist Michael Sturgeon who, by chance, had been looking for something to do with his land. A deal was struck, with family and friends included, and planting began in the spring of 1986.

Today vines cover 40 hectares of the property with the white varieties — semillon, sauvignon blanc, chenin blanc and chardonnay — making up 65 per cent of the total, and reds — including cabernet sauvignon, cabernet franc, merlot and shiraz — the rest.

An initial crop of 50 tonnes in 1989 was sold to Cape Mentelle and Evans and Tate, but an impressive new winery (including cellar door facilities and a garden restaurant) was constructed in a picturesque setting among trees adjoining the vine-

AMBERLEY ESTATE

Thornton Road, Yallingup
Cellar door sales: Daily 10 a.m. — 4.30 p.m. À la carte restaurant, luncheons

1993
CHENIN

AMBERLEY

1993
MARGARET RIVER
WHITE BURGUNDY

Amberley's attractive garden restaurant, adjacent to the cellar door sales area and winery, is a popular venue among visitors to Cape Naturaliste

AMBERLEY

1993

SEMILLON
SAUVIGNON BLANC

yard, to cater for production from 1990.

The man charged with the task of making the wines is West Australian Eddie Price. The son of a former Bindoon currant grower, he was the dux of Roseworthy in 1982, winning the three prizes made available in the oenology and viticulture course. Eddie was immediately recruited by Brown Brothers in Victoria where he worked continuously until his return to Western Australia.

In 1994 the Amberley crush was 350 tonnes, including 100 from contract growers with eight wine styles made. Among them is the popular, slightly sweet but fresh and fruity chenin-sauvignon blanc, a 70-30 blend, the winery's main seller. The extremely palate-pleasant style has proved an excellent introductory and lunch-time wine, a joy to sip chilled while gazing out over the vineyard from which a lot of the fruit has come.

A more serious wine, however, is the white burgundy, a blend of mainly semillon, sauvignon blanc and chardonnay. Fermented in part in French and American oak, and left on lees for between four and six months, it is a big, ripe, soft and round food wine, unctuous says Eddie.

The semillon-sauvignon blanc, however, is leaner and more herbaceous, its light, crisp freshness enhanced by attractive tropical fruit flavours, making it appealing as a restaurant style. Sipping this wine reminded me of a quote in an Amberley newsletter in which its fruit was described as being like a woman. 'It responds to love and care', the author said. 'Its mother vine needs to be laid gently, preferably on an eastern slope. It likes to be caressed by trellises which lift up so that its splendid, juicy body is revealed to the sun. It can become acid unless you treat it nicely.'

The Amberley semillon — once described by a colleague as a hero's wine — has become slightly lighter, more subtle, to create more of a difference to the chardonnay. To me it is the classiest wine of the whites with finer, intense fruit characters and better quality oak flavours.

Of the two reds, I preferred the cabernet-merlot, a combination of berry characters and generous, fleshy, slightly plummy flavours, soft tannins and a long finish. The Amberley nouveau, in comparison, is a light, early, easy-drinking red, a partner to the chenin and released together on 1 July each year.

Despite its short history, Amberley has gained an early reputation for innovation in the vineyard and winery in the search for better quality from each variety. Included have been trials with trellising and minimum pruning, and experiments with wild yeasts.

Albert and his wife Bridget chose Amberley Estate as their label, inspired by her grandparents' farm in South Africa which was so named because they had come from Amberley in Sussex, England. 'When we found our new property was in the Sussex location of the Busselton Shire, it seemed ideal', Albert said. 'Besides, we think the name is soft and musical.'

Albert believes that the 1994 production of 350 tonnes can be trebled, with market consolidation and export development. In 1994, when predictions of the first shareholder dividends to be paid were made, the first overseas order of 1100 cases to the UK was achieved. Important to Amberley's need for new equity capital was the 25 per cent shareholder inclusion in 1993 into the private company partnership of Oxford University economist John Brunner, of the Perth suburb of Dalkeith. Expressing happiness with the investment, he said, 'I have no illusions. Only the efficient with good products and marketing flair will survive. The wine industry is, however, one of the few Australian industries where the technology is first class.'

In an area where vineyards and native trees stand side by side, Amberley Estate differs in one unusual respect — the impressive sweep of the vineyard is dotted with rows of pine trees planted in various places. Albert says they serve a special purpose as windbreaks, and because they have no nectar they do not attract the birds like native trees — a real bonus. Also, their roots can be pruned so that they do not invade the vineyard.

But a visit to Amberley is far more than pine trees and chenin blanc. It is an experience of sweeping vines amid the bush, of stimulating wines and good food in a setting that spells relaxation.

A TWISTING gravel road through about a kilometre of bush leads to the tasting facilities and vineyard of Arlewood, a development by Liz and John Wojturski. They have established their vines on a property that should realise wines of quality, given the pedigree of surrounding producers. Among them, for example, are Ashbrook, Willespie, Vasse Felix and Cullens, some of the best in the business.

The couple's property name preference originally was Harwood. This was because of John's home town, Great Harwood in Lancashire. But legal advice directed them elsewhere, for fears of problems with McWilliams Henwood at some future date. So they recalled a trip to France in 1986 when the school teaching couple were on long service leave. A favourite small town was Arles in the Rhone Valley of Provence with rich winemaking history dating back to Roman times. In addition, master painter Van Gogh, whose work John and Liz greatly admire, lived and worked in the area. Thus was born Arlewood from a list of about 20 names.

The couple purchased their 90-hectare property, which appealed for its mixture of grazing and bush country, in 1984. Brian

ARLEWOOD ESTATE

Harmans Road South, Willyabrup
Cellar door sales: Weekends, public and school holidays, 11 a.m. — 4.30 p.m.

Above: Teachers-turned-vignerons Liz and John Wojturski sample some of their estate semillon

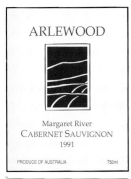

ARLEWOOD

Margaret River
CABERNET SAUVIGNON
1991

PRODUCE OF AUSTRALIA   750ml

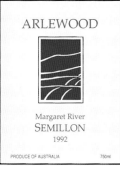

ARLEWOOD

Margaret River
SEMILLON
1992

PRODUCE OF AUSTRALIA   750ml

ASHBROOK ESTATE

Harmans Road South, Willyabrup
Cellar door sales: Daily 11 a.m. — 5 p.m.

Devitt (of adjacent Ashbrook Estate) had cleared part for a vineyard for a previous owner, but nothing was done. 'We had considered a vineyard when we had land in the Porongurups prior to our move to Willyabrup', Liz said. 'Now that we were in the dress circle of vineyards, it seemed a logical move.'

Planting began in 1988, two hectares of cabernet sauvignon and semillon. John and Liz acknowledge it is a small area, but there is pride when they reflect on the thriving vineyard, having done all the work themselves. Only 40 of the first 4000 vines did not take, remarkable for rank amateurs.

The trickle-irrigated vines grow on well-drained clay loams and produced their first fruit in 1991, a total of 6.5 tonnes in all. A setback, however, was losses estimated at 50 per cent due to birds. With planned plantings to include other varieties such as sauvignon blanc, merlot and perhaps verdelho and chenin blanc, the Wojturskis are expecting 50-60 tonnes, or 3000-4000 cases at full production.

There are four wines in the range, two from home-grown grapes and two sourced from purchased fruit. This includes the sauvignon blanc-semillon, a 50-50 blend in 1994. John views this partly wooded,

slightly grassy dry wine as a clean and lively, easy-drinking lunchtime style that will also age gracefully. The estate semillon (also part barrel-fermented) is a more full-bodied wine for which seafood restaurants have been targeted. Its cellaring potential is about five years.

The 1991 cabernet sauvignon was a very credible first-up red. A medium-bodied, supple and smooth style, softened with egg white fining, it certainly would have complemented lamb chops done on the barbecue.

The sweeter-style Liaison made from frontignan often sees a male taster turn to his wife and say: 'This is a wine your mother would like'. Though a fun wine, it has an important role at cellar door where so many people talk dry but drink sweet.

And when the visitors are gone, John and Liz might at crop ripening times offer a prayer for a successful jarrah and marri flowering season. This means the birds will feast on that natural food source, and not the grapes of Arlewood.

Establishment of the project has been based on John taking leave from his maths-teaching duties, while development and living funds have been provided by Liz, who has been a deputy principal of various state senior high schools for 15 years.

THERE WAS no fanfare, no ritzy celebration when Margaret River producer Ashbrook Estate came on-stream in 1979. The wine quietly appeared in the marketplace, the result of a strong family commitment to premium wine production centred on brothers Tony and Brian Devitt. Like John Kosovich in the Swan Valley, they are the no-fuss achievers of the industry, confident in the quality of their range.

The Margaret River family connection really began with a grandfather the boys never knew, Theodore George Kitching, a pastoralist for most of his life who died in 1933. A love of the South West encouraged him to acquire a hectare of land on the coast between Dunsborough and Quindalup, which became the focal point for family holidays from the early 1950s. It was the start of hundreds of trips by the Devitts to the region, multiplying rapidly as land was purchased in early 1975 for a vineyard and the hard work of establishment began.

Although the family had no links with wine production, the brothers' parents, Harold and Henrietta Devitt, were both born on West Australian farms and had

strong rural backgrounds. Involvement in wine came about through a series of events affecting Tony who in a few short years was to become State Government Viticulturist (later called Principal Officer, Viticulture) in 1979, following the retirement of long-serving Bill Jamieson. A university graduate in agricultural science with an honours degree in agronomy, Tony Devitt joined the Department of Agriculture as a research officer in 1966. During his university days, he and Brian played A-grade cricket with Tony Mann (son of legendary Houghton winemaker Jack) so that a lot of post-match entertainment took place at the winery or with some of its fine wines. At the same time his honours degree supervisor, Dr John Gladstones, was to provide another influence. Dr Gladstones published a paper in 1965 that was to alert many for the first time to the potential of Margaret River as a wine producing area, through its soils and climate. Meanwhile, at work Tony had contact with Dorham Mann (another of Jack's sons) who was working with the Department of Agriculture as a viticultural adviser.

The interest kindled and led to the

successful completion of basic and advanced courses with the Western Australian Wine Information Bureau (now Wine Education Centre). When Dorham Mann announced he was leaving to take up the position of winemaker with Sandalfords, Tony sought talks on his future with former department director Noel Fitzpatrick. Keen wineman though he was, Fitzpatrick pressed him closely about his motives in seeking Dorham Mann's position, warning that horticulture was then an 'agricultural backwater'. But he added some advice: 'Whatever you do, do it well'.

It was an exciting time for Margaret River as Perth heart physician Dr Tom Cullity had just released his first wine and interest was high. Tony Devitt was determined. He got the job and part of the deal was that he go to Roseworthy Agricultural College in South Australia to study winemaking.

It was a move he warmly embraced because he had already decided that this was something he badly wanted to do.

His keenness to learn and willingness to work was rewarded at graduation when he won the Leo Buring Medal as dux of the course with first class honours, as well as a special commemorative award for the student who contributed most to college life. By this time he had the support of the family to set up an operation. Tony had no trouble convincing brother Brian, an organic chemistry graduate from the University of Western Australia. He had returned from an 18-month stay in England convinced that the happiest people were those on the land.

Back in Western Australia in late 1975, Tony found things had really started to move at Margaret River, and the wines produced heralded a bright future. It inspired the brothers who began planting in September 1976, expending a lot of weekend sweat. The family had sold off the holiday home to help fund the 100-hectare block to which subsequent purchases of two adjoining properties have been added, doubling the area. Now the vineyard contains 12 hectares of semillon, chardonnay, sauvignon blanc, verdelho, riesling, cabernet sauvignon, cabernet franc and merlot. The fruit is processed in a functional and attractive winery, built in busy-bees by the family making their own mud bricks with raw material from a nearby creek.

The vines flourish on gently undulating slopes of loamy gravel soils, once covered in stands of large redgum and jarrah forest. The rows are conventionally spaced with most of the vineyard irrigated. Wa-

tering is considered necessary to establish young vines and to provide an insurance against exceptionally dry conditions during fruit maturation. 'I have seen fruit literally fall off excessively stressed vines', Tony said. 'Vines under stress do not direct sugar to the grapes or develop the flavours so keenly sought.'

Contrary to advice at the time the Devitts planted numerous eucalypts around the vineyard to act as windbreaks and to provide an alternative food source for birds. 'Silvereyes enter vineyards only when there is not enough to sustain them in the surrounding bush', Tony noted.

The Devitts also introduced guinea fowl to control insects, eliminating the need for insecticides.

The Devitts have planted a range of varieties because they believe it will be some time before those best suited to their environment are more clearly defined.

In the future they believe soil type differences will be more important than considered in the past in variety selection. So will trellis design, to get the best fruit quality. The Devitts' vineyard includes experiments with the Scott Henry system, along with Lyre and vertical trellising in the search for the best structure.

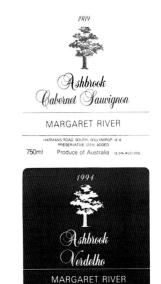

To brothers Brian and Tony Devitt, the strength of the style is seen in the raw material, the fruit quality nurtured by the conditions

The first commercial Ashbrook vintage was in 1979 with an annual crush now of 100 tonnes. As new plantings develop this total will increase to 120-130 tonnes.

The steady development at Ashbrook enabled Brian to retire from teaching at Busselton and with his wife Carol (Jay), the State's first female Rhodes Scholar, to move full-time on to the property. He has since become manager of the estate.

The winery is constructed on simple lines with separate areas specified for the various winemaking functions. Included is a 20 by 16 metre refrigerated underground concrete cellar where all barrels and bottled wines are stored, so that in the event of a disaster, an opener and glasses would at least ensure a pleasant wait!

Although the business expects to increase to 8000-10,000 cases a year, it will still be relatively small, for the Devitts are keen to maintain control over the crucial aspects of management and production.

Ashbrook has sought to ensure the marketing of their wines have kept a little ahead of production. The importance of this was bought home in 1989-91 with a tightening of the domestic wine market coinciding with a doubling of production at the estate. A major effort to develop markets has led to Ashbrook selling wine nationally with 15 per cent being exported to the United Kingdom, Switzerland, Japan and several provinces in Canada. This success was tempered, however, on a Thursday morning in late November 1992 when a devastating hailstorm wiped out more than half the potential crop for the 1993 vintage, creating a very different set of marketing problems.

However, the 1994 vintage returned to more normal levels, the long, dry summer providing for excellent flavour and sugar development in the grapes. This is necessary to meet the Ashbrook philosophy of translating grape flavours into their wines.

The unwooded riesling, verdelho and semillon all display strong varietal aroma and flavours and crisp, clean acid finishes.

Unlike many of their Margaret River colleagues, the Devitts believe riesling has a place in the region. 'It is the world's best aromatic variety and produces wines of lovely floral aromas and strong flavour', Tony said. The wines also have the capacity to age gracefully over long periods. I have seen ten-year-old Ashbrook rieslings showing attractive developed characters and great life.

The sauvignon blanc, chardonnay and a new edition, the semillon reserve, are fermented and stored in French oak. Only new oak is used with the chardonnay but it is still dominated by fruit flavour, for the grapes are picked fully ripe, yielding full-bodied wines of great character.

The dry red based on cabernet sauvignon, with a five to ten per cent dash each of cabernet franc and merlot to add extra flavour components, is kept in wood for two years and then matured in the bottle for the same period before release. The wine is never marketed unless it is at least four years old.

BROOKLAND VALLEY

Caves Road, Willyabrup
Cellar door sales: Daily 10 a.m. — 5 p.m.
Flutes Café, lunches daily, dinners Saturdays

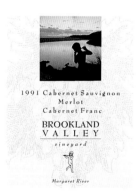

THE LABEL of Brookland Valley at Margaret River, developed by Malcolm and Deidre Jones, features Peter Pan, hero of that evergreen play by Scotsman Sir James Barrie. Many readers will no doubt recall he was the boy who refused to grow up, persuading three children to fly with him and fairy Tinker Bell to the Never Never Land, to have adventures with the pirate Captain Hook, an Indian princess, and a crocodile.

To many of Western Australia's financially battling vignerons, Brookland Valley may well be Never Never Land, for it is a mint development where no expense has been spared and only the best will do.

Peter Pan, a lovely flute-playing nude statue set in a landscaped garden, overlooks the lake formed by the damming of the Willyabrup Brook and a bridge which leads to a bush walk to the beach, and seems in total harmony with his new location. Behind him is the Flutes Café the family has built, with a balcony from which guests can feed wild ducks, and a gallery with exquisite items for sale, based on a grape and wine theme.

The family bought the land in 1982 as a place 'to get away from it all', and the first thing they did was to dam the brook to provide an attractive setting for a new home. But they decided against a life of total relaxation and elected to go commercial, initially thinking of building a cheese factory. On to the scene came Vasse Felix principal of the day, David Gregg, a former dairy technologist who promptly talked them into planting a vineyard.

The thought appealed, for Malcolm was trained in agriculture in his native New Zealand and had come to Australia as a farm management consultant before turning to the corporate world for a career. His strong yearning for the land had never disappeared.

The first two hectares of chardonnay

were planted in 1984 with the initial guidance by David Gregg, and subsequently leading Australian vine and wine people Brian Croser, Tony Jordan, Gary Crittenden, Gary Baldwin and Di Davidson, something of a Who's Who of the Australian industry.

Today the vineyard covers 20 hectares of closely planted vines, looking more Germanic than Australian, with about twice the number of vines of the average development. About a third grow on lateritic gravel and the rest on granite loams and river silts, apart from a small corner of hungry looking sand, the site for experimentation with sauvignon blanc to control the vigorous growth. Other varieties include cabernet sauvignon, merlot and cabernet franc.

So far several million dollars have been invested in the beautifully maintained hedged vineyard and the dam, but excluding the cost of the land.

On an early visit, I put it to Malcolm, was Brookland Valley a rich man's toy?

He confessed it started out as an indulgence, but is adamant now that it is geared firmly towards profits, with a crush in 1994 of 200 tonnes, returning about 6000-7000 cases of finished wine from Cape Mentelle which retains the balance under contract arrangements that have applied since the inception.

The Brookland Valley marketing strategy is based on restaurant sales and selected liquor outlets in Perth, Sydney and Melbourne. Flutes is also a major outlet and set to expand with a 12-unit chalet project in a hidden valley on the property,

to be in place in 1995. 'It will strengthen the experience in wine for visitors', Malcolm said. 'As well as bush walks people will be able to browse through the vineyard and get a good feel of the whole operation.'

Daughter Liza, the driving force behind the Flutes project, is the marketing arm of the operation, handling a small but quality range of wines. Included are a chardonnay, sauvignon blanc, a cabernet sauvignon, cabernet franc and merlot blend, and Flutes Café (soft) red, introduced for the first time in 1994.

A feature of the sauvignon blanc style, despite or indeed due to the struggle in the sand, is its fruit salad sweetness. Blessed with excellent balancing acid, the dry early drinking style fits the Flutes atmosphere of pleasure and relaxation to a cork. The chardonnay is the more serious wine, thoughtfully oak-crafted and usually a combination of attractive riper tropical fruit flavours, perhaps melon and passionfruit with cashew nuts and toastiness enhancing the palate sensations. Both whites and the cabernet-merlot blend have been highly recommended at different national tastings.

The full-bodied red blend is released after three years, though the aim is for four. At first the richer plummy characters of the merlot with a touch of spiciness from the cabernet franc are most evident, but with time the cabernet begins to assert itself. To me the sweet fruit, black cherry style of the red with its long, delicious palate and fine, soft finish is the wine I like to savour when visiting Peter Pan.

The ubiquitous flute-playing Pan is an apt symbol for Brookland Valley, and is seen here against a backdrop of vine rows, and the lakeside restaurant

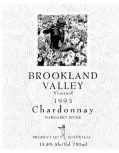
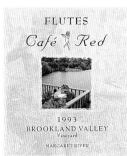

CAPE CLAIRAULT

Henry Road (off Pusey Road), Willyabrup
Cellar door sales: Daily 10 a.m. — 5 p.m.

THE EARLY years of Cape Clairault at Margaret River could best be described as growing grapes and making wine by telephone. For while geologist Ian Lewis was out in the bush pursuing his profession to provide vital cash flow for his family and property development, wife Ani was home on the farm keeping the operation going and bringing up four sons. During much of the early 1980s, Ian was away many months of the year, sometimes making a 300-kilometre round trip to telephone Ani with instructions.

'He would ring to say today was the day to rack the cabernet, but I did not know what that meant', she recalled. 'So he had to go through it step by step while I took notes. Then he might say something like "Remember, that has a left-hand thread" — again, a mystery to me.'

She recalled the messy job of cleaning out smelly sludge (cabernet gross lees) from some borrowed stainless steel tanks. Fearing she would be overcome by the fumes inside, Ani asked her octogenarian father-in-law to have ready the outlet hose of the vacuum cleaner, to dangle near her face. Instead he preferred to tie a rope round her armpits — to pull her out, if needed, as if he could! Anxiously, he waited at the top and when she slipped in the sludge he thought she had passed out. 'So he pulled like mad, and when I got to my feet he pulled me off balance and I slipped again', she said. 'I came out with purple sludge all over me. We sat on top of the tank and laughed and laughed.'

Regardless, the couple have prospered strongly since the early stumbling days, when $200 was all they had left after selling their Perth suburban home to pay for their 64-hectare property and a tractor. For the next 13 years, while funds for the vineyard and winery were the first priority, the family lived in a simple two bedroom timber cottage that came with the property, before a modern home was built.

Sydneysider Ian had come to Western Australia to complete his degree at the University of Western Australia, and later met Ani, from Cape Town, in a London pub. She had already shown her versatility, being at the time one of the first female bus drivers in England. She equipped a double-decker bus as a kindergarten for the poorer sections of Sheffield, and even sported a sandpit on the upper deck.

It was when the bearded, retiring geologist happened much later to be sitting alone in the remote West Australian goldfields, seeking relief under a tree from the intense heat, that he began seriously to contemplate a cooler way of making a living, and the idea of a wine cellar in Margaret River was born.

Although their land, then north of the mainstream district vineyard country, had never grown grapes before, that initial risk was well worth their sense of adventure. The first vines were planted in 1976, and the first wines appeared four years later — made in the farm milking shed.

The initial emphasis was on cabernet sauvignon, a passion of Ian's, and it was not long before show success came their way. The first trophy, for example, was at the 1984 Canberra Wine Show, where the 1982 cabernet was adjudged the best dry red table wine with a firm finish in the premium classes. This was a tremendous boost for the battling couple, well worth the drive across Australia (complete with four sons) to collect the memorable award.

Since then they have gained a further 90, including a bronze medal for the 1985 cabernet at the 1988 International Wine Challenge in London. In the same year three Sheraton Perth trophies were achieved, for the 1986 cabernet and the 1988 sauvignon blanc — the latter being the chairman's selection as the wine of the show.

The annual Cape Clairault crush is about 90 tonnes from nine hectares of vines that also include merlot, cabernet franc, semillon and rhine riesling.

The fruit is processed in a modern, attractive, white Cape Dutch building set in natural bush amid tall redgums and jarrah trees, an important part of the Lewis philosophy. Ian is convinced that such an environment helps to encourage natural predators of vineyard pests. For example, he says the vineyard should have tremendous bird problems being surrounded by bush, but it does not suffer as much as others because hawks nest regularly in the tall trees. These birds, and their noisy young learning to fly, scare away the grape-eating birds.

On one occasion he sprayed three times to control grasshoppers, but in so doing allowed for a tremendous explosion of caterpillar numbers later in the season. This in turn led to a significant area of cabernet being defoliated and even the grapes eaten. Ian now believes that the spraying killed many small lizards, natural enemies of the caterpillars.

'We want to work with nature, not against it', Ani said, explaining how the property has been planned to leave corridors of natural bush, providing a haven for their 'attacking allies'.

The property is also fortunate to have three creeks and a permanent forest soak.

One of the natural advantages of the property is its elevation — 120 metres above sea level.

'Cool winds from the sea are channelled up to the highest part of our block', Ian said. 'This helps give us a longer ripening period and a later picking than other vineyards around us.'

The cabernet on the property grows on heavy gravelly soil, a combination that produces elegant, balanced wines which are very drinkable when young, but have the necessary structure for long living. In some years they have strong mulberry characters with a touch of cassis, and cherry flavours in the lighter years. The semillon and sauvignon blanc grow in more loamy gravelly soils, resulting in a fuller blend that can certainly take bottle ageing, while an unwooded sauvignon is a crisp, zesty wine designed for early summer drinking.

Cape Clairault has two ranges of wines, the top varietals sold under the Estate label and the lighter, fruitier wines made for earlier drinking, under Cape Range. Wines are sold in Perth, Sydney and Melbourne with most, however, at cellar door and through a mailing list.

Innovations for visitors to Cape Clairault include a refreshing warm or cold towel before tasting, a luncheon facility available by Christmas 1994, bush excursions and an inspection of the operations of a small winery.

Ian, with eldest son Matthew joining the business, now looks beyond the year 2000 for a quantum leap forward in wine quality, through improved trellis design and new winemaking equipment. He has split vine canopies to reduce dense growth in favour of greater sun penetration for more flavour and harmony in the grapes.

A turning point for the couple came in 1993 when the property was put up for sale, and then withdrawn. At the time, they were able to step back and look at 18 years of achievement. 'This soul-searching has made us realise that what we want is the best block of land in the best area with the best vines and a lovely hands-on little winery where we can do almost everything ourselves with some time off as well', Ani said.

As she spoke, I recalled their early dreams from that first walk around their new block on a moonlight night not really so long ago. As they headed out like excited children they talked about making the best wines in the area; then it became the best in the country; and by the time they reached home they had stretched their horizons to the best in the world.

Understanding the eco-system and micro-climate is vital, says Ian Lewis

FORMER West Australian wine writer David Foster once dubbed David Hohnen the 'Squire of Cape Mentelle'. I followed this up by suggesting he should be called 'King of the West Australian wine industry' after the tremendous success at the Melbourne Wine Show of 1983 when the nation's best were eclipsed in the battle for the prized Jimmy Watson Memorial Trophy. It was the first time the award, presented to the best year-old dry red at the show, had been won by a West Australian producer. And when Cape Mentelle proved it was no fluke the following year by winning again, any lingering doubts over Margaret River's tremendous potential were dispelled.

The winning wines were the 1982 and 1983 cabernet sauvignons, and their awards, glass claret jugs, sit proudly on a shelf in the winery's tasting room. In actual dollar terms they may not be worth much, but the image boost was considerable — 'a lot more than $1 million' according to a leading winery which won the same accolade in 1988.

The remarkable thing about David Hohnen's success was that it came so early in a new career. He was not born on a vineyard. He had no family connection with wine (although distant relatives in Germany are in the wine business in that

CAPE MENTELLE

Wallcliffe Road, Margaret River
Cellar door sales: Daily 10 a.m. — 4.30 p.m.

An impressive line-up of stainless steel fermenting tanks at the Cape Mentelle winery

CABERNET MERLOT 1992
TRINDERS VINEYARD

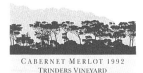

SEMILLON SAUVIGNON 1993

country's famous Mosel Valley) and had no hobby interest in the subject.

David was born in New Guinea, where his father worked as a mining engineer. One of Mr Hohnen's transfers brought him to Perth for a spell, during which time he purchased land in Margaret River as an investment.

David spent a year as a jackaroo after leaving school, and later took a job with the South Australian winery, Stonyfell. Convinced that wine was his cup of tea, he subsequently studied oenology and viticulture at the University of California in Fresno, worked in the Californian industry, and helped establish Taltarni in Victoria in a four-year stint.

By this time brother Mark, a finance specialist, had returned from London and asked David to come back to Western Australia to rehabilitate the initial vine plantings at Cape Mentelle, a name taken from a nearby coastal feature. He joined the venture in 1976 in time to crush the 1977 vintage, and has been responsible for all subsequent vintages.

It was a humble start, just a few hundred gallons made in the tractor shed, and certainly a far cry from the sophisticated, professional operation that now stretches across to New Zealand to include the bold Cloudy Bay vineyard and winery development at Marlborough, at the northern end of the South Island.

Mark (who has since left Cape Mentelle) described his brother as a perfectionist who, even under the severest pressure to change, will 'stick to what he believes is right'.

Although enjoying an excellent reputation for white wines today, with the Cloudy Bay sauvignon blanc a benchmark, David had originally set out to make re-

ally good red wines because he believed there was more art involved, particularly in ageing and blending. Early positive national reviews opened the door to the valuable Eastern States markets, especially Sydney and Melbourne, and with the Jimmy Watson award he was on a roll.

During this period vineyard plantings were gradually being increased, but the potential was seen for selling more than could be produced, hence the focus on New Zealand and the decision to go ahead, regardless of high interest rates. By 1994 this vineyard extended to more than 50 hectares with the 45,000-odd cases made annually from a 800-tonne crush, almost sold before the grapes are processed.

Margaret River production in 1994 amounted to 700 tonnes, about half supplied by contract growers. A new vineyard development, Chapman Brook at Witchcliffe, will help boost the quantity to 1000 tonnes by the year 2000.

Six wines are made, four reds and two whites with cabernet sauvignon ruling the vineyard roost. Shiraz and zinfandel are important contributors, however, with chardonnay and a semillon-sauvignon blanc blend the main whites.

It must be remembered the emphasis on red wines at Cape Mentelle was at a time when the country had swung strongly to whites, leaving significant stocks in reserve around Australia, and wine grapes on the vines in the Eastern States.

But to David the Margaret River area was special and the cabernets memorable, particularly for their lovely intense fruit flavours and length of palate.

The early wines from Cape Mentelle were big and particularly firm in tannin. Later vintages were more elegant and refined, better structured and balanced with improved use of oak. Longer fermentations have provided the tannin muscle for long life, though earlier wines also aged well. Under good cellaring conditions (twelve to seventeen degrees Celsius) Cape Mentelle cabernets have the capacity to live for 15 to 20 years.

Of the wines of the 1980s, I especially enjoyed the '83 — for its concentrated eucalypt/cassis aroma and a firm, full palate. The 1986 and '87 were not far behind, while of later vintages the 1991 was memorable. From what some see as the perfect vintage, it has incredible extract and density, resulting in a huge weighty palate. Younger wines usually show typical Margaret River characters — cassis, herbaceous greenleaf aromas and full flavour. Their style is Cape Mentelle — full, firm tannins, a long finish. Recent vintages have added refinement and are more blackberry and mulberry than herbaceous.

Trickle irrigation is an important part of vineyard management, aimed at reducing stressed conditions without increased vigour. Mechanical harvesting was introduced in 1987, adding flexibility as well as providing cost savings. During hand picking days, the cabernet fruit, such as the 1982 vintage, was picked over three weeks, the early grapes to give the wine herbaceous, aromatic qualities, the middle pick for varietal flavour and the last for richness through the extra ripeness. The picking practice has been followed with the mechanical process.

The oldest vineyard vines produce the fruit for the straight cabernet, adding power but with finesse. Younger cabernet is used in a blend with merlot to make a more approachable earlier maturing style. It is marketed under the Trinders label, taken from a Group Settlement school site, and now a Cape Mentelle vineyard.

Shiraz from the property is also bred to stay, but they are softer as young wines. French techniques modelled on the northern Rhone are used in processing, including partial whole berry fermentation and ageing in big wooden casks. In some vintages, says winemaker John Durham, the result is intense pepper, sometimes chocolate, cherry and creamy, like Black Forest cake. I have enjoyed the berry-fruit richness of the wines, and the occasional spicy and plummy characters, with the 1989 and 1990 among my favourite vintages.

The zinfandel, a specialist wine, is spicy and plummy as well. Overall, however, it is more robust, offering enthusiasts a totally different style. While not a popular variety in Australia, it is a dry red alternative based on full ripeness and even partial raisining and high acidity.

The semillon-sauvignon blanc blend, which includes a dash of chenin blanc, is a favourite of mine, and obviously with other people as well, for production is greater than that of the cabernet. About 20 per cent is barrel-fermented with the characteristics of the more grassy semillon providing for bottle development and the sauvignon blanc tending to tropical fruit flavours, for earlier drinkability. The 1991 was a very good example. Three years later it was still drinking as a fresh vibrant youngster and it was an excellent complement to Rottnest Island barbecued whiting.

The 1992 vintage won the SGIO WA Winemakers Exhibition award for the best Margaret River dry white wine.

Such Bordeaux varieties do well in the maritime climate of Western Australia's South West, though Cape Mentelle is an exposed vineyard, prone to wind damage. So is Cloudy Bay, a wholly owned subsidiary of Cape Mentelle Vineyards Ltd of which David and Mark had owned 50 per cent and investors the rest — until the French connection.

In April 1990 leading French champagne house, Veuve Clicquot Ponsardin, bought a controlling interest in the venture. It followed a two-year search by the French producer for a 'New World' base to produce top-quality table wines for sale alongside its champagnes in major export markets. This will see the focus at Margaret River on cabernet sauvignon and in New Zealand on chardonnay and sauvignon blanc with David remaining at the helm in the arrangement, and having complete autonomy.

Given the arrangement, the Cape Mentelle chardonnay is nonetheless a very worthy wine, usually full and voluptuous, grapefruit and peachy combined with oak char flavours and buttery characters. Usually time is needed for the wine to evolve and reach approachable flavours.

No discourse on Cape Mentelle would be complete without reference to the Great Cabernet tastings, introduced some years ago to see how Margaret River and Australian wines of the same vintage compared with those produced elsewhere. Leading identities are brought to the winery from the Eastern States and overseas to take part.

Cape Mentelle cabernets have usually performed very well, no doubt helping the successful export performance. About 20 per cent is marketed abroad.

David Hohnen — seeking perfection in wine

CARBUNUP ESTATE

Bussell Highway, Carbunup
Cellar door sales: Daily 10 a.m. — 5 p.m.

Phyllis and Robert Credaro prepare for tastings at Carbunup Estate's cellar door sales area

AN OLD broadaxe is a significant part of history at Carbunup Estate, the first winery on the road south from Busselton to Margaret River. It belonged to Cesare Credaro who used it to clear the virgin land in the area the family still farm. Included is the vineyard, established by son Albert (backed by wife Ruby) and grandson Robert which provides for their Carbunup and Vasse River labels.

Before migrating in 1922, pioneer Cesare worked in a Swiss chocolate factory just across the border from his North Italian home. It was a much different, and tougher, story in Western Australia; here he cut sleepers from trees on the property, and worked on bridge building for the Busselton to Margaret River railway line, long since closed. But Cesare persisted, bringing out his wife four years later in the normal pattern of Southern European migration. He worked on an historic vineyard at Yallingup and later, on the dairy farm he had cleared, grew grapes to make his own wine. Albert did the same, quitting cows, however, to graze sheep and cattle for beef.

When Albert became bored with retirement after handing over the farming operation to Robert and his wife Phyllis, he decided to extend his small patch of vines. Initially, it was going to be two hectares, with the fruit to be sold. Then Robert became interested and the plantings were doubled. That was in 1988. Today, a substantial 18 hectares thrives, mainly chardonnay, semillon and cabernet sauvignon with smaller areas of verdelho, merlot and shiraz. The vines are not irrigated and grow mainly on red gravelly loams.

At full production the family is expecting about 180 tonnes of fruit. But there is a vast area of the property suitable for further plantings, expected to be undertaken after a consolidation period. Meanwhile, Robert says, fruit surplus to winemaking needs will be sold off.

There are five main wines made at the estate in an old potato shed converted to a winery and cellar door sales centre. But such a basic facility should not deter a visit. For despite the youthfulness of the modern development, some very good wines are made. Included is the (unwooded) 1993 chardonnay, a big, generous mouthful of tropical fruit and melon flavours — in a word, delicious. At the first judging for the family (the 1993 Mount Barker show) it won a silver medal, a proud moment indeed and a good indication of things to come. It is marketed under the premium Vasse River label, along with a semillon and cabernet sauvignon, while others carry the Carbunup Estate brand.

I especially enjoyed the 1993 (unwooded) semillon. It revealed attractive, lifted, fresh and lively, grassy, herbaceous characters that really filled out the mid-palate. A beautifully clean, refined wine with a firm finish, ideal with seafood It certainly made no bones about being a semillon, and proud of it.

IT IS AN unusual combination, the Irish and wine. Not in the drinking sense, to be sure, to be sure, for I have known them to enjoy many a glass. But their consuming strength is more in the product of the grain rather than the grape.

As Dr Ken Lynch, of Chatsfield Wines has done at Mount Barker, doctors John Lagan and his wife Eithne Sheridan have established an impressive operation at Chateau Xanadu at Margaret River. Their vineyard and winery, tucked away between the town and Caves Road, is now a substantial operation for small wine producers, one that is destined to continue expanding for the rest of the decade, and beyond.

The couple came to Margaret River with their three children for a year in 1968 and, attracted to the tranquillity of the South West, decided to stay. At the time youngest son Conor was just three — but 21 years later, he was to be made general manager of Xanadu, a task assisted by studies in winemaking at Roseworthy Agricultural College in South Australia.

Wine, however, was not the motivating factor when the Lagans bought their 160-hectare virgin block in 1970. For when cleared it was home for the beef cattle to graze upon and grow. But this was an exciting time for the wine industry, and inspired by other medicos — Cullity, Cullen and Pannell — in establishing vineyards and wineries, the Lagans decided to follow suit. It was a bold decision for they had no knowledge of what was involved, or how much money would be needed.

Yet in a few short years their wines have set high standards, showing the way for many others to follow. At Xanadu various show awards gracing the walls of the cellar door sales area reflect its success. Initially, their semillon set a standard many other winemakers dearly wanted to match. Indeed, the wines made from the variety by bearded winemaker John Smith during his time with Xanadu have done much to convince the industry that semillon is definitely right for the region.

Later, however, under the guidance of Swiss winemaker and viticulturist Jurg Muggli, Xanadu was able to impress with chardonnay and cabernet sauvignon, claiming with the latter the right to be part of the elite high quality 'cabernet club' of Margaret River.

The unusual name for the winery derives in part from the ancient Xanadu, which was Kubla Khan's summer palace near Beijing and founded in the 14th century. It has always been advocated as a mythical place of contentment and beauty, inspiring the poet Samuel Taylor Coleridge to pen his immortal poem 'Kubla Khan' in the late 18th century. The Lagans were struck at how its dreamy lines so aptly described Margaret River and its close association with great wines, and they are fond of quoting excerpts:

> *Five miles meandering with a mazy motion*
> *Through wood and dale the sacred river ran,*
> *Then reached the caverns measureless to man,*
> *The shadow of the dome of pleasure*
> *Floated midway on the waves;*
> *Where was heard the mingled measure*
> *From the fountain and the caves.*
> *It was a miracle of rare device,*
> *A sunny pleasure-dome with caves of ice!*
> *For he on honey-dew hath fed,*
> *And drunk the milk of paradise.*

Their residence in Ireland was also called Xanadu while the Chateau prefix acknowledges the many famous chateaux of Bordeaux and Cognac founded by the Irish such as O'Brien, MacCarthy Lynch-Bages, Barton, Kirwan and Hennessey.

The first vines, four hectares of cabernet, were planted in 1977 and followed by four hectares of semillon the next year. These areas were subsequently increased with other varieties including chardonnay, sauvignon blanc, merlot and cabernet franc. The production of 10,000 cases in 1993 is expected to be 15,000 by 1995, from 200 tonnes.

The early wines were made by Bill and Paul Ullinger, of Redgate, and Roseworthy graduate Theodore Radtke before the appointment of John and Dina Smith, and then Jurg.

Initially, the aim was 'modern wines' that were clean and elegant but with lots of fruit power, without coarseness and not dominated by oak characters. An underground cellar featured an ancient Egyptian method of cooling where cool humidified air is wafted through carbon 'port' holes to keep cellar temperatures constant.

By vintage 1989 it was time for the return of the 'prodigal son' from his studies in South Australia, to take over the winemaking helm. A young man in a hurry, Conor quickly realised that in the wine business you can only go so fast. Nevertheless, he maintains that diversity and innovation are the keys to maintaining consumer interest.

CHATEAU XANADU

Terry Road, Margaret River
Cellar door sales: Daily 10 a.m. — 5 p.m.

So in 1993 Secession was introduced into the Xanadu range. A blend of 65 per cent semillon and the rest sauvignon blanc, it is an early drinking style, unashamedly 'full frontal' — with loads of fresh, sub tropical fruit flavours, 12.5 per cent alcohol by volume, and a crispness without being acidic. 'People thought the label was a political statement', Conor said. 'It was not. It was a statement against the traditional, the use of a classic dry white label or just the varietal name.'

Cabernet is the flagship of Xanadu with the 1990 reserve and the 1991 winning the best dry red trophies at the 1991 and 1993 SGIO wine awards. I was associate judge to Sydney Master of Wine Nic Bulleid in 1993 and the 1991 Xanadu cabernet reserve proved outstanding. And it had to be, for it competed against an impressive line-up of Margaret River reds. The wine, reflecting a dry year, was big rich and full, a marvellous collection of complex, beautifully balanced fruit and

In 1990 the Xanadu chardonnay of that year won the SGIO best Margaret River dry white trophy, a reflection of the winery's rich, complex, wooded styles. While semillon, the original Xanadu pacesetter, has taken something of a back seat, a full-bodied, wood-aged wine for the specialist is still made, as well as a gold-medal winning sweet botrytis noble semillon. I well recall my first taste of a Xanadu (dry) semillon. It was the 1985 vintage, and I can still taste the superb depth of fruit flavour and the long aftertaste, with its subtle, grassy characters and lovely touch of oak. What a great Australian style, I thought, ideal for summer drinking, especially with salads. The fact that it became a trophy winner, best semillon in open classes at the Perth Show, came as no surprise. Xanadu buys in fruit from Rosa Park at Rosa Brook, south of Margaret River township, a vineyard developed by retired Perth architect, Ed Whittaker. Conor says the move is to add

This aerial perspective of Chateau Xanadu, where forest, farmland and sea are in close proximity, typifies the distinctive character of the Margaret River winegrowing area. Opposite: Winemaker Jurg Muggli with Conor Lagan

integrated new French oak flavours generating enormous length that would see it live beyond the year 2000. Slightly higher in alcohol than the norm at 14 per cent by volume, the reserve includes 20 per cent cabernet franc. Merlot is to be added in the future to make it even better, says Jurg.

The red range includes another cabernet, of good life, but earlier drinking than the reserve, a ripe, plum, cherry shiraz and Featherwhite, an intriguing rosé style made with cabernet. Fermented in old cabernet barrels, its salmon pink glow belies its fruit intensity and surprising full palate. Nearly 40 per cent goes to Switzerland, an indication of its quality.

flexibility, helping maintain the aim of consistency from modest yields.

Jurg is also introducing integrated production (IP) in seeking to make the vineyard more in harmony with nature. This means using organic-based fertilisers, predator friendly spray programmes, the minimal use of herbicides and irrigation. The change from conventional vineyard management in pursuit of organic production is scheduled over five years.

Another dimension was added to Xanadu in 1992 with an artist-in-residence. Robert Lawson painted WA scenes from the rugged red ranges of the Pilbara to the cool gentle forests of the South West on

ONE OF Western Australia's most popular wineries, host to a constant stream of visitors, had its origins as a coastal hideaway. That was the intention of the late Dr Kevin Cullen and his wife Di who lived in Busselton when they bought their first land in the Margaret River district in 1951. This was to result in the establishment of Cullen Wines, one of the pioneers of what is now a thriving and valuable local industry.

Initially, the Cullens grazed sheep and beef cattle, an activity which led to contact with Agriculture Department scientist Dr John Gladstones for advice on lupin growing. But while an expert in lupins, Dr Gladstones had also highlighted Margaret River as a place ideally suited to vineyard development, and he suggested to the Cullens that they plant vines.

The idea appealed immediately, especially to Kevin whose grandfather, Ephraim Mayo Clarke, planted a vineyard in 1890 in tuart country just south of the then Bunbury township.

The area, which now includes Clarke Street, near the Hands Memorial Oval, was planted with the varieties shiraz, muscadelle, doradillo and black constancia from cuttings brought from the Eastern States and Italy because a fungal disease had destroyed most of the small areas of vines in the South West.

Sweet red and white wines produced at the vineyard were sold in Bunbury from the family's general store. When Mr Clarke died in 1921 at the age of 75, the vineyard and winery was inherited by A. H. (Tubal) Clarke.

Tubal's sister, Elvie Alice Clarke, who was involved in the vineyard and general store, married Dr A.E. Cullen. They were to become Kevin's parents.

In 1971, 81 years after Mr Clarke began his venture, the Cullens started with an ambitious 6.5-hectare planting at Willyabrup, choosing cabernet sauvignon, rhine riesling and traminer in the first year. Today their vineyard extends to 28 hectares and includes chardonnay, semillon, sauvignon blanc, chenin blanc, merlot, cabernet franc and pinot, with cabernet sauvignon the biggest area at just under eight hectares. Chardonnay is the next largest with 7.2 hectares. The vines grow on gravelly sand over laterite and clay with a lot of granite on the property. The vineyard is not irrigated.

The family laugh now when they think of their first vintage, about 45 litres in 1974, definitely not something they could put down for their grandchildren.

The following year's production

magnums of cabernet sauvignon, a move thought to have created Australian industry history. The colourful additions had their marketing rewards, with the bottles selling for $100 in WA and for $130 in the Eastern States, to a keen demand.

Any visitor to Margaret River should include Xanadu in their tour. The pleasant drive through forest and farms leads to a sturdy gateway and buildings constructed from granite excavated during preparation of the vineyard area for planting. Antique leadlight windows in the small cellar door sales area generate an atmosphere of calm and charm, combining tastefully with local hand-crafted timber work.

CULLEN WINES

Caves Road, Willyabrup
Cellar door sales: Mon — Sat 10 a.m. — 4 p.m. Light luncheons available daily

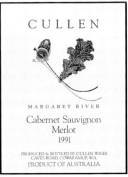

A family tradition continues — Di Cullen with daughter Vanya

gested she do winemaking at Roseworthy because he believed somebody in the family had to develop the skill besides Di.

Vanya liked the idea, completing a post graduate diploma in winemaking in 1986, making industry trips to New Zealand, the United States and France, with the icing on the cake coming when Californian industry giant Robert Mondavi invited her to work a vintage at his famous Napa Valley winery.

At full production Vanya expects to produce about 12,000 cases by 1996, from some 200 tonnes of fruit. Previously, however, Cullens like other producers in the district suffered from declining production. For example, only 80 tonnes was harvested from 20 hectares in 1988, resulting in heavy emphasis being applied to soil management techniques, fertilising and trellising. The aim was to produce more economic yields while maintaining full-flavoured wines from the earliest picked grapes in the harvest to the last.

There are 12 wines in the Cullen range, the main whites being chardonnay, sauvignon blanc (including a blend with semillon) and a classic dry white. A cabernet sauvignon-merlot-cabernet franc blend and a pinot noir are the main reds.

Reserve styles, of exceptional intensity and length of palate, are made of the cabernet blend and the sauvignon blanc semillon. The best fruit is selected and the wine is given 'princely' treatment.

Vanya says merlot grown by the family since 1976 adds rich mulberry characters to the red blend and, in the finest wines, a distinctive liqueur cherry touch, in helping to provide early drinkability and the long palate. The cabernet franc adds raspberry while the cabernet itself contributes more blackcurrant. The wine is matured for about 22 months in new and used French oak, adding to the backbone and structure for graceful ageing, different indeed to the greener herbaceous characters of some other wines from the district, especially prominent in the early 1980s. The 1986 was the first joint effort by the two ladies and a fine wine they produced, with five to ten more years ahead of it, given good cellaring conditions. In a worldwide assessment of the 1984 year by the London magazine *Wineyear*, reviewer Stuart Walton said of the Cullens wine: 'This low profile Estate produces wines with high profile results. The wine's deep, well-extracted colour heralds a brilliant roasted meat nose. This in turn gives way to rich, deep, thick, plum pine and mint Australian flavours. This serious loganberry fruit is teamed up with a gorgeous balance of acid

amounted to about 100 cases, and 500 in 1976. Despite the interest created in the area, sales were slow and difficult.

Then came the first trophy for the Cullens, for a 1977 rhine riesling in Canberra, a marvellous initial success for the district that certainly made selling a lot easier.

More West Australian industry history was later created when Di became the first woman to win a trophy at the Perth Show — a 1981 chardonnay and a 1981 sauvignon blanc made her the most successful exhibitor in varietal classes.

A mother of six, she took up winemaking when most women would be looking to tending flowers, perhaps a game of bridge or bowls, or looking after grandchildren. To me, however, she seemed totally at home dashing around the winery in gumboots and jeans with boundless energy and enthusiasm, getting great satisfaction out of making wines that people really enjoyed. Daughter Vanya has since taken charge though Di is still very much involved, with another daughter Shelley running cellar door sales and providing a very tasty lunch at modest prices.

But wine almost played second fiddle to music for Vanya, who graduated in zoology from the University of Western Australia. She was heading for Adelaide for music studies when her father sug-

and tannin, making for very sophisticated stuff.' The wine, under the banner 'exceptional', was reviewed ahead of the Penfolds 389 and Grange.

Vanya believes in super ripe fruit for the pinot noir, helping maintain colour stability. Later vintages like the 1992 and 1993 are lightly oaked, high in alcohol and consistent with the estate style of full, rich and generous wines. Some of the 1992 pinot and 1991 cabernet was even sold to an importer in Paris!

The 'chicken and hen clone' of chardonnay, which came from Houghton, produces big and small berries, resulting in gentle flavours. This, combined with barrel fermentation, lees stirring and 11 months of oak maturation, produces complex, slightly nutty, rich, big, generous, harmonious wines that are among the best in the State. Preferably drunk three to four years after vintage, they often show grapefruit and peach characters with vanilla from the oak.

I really enjoyed the classy, big, ripe 1993 Cullens sauvignon blanc. Features included the quality fruit and oak integration and the freshness, with a third fermented in stainless steel. This makes it more approachable as a youngster, and it proved ideal with grilled fish at Rottnest. Had I been judging, however, I would have put the 1993 sauvignon blanc-semillon blend slightly ahead, the combination of the two varieties generating elegance and strength, big, ripe but refined flavours at the passionfruit and tropical fruit end of the spectrum.

The Cullens' classic dry white, a blend of semillon, sauvignon blanc, chardonnay and rhine riesling, is fresh, clean and fruity, a wine that sells very well at restaurants.

With white wines, no sulphur is added until fermentation is finished, sometimes up to a month later. It sees the must go brown, like dark jarrah.

'I would not have done it had I not seen the technique, called oxidative must handling, used in the United States, and the wines that resulted', Vanya said. 'It really makes a difference, reducing the potential for oxidation of the phenolics in a young wine by removing them from the solution. But I stress that I am not changing the very drinkable wines my mother produced, just refining them.'

Vanya bases her winemaking techniques on a key word to Burgundians, 'doucement', meaning to be gentle.

(Kevin Cullen, who passed away in 1994, has been honoured for his contribution to medicine in the Busselton-Margaret River district and to the wine industry.)

THERE WERE no happier people in Perth on the night of 22 November 1992 than Phil and Allison Sexton, and with very good reason. Their 1990 cabernet sauvignon-based blend, the first from their new Margaret River development, had just been awarded WA's richest wine prize, a trip for two to America or France, plus $2000 in spending money for having the top wine at the SGIO Winemakers Exhibition. I was associate judge for the event to Dr Tony Jordan, of Victoria's premier Domaine Chandon, and he was ecstatic about the wine. As we moved down a line-up of very good reds, he turned to me and said: 'There is one outstanding wine here. Look for the quality of fruit structure. It is a young wine but it has the potential to age for many years.'

I had come to know Phil Sexton some years earlier, mainly in his role as a boutique brewer, for it was in the beer business in the 1980s that he had made his mark in WA.

Prior to this, a love of wine had seen him take a job at the Swan Brewery in Perth to earn the money for a course in oenology at the Charles Sturt University. Instead, the University of Western Australia science graduate with a bio-chemistry major was taken on as a trainee brewer, later completing a masters degree at Birmingham University. It was while travelling in Europe with Perth mates that the concept of a specialty brewery was born, and the successful Matilda Bay business was subsequently established. But despite the demands of competing with the giants of Australian breweries, and buying and running hotels, Phil Sexton never lost sight of his real goal, a vineyard and winery. In 1981, after a long search, 112 hectares was purchased 20 kilometres south of Margaret River.

His intention was something different to the usual fruit produced at Willyabrup, despite its success, and it was certainly a different location. Part of the property, for example, had been used as a gravel pit to provide ballast last century for the Hamelin Bay railway. Initial efforts were disastrous; attempts to establish a 12-hectare vineyard failed dismally, inadequate moisture a problem in the deep, gravelly, rocky country. But a determined Phil Sexton was not about to let targets slip away. In 1985 a water resource was leased from a neighbour, and this time the planting took. 'It was the gravel I wanted, rather than loam', Phil said. 'I wanted deep, draining country to allow deep root systems to be established — the development of maximum flavours through low-

DEVIL'S LAIR

Rocky Road, Forest Grove
No cellar door sales until 1996

The new winery, with an ultimate capacity of 500 tonnes, is worked round the clock at vintage time
Below: Messy, but fun — Phil and Allison Sexton during crushing

yield viticulture.' Adjoining land was bought and a 15-hectare 'lake' created to provide for the planting of more young vines, established on picturesque surrounding slopes like a huge Roman amphitheatre. Once established, the vines are not watered.

Today Devil's Lair has 36 hectares flourishing with chardonnay and cabernet sauvignon making up 75 per cent of the area, the balance merlot, pinot noir, cabernet franc and petite verdot.

The first vintage in 1990 produced 2000 cases. By 1994 it had increased to 10,000 and at capacity, by 1996, is expected to have doubled to 20,000 cases, catered for in a winery modelled on the German Bauhaus tradition.

Besides the cabernet, which includes blending of other red varieties to help generate the powerful, intensely flavoured fruit and fine tannins from low-yielding vines, a chardonnay and pinot noir are also made.

In the search for ripeness from the cooler area, just 10 kilometres from the Indian Ocean, the cabernet is not picked until mid-April. This means, of course, that the birds have a ball on the last remaining fruit in the area. Netting is seen as the only answer, costly and cumbersome as it is to erect and move, though the 30-odd kangaroos which live in bush on the property require a tougher fencing barrier to protect the succulent leaves and fruit they have enjoyed so much.

Chardonnay is machine-harvested except on the steep slopes where the fruit is hand-picked. The wine gives off pungent, citrus-like characteristics as a youngster,

lime-lemony flavours that soften with age. This barrel-fermented style spends a maximum of 12 months on oak with the high alcohol enhancing fruit sweetness to make an excellent food wine.

The 1993 pinot represents the style being sought with the variety. Deep in colour with oak complexity from barrel fermentation of part of the fruit, the bouquet and palate finds intense cherry and strawberry characters and subtle tannins. But the wine is slightly lower in alcohol than the previous vintage and has less sappiness, with the stems removed. A tasting at the winery revealed a common theme with the reds — ripe, sweet fruit, excellent balance and stimulating characters developing with time, such as chocolate and cigar box in the cabernet, enhanced by dusty oak.

Initial wines were made at Plantagenet. Since 1993 they have been processed on site, with the 500-tonne capacity winery being established over three stages.

By 1996 an operating profit is expected, but it would be many more years before there was a return on the investment. Meanwhile, interests in some of Perth's most popular dining and drinking facilities ensures that the Sextons have plenty on their plate.

And why the name Devil's Lair? Phil explained that as a university student, he studied anthropology which involved a 'dig' at an archaeological site right by their vineyard. Called the Devil's Lair cave, it is believed to have been frequented by the now-extinct marsupial, the Tasmanian Devil, and also used by Aborigines for thousands of years.

EVANS & TATE WINES

Cnr Caves & Metricup Road, Willyabrup
Cellar door sales: Daily 10 a.m. — 4.30
p.m.
(For full entry on Evans & Tate, see page
35, Swan Valley section)

*Some of the 20 hectares of vines at the
company's Redbrook, Margaret River,
property*

FERMOY ESTATE

Metricup Road, Willyabrup
Cellar door sales: Daily 11 a.m. — 4.30 p.m.

THERE IS for ever a little slice of old Ireland at Willyabrup as far as John and Beryl Anderson are concerned. John's great great grandfather of the same name came over from Scotland in the latter part of the 18th century to set up business in the town of Cork. Later he bought part of Fermoy Estate, donating land for the military barracks which in turn provided a base for the prosperity of Fermoy after it was established. Not one to rest on his laurels, he also founded the Irish Mail coach system, laid a series of major roads in the country to carry his coaches, and set up several industries in Fermoy, which is just north of Cork.

The success and the obvious talent and drive of his forebear have certainly been matched by John Anderson, a leading Perth businessman and company director. During a trip back to Ireland he and Beryl were fêted at a civic reception at Fermoy. In a responding speech, John told the gathering he would name his West Australian vineyard and winery after Fermoy, a gesture that acknowledged the importance the past holds for the Andersons.

One of the posts John held as chairman over about a decade was with Sandalford Wines which owns a major vineyard directly opposite Fermoy Estate, purchased by the Andersons in 1984. The following year 11 hectares were cleared and planted by Ellis Butcher, a successful local farmer and experienced vineyard contractor. The cuttings came from neighbour Moss Wood (cabernet sauvignon, pinot noir, chardonnay and semillon) and from nearby Evans and Tate (merlot) and Pierro, (sauvignon blanc).

A winery was built in 1987 to the specifications of winemaker Michael Kelly who has been allocated a share of the Fermoy Margaret River Unit Trust with other units issued to the families of Perth businessmen

Bill Caldow, Bill Mitchell, Justin Seward and Antun Triglavcanin.

And the group did not have long to wait for an early industry thrill when the 1988 Fermoy Estate cabernet sauvignon won the gold medal at the 1989 Sheraton Perth wine awards in the light-bodied red wine class. In a sense, however, it may have come too soon for the fledgling venture, for at such an early stage of development there was just not the wine available to capitalise on the interest the award created.

Even so Michael Kelly, who came into the industry by chance, was on a high because he believed the gold medal reflected the potential of the quality of fruit he was convinced the property could produce.

The son of a farmer and woolbuyer, he travelled frequently as a youngster to Victoria for school holidays where an uncle introduced him to prominent modern-day Yarra Valley pioneer Dr John Middleton, of Mount Mary. The doctor talked Michael out of studying economics and into winemaking.

This must have been sensible advice for in 1982 he was awarded a cadetship by the Riverina College of Advanced Education in New South Wales (now the Charles Sturt University) for studies that resulted in a Bachelor of Applied Science (wine science) degree in 1986. Vintage experience continued at Mount Mary with other work at Leeuwin Estate, Sandalford and in the Burgundy region of France, at the Domaine Louis Chapuis in the village of Aloxe-Corton.

My first contact with Michael was when he managed one of Western Australia's leading retailers, John Coppins at Cottesloe. But with dirt in his veins it was no surprise that he took up the challenge with Fermoy, and to call on family cropping experience by growing hay to roll

Winemaker Michael Kelly checks a Seitz filter used to remove sediment from the young white wines contained in the 3000-litre stainless steel tanks behind

out among the vines like a carpet. The idea, of course, is to provide valuable mulch and to retain moisture.

This may seem unnecessary when one takes into account one of the vineyard's problems is abundant vigour. As a result split canopy trellising like that designed by Professor Carbonneau, formerly of Bordeaux, and adopted successfully by other producers, was introduced.

There are now some 16 hectares of vines at Fermoy, with four hectares planted in 1994. The main varieties are cabernet sauvignon and semillon with others sauvignon blanc, chardonnay, pinot noir and merlot. They provide for six dry wines, three white and three red.

The initial crush of eight tonnes in 1987 has built up considerably, to 100 tonnes in 1994. By the year 2000 it is expected to be 150 tonnes.

Soils on the property are made up of gravelly loam on a clay base and though water is available the vines are not irrigated. Michael believes there is more to be gained in soil management practices than in boosting vines with water. 'We do not cultivate in spring', he said. 'You would be surprised how much soil compaction there is in driving tractors up and down at that time of the year. Come summer and it is like concrete and that really restricts the root growth. Then when you get a bit of warm weather the vines stress straight away.'

The Sheraton success confirmed the sweet-berry cabernet as the Fermoy flagship. However, a gold medal at the 1993 Perth Wine Show for the 1991 merlot stamped it as a potential challenger. It is a wine of strong raspberry characters, and Michael believes its soft, opulent, up-front flavours mask its tannin structure, leading many people to think it will not last. 'I believe it has as much life as our cabernets, five to ten years in good cellars', he said.

Patience, Michael says, is needed with pinot noir. For a long time he was unconvinced about the variety, but the gamey, spicy 1993 vintage changed his views. 'The lesson is that the vines need some years to mature, to produce fruit of the required flavour and balance', he said.

Semillon from the vineyard has proved a big winner in Sydney. In 1994, 100 cases a month were being sent there, reflecting the quality of the wine and the greater understanding of the variety in New South Wales from its excellent history in the Hunter Valley. About ten per cent of sauvignon blanc is added to the barrel-fermented semillon. This provides fresh tropical fruit salad flavours to the fig characters of the semillon. About 2000 cases are produced a year, the same as the cabernet, the two biggest wines in the Fermoy range.

All new French oak is used for the barrel fermentation and maturation of the chardonnay, usually producing cashew nut flavours to go with the peachy characters of the fruit. The (limited production) wine fits in between the unwooded and more intensely wooded wines available in the market place. Since 1990 it has been released in mid-September of the year of vintage, much earlier than many others. But it hits a popular marketing note, for the winery sells out by Christmas.

The sauvignon blancs, based on natural acids, are fresh and fruity, made to be drunk early.

Netting was introduced for the first time in 1994 to protect chardonnay from birds. Like other vineyards in the State, Fermoy has had its problems. In 1988, for example, losses were estimated at ten tonnes, especially disappointing at such an early stage in the project. An alternative scare tactic could be John Anderson swinging a golf club among the vines. He is a member of the Royal and Ancient club of St Andrews in Scotland, an important contact base for exports to the United Kingdom, and other markets.

GRALYN CELLARS

Caves Road, Willyabrup
Cellar door sales: Daily 10.30 a.m. — 4.30 p.m.

ONE OF the biggest ranges of wines in the Margaret River district is available from one of the smallest producers, Gralyn Cellars. It offers a smorgasbord of styles including dry and sweet whites, rosé, light and full-bodied dry reds, liqueur rhine riesling in the years of botrytis infection, and a range of ports. These include vintage, tawny, ruby and liqueur styles as well as a white port made from rhine riesling.

With such a diversity, it may well be imagined that the principals are long- established wine people. They are not.

Graham Hutton is the son of a Capel dairy farmer, while his wife Merilyn is a former teacher. After marriage they decided to turn their attention to the land for their future, developing a 240-hectare bush block to fatten cattle for the Perth and local market, and to grow grapes to make wine. Their interest in the latter pursuit was triggered by a severe decline in the beef market, while at the same time they were sampling some of the new wines produced in the district and enjoying them. In particular a bottle of Moss Wood red caught their fancy at a dinner party. 'We thought we would like to make a bit for ourselves', Graham told me.

Now they crush about 20 tonnes a year in a modern winery complex, a far cry indeed from the conditions of the first vintage in 1978. Stainless steel tanks have replaced wax-lined concrete fermenting vats, and computerised cooling controls the making process. Mind you, there was a time when cooling methods were anything but conventional. A beach umbrella was used in the initial vintage to protect a tank of crushed grapes from the hot sun.

The first vines were planted in 1975, leading to a vineyard of 4.5 hectares with just over half cabernet sauvignon. Rhine riesling and shiraz are the other main varieties. 'The industry gave us a new direction in life', says Merilyn contentedly. 'It is a special feeling to plant a vine, make wine from it, and to know it could go anywhere in the world.'

The Huttons rely mostly on cellar door sales to dispose of their stock, though an active mail order business sends wines around Australia. Mostly, wines are made to meet demand as supplies run down.

The couple are self taught, apart from a short course in wine quality control completed by Merilyn. They believe their best wines will be produced in the 1990s.

Rieslings from the winery have proved popular. More passionfruit than lime, they have a good level of natural acidity to balance the touch of residual sugar which lifts the palate.

The sweet, dessert-style white port from the variety is the vineyard's biggest seller. Made first in 1984, it is picked as late as possible, depending on the birds and rain.

This wine and other well made fortifieds in the extensive Gralyn range —

Considerable experimentation in different techniques has resulted in these healthy Gralyn vines

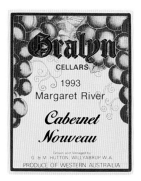

eight in all in 1994 — shows that areas beside the well-established Swan Valley, have a sound potential for such wines. First made in 1978, the production of the pioneering fortifieds were stimulated by the flavours and tannins of red wines being made in the district, characteristics the Huttons believed that were ideal for fortified styles. About half the Gralyn production goes into such wines, making the winery an exception in the table wine-based Margaret River industry.

Ports have also resulted from an unusual innovation. The couple have given their two sons a tonne of grapes on their 21st birthdays to make any styles they like. I especially enjoyed Michael's St George's College 1991 Anniversary port, plummy and liquorice on the nose, smooth and flavoursome on the palate with a dry finish.

Michael, an architect and resident of the college at the time, had the satisfaction of seeing the wine selected for its 60th birthday celebrations as well as winning a bronze medal at the Perth Show. Not far behind was horticultural scientist Bradley's 1991 pink port. Made from shiraz, it is light, fresh, clean and very sweet, ideal served chilled with fruit after a dinner party. The boys also designed their own labels and picked their fruit in a week-long Easter exercise. 'I suppose it shows that our family likes to make different things', Graham said. Daughter Annette's challenge comes up in 1995.

Another popular table wine in the Gralyn range besides the riesling is a light, lively, unwooded, slightly sweet red made from cabernet. Served chilled, it is an ideal summer wine, especially enjoyable with lightly flavoured foods.

Vineyard experimentation over the years in the search for better balanced vines, rather than those producing a lot of growth and not much crop, has involved trials with fertiliser, adding lime, clover mulching, ceasing cultivation between rows, soil and leaf analysis and hedging three to four weeks before picking. 'If we hedge earlier than that, we find the crop is down the following year', Graham said. 'We do not get as good a setting of fruit.'

As the combination of their Christian names for their label indicates, the couple like to do things together, including the maintenance of the garden and lawns around their home and winery complex, an attraction in itself. On the day of our visit, colourful blooming petunias seemed to be reaching across the narrow path leading to the tasting area, and to the nearby thriving grapevine shoots.

The display helps set off a winery dug about a metre into the ground with the earth banked up on the western side and covered with lawn to keep the premises cool. The winery was built from local material and embraces an unusual feature. It surrounds an above-ground concrete water tank. 'We believed it would also have a cooling influence on the winery', Merilyn said. 'We are well satisfied now that that has proved correct.'

PERTH weatherman Ed Green, developing a vineyard at Forest Grove, 15 kilometres south of Margaret River, nearly called his first wine 'after tennis'. He and wife Elenore thought the name appropriate, for the wine concerned, made from the variety müller thurgau, is crisp and refreshing, ideal they thought, after an energetic work-out on the court.

Grown extensively in Germany and New Zealand, müller thurgau is one of the less fancied varieties in Australia, though this does not worry the Greens, or for that matter, Mount Barker advocates Ian and Linda Tyrer who have enjoyed significant success with the style, made slightly sweet.

The Greens became fans during travels in Europe, but instead of 'after tennis' they resorted to using the varietal name for their wine, under the Green Valley label. 'Müller thurgau may have an image problem in Australia, but when people try it, they buy it', Ed said.

Cabernet sauvignon and chardonnay lead the way in Green Valley's development

When eyesight and stress-related problems stopped him from further tertiary studies, Ed Green, manager of aviation and defence weather service programmes with the Bureau of Meteorology, turned to something 'more relaxing' — establishing a vineyard. Each weekend, the couple would make the three-hour-plus trip to Forest Grove to work the picturesque sloping property, where planting began in 1980. For a decade Ed spent his annual holidays at Vasse Felix, to 'learn the ropes'.

I first visited the property when the vineyard was flourishing, to find an unusual scene. Swinging in the breeze, above and among the rows of vines, were the silvery inserts of wine casks, featuring drawings of eagles' heads and eyes, the Greens' anti-bird device. 'The grape eaters squealed and squawked when they first saw them and disappeared', Ed said. 'Unfortunately, they get used to all the scaring devices pretty quickly.' For Green Valley, that has proved costly. Early crops, such as the first three, were wiped out totally as birds swept in from the adjoining Boranup forest. In following years, they have taken as much as 35 per cent of the expected harvest. This was desperately disappointing, given the enormous work commitment. Finally, in 1994, just under half the vines were being netted to protect the precious fruit.

Chardonnay and cabernet sauvignon are the strengths of Green Valley, despite the müller following. I especially enjoyed the 1992 cabernet, an elegant, stylish wine with excellent varietal fruit flavours, fine tannins and a lovely soft pleasant finish, ideal with lamb or veal. It won a silver medal at the 1993 Perth Show, maintaining a medal-winning performance by all Green Valley reds since the first in 1990.

GREEN VALLEY

Sebbes Road, Forest Grove
Cellar door sales: Weekends and holidays, Saturday 10 a.m. — 6 p.m. Sundays, 10 a.m.— 4 p.m.

HAPPS

Commonage Road, Dunsborough
Cellar door sales: Daily 10 a.m. — 5 p.m.

Erl Happ and wife Roslyn on an inspection tour of the vines

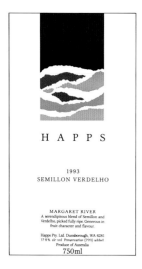

DUNSBOROUGH producer Erland Happ is a serious, studious man who backs action in life with a lot of thought. Yet some rather unusual incidents helped to direct this economics graduate and former teacher on the path to the wine industry. One involved a truck-driving stranger, and the other an off-hand comment by West Australian show judge John Hanley.

As a young man in South Australia, Erl was given a lift by a truckie. They stopped for a drink and the driver suggested he try hock and lemon. 'I liked it, and it opened the door to wine for me', he recalled on my first visit to his winery.

Some years later Erl was visited at his Vasse home, south of Busselton, by John Hanley who suggested he should try making wine from the fruit of a single sultana vine in his backyard. The thought appealed, and stimulated by the increasing success of the early wines from the district, Erl moved fulltime into the industry, planting the first vines in 1978 and combining the new challenge with another love, pottery

So a visit to Happs means much more than a tasting of fine wines, even though

Erl gave up potting in 1990 because of the demands of seeking wine perfection. Others, however, like US sculptor Hobart Brown and local craftsman Kim Potter, were quick to step in, their skilful work displayed in a picturesque mud brick complex built by Erl and his music teacher wife Roslyn in 1977.

Ever keen to minimise the wayward element of chance with proper knowledge, Erl once made a pilgrimage to the premium producing areas of France. And back with him came the 'glass with no pity'.

He had bought the unusual tasting glass in Burgundy where it had been developed by a Frenchman who ran a centre to help people understand wine. The distinctive wide-bodied glass contracts to a narrow top so that every bit of the bouquet can be assessed. Faults are quickly revealed — hence the name.

'A lot of people complain they cannot get any nose on a wine', Erl told me. 'But you need the right tools. The glass traps the aroma from the big surface area of the wine, concentrating the flavours as they rise.'

The red varieties cabernet sauvignon, merlot and shiraz make up nearly half the eight-hectare plantings at Happs, and these are supported by areas of chardonnay, verdelho, muscat à petit grains and the Portuguese port varieties touriga, tintacao and souzao, for an average crush of about 140 tonnes, yielding about 10,000 cases.

Netting to prevent bird damage, especially of chardonnay, has been important to generate ripeness and fruit flavour. Without such protection, losses could be as high as 50 per cent. 'You have to let the flavour of the grape express itself', Erl said. 'Initially, I tried to do it the academic way of the chemistry books. My philosophy has since been based on giving people something in the glass they are going to enjoy. There should be no elbows in the wine, like obtrusive acids and tannins.'

The Happ property is situated at the northern end of the Margaret River zone between Yallingup and Dunsborough, on the north-east slopes of the Leeuwin Naturalist Ridge, with the sea about five kilometres to the north and to the west. The vineyard is often misty with salt drift off the ocean, light rain, smoke blown in by an easterly, or winter fog carried in by the sea. The vines grow on gravelly and sandy loams of varying depths, with the ancient uncultivated soils well leached and easily eroded, making nutrition a critical factor. In the quest for organic ideal, the soils have been improved through the growing of winter cover crops such as lupins, oats, clover and cereal rye, and from mulching and spraying of weeds, the addition of sawdust or straw and the return of prunings, along with winemaking residues.

The vines are not irrigated, for Erl firmly believes they will produce greater concentrations of flavours this way. He argues that vines do their best with sound soil management in gradually adapting to natural moisture deficiencies that happen in a season (a contentious matter many of his peers no doubt would challenge).

But he regards himself as an adventuresome type as the move into fortified wines would suggest. For few would think of Margaret River a suitable area for such wines, like the Swan Valley for example, or Victoria's Rutherglen district.

Yet it really happened quite accidentally — neighbour Ian Lewis of Cape Clairault had asked Erl if he had any space in his winery for he had run short. The duo feared, however, that the cabernet fruit it was needed for may have become too ripe to make a dry table wine, and instead decided to try a port. The result — a gold medal! That was in 1981 and Erl's interest was really stimulated. 'I decided later as

we won more awards that we must have something special here', he said. 'But I decided I wanted to make port in the Portuguese style, not sweet like many Australian wines.'

The move to plant muscat was generated by (retired) Department of Agriculture scientist Dr John Gladstones who, in a review recommending areas in the South West suitable for the production of various wine types said: 'The area around Busselton has a climate closely resembling that of Frontignan, in the south of France. It could be particularly suitable for producing sweet, lightly fortified wines from muscat à petit grains.'

Over the years Happs has had its fair share of show successes, with some being very special, like the 1984 merlot winning gold at the Sheraton Perth wine awards and the following vintage gaining gold in Melbourne. Then there was the 1990 which won a Sheraton silver trophy and the 1991, gold at Perth. Other wines of which Erl is particularly proud include the 1991 and 1993 chardonnay, and the 1986, '88 and '91 cabernet merlot. Merlot, which retails for about $19-$20 (1994 prices) is the flagship and the dearest wine, with the popular, slightly sweet, drink-anytime pink Fuchsia, a red wine made to a white wine formula, the cheapest at $11.50

The estate's dry reds are not fined and show full fruit flavours, soft acidity and a generous finish, made to drink well at three years and to mature between five and ten years. The long palate sweet fruit, dry white chardonnay relatively high in alcohol (at 13-14 per cent by volume, a reflection of its ripeness when picked) is oak fermented and matured on lees for about four months. The unusual combination of semillon and verdelho fermented in tank and barrel yields another dry wine, with lovely sweet fruit, while a sweet white verdelho accommodates the dessert drinker. The fortifieds are Garnet, from the aromatic intensely flavoured muscat, and Fortis, a smooth and integrated port style from Portuguese black grapes.

Initially, Erl Happ was touchy about his ability. While he felt he could back his own palate, he would sometimes wonder whether a wine being bottled was as good as it should be. Today he is relaxed, confident about the future, acknowledging though that marketing is a permanent problem. But with a wide range of well-made wines, and with export interest growing, such as in South East Asia and Japan for Fuchsia, he reflects with pleasure on his decision to quit teaching, to be his own man in control of his own destiny.

HAY SHED HILL

Harmans Mill Road, Willyabrup
Cellar door sales: Weekends, school and
public holidays, 10.30 a.m.— 5 p.m.

*Above: Bright yellow sunflowers in front of
vine rows and winery lend a splash of colour
to this bucolic scene*

THERE could scarcely be a more rustic name for a label in the WA wine industry than Hay Shed Hill. Added to that, a pitchfork is its label emblem and one of its wines is called Pitchfork Pink. But there is nothing 'hickish' about the operation or the people involved. It is a serious, professionally run business in which owners Barry and Liz Morrison have invested heavily.

Perth orthodontist Barry and former teacher Liz decided in the 1980s that they wanted property in the Margaret River area, purchasing a 48-hectare block and small vineyard, initially established as Sussex Vale, in 1989 after a 12-month search.

They knew the property (originally part of a major dairy) had to be on good ground, for neighbours included the premium vineyards of Willespie and Ashbrook. But Hay Shed Hill was run down, so a major rejuvenation programme, began by a previous owner, was pursued. But why Hay Shed Hill?

Barry explained that the original wines were made in a hay shed, part of the old dairy situated on a hill and still in place. 'We wanted something different, not plain like Morrison's wines. Like it or not, you will not forget it.'

The original plantings of some nine to ten hectares have since been extended to 13, and a new winery established.

No Chateau Lysaught this. Through a stone entrance, visitors head up a winding driveway, past immaculately tended rows of vines, rose bushes planted at the end of each. They pass by the main house, an old

settler's cottage, extended and given a coat of white paint with surrounding white pickets, to the weatherboard winery, higher up Hay Shed Hill. It features a tower above which flies a 'corrugated iron' flag that is also a weather vane.

The winery, pleasing to the eye and yet functional, was designed by architect Chris Willcox, noted for the rammed earth Catholic Church in Margaret River and other buildings, including the Amberley winery. At full production in about 1997 a crush of 100-120 tonnes of fruit is expected (or 7000 — 8000 cases) with 30-40 per cent exported.

Meeting Barry Morrison for the first time, one gets an impression of a solid, no frills, down-to-earth guy. And, when talking about wine styles from Hay Shed Hill, a super-confident one. 'I believe we can be the next Moss Wood of Margaret River', he said. Later, I realised this was not a boast, or a beating-of-the-chest claim. Barry Morrison has total belief that the vineyard fruit will produce the quality he and his wife are seeking. One unusual feature is that the grapes are picked a week or two later than neighbouring properties, because it is cooler on Hay Shed Hill. Barry is not sure why, perhaps the lie-of-the-land to the wind, or that there is plenty of water about the place.

The main varieties grown are cabernet sauvignon, sauvignon blanc, semillon, chardonnay, pinot noir and surprisingly, some muscat of Alexandria. This latter variety, better known as a luscious, sweet, flavoursome table grape, provides for the birds, and for Pitchfork Pink. A 10-15 per cent dash is added to a base cabernet, so in essence it is a white wine made from red grapes, gaining a blush of colour from minimum skin contact. Though it may look cordial-like, it is a mouthful of wine with a pleasant touch of sweetness and spiciness. Served chilled, its crisp acidity sees it go very well with Asian food, and it has proved extremely popular with female and younger consumers.

Light oak treatment softens the sauvignon blanc produced at Hay Shed Hill, and adds a touch of complexity and smoky overtones. More tropical fruit and gooseberries, the 1993 was a big wine though the aim will generally be a light to medium-bodied style. The semillon is more intense. Half barrel-fermented, it is more in the chablis style, higher acidity adding crispness. The first chardonnay and pinot were made in 1994, the former from low-yielding vines, and not due for release until 1996, as a big, rich, full and complex style. Of the pinot, said winemaker John Smith: 'We are aiming at a rich, earthy style based on fruit showing bright red cherry flavours'.

The cabernets have shown a consistent soft mid-palate, a style that is elegant, full, ripe and rich. Dusty, smoky, coffee flavours show through from the oak and fruit, voluptuous characters certainly reflected in the very successful 1990 vintage.

HUNT'S FOXHAVEN ESTATE

Canal Rocks Road, Yallingup
Cellar door sales: School and public holidays and most weekends, usually 11 a.m. — 5 p.m.

Libby and David Hunt in their cellar, busily patronised by tourists heading for the area's popular beaches

LYING under a vine, David Hunt watched a fox take a bunch of grapes in its mouth and tear off the berries from the bottom half. Others have done the same, their constant visits from the surrounding bush leading to the unusual name. Family dogs now keep the intruders at bay, protecting the precious fruit.

The vineyard development meant a return home for David, a Perth real estate valuer who runs the property with school teaching wife Libby. The land, on the road to popular Smiths Beach and Canal Rocks, was purchased by his father in 1946. For Mr Hunt sen. had decided there was a better future in milking cows than wheat and sheep farming at Narrogin, the family's previous base. Their new home and adjoining shop, in fact an old mud-brick building, was subsequently to become one of the best known restaurants on Caves Road, the Crayfish Inn, and before that, the Lobster Pot.

In the 1960s part of the property was sold, with David's mother Greta running a small tearooms to earn income. On some occasions, David recalled, she would bake as many as 70 dozen scones on a wood

stove as well as countless pies and pasties, while he would wash dishes all weekend.

David ultimately purchased the remaining 11 hectares from the family in 1976 and planted rhine riesling two years later, keen to be involved in the new Margaret River wine industry that was creating widespread interest at the time. Later plantings, including some in 1994, established a vineyard of 4.5 hectares made up of cabernet sauvignon, merlot, semillon and sauvignon blanc.

The first wines, a dry riesling and a dry red, were produced in 1985 with David taking up the winemaking challenge himself on a hands-on, often weekend basis. For much of the period he maintained his professional life, living in the family house at Lesmurdie and commuting. In 1994 he became fulltime, concentrating on a crush to realise 1000 cases at peak production, in 1997-98.

Setbacks have included damage by the South African garden weevil, birds, hail and botrytis rot resulting from heavy dews, the vineyard being only 1500 metres from the sea. 'You can feel the air', David said. 'If it is 19 degrees Celsius at 6 a.m. with over 50 per cent humidity for two days in a row, you get botrytis and I have to control spray.'

The soils at Hunts vary from brown limestone sands to red clay loams with some grey sand. New vines are irrigated for establishment; so too, on a more regular basis, are those on higher ground where there is a lack of moisture retention.

Wine styles include a rhine riesling with a touch of residual sugar, a sweeter style, a dry semillon with a small addition of sauvignon blanc, and a cabernet sauvignon which has 12-18 months on new and used American oak. Prices (1994) range from $9-$15, with about half sold at cellar door.

The rieslings are aromatic floral styles with a high level of natural acid — so much so that David has had to add only once, in 1985. High natural acids — David believes because of the proximity to the sea — are also a feature of the semillon-sauvignon blanc blend, a ripe, subtle, tropical fruit salad style that develops complexity with age, wooded or not.

The cabernet is open-fermented and taken from skins in four days, time enough to generate plenty of colour. The wine usually shows vanilla from the oak and pleasant berry fruit flavours — with the 1988 vintage one of the best, David says. Other vintages of which he was particularly pleased included the drier 1990 riesling and the intense 1992 semillon-sauvignon blanc.

By the early 1990s David felt he had completed his winemaking 'apprenticeship' and was looking to his best wines to come. The operation is low key with a natural market among the vast numbers travelling to the nearby extremely popular beach area. Some visiting surfies come to pick grapes at vintage for Hunt's Foxhaven, and to enjoy the scones Greta has continued to bake for the occasion.

LEEUWIN ESTATE WINERY & RESTAURANT

Stevens Road, Margaret River
Opening times:
Wine sales: Daily 10 a.m. — 4.30 p.m.
Winery tours and tastings: Daily 11 a.m., 1 p.m., 3 p.m.
Alfresco dining: Daily 10 a.m. — 3.30 p.m. (Light lunches and morning and afternoon teas)
BBQ facilities: Daily 10.30 a.m. — 3.30 p.m.
À la carte restaurant: Daily 12 p.m. — 2.30 p.m. Saturday evenings from 7 p.m.
Bookings can be made in advance for the restaurant, and information for functions is available on (097) 576 253

STANDING on the bare slopes of Leeuwin Estate, watching the first vines being planted, it was impossible to imagine the development that was to come. Who would have thought, just a decade later, that thousands of people would crowd the property to watch international alfresco concerts, sipping estate wines to match the music?

Involved in those early days was John Horgan, brother of principal Denis, and a bouncing little bloke from South Australia, viticulturist Stan Heritage. There was not much more than a tin shed on the place then, and a heap of vine cuttings all ready to take over some of the long-held domain of grazing cattle.

Today 93 hectares of vines grace the land, providing the raw material for a fine range of wines — chardonnay, cabernet sauvignon, pinot noir, sauvignon blanc and rhine riesling. They are the result of what can best be described as a 'Rolls-Royce' development, with prices setting new horizons for table wines in Australia.

It all came about by chance, Denis explained. He had taken over a business which included the 650-hectare property, and when quitting the former he decided to keep the land and continue with the cattle.

Then into the scene stepped leading Californian producer Robert Mondavi who was looking for a vineyard and winery project for a group of United States investors. A deal was struck, and the first West Australian joint venture of its kind moved into gear. Forty hectares were planted in 1975 and another 40 in 1976 with the Australian interest (a controlling 51 per cent) supplying the land and management, and the Americans the funding and technical expertise.

As a result Mondavi, a great wine enthusiast who infected all about him with his verve, made numerous trips to West-

ern Australia with sons Michael and Tim. He was convinced about Margaret River's great future, lamenting only that it was so far away.

Denis describes Mondavi as his mentor with the American connection lasting about four years before it ended, and Leeuwin Estate became a total Denis Horgan West Australian venture.

But this was more than another business interest. It became an outlet for Denis's

creative energies and a personal involvement for the family. The long-term plan for Leeuwin saw it closely linked to nature, with the winery, restaurant and cellar door sales complex set among the karri trees, a tourist attraction in itself.

During its establishment, and that of a superb residence hidden away among the trees, Denis was learning as much as possible about a totally new industry. I recall in an address to *The West Australian* Wine Press Club how he said he would watch closely at tastings to see which bottles were emptied first, taking that as his direction for the best wines.

The two men charged with nurturing Leeuwin have been winemaker Bob Cartwright, who joined in 1978, and viticulturist John Brocksopp, 1979. If one is to follow the oft-quoted industry reference that good wines begin in the vineyard, then we should talk about John first.

A tall, lean man dedicated to his profession, he gained experience in New South Wales, Victoria and South Australia before heading west. Every bit the realist, he reacted to the Leeuwin vineyards at the time by likening them to a 'fairly windblown desert'. Immediately he set about growing trees and establishing windbreaks, anything to stop the effects of

Above: The distinctive entrance to Leeuwin's winery, sales area and balconied restaurant, reached after a long, curving approach through the extensive vineyard
Below: Winemaker Bob Cartwright (left) and production manager/viticulturist John Brocksopp

equinoctial gales damaging the young shoots as they emerged.

In 1981 the practice of growing cereal rye was introduced for protection, also providing valuable mulch for the light, warm soils which extended some two metres to clay — perfect, John believed, for grape vines. 'After about four years, the roots hit the clay layer which has plenty of nitrogen and moisture, grabbing everything as it comes down from the surface', he said.

His target for the winemaker is balanced fruit allowing for distinctive flavours, without coarseness. Excessive heat during ripening is not wanted, rather the aim is for a cool finish to preserve the acid balance.

John uses different trellising techniques for the individual varieties in seeking a balance between character and crop. Once, though, when he demonstrated the two-catch wire foliage trapping and hedging system in the pinot noir, he raised a few eyebrows. He told a group of visitors that minimally pruned vines in Coonawarra resembled the cross section of an emu. 'The bunches tend to hang on the outside like oranges on a tree', he said. He went on: 'There has been too much emphasis on crop level rather than quality, with the belief that the winery will produce the great wine. We have found that we can increase wine quality through manipulation in the vineyard. We seek more gentle sun exposure. Sun has a great deal of influence on pinot noir and chardonnay especially.'

Bob Cartwright has about 500 tonnes of fruit a year to process from the vineyard, and some outstanding wines have been made. For me the chardonnays have been memorable, and it was no surprise to receive an excited telephone call from the vineyard to say that the 1981 vintage was judged the best at an international tasting in London. Its success was against tough competition, with 80 wines entered by 12 countries — and it was only Leeuwin's second commercial release!

But the success did not alter the basic vineyard policy of not taking part in Australian wine shows. The philosophy has always been that Leeuwin wines are released when they are ready for the market, and not to meet show requirements. (The 1980 vintage, however, did go before the judges in Sydney, winning a gold medal.)

Such early success may suggest that the winemaker comes from a long family involvement with strong industry ties. He does not. Bob Cartwright's beginnings

were humble, his home being at Nuriootpa in the Barossa Valley where his father was a painter and decorator. Bob joined Kaiser Stuhl when he left school, and a chance spell in the laboratory led to studies in winemaking at Roseworthy. His wine career took him back to the Kaiser before Wolf Blass, a good friend, suggested he try his skills with Houghton-Valencia in Western Australia. For three years he worked with well-known identity Charlie Kelly. At that time, Bob recalled, the only cooling at Houghton was by the 'Coolgardie safe' principle of hessian bags wrapped round tanks with water run over them.

His first Leeuwin crush amounted to 19 tonnes. With chardonnay Bob looks to intense but subtle fruit flavours that do not 'come up and hit you in the nose'. These are big wines, but not too obvious, having tremendous depth of flavour enhanced by wood, all new and all French.

For me the feature of the wines has been the richness of the mid-palate, balance and complexity with some buttery character from the malolactic fermentation. Usually, the fruit is picked fairly ripe with the final judgement depending on a walk through the vineyard — a berry tasted here, another there.

The wine is totally barrel-fermented and left on lees, with stirring as required. And when released it has to be just right, rather than when the marketing pressures dictate. For example, the 1985 vintage was

The annual Leeuwin Concert, held outdoors against an imposing backdrop of karri trees, has become a mecca for audiences who enjoy adding fine wines to an unusual cultural feast

Part of the 'Rolls-Royce' development at Leeuwin Estate, where 93 hectares are planted to vines

Visitors to Leeuwin can test the estate's extensive wine list at the à la carte restaurant, which overlooks a sweeping grassed area

About half the wine is barrel-fermented in wood used previously for chardonnay, with a final three-month kiss of wood before bottling.

A preview of the 1993 wine revealed a fresh, lively mouthful, with hints of tropical fruit and melons, excellent with or without a meal.

Bob once told me he thought that pinot from Leeuwin could eventually outpoint cabernet as the winery's top red, a view I never shared. While he concedes it is a contrary variety, perhaps the most difficult there is, he argues it can be sculptured and moulded. 'The trick is trying to work out how to do it consistently each year', he said.

In colour, the pinots have often been lightly brown, giving the impression of wines two to three years older. Certainly there have been some lovely wines produced, like the 1982, 1983, 1985 and 1989, for example. But I did not like the 1984, a hard wine, no doubt a hiccup every producer of the variety tends to get — even the Burgundians.

Then again, I am a bit cautious because wines can change. Take the 1979 cabernet — it was an aggressive tannic brute of a youngster, so harsh to the taste that it was thought at one stage it might never be released at all. Yet ten years later it had become a graceful, smooth, superb wine, one of the best reds I had tried in 1989 from all over the country. It reflected the Mondavi touch and the Californian approach at the time, to extract bigness, certainly not needed at Margaret River as time has shown.

Bob Cartwright recalled how the juice had been pumped from the bottom of the tank over skins at about twice the usual frequency resulting in a big, gutsy, hard wine that left a gritty furriness on the tongue.

'We kept looking at it again and again, and then ignoring it for 12 months', he said. 'Then we would look at it again.'

Along came luck to take a hand. The corks involved were not of very good quality and were starting to leak, so a decision was forced upon the winemaker — dump it, or pull the corks, top up the wine and reassess the situation. Opening the bottles allowed some air exposure which modified the tannins, removing the hard grittiness. Six months later and there was a big change to the wine, which was released with relish and enthusiastically sought by buyers.

Today older vines and changed techniques have resulted in wines with much softer, velvety tannins and rich fruit, her-

marketed in 1989, and that may well be some sort of a record in Australia for a dry white table wine

I believe the chardonnays have been the outstanding Leeuwin wines, West Australian ambassadors of world class. They have been widely recognised by critics and competitors with many international accolades throughout the 1980s. Perhaps the most memorable have been the 1986 and 1988, the former the 1992 International Wine challenge winner in London against the best from anywhere. To me, the 1988 was a classic, a wine with a stunning rich, silky palate. The marriage of fruit and oak generated great length and exquisite balance, an ideal example for a tasting beginner looking to a wine that is totally opposite to thin and watery.

But then there was the 1987, arguably Australia's greatest, said Sydney critic Huon Hooke. 'In typical Leeuwin style, it exudes tropical fruits (pineapple, passionfruit), butter and grilled nuts with subtle well-married oak, a wine of charm and complexity.'

While rhine riesling from Leeuwin is a popular bread-and-butter performer, representing about 30 per cent of production, the sauvignon blanc is real quality. Introduced in 1984 into the range, the 1985 vintage really impressed with strong, green, grassy characters rather than capsicum and asparagus. Later vintages retain the grassy flavours, but without the intensity, making them perhaps more suitable with food.

baceous and minty in some years.

Asked about his best wines from Leeuwin, Bob became philosophical. 'They are like your children', he said. 'They all have good things going for them, but in different ways.'

He rated 1982 a brilliant year with the weather conditions ideal, generating a beautiful, slow ripening to produce excellent flavour intensity. The 1987 vintage was almost as good.

Then there was 1991, some rate one in a hundred, especially for cabernet. The Leeuwin wine, due for release in 1995, is potentially its best yet. Elegant and herbaceous with a long structure benefiting from vine maturity, it has an enormous depth of fruit and overall qualities to be a trophy winner, a benchmark. Included with the usual malbec and merlot for the first time is the merest dash of petite verdot, regarded as a concentrated version of cabernet. In tiny quantities, it adds to the flavour and soft tannins and provides fresh natural acids. 'It is so intense you could stand a spoon in it', John said. So far the 1989 has been a favourite, impressive for its powerful concentrations of rich and ripe flavours, touches of spice and dusty oak.

The finest wines from Leeuwin become part of the Art series, featuring a painting on the label that reflects the estate's aims of savouring fine wine, good food and culture.

Many visitors may regard some of the wine prices as princely, for Leeuwin has never hesitated in charging what it thinks the wines deserve. At the winery Denis Horgan once told me: 'If we do not set such prices, we would have to cut corners, and I do not want to do that. Our production is labour-intensive and costly. The wines rank with the best the French can produce, and are not nearly as expensive.'

Well, then, does Leeuwin return a profit? 'It does now', said Denis, 'but it took 11 years. This is a long-term business.'

A second Leeuwin label called Prelude was introduced in 1990. More modestly priced, it provides for wines not regarded as Art series quality and that could be released earlier.

At least the birds are not causing the problems of a few years back when chardonnay in particular suffered some savage losses. John Brocksopp puts it down to plantings of sunflowers, preferred to grapes by the parrots, and a remedy that 'works like a charm'.

Problems in getting pickers has seen Leeuwin turn to mechanical harvesting, but not for chardonnay, sauvignon blanc and pinot noir.

THERE would be few vineyard developments in the world where the owner would pull out nearly half his vines just as they were about to bear their first fruit. But that is exactly what Bruce Tomlinson did at Lenton Brae, his Margaret River property. He felt he had to heed the advice of former State Government Viticulturist Bill Jamieson and replace the carefully planted pinot noir with cabernet sauvignon.

Bruce admitted it was a tough decision, for the vines were thriving. 'But cabernet has done so well in Margaret River and I believe it can produce wines comparable with the best of Bordeaux', he said. 'Unfortunately, after making a visit to Burgundy, I do not believe that applies to pinot noir.'

An architect and town planner by profession, he had spent much of his time involved in mining town developments in the north of Western Australia (such as Karratha, Argyle, Pannawonica and Leinster) before turning to wine. In 1982 he purchased 17 hectares — part of a subdivision he had organised. 'I liked the look of the soils', he commented. 'They were uniformly excellent over the whole property. 'And to be next door to Moss Wood was a recommendation in itself.'

He began planting the following year, almost exclusively pinot noir and chardonnay, when Bill Jamieson stepped in. Today the ten-hectare vineyard also includes semillon, sauvignon blanc and merlot, with the initial crush in 1987 processed at Redgate. The first significant harvest, of 20 tonnes in 1989, was made by Rob Bowen on the property, with John Smith undertaking the 1990 vintage in a modern rammed earth winery. This, the family residence and cellar door sales centre were all designed by Bruce; visitors can look down from three balconies on some of the producing equipment and work area, and so feel more a part of the wines they are trying (usually poured by wife Jeanette).

Among the styles are a chardonnay, early release cabernet-merlot blend, a reserve cabernet, sauvignon blanc, and a semillon-sauvignon blanc blend, top wines that have generated great success for the operation. The pinnacle was the 1990 SGIO Winemakers Exhibition when the 1988 cabernet won best Margaret River red and then the major prize, of top wine of the show, winning for the Tomlinsons a trip to California and Bordeaux. As well, it enabled them to visit the London Wine Fair, resulting in export orders to Wales and England and justification in the best

LENTON BRAE

Caves Road, Willyabrup
Cellar door sales: Daily 10 a.m. — 6 p.m.

The Lenton Brae winery at night, with lights ablaze. During the day, bells in the tower peal out at chosen intervals

SEMILLON
SAUVIGNON BLANC
LENTON BRAE ESTATE, CAVES ROAD, MARGARET RIVER, WA.
750ml PRESERVATIVE (220,300) ADDED 12.5% ALC/VOL

possible way of the vineyard's change from pinot.

Another great victory for Lenton Brae was with the 1992 chardonnay when it won the inaugural West Australian Wine Press Club award for the best WA wine at the Perth Show in a taste-off against the best red, after it was judged the leading white table wine.

The wine was also judged best WA chardonnay, making it a record triple trophy winner on the one day!

Son Edward, a Roseworthy graduate in oenology and home for the 1992 vintage, had a key role in the making of the chardonnay. The family hope is that he will eventually take over winemaking duties, after experiences in other parts of Australia, South Africa, California and Europe.

In 1994 the Lenton Brae crush was 90 tonnes and despite the successes of the chardonnay and cabernet, my favourite wine from the estate is the semillon-sauvignon blanc blend. Initially, it was labelled Graves, but French pressure led to the name being dropped. 'They told me I would be pursued to the highest court in the land, if we persisted', Bruce said.

The varieties are picked as close together as possible and fermented as one, some in oak and some in stainless steel tanks. Bruce described them as synergistic. 'They love being together', he said. 'In this way you get the aroma and vigour of sauvignon blanc, with the length and base of the semillon. Sauvignon on its own does not last consistently. We want the best of both varieties, like they get in Bordeaux.'

It is a lively, stylish wine, soft and gentle with strong palate appeal. For me the 1989, which seemed a touch riper, has been the pick.

The trophy-winning chardonnay of the lighter style appealed for its excellent, elegant length of fruit flavour and exquisite balance, a great early drinking wine unlike a lot of other Australian, more heavily oaked styles. Generally, the chardonnays have been lighter-medium bodied with sometimes melon and nutty characters evident. Bruce believes that the variety in Margaret River, planted on slopes away from the wind, will produce a truly internationally acclaimed wine.

The trophy-winning 1988 cabernet was from first crop fruit, parallelling other Margaret River initial vineyard successes with the variety when the first fruit produces rich, generously flavoured soft wines with very good keeping qualities. At first the wine is closed, but left for a few hours it opens up with buckets of beautiful bouquet and mouth-filling flavours. 'They are of such quality I have no regrets about pulling out the pinot', Bruce said.

One of the most popular wines with consumers is the straight, unwooded sauvignon blanc, a fresh, crisp, bone dry wine made for early drinking, ideal for Perth summers and usually sold out by Christmas in the year of vintage!

The Lenton Brae winery facility allows for trailer loads of white grapes to be chilled overnight, before crushing.

Bruce has adopted near neighbour Mike Peterkin's trellising system which involves using wires to lift the canopy in the growing period to allow hedging for plenty of fruit exposure to the sun, and more even maturation. Watering is selective and mainly applied to high-yielding semillon to avoid stress. The vineyard flourishes on about a metre of gravelly loam over clay and limestone, allowing for good quantities of sub-soil moisture throughout the summer. Cover crops of lupins, cereal rye and clover are also part of the vineyard's husbandry programme.

Such demands, however, have not prevented Bruce from taking an active industry role, such as serving as president of the Margaret River Industry Association where he quickly established a reputation for being forthright when required.

As to the name of the vineyard, its origins have intrigued many a visitor. Lenton was the chapel district in Nottingham, where the family originated. They came to Western Australia in 1884, and the custom was to name all their homes Lenton. 'Brae' is a northern English-Scottish word meaning hill on which the property is situated.

Featured on the label is the winery's belltower which houses five bells made in Perth to peel three times a day, in the way the French use bells for vineyard celebrations and to herald picking times.

T HERE ARE numerous reasons why people enter the wine business, if they are not born into it. Jeff Moss can put up a couple that perhaps no one else can claim.

As a boy he lived west of Mildura, close to the South Australian border, and his father, a public servant and farmer, would buy full-bodied dry reds from the Barossa Valley in demijohns, packed in cane wicker baskets. They were put into the bottom of the linen press, but it did not take young Jeff long to sniff them out, take a sip or two, and to decide this was the stuff for him.

If he needed further confirmation, it came some years later when, at the age of 12, he was travelling with his father on holiday in Victoria. There they visited an old Yarra Valley winery and when the manager opened the big cellar doors on what was a warm summer's afternoon, out wafted a magical smell. It was a combination of rich flavours based on wines of the past, old wood and a touch of vinegar. The cellar had a cobblestone floor which showed where the wagons carrying the grapes had once entered, along with an old press. 'I walked around sniffing and feeling the beautiful old shiny wood and I was hooked, committed', he recalled.

But it was to be an unhappy start. On leaving school he joined an established winery to learn the basics of the business in the cellar. Three years later he was put off along with about 60 others following a disastrous collapse in export sales to the United Kingdom. Quality had dipped, it was felt, and the market reacted accordingly.

After a stint with the Victorian Government he purchased a sultana block at a place called Red Cliffs which he was to operate for 15 years. After three consecutive wet seasons when there was not much fruit and not much money coming in, he accepted an offer to join Seppelts to look after vineyards at Qualco, near Waikerie. Nine years later Jeff was recruited by Hardy Wines and headed west, this time as company viticulturist for Houghton.

Naturally enough, bringing new ideas into established, traditional ways caused local consternation and raised plenty of eyebrows. But 'Mossy' (as he had become known) had been given a firm brief, to modernise the vineyards in line with the latest developments elsewhere in the world, to boost production but not at the expense of quality.

However, the urge to 'do his own thing' remained strong and in January 1987 Jeff left Houghton for Margaret River to start up a family enterprise in which sons Peter and David, and later daughter Jane, a Roseworthy graduate in oenology, all took an active part.

A 100-tonne winery was established for the 1992 vintage with contract growers supplementing the family's own seven-hectare vineyard. The main varieties planted include semillon, sauvignon blanc, pinot noir, cabernet franc, merlot, chardonnay and grenache.

The vines grow on what Jeff describes as particularly mean, hungry, gravelly soils, the advantage being in the flavour intensity generated with vine maturity. Limited irrigation keeps the vines in a healthy working condition.

Moss Brothers produces a premium range of wines to appeal to the connoisseurs, and others for consumers who want uncomplicated, easy drinking styles that are not expensive.

An unusual feature of the vineyard is that two cuttings were planted in the same

MOSS BROTHERS WINES

Caves Road, Willyabrup
Cellar door sales: Daily 10 a.m. — 5 p.m.

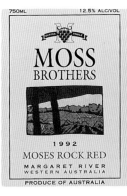

When it comes to expertise, there is no lack in the Moss household. Pictured are Jeff Moss with daughter Jane and sons Peter (left) and David

hole, and trained in opposite directions. Such a move sought to cut vigour with the vines competing against each other, while reducing the risk of 'misses' where a single vine has failed to strike.

Plantings began in 1985, and on this subject Jeff has mixed feelings. He regards chardonnay as a pain to grow because bud burst is early, and the variety suffers wind damage in spring, at flowering time. 'But it produces magical wines', he said.

I enjoyed the 1991 vintage of butterscotch, melon and hazelnut, more fruit generosity than the 1989 and 1990, styles of power and complexity.

Chardonnay is part of the premium range, along with semillon, sauvignon blanc, cabernet and pinot noir.

The family has been especially proud of the latter even though Jeff believes that Margaret River is a shade too hot for the refined variety.

The winemaking involves whole bunches, some crushed, varying proportions of stalk inclusion, hot fermentations with ten to 12 months in wood before bottling. I marked the 1992 highly at the 1993 SGIO Winemakers Exhibition judging, for its fruit depth, complexity and balance. The previous vintage contributed to a Perth Wine Show trophy for the family (with the 1990 cabernet merlot) while

the 1990 featured prominently at the Sheraton awards in 1991.

The cabernet-merlot blend varies from year to year in percentage terms, usually showing blackcurrant and blackberry from the cabernet, plum from the merlot with a dash of cabernet franc adding a pleasant raspberry lift to the palate.

Jeff has a lot of faith in semillon and sauvignon blanc, varieties he is certain will bring fame to the district. A blend of the two labelled CD white certainly keeps the cash register chattering.

The Moss Rock range, a white and a red, are the popular modest-priced wines. The red, made up of cabernet, pinot and grenache, quickly established its consumer appeal as did the slightly sweet white, a blend of frontignan, semillon and sauvignon blanc. Fun wines include non-wooded fortifieds, Bona Vista white and ruby. The white is quite sweet, a fruity blend of frontignan and semillon. The ruby is made from cabernet franc, a light, crisp sweet red.

Visitors to Moss Brothers often ask about the connection with neighbouring high profile Moss Wood. 'We share the air and soils', Jeff tells them. During establishment days, it was more than that. Before the family home was built, they camped in the Moss Wood cask cellar!

THE 1976 Perth Wine Show was more than another annual event as far as Margaret River was concerned. It marked an historic event in the fledgling district's short history — the first gold medal for a South West wine in open classes. It was awarded to Moss Wood, established by Dr Bill Pannell and his wife Sandra, and was one of three gold medals and two silvers they gained from seven wines entered. I remember reporting that the Pannells had trouble sampling wines that day because they could not stop grinning!

The medals were a fitting reward for a couple dedicated to a new industry and who had set personal standards for the highest quality, with a vision for their wines that knew no horizons.

To me Bill Pannell showed rare talent in his search for great Australian wine styles; his perfectionist attitude was reflected particularly in a long line of outstanding cabernets, notably the 1978 vintage. It was not released as a cabernet because it was not considered up to standard. It was simply called dry red and it sold from the winery at $3 a bottle, or $35 a case. At the time Bill explained that like other producers he had yeast problems with the vintage. But I recall clearly the wine performing very well at one of my tastings, being rated one of the best value-for-money wines we had tried in months. In those days there were a lot of wines selling around Australia for much more without being nearly as good.

Then there was the chardonnay. It shocked me, and many other enthusiasts, when a Moss Wood entry scored only eight points out of a possible 20 at another Perth Wine Show.

I remember looking at the wine at the show with wine buff Stephen Leslie — it was cloudy, like a wine sample drawn from a tank during processing. Winemaker Keith Mugford, who joined the Pannells in January 1979, identified the problem as an attempt to be different which just did not come off. 'It would have been better not to have entered the wine because it was just not understood', he said.

Bill and Keith had decided to use French methods, like allowing the wine to mature on the lees, common practice in the industry today. I am happy to report that the ugly duckling became a beautiful swan when released, a brilliant, clean wine with flavour and complexity rare in Australian chardonnays. Its extra depth and richness was generated by not clarifying the wine after fermenting before it was returned to the cask for maturing, a practice still continued.

The Pannells, who began planting the vineyard in 1969 with cabernet, leased Moss Wood to Keith Mugford for a year before he and his wife Clare purchased the property and business, taking over in July 1985. The Pannells later became involved in Domaine de la Pousse d'Or in Burgundy and a vineyard at Pemberton.

Originally from McLaren Vale in South Australia, where the local wine industry whetted his appetite, Keith graduated from Roseworthy and looked to Western Australia for a career opportunity.

At the college there was strong interest in new cool climate viticultural areas like Margaret River. Then at dinner one night Keith was introduced to his first wine from the district, a 1977 Moss Wood semillon, by fellow students John Elliott (now with the Department of Agriculture) and Dr Mike Peterkin (Pierro).

'I was quite taken by the wine', he recalled. 'It was tremendously rich in flavour, a dimension I had not seen before.'

Today there are nine hectares under vine with cabernet sauvignon making up half; chardonnay, semillon and pinot noir dominate the balance with a small amount of cabernet franc and merlot. The crush is 75-80 tonnes, Keith says. There is no irrigation at Moss Wood where the vines grow basically in a gravelly red loam over clay to varying depths.

Five wine styles are made, a wooded and unwooded semillon, chardonnay, pinot noir and cabernet, with about 40 per cent sold in Perth and the rest around Australia and overseas. The United Kingdom is the biggest export market.

Cabernet is the flagship, carrying the label's reputation. A vineyard characteristic is the richness of flavour — generous, smooth, long and consistent wines, very enjoyable when young. For some, however, this has been a criticism; they have expected more 'spine' in the style, and have expressed concern that the wines lack good cellaring structure. 'Early vintages like the 1975, 76 and 77 are still sound and drinking beautifully', Keith said. 'If they do fall apart, it will be after 20 years, and for that period, I will be quite thankful. We are not looking at 50 years like some of the great wines of Bordeaux.' After 15 years in the bottle, however, leaking corks can be a problem. These will be replaced by Moss Wood, free of charge, for anyone concerned.

Pinot noir has proved the most challenging variety to grow at Moss Wood, requiring more perseverance than cabernet. Much more time has been spent analysing grape growing methods and

MOSS WOOD

Metricup Road, Willyabrup
Tastings by appointment

Keith Mugford takes count amid the racks of stored wine

fine chablis styles, being fuller and riper with peach, melon and sometimes lime flavours. Complexity from wood treatment develops buttery overtones, marmalade, dough and bread flavours. The variety is fermented in oak and left sitting on lees, with about nine months' oak ageing. In severe wind years at Moss Wood the chardonnay has suffered badly with losses up to 90 per cent.

The semillons fit two distinct markets. On the one hand there are the fresh, clean fruit characters of the variety which sometimes include honey, fig and gooseberry; on the other the wooded style is more spicy and complex, perhaps longer living and more of a food wine. The fruit is picked at the same time and processed identically, apart from barrel fermentation and wood maturation. Hail storms in 1993 reduced the crop such that no wooded style was made.

Keith is always on the lookout for any innovation which will help with wine quality, including varying picking times, considering new varieties and trellising methods to control vigour and the exposure of the sun to leaves and fruit. He has also turned to the Pemberton-Manjimup area for fruit supplies, especially pinot noir.

Keith regarded the 1993 vintage as outstanding for semillon, the unwooded wine blessed with tremendous intensity and intense complexity. It was also a good year for chardonnay, resulting in a wine of tremendous richness with a lively palate from the natural acid. About one year in four, the acidity is such that none has to be added. With semillon, it is one year in three.

In common with so many Margaret River estates, Moss Wood enjoyed an outstanding year for cabernet in 1991, producing a wine that appealed for its strong, attractive lifted bouquet, its refined structure and great length of palate. And the 1990, said Keith, was not far behind either.

Nature helped the 1992 pinot when hail reduced the crop, in effect thinning out the fruit to concentrate flavours in the remainder.

Surprisingly, during tastings marking the 21st birthday of Moss Wood, it was not the reds that drew the attention but the old semillons. Age had seen the development of honey, caramel and toasty characters, and the return of fig and quince flavours. 'The event revealed that our semillons were at their best in the ten to 15 year range', Keith said. In 1994 he described the 1981 vintage as 'just hitting its straps'.

yield, while in the winery different vinification techniques are used such as warmer fermentation, longer contact with skins, and the inclusion of uncrushed bunches.

Yet today the outstanding 1981 vintage remains the benchmark, a wine that received accolades from many quarters. I recall receiving a telephone call from an excited Sandra Pannell saying that an eminent Frenchman who tried the wine at Moss Wood compared it favourably with the best from Burgundy. The season resulted in low yields but produced grapes of tremendous depth of colour and flavour.

'I estimate we are about 90 per cent down the pinot learning curve', Keith said. 'But people have to accept that the variety will vary from year to year. That happens in Burgundy and they have had several hundred years start on us.'

New wood treatment, all French, varies for the reds with the cabernet maturing in about half new oak and the pinot about 30 per cent, depending on the year. Trellising changes to the Scott Henry system have increased depth of fruit, allowing for more oak if required.

The Moss Wood chardonnays are not

IT WAS labelled an abandoned vineyard in the Government Gazette. These were the first plantings of Palmers, hit by cyclone Alby and then grasshoppers, to such an extent that wild oats smothered the struggling survivors. However, there was to be a rebirth and today, a flourishing vineyard produces award-winning wines.

Principals Stephen and Helen Palmer joined the industry in a sense by default, for their picturesque property was to have been part of a major development by major national producer Seppelt. But the deal fell through and the big property was subdivided and now includes leading producers Pierro, Evans and Tate, part of Sandalford and, of course, Palmers.

On our visit Stephen, a farm adviser, recalled the early vineyard setback which saw the couple instead turn to the thoroughbred horse industry, developing a stud on the Old Coast Road at Myalup. But their ties with the Willyabrup land were strong and the Government Gazette record of their vines, two hectares of cabernet sauvignon they planted in 1977, rejuvenated their interest. 'The vines were on the ground but we found as many as we could, stood them up and began again from there', Stephen said.

By this time Helen, a former Channel Seven make-up artist and public relations consultant, had had a strong taste of the wine industry, being involved with Vintage Festivals run over a number of years at Lilac Hill Park in Caversham.

Under an arrangement with neighbour Dr Mike Peterkin (Pierro Wines), a vineyard management plan was put in place and plantings extended over five years to 12 hectares, slightly less than half the property. Besides cabernet, other varieties include chardonnay, semillon, sauvignon blanc, merlot and cabernet franc. There are five wines in the range with a target production of 6000 cases by 1996.

A highlight for the Palmers in 1993 was a West Australian and South Australian design award for their striking labels, based on different coloured vine leaves representing seasons of the year. But as pleasing as that was, it was even more gratifying to win a series of awards for their wines, proving to consumers that there is as much quality inside the bottle as outside. The pinnacle was the Mount Barker show trophy for the best chardonnay for the 1991 vintage.

The chardonnay is the Palmer flagship. Barrel-fermented in new French oak and

PALMERS

Caves Road, Willyabrup
Cellar door sales by appointment

Stephen and Helen Palmer (above) toast the latest vintage

made by master craftsman Mike Peterkin, the trophy-winning wine is full-flavoured, rich and refined, a light, toasty and melon style with a long, stimulating aftertaste.

At a tasting on the property, it was easy to understand the enthusiasm for the classic dry white, an unwooded blend of semillon and sauvignon blanc. A lively wine of generous up-front tropical fruit flavours, especially suitable for summertime consumption, it is fresh, crisp and dry, an excellent seafood style or accompaniment to Asian food.

I especially enjoyed the 1991 cabernet sauvignon, an excellent claret style. A medium-bodied wine with plenty of clean berry character and fine tannins, its texture and weight is enhanced by the addition of merlot. A silver medal winner at the 1993 Perth Show, it went very well with roast lamb but would add to any red meat dish, or a pasta or cheese board for that matter.

PIERRO

Caves Road, Willyabrup
Cellar door sales: Daily 10 a.m. — 5 p.m.

I FIRST met Dr Michael Peterkin in the early 1970s, soon after he had graduated in medicine. We had attended a wine industry seminar at Yanchep and I had come across him sitting on the edge of a garden table, gazing out towards the horizon deep in thought. It transpired he was weighing up his future: was it to be medicine or the wine industry? In fact, it evolved as a combination of both.

Today he tends vines and wines at the impressive Pierro development in the Margaret River district, and patients in Busselton.

The initial interest in wine was stimulated by adult education courses and tastings, and visits to Houghton as a medical student to meet Jack Mann, to listen to his stories and taste his wines. Then came the initial Vasse Felix wines, such an exciting development that Michael headed for Margaret River the following weekend for his first visit to the district.

Having decided he wanted to be part of the wine industry, Michael went to South Australia to attend Roseworthy Agricultural College in 1976 and 1977, gaining a degree in grape growing and winemaking.

In 1980 he began establishing Pierro in one of the most attractive settings in the district, on the banks of Willyabrup Brook.

Visitors to the estate are well advised to sample the beauty of the location as well as the wines.

But he was not prepared to sit by and wait for his first vines, mainly chardonnay,

pinot noir and sauvignon blanc, to bear fruit. He made wines for Cullens, Alkoomi and (the former) Chateau Barker, and helped set up Capel Vale, ending consultancy work after his own first vintage in 1983.

It was a significant time, for his vineyard methods were radical to say the least. They involved close plantings, 4000 vines per hectare one metre apart in rows of 2.5 metres on reasonably steep slopes, similar to many German vineyards. Subsequent plantings, which have included cabernet sauvignon, merlot and cabernet franc, are even more dense with 5500 vines per hectare, still a metre apart, but in rows 1.75 metres wide. While the total area is small, given further plantings, the density rate is two and a half to three and a half times that of the traditional vineyard.

Michael's idea is to elicit better fruit quality through vine competition. 'Smaller grapevines produce less fruit per vine', he told me as we drove among the vines. 'But overall the vineyard produces economic yields through having more vines.'

He argues that the improved quality comes from more fruit, shoot and leaf exposure to sunlight, made possible by trellising with movable wires to lift up the growth for close hedging.

Such management is part of an integrated system of canopy, soil and water control. The vineyard is trickle-fed from a dam in the Willyabrup Brook — crucial, Michael believes, to provide flexibility in soil care. 'You do not have to cultivate, which is a major bonus', he said. 'Most of the nutrient exchange is in the surface area where the vine's shallow root structure exists. Cultivating chops them off and oxidises the organic matter.'

This technique, he says, is well suited to blocks like his where poor soils occur, in places very gravelly and rocky, with some vines planted on sheet granite.

Yet healthy crops on vines bearing chardonnay — with higher yields than those achieved on better land — reflect how infertile soils have been made to produce.

Mulching between vines with oats, cereal rye and prunings is another vital factor in the husbandry chain, providing

go 'over the top', the more desirable the flavour development, Michael explains, adding that many great vineyards, especially in the northern hemisphere, have rocks or very dark soils to retain the heat.

Michael says he was regarded as a crank in the early days for his vineyard innovations, but now others follow his lead. And a bonus is that the silvereyes are not the problem they are in other vineyards. He believes this is because they do not have the canopy under which to hide from predators while pecking away. 'I lose about 10 per cent on average, but I can live with that', he said.

The wines produced by Pierro cater for two distinct markets, with the pre-

for the build-up of armies of earthworms, helped by an earthworm 'factory' on the property. 'We throw them by the bucketful around the place', Michael said. 'Besides aerating the soil, they fertilise it as well.'

Another interesting aspect of Pierro is that the bigger rocks have been collected and placed near the vines to retain heat at night. The theory is that during the day photosynthesis by the leaves produces sugar in the grapes which at night is converted into other compounds including flavour and aroma, a process that is temperature-dependent. So the warmer the night for the fruit, provided it does not

mium end based on chardonnay, pinot noir and a blend of sauvignon blanc and semillon. Three other styles, including a white wine made from red grapes (pinot noir) and a late-harvest rhine riesling, are specials for cellar door visitors who can relax while sipping in the attractive rammed earth cellar. Its high, slanted roof provides a cool interior even on the hottest summer days, and inside local jarrah has been used to line the whole ceiling of the winery, and for a bar.

But for me it is the chardonnay that is king at Pierro, certainly among the best produced anywhere. In the winery's short history, the various vintages have been

Huge jarrah doors are a feature of Pierro's rammed earth winery, set in verdant gardens

Punching down whole bunches of pinot from the 1994 vintage is an appealing task for these youthful fermentation helpers

lauded at tastings and awarded top trophies at judgings. For example, Pierro chardonnays have won three SGIO and three Sheraton awards, the 1991 selected by leading French Champagne producer Möet and Chandon for 250th celebration dinners in Sydney and Melbourne while the 1989 topped the Great Cullens Chardonnay taste-off in 1993, heading 20 of the best wines from round the world. With 1100 points, the Pierro wine was a clear winner from the Leeuwin entry, 1060 points, a particularly pleasing result for Western Australia especially given the leading French wines assessed. It must also be remembered that there was hardly a decent chardonnay made in Australia 15 years ago. I preferred the 1992, a subtle and sophisticated classic of excellent strength of flavour complexity and length, with up to a decade of graceful ageing ahead.

Michael seeks drinkability — and that means six months after making — with the complexity of overall flavours on a light to medium background. 'I want them to evolve in the mouth, so that each time a sip is taken, there is something a little different, as opposed to the wine with a tremendous initial impact, but nothing else.'

Vineyard changes in the early 1990s sought even more fruit and aroma.

Introduced was leaf plucking, growing and mowing clover cover crops for nitrogen, and irrigation manipulation at the right time for the watering to benefit the fruit, and not to generate further vine growth.

The chardonnays now are made in exactly the opposite manner used in the early years; basically a switch from hi-tech to low-tech methods like those evolved by the Burgundians.

And it happened by chance. In 1986

pressure at the surgery resulted in the chardonnay being left almost to the end of the year, maturing on lees in oak because Michael did not have the time to attend to it. He thought he had 'mucked it up', but when he came to try the wine he was impressed, and the following year tried half and half. Now the process is total, with complete barrel fermentation and no stirring of the lees. He is not concerned about the build-up of temperature during fermentation, doesn't worry about a bit of oxygen getting in, allows for a total malolactic fermentation and does not add sulphur until just before bottling, and provides only a coarse filtering. The result is a wine with hazelnut, almond and peachy characters — with melon in cooler years.

The other great winemaking challenge for Pierro is pinot noir. Once the vines were nearly pulled out because Michael began to doubt their worth.

He has found it an extremely difficult variety to handle but experience is generating more comfort with low-tech methods even more important than for chardonnay.

'I believe the less you do to it, the better you are', he said. 'That means controlled dirt, not taking the wine off gross lees straight after fermentation, contrary to what we were taught for red winemaking. But they seem to develop nicer flavours and aromas this way. Sometimes they might be a bit pongy, but you have to accept that. We are not looking for fresh, fruity wines that so many Australian makers produce.'

However, the future could see the Pierro pinot a blend of estate-grown grapes, with fruit from Denmark and Pemberton adding aroma and sappiness to the Margaret River structure.

Seafood lovers would do well to try the semillon-sauvignon blanc blend which has a dash of chardonnay. It has a crisp, light, dry, attractive palate with a touch of herbaceousness, and the ability for some ageing.

The wine has done exceptionally well in the Eastern States. Late in 1995 Pierro planned to release its first rich, full-bodied red, to be called Cabernets. Made in 1994 it involved a real mixture, of cabernet sauvignon, cabernet franc, petite verdot, malbec and merlot.

In 1994 Pierro crushed 100 tonnes of fruit and this is expected to double by the year 2000. Small shareholders in the operation include prominent Perth lawyer Bevan Lawrence, brother of former premier Dr Carmen Lawrence, and Perth cardiologist, Dr Peter Thompson.

REDGATE

Boodjiup Road, Margaret River
Cellar door sales: Daily 10 a.m. — 5 p.m.

*Honest value-for-money wines are available
at Redgate's Margaret River cellar*

IT IS A bit disconcerting wandering around parts of the European wine world with Bill Ullinger of Redgate Wines at Margaret River. The former World War II Lancaster pilot is likely to recall suddenly where some of their bombs had fallen. Well, whatever his targets were then, they were vastly different on our travels as we sought out the secrets of the great vineyards of Germany and France, and their fine wines.

It was, however, the Royal Australian Air Force which indirectly introduced Bill to wine. While training in South Australia, he began visiting wineries in the Barossa Valley and McLaren Vale, near Adelaide. After the war he turned to engineering, and it was not until 1976 that he purchased Redgate, one of the southernmost vineyards of Margaret River. He had searched for five years for the right block, from Gingin south, and when he finally found what he was looking for, he made up his mind and made an offer within a mere 20 minutes.

At an age when most are planning retirement, Bill set about establishing Redgate, a name taken from a nearby beach. The property is only three kilometres from the Indian Ocean which makes it, Bill confesses, one of the windiest in the State. But he was unperturbed. After all, his family had had rural interests over four generations and his father, Mr W.H. Ullinger, was a pioneer banana planter in

Carnarvon. Bill was confident good vineyard management and techniques would ensure a healthy production of quality fruit.

Planting of the 80-hectare property began in 1977, and today there are 18 hectares under vines. The white varieties of semillon, sauvignon blanc, rhine riesling and chenin blanc make up just over half, while the main red grapes are cabernet sauvignon, pinot noir and cabernet franc, with small areas of merlot and shiraz. They grow on soils varying from heavy gravelly loam to light sandy country with a clay base. A spring-fed dam supplies about 100,000 litres a day from late November to February, depending on the season. At full production Redgate expects to crush 150 — 180 tonnes of its own fruit, with about 80 tonnes processed into wine for other growers.

Progress in the early years could best be described as steady as experience in a new vocation was slowly gained. Then came 1984, the agony and ecstasy year for the fledgling winery. The Ullingers (Bill had been joined by son Paul) had decided to close their doors, dejected by the introduction of a ten per cent sales tax on wine by the Federal Government. Bill believed it would make the difference between profitability and going down the drain.

But at the Adelaide Show their 1982 cabernet sauvignon was awarded the

Former pilot turned winemaker Bill Ullinger,
with son Paul

with barrel fermentation and lees stirring because, says winemaker Virginia Wilcock, it has the fruit power to carry the wood treatment, generating a full, creamy, rich palate. 'It is a style of the future', she said.

The 1993 vintage was a full-bodied, herbaceous, tropical fruit wine, more opulent than the previous vintage, suiting consumers who enjoy a solid mouthful of fruit and gentle oak.

While chenin blanc may be a down-market variety for some producers in the area, that is not the case at Redgate which makes a fresh, fruity, slightly sweet early drinking style, selling it to a keen demand. All vintages have sold out just months after release with extra grape purchases having been made to supplement vineyard supplies.

The cabernets from the winery are much more approachable as younger wines than they used to be. More mature vines are resulting in wines of softer tannins and more finesse But they still have plenty of cellaring potential, up to ten years Virginia believes. Most of the cabernet comes from a sheltered valley where there is a concentration of heat.

The 1992 vintage saw a cabernet franc introduced for the first time. A supple, refined wine, it has a more uplifted perfumed bouquet than the cabernet. While I remain unconvinced about pinot noir in Margaret River generally, there have been some good wines made. Redgate's 1991 release won a gold at the Perth Wine Show and a silver Sheraton trophy.

Like other vineyards Redgate suffered heavy losses in 1993 due to hail and heavy rain, and there have been other disappointments. Over a glass or two one night, Bill recalled how in 1985 some 4500 litres of semillon was dumped into a nearby paddock when a technical mishap led to methylated spirits being leaked into a tank. 'I knew something was wrong when I tasted it, for it was very bitter', he said. The loss represented about $16,000 worth of wine.

Previously just over 2000 litres of cabernet (about half the production) had been dumped from the first commercial vintage in 1981 — judged not worth keeping. 'We put the rest through a malolactic fermentation, and three years later sold the lot at $17.90 a bottle', Bill said. 'It was a big tannic wine, one of the biggest we have ever made.'

Redgate has not been one of the high-fliers of the region but its wines have come to enjoy a solid following as honest value-for-money products.

prized Montgomery Trophy for the best full-bodied, dry red table wine of any vintage with a firm finish, made by a small producer. This quickly changed despair into delight. It was a huge result, against the nation's best, opening the marketing door to Redgate wines and putting the label firmly on the Australian wine map.

But the sales tax issue was to raise its head again and again, and has remained a sore point in the industry, especially with an audit in 1989-90 that resulted in some heavy bills for small wineries. Like others Bill Ullinger has condemned the tax, and later impositions, as a terrible disincentive to people trying to establish a new industry with so many side benefits to the general community, and especially to tourism.

Redgate makes more wine styles than most wineries in Western Australia including a bubbly and reserve chardonnay and pinot in special years, only available at cellar door. The main whites are sauvignon blanc, semillon and chenin blanc. Bill believes sauvignon blanc is on its own in Margaret River for a full-bodied, wooded wine style. 'It is economically superior to chardonnay and will develop very well,' he said.

The wine is made like a chardonnay

JOHN JAMES of Ribbon Vale Estate can claim a unique record in the West Australian wine industry — 35 years between vintages. As a schoolboy of 15 he made wine from a single vine growing next to a tankstand in the backyard of a Moora hotel run by his father. 'I used an enamel bucket to ferment the grapes and a felt pad used in the soft drink making process for filtering', he recalled. 'My father drank the two bottles at Christmas, and said he liked them. Anyway, he survived!'

Now John makes premium wine at his Caves Road property named Ribbon Vale because of its shape. The narrow strip measures 1.3 kilometres by 185 metres and runs in an east-west direction, with the winery on a high hill and taking in commanding views. It makes no pretence at being lavish, nor does it boast spectacular landscaping like some in the district — but it provides for the necessary modern equipment, with a layout that certainly does the job.

Considering his background, wine represents an unusual career shift for the former industrial chemist from Perth who once worked in an oil refinery, and then in businesses making soap, gas and bricks. But John's enjoyment in wine consumption dates back many years, to his university student days.

In 1973 John visited Margaret River to inspect a property advertised in a newspaper, and though he did not purchase the land the visit clearly cemented his thoughts towards a new life, for he was much taken by a rhine riesling made at Vasse Felix. Four years later he purchased Ribbon Vale, impressed with the gravel over granite gneiss soils which he says do not need any irrigation because of their moisture retention capacity when combined with soil management and contour planting.

There are seven hectares planted at Ribbon Vale with semillon the biggest, then merlot, sauvignon blanc and cabernet sauvignon the main varieties. The crush is 50-60 tonnes with six whites and two reds produced.

For John 1993 will go down as his more remarkable year. It saw his first trophy — indeed, a hat-trick for the one wine, the 1993 sauvignon blanc, at the Perth Wine Show. After 11 years, and so much toil, it was a marvellous moment.

'We get more passionfruit and tropical fruit characters in our wine than anywhere else in the country', John said. 'People like drinking them for it gets away from the meaner styles of cooler areas and the often washed out wines of warmer regions. Af-

ter semillon, I believe it is the variety for this area. Good chardonnays are being made and crafted all over the country, including Margaret River, but few areas are producing sauvignon blanc of quality.'

The outstanding triple-trophy winner was a mouthful indeed, swamping the palate with its glass-brimming fruit flavours. Like the lively, slightly herbaceous, unwooded semillon from Ribbon Vale, its other features include freshness, and a clean and crisp finish.

These are picked earlier than the wooded styles, usually barrel-fermented and with extended lees contact because the extra flavour is considered necessary to balance the oak. 'We do not want the natural grape flavours dominated by wood contact', John said.

But while the judicious use of quality oak certainly adds greatly to various white wines, adding significant cellaring potential, sometimes one can only wonder. For as we proceeded through a tasting of Ribbon Vale wines, John pulled the cork on an unwooded semillon made by Di Cullen from his first vintage in 1982. It was a treat with lovely development and a light, toasty character, suggesting a more complex wine as a youngster than the fruity, high acid style it was.

Semillon at Ribbon Vale is a healthy producer, though more prone to wind damage than sauvignon blanc because of an earlier bud burst. It cannot be manipulated through pruning to avoid critical periods, like the fuller-flavoured aromatic sauvignon.

John keeps a close eye on vigour in the vineyard, especially with sauvignon blanc. He has taken a tack that is different from most by pruning to increase fruit yield to control growth. The adoption of this method followed a visit to the Geisenheim Research Institute on the banks of the Rhine River in Germany, and discussions with the eminent Professor of Viticulture, (the late) Dr Helmut Becker. His advice to John was 'put fruit on the vine, that is the way to keep vines in check'.

I had come to know Professor Becker from interviews on several trips he made to Australia, and from a visit I had also made to Geisenheim. There he had shown me some of the 800 varieties from round the world being investigated, from frost-

RIBBON VALE ESTATE

Caves Road, Willyabrup
Open weekends and public holidays 10 a.m. — 5 p.m.

John James's discerning nose exerts some traditional quality control

resistant Siberian plants to thorny vines from China. The institute makes wines from about 500 of them, and as we tried some in the tasting cellars Professor Becker recalled his last visit to Australia in which he had tried some of the wines from the new southern areas of Western Australia. His conclusion then was Australians were getting to be a danger — 'They are starting to make wines like us'. But on a previous occasion, while working briefly with the CSIRO, he had not been so kind. 'The whites are horrible, while the reds are drinkable', he had said.

That red description would not do justice to Ribbon Vale wines, based on cabernet and merlot in varying proportions. Basically, and depending on seasons, they fall into two distinct categories: a big, gutsy, rich, full-bodied wine with firm tannins, excellent with a roast dinner on a winter's night, and an alternative lighter style, but having plenty of flavour and good structure for cellar development.

Picking times for such wines vary, and in the early days John knew from foxes when to go ahead. 'They attacked the fruit as it was ripening', he said. 'They pulled at the berries of the hanging bunches, leaving footprints and other evidence so there was no doubt who the culprits were.'

The cunning freeloaders are still around today, but there are lot more vineyards competing for their attention.

As if running Ribbon Vale was not enough, John chooses to do his own wholesaling in Western Australia, and that includes dealing with some 100 outlets between Margaret River and Perth. This helps him keep a finger on the market for, as he says, 'While everything else about the business may be seasonal, marketing is not and it is something you have to be at all the time'.

RIVENDELL GARDENS

Wildwood Road, Yallingup
Cellar door sales: Daily 10 a.m. — 5 p.m.
Includes tearooms for lunches, morning and afternoon teas

Mark Standish shoulders the rewards of a fruitful family venture

PETER STANDISH was born to be a horticulturist. Though brought up in suburban Melbourne where his father was a prominent journalist, he says he knew from a very small boy that he wanted to grow things. But it took a long time to realise the dream and it involved a family transplant. For Peter, who had come to Western Australia to work as a farm overseer at Esperance, was encouraged to seek his own land. Somewhat to his surprise, considering his tender (20) years at the time, he was allocated an 800-hectare conditional purchase block at Munglinup, where virgin land was being opened up. For 25 years he and wife Lu grew crops, grazed stock and raised a family.

But there was a yen for something more intensive, an appetite for vines and wine whetted by a long association with the Hohnen family of Cape Mentelle where they had helped plant early vines. So the move was made in 1983, initially to grow tomatoes, snowpeas and strawberries and to run stock. Gradually, the family realised they needed a cash flow to support their vineyard development plans, and a tearoom was opened. Property was sold off for extra funds and son Mark returned from Muresk Agricultural College to join the family venture.

As father and son shared a good palate for wine, it was not long before plantings began. That was in 1987 and included the varieties semillon, sauvignon blanc, verdelho, cabernet sauvignon, cabernet franc, shiraz and merlot, established in a three-year programme. The closely spaced vines flourish today in the midst of bush, on ironstone country, 13.4 hectares of mainly gravelly loam over clay. They are serviced by an impressive dam in the valley below.

The first vintage of four tonnes was harvested in 1990. At full production 200 tonnes is expected, the main wine styles a semillon-sauvignon blanc blend, in 80-20 ratio, verdelho, a red blend, a straight shiraz and Honeysuckle, the biggest seller of all. This is a late-harvest, fruity and unpretentious semillon which really appeals to people with a sweeter palate. High in acid to make it fresh and clean, it is ideal served chilled as a late afternoon beverage wine.

Mark says in the unoaked classic white blend, the flagship, length of palate is the aim. This is provided by the weight of the semillon with the sauvignon blanc adding early, riper tropical fruit lift.

The first release red was the 1992 cabernet shiraz, a pleasant picnic wine from the young vines, and priced accordingly. In time cabernet franc from the vineyard is expected to generate lovely cherry flavours to enhance the blackcurrant of the cabernet.

Initially, the Standish family controlled 50 per cent of the vineyard and local investors the rest. However, it was subsequently sold and leased back by Mark for five years to sell fruit to a family syndicate for winemaking (under contract at Ribbon Vale) with the rest sold to other producers. About 80 per cent of the Standish wine is sold at the Rivendell Gardens facility.

RIVENDELL

1993
SEMILLON
SAUVIGNON BLANC

A classic
Margaret River dry white -
fruity, with a fresh clean finish.

750 ml
WILDWOOD ROAD, YALLINGUP
WESTERN AUSTRALIA 6282
PRODUCE OF AUSTRALIA
PRESERVATIVE 220 ADDED   12.5% ALC/VOL.

RIVENDELL

1993
"HONEYSUCKLE"

A late harvest
Margaret River Semillon
with a fruity sweet finish.

750 ml
WILDWOOD ROAD, YALLINGUP
WESTERN AUSTRALIA 6282
PRODUCE OF AUSTRALIA
PRESERVATIVE 220 ADDED   12.5% ALC/VOL.

A CONVERTED abattoir built around 1930 during Group Settlement farming days is the rustic cellar door sales facility for Rosabrook, just five minutes south of Margaret River. Inside is a very different feature indeed from any such centre I have visited around Australia — a cattle crush into which the beasts were put before slaughter.

While such historic memorabilia is certain to interest visitors, it is the wines of Rosabrook that principal Dr John Shepherd, a Perth radiation oncologist, and wife Joan hope will be the ultimate attraction.

John migrated from the UK in 1974 looking to Australia for new opportunities in medicine. A Cambridge graduate, he initially went to Hobart before moving west in 1976 to join a Perth practice. The couple purchased Rosabrook, a 34-hectare part vineyard and part orchard property, as an investment in February 1993. Though John loved wine, he knew little about the industry at the time.

A year later, and he is looking to wines that will be delicate, approachable as youngsters, but with the qualities of sound ageing.

Planting of the property was begun by previous owners in 1980 and extended in 1989. Further expansion plans for 1994 and 1995 aim for a production of 150 tonnes by the year 2000.

A premium range of wines is produced under the Comfort Hill label from the pick of the fruit, mainly from vines growing on the unirrigated, almost pure gravelly soils on the eastern part of the estate. These include a semillon, merlot and shiraz with perhaps a chardonnay in the future. They sell in the $15-$20 range (1994 prices) with wines under the Rosabrook label, $10-$15.

The unwooded semillon is a dry, crisp,

ROSABROOK ESTATE

Rosabrook Road, Margaret River
Cellar door sales: Daily Nov. — April 11 a.m. — 5 p.m. Other times, Fri, Sat, Sun 11 a.m. — 4 p.m. or by appointment

Visitors sampling Rosabrook wines get a taste of history as well when they enter this one-time abattoir, now used for cellar door sales Right: Winemaker Dan Pannell empties a fermenter of merlot into the press

green apple style. With vine maturity, especially on the drier eastern block, it is hoped light tropical fruit characters and herbaceousness will develop. There are problems, however, with fruit ripeness on a wetter part of the property where the vines are heavy yielders. In 1993, for example, this block was picked in early to mid-May in the search for higher sugar levels. At the time it was raining. However, trellising changes providing for greater fruit exposure to sunlight is expected to improve the situation.

Young winemaker Dan Pannell, whose parents Bill and Sandra established Moss Wood at Willyabrup and whose owner, Keith Mugford, consults to Rosabrook, believes merlots will be intense mulberry styles. The shiraz he wants will be a big, soft, full-bodied, long-living wine having distinct sweet berry fruit flavours. It will be enhanced by French oak and should generate attractive pepper and spice characters. 'We will put wines in and out of the Comfort Hill range, depending on quality', he said when preparing for the first wines to be made on the property from the 1994 vintage.

On average, there will be four to six wines under the Rosabrook label with some special cellar door wines to enthuse visitors. Generally, these will be softer, early-drinking wines to be enjoyed with or without food.

SANDALFORD WINES

Metricup Road, Willyabrup
Cellar door sales: Daily, 11 a.m. — 6 p.m.
(For full entry on Sandalford Wines, see
page 60, Swan Valley section)

*Entrance to the estate's Margaret River
vineyard and cellar door sales facility*

SANDSTONE

Corner Caves and Johnson Road,
Willyabrup
Cellar door sales by appointment

L OADED with furniture and other
goods, Mike and Jan Davies had plenty
of time for contemplation back in 1987 as
they rattled across the continent, heading
west in their hire truck. Having left Sydney, the couple were on their way to take
up winemaking duties in the Margaret
River area, as consultants to Cape Clairault,
Willespie and Ribbon Vale.

The harshness of the New South Wales
outback plains through which they passed
made a strong impression — so much so
that later, in more verdant surroundings,
they decided on the unusual name of
Sandstone for their label.

Now they consult to a range of producers, having become an integral part of
the West Australian wine industry. Said
Bernard Abbott of Virage Wines: 'They
have become one of the most influential
factors in the improvement of small
winemaking in Western Australia'.

In addition, they established the
Portavin Group. With fully equipped
mobile plants, Mike and others in the
business travel to wineries to do their

bottling and packaging under the most
hygienic conditions. By 1994 they had five
units operating, two in WA, two in Victoria and one in South Australia, with millions of bottles processed for more than
100 labels.

Mike and Jan met at the Roseworthy
Agricultural College where they were
pursuing Bachelor of Applied Science de-
grees in oenology. Successfully completed,
they followed separate paths, Jan to
Tollana in the Barossa Valley and Mike to
Tyrrells in the Hunter Valley and Chapel
Hill, McLaren Vale. Their next move was
to Coonawarra, to work at Wynns and
Katnook respectively, before travelling to
Bordeaux to work a vintage at the prestig-
ious Chateaux of Bonnet and La Louviere.

Such diverse knowledge gained has
been applied to Sandstone under which
two wines, a semillon and cabernet
sauvignon, are made from purchased
Margaret River fruit.

Sandstone was first introduced in 1988
with early show success when the 1989
semillon won the trophy for best Western

*Principal Mike Davies in front of one of the
mobile bottling units*

Australian dry white wine at the 1990 Perth Show.

Jan says with this variety they look to make a style with ripe fruit vibrancy and weight, elevated by soft oak. They also want sufficient development so that the wine can be enjoyed with Christmas lunch in the year of vintage, yet be capable of improving in the cellar for up to ten years.

As to cabernet, Mike says he seeks the Margaret River berry and earthy flavours with early softness generated by long maceration on skins. 'We want them to be approachable as three-year-old wines and still looking pretty good as ten-year-olds', he said.

The semillons I enjoyed most were from the 1988, 1991 and 1993 vintages, and the cabernets, the 1990 and 1991. This latter wine, rich, full and elegant, demon-strated once more what an outstanding vintage this was for the variety in the area.

Wine buffs should be gratified to learn that Mike has particular concern about cork taint — a problem he says affects the industry round the world. The faulty corks in question give off a distinctive smell which he likens to wet football boots or ballet shoes that have been left in a damp cupboard for a couple of weeks.

'Cork taint is believed to be caused by a reaction between wine and some chlorine based compounds that are used in the cork washing process', he said. 'A lot of research is being done on its formation and how to avoid it. So if you taste a wine with damp footwear syndrome, it is probably cork taint and there is no question that the producer will replace the bottle. I believe the industry average is about five per cent, and rising!'

SERVENTY

Valley Home Vineyard, Rocky Road, Forest Grove
Cellar door sales: Fri — Sun 10 a.m. — 4 p.m.

'Organically grown' and 'rustic environment' are virtually synonymous in the timbered surrounds of Valley Home Vineyard

THE NAME Serventy is synonymous in Australia with care of the environment. So it is no surprise then that Peter and Lyn Serventy do not like any chemicals used on their operation, apart from sulphur. Indeed, they feature on their label the words 'organically grown wines'.

Peter, the son of ornithologist Dominic and nephew of naturalist Vincent, and Lyn decided on a move from Darwin after losing their house to Cyclone Tracey. In 1976 they purchased 50 hectares of land tucked away in the bush 14 kilometres south of Margaret River as the basis for a new venture — and a significant change of lifestyle. For Peter had been involved in tin prospecting and mining, and Lyn in theatre production and education.

Originally, the cattle grazing property in former dense karri country had been opened up under the Group Settlement farm scheme in the early 1920s and called Valley Home. At first they ran sheep but decided then they could produce grapes without using chemicals, encouraged by Leeuwin Estate viticulturist John Brocksopp. They planted 7000 vines, suffering early losses from black beetle. The couple persisted, however, and today after several inspections have been certified level A by the National Association of Sustainable Agriculture of Australia.

Each autumn tonnes of compost from mown farm pasture is spread among the vines, and in winter, seaweed and fish fertilisers. Peter says he makes sulphur the only concession to combat mildew — as used in vineyards over the centuries.

The couple began planting in 1984 with four hectares of shiraz, pinot noir and chardonnay now tended and trickle-irrigated. Wines are made on the property by Frank Kittler who learnt his craft working vintages in the Santa Barbara vineyards of Au Bon Climat and Qupe in California.

The first modest vintage of 100 cases was produced in 1989 with a target of between 3000 and 3500 by the year 2000.

I enjoyed the big 1991 shiraz for its sweet, soft, full fruit and enhancing pepper characters, and was not surprised when the 1992 won the couple their first gold medal, awarded at the 1993 Mount Barker Show in the full-bodied dry red class. This was a significant achievement, given the competition from so many good reds now made in Western Australia.

The first pinot noir release, of cinnamon and strawberries, was the 1992 and judges at the Perth Show considered it good enough for a bronze medal. The chardonnay is barrel-fermented. Picked ripe, it generally shows melon and citrus characteristics with the 1991 having an intense flinty palate.

The couple's confidence in organic viticulture is mounting despite the extra work involved. Lyn says she is developing a feel about the vineyard, using her senses. 'There is a lot of difference between a green, vibrant vine that is healthy and one that is not', she said. The wines sell for about $14-15 (1994 prices) at selected Perth retail outlets. But anyone visiting the Margaret River area would do well to include Valley Home, whether they like the wines or not. It is an attractive rural setting with the Georgian-style two-storey home a feature. It has been a labour of love for Peter, using some excellent recycled material including a sweeping timber staircase from an early building at Princess Margaret Children's Hospital.

TREETON ESTATE

North Treeton Road, Cowaramup
Cellar door sales: Daily, 10 a.m. — 6 p.m.

DAVID McGOWAN flies kites, up to 20 at a time. But this has nothing to do with boyhood passions — it is a counter to birds which frequent the surrounding bush and attack his ripening grapes. 'The kites really work', he said, fixing one to a pole with about five metres of line to demonstrate. 'With gusts of wind they soar into the air and thrust about, frightening away the invaders. It unsettles them, makes them nervous for about two weeks.' In that time, he hopes his fruit will be ready for harvesting and processing.

David is a man-of-the-sea turned wineman. His life has been based on long years of turtle and crayfishing around the West Australian coast, of skippering tugs and seismic survey work as well as teaching seamanship. But so much time aboard bobbing boats, however, generated the desire for firm ground and when an old shipmate telephoned to tell him about the Cowaramup block, he jumped at the chance. The former cattle grazing property of 30 hectares was purchased in 1982 with planting beginning two years later.

Sitting in his unpretentious winery, David recalled a 1972 holiday grape picking trip to France in which his task was to carry the fruit in a basket on his back. When he would bend forward to tip out the contents into a cart, his neck and head would be covered in juice. On standing up, it would trickle down his back. Other workers referred jokingly to him in French as 'the donkey'. 'If that did not turn me off the business, nothing would', he said. Rather, it was to be the beginning, the setting of the vine and wine seed.

First, love of the sea . . . then wine. For David and Corinne McGowan a change of tack has proved challenging

But contact with wine had come much earlier. On the first boat he bought, called the *Carmela*, there were three taps over the sink, one for fresh water, one for salt and one for wine! They were connected to stainless steel tanks with volume indicator meters running as for fuel, when filled by a supplying truck. 'So you paid on the gallonage that went in', David said. 'I soon got used to red wine.'

Back on shore, aged 33, David returned to school and gained an associate diploma in applied science, majoring in recreation, of all things. But once the vines began to grow, life was not so easy for David and his wife Corinne. It involved weekend trips to the property over six to seven years while still teaching and lecturing at Fremantle.

Firstly, ring-barked trees had to be cleared, water provided and a home built. Then twice they thought they had lost the entire planting when gates were left open, presumably by shooters, and neighbouring cows had a real party. On the first occasion they stripped every leaf. The second time damage was more physical, with vines and trellising trampled and pushed over. But somehow the hardy plants survived, as they did on another occasion when city work pressures prevented the couple getting down during a particularly dry spell. 'The leaves were so brown they crumbled in your hand and this was just before Christmas when they should have been at their greenest', David said. Furi-

ous watering, however, just saved the day.

The ultimate vineyard plan is for 10 hectares on the pick of the gravelly loam over clay soils, producing 100 tonnes of fruit.

Located as it is three kilometres east of Bussell Highway, the vineyard could well be regarded by some as on the 'wrong side of the track' and a long way from the high fliers of Willyabrup and elsewhere in the district. But David sees this is an advantage, giving people an alternative with wines of good quality at modest prices. In addition, he says, the area is generally frost-free and there are no problems with salt spray which affects some vineyards closer to the sea.

On our visit, David took pride in the pouring of a concrete pad for a new snack area adjoining the big corrugated-iron shed winery where visitors can sit and sip, and taste a little cheese.

Initial wines were made at Woody Nook, another Margaret River producer, but since 1993 the fruit has been processed on the property where David has been helped by a local consultant. The wines include a chardonnay, semillon and shiraz from the estate, a sweeter style chenin blanc from purchased fruit, and a port. This is based on Swan Valley material with Treeton shiraz added.

Of those tried, the shiraz was my preference. With some pepper and spice it was soft and flavoursome, ideal in my view with pasta.

VASSE FELIX

Cnr Caves and Harmans roads, South,
Cowaramup
Cellar door sales and à la carte restaurant:
Mon — Sun 10 a.m. — 5 p.m.

*Stone and warm timbers set the scene at the
Vasse Felix cellar door*

B EFORE I met Tom Cullity, the pioneer
of the modern day Margaret River
industry, I had often thought of him as a
passionate man of the land. Surely, I would
muse, behind the heart physician exterior
lurked a basic agriculturist, finding at last
his true vocation.

I was wrong. Sitting in his Peppermint
Grove home, he told me he had no practical bent at all, had never changed a car
tyre, could scarcely identify a weed, and
knew nothing about vines or winemaking.
Furthermore, he had not been south of
Bunbury in his life. This, then, was hardly
the picture of a man whose grit was to lead
to hundreds of hectares of vineyard being
established, and some of the finest wines
in the world produced.

Even so, Tom confessed later, he wondered whether it was all worthwhile. 'But at
the time', he said, 'it seemed almost a disgrace
that nobody was actually doing anything to
prove a golden opportunity that would be
the envy of most other countries'.

His original plantings were in fact on
the property of his sister Margaret and
brother-in-law Frank Wilson at Tynedale,
five kilometres east of Roelands. That was
in 1966 and it involved half an acre of
cabernet sauvignon and hermitage.

'I made 30 gallons of wine in 1970, but
in my ignorance, and due to the silvereyes,
I picked the grapes at a Baume reading of
ten', Tom said. (Baume is a measure of the
sugar content of the grapes and closely
approximates the potential alcohol level

of the finished wine. At ten degrees Baume
the grapes could be considered to be un-
ripe.)

Tom then turned his attention further
south, inspired by the work of Dr John
Gladstones who, in an article in the Australian Institute of Agriculture Science
journal of December 1965, highlighted the
soil and climate of the area south of
Busselton as ideal for the production of
high-quality table wines.

So, armed with an auger for digging
holes, Tom began his search for a well-
drained block, with small gravel, growing
'large redgums and little jarrah'. He was
helped by newfound interested friends
such as the Cullens, Minchins, Junipers,
Stan Dilkes, Jim McCutchen and Alec
Hamilton, of the Department of Agriculture. Continued encouragement came
from Bill Jamieson and Jack Mann.

His idea at the time was to buy a small
area, planting less than half a hectare,
convenient to a farmer who would work
with him, accepting payment and performing faithfully. 'This was to be at the
behest of somebody like myself whose only
knowledge was what he had read in books
or been told by "experts"', Tom said. 'It was
idealistic, poorly conceived logistically and
in an area where it was common to see
people with bright ideas founder.'

To complicate matters further, he
looked to people used to grazing cattle
and milking cows rather than being involved in intensive agriculture and so-

Opposite: Senior winemaker Clive Otto

phisticated winemaking.

Finally, Tom bought 3.2 hectares of land at Sussex location 1668, adding other lots later at an average price of $150 per hectare, fenced and under pasture. By 1990s standards it seems a pittance but for the busy physician it meant the start of thousands of kilometres driving at weekends and holidays to establish and attend to his vines and wine, living under difficult conditions in a tin shed. Regularly he left Perth at 3 a.m. on a Saturday to start work on the vineyard at 8 a.m., returning late on Sunday. It truly seemed a labour of love considering the motive behind the first plantings was not commercial, rather just to make the best possible wine.

In August 1967, after site and soil preparation, about 1.6 hectares of rhine riesling, 0.8 hectares of cabernet sauvignon and some malbec and hermitage were planted by Tom with the help of Tony, Joe and Dominic Rossi. The cuttings were from the Department of Agriculture cool store, originating from Swan Valley vines, treated against nematodes but not clonally selected. They were not rooted cuttings, but the strike rate was high, with an estimated 98 per cent success.

Tom said that the methods of nurturing, pruning and fertilising the vines were standard, though all new to him and his team. 'If I had my time again, the trellis would have been different, and possibly I would have irrigated to support the vines in summer drought', he recorded.

Initially, he employed the Junipers and then the Merchants to manage the developing vineyard. The Rossis travelled from Burekup each weekend as the labour force.

The first vintage from four-year-old vines was in 1971, and it was a disaster due to bunch rot and silvereyes. 'I will not forget the exhaustion and disappointment', Tom ruefully said. To cap it all, he had an estimated 300 bottles, half the vintage, stolen from his Perth home cellar.

But it was not all bad news. The wine won a bronze medal in the local small winemakers section at the Perth Show and was the highest point scorer in its class.

I made my first visit to the vineyard soon after, meeting new manager Murray Neave. He was busy putting the finishing touches to a hawk house for a peregrine falcon he hoped to train to protect the vineyard from bird damage by scaring them away. The falcon had other ideas — when released it disappeared into the heavens.

Then came the 1972 Perth Show when the Vasse Felix riesling entry really caused a stir. At its first showing in open classes the wine won a silver medal against tough national competition. It also won a gold and silver medal in the local small winemakers section. Tom told me the wine was treated with bentonite in the fermenter and filtered off its lees. Similar success followed with cabernet the following year, focusing further state and national attention on the potential of the Margaret River area.

The next significant stage in the history of Vasse Felix came with the arrival in March 1973 of a young, broad-shouldered British dairy technologist, David Gregg, and his wife Anne. For years they directed its destiny with tireless effort and enthusiasm, as workers, then leaseholders and eventually, in 1984, as owners.

At the time of their involvement, cabernet made up more than half the 7.3-hectare vineyard, with other varieties including verdelho and traminer. But it was riesling that attracted David Gregg. After tasting the 1972 Cullity wine, he later told me: 'I thought this was something special. It had a fruit intensity and balance I have not seen in many wines since.'

A huge crop in 1980, with average yields of 17 tonnes per hectare, nevertheless had its disappointments. The wines were lacking, especially in comparison to other new developments, leading to the observation that new vineyards produce stunning wine in the first few years, only to fall away. 'I put it down to soil nutrition', David said. 'While we got the yields, the intensity of flavour was lost.'

Three years after they had bought Vasse Felix, the Greggs sold the estate to Heytesbury Holdings Pty Ltd, the private company of Perth magnate Robert Holmes à Court and his wife Janet. Later this group purchased the Great Southern vineyard Forest Hill, at Mount Barker, to be sold in 1994 (see Forest Hill entry) with Vasse Felix retaining long-term fruit supplies.

In 1989 Clive Otto was made senior winemaker at Vasse Felix, a daunting challenge for this was his first industry job. Born in Tanzania where his father was a judge in the Colonial Service, he lived later in several Arab countries and was educated in New Zealand, gaining a degree in horticultural science. This was to be the vehicle for a career in the kiwi fruit industry, but a vintage holiday job at the Matawhero winery at Gisborne led to postgraduate winemaking studies at Roseworthy, and the world of wine.

The Vasse Felix crush in 1994 was a record 420 tonnes. Of this, the estate vineyard produced 50 tonnes and Forest Hill

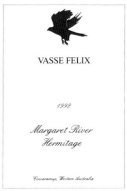

120 tonnes. The rest was purchased from contract growers, like former vineyard manager Alister Gillespie who has a vineyard at Witchcliffe. Other sources include new vineyards in the Pemberton-Manjimup area.

In all, ten wine styles are made with the biggest seller, the classic dry white, a blend of semillon, sauvignon blanc and chardonnay. The wine really took off in 1992 with the award-winning vintage appealing strongly for its fresh tropical fruit flavours, touch of residual sugar and acid balance. Two years later the production was up to 11,000 cases, nearly half the winery's total output

For me, however, cabernet and hermitage have been the classics of Vasse Felix.

Over the years the cabernets have been elegant, finely extracted sweet fruit wines with lighter than usual tannins, soft and silky styles and reasonably early drinking. Clive says a five to eight per cent dash of malbec (depending on the year) adds cherry and rose petal flavours to the mulberry, chocolate and blackcurrant of the cabernet, and makes the tannins more subtle. 'We will be looking to make it a bigger bodied style', Clive says. 'Still soft, but fuller. This is what people expect from a $25 bottle of wine. This will come from extended maceration and increasing the temperature of the ferment.'

The 1988 Vasse Felix hermitage, a major award winner, has been one of the great wines to be made in Margaret River. The richness of fruit on the palate enhanced by new American oak will see it remain memorable. Generally, the style (called shiraz in 1994) is soft and round, more spicy than peppery.

Another favourite from the winery is the noble riesling from Forest Hill fruit and only made in years of botrytis infection. Made first in 1990 and picked very ripe, it is a luscious dessert style with excellent natural acid and loads of attractive apricot characters.

The winery's extra brut sparkling wine sees the fruit sourced from Pemberton-Manjimup, though initially it came from Margaret River pinot. As well, whole bunches are used instead of machine-picked fruit.

This is an unusual bubbly for it contains a dash of vintages going back years, in a Gregg-evolved solero system with the blending each year of half the previous base wine vintage with the fermenting new crop, in the search for complexity and consistency. Pinot (mainly) and chardonnay are fermented together, with moderate extraction and three years on lees. Light salmon pink in colour, some say partridge eye, it is a full yeast-influenced wine, dry and firm and unliqueured after disgorgement. It can be bought by the glass in the delightful development built at the rear of the winery from local stone with some wooden beams from the old Busselton jetty.

Visitors enjoy commanding views across the vineyard from the winery's first floor location. No doubt many sip the sparkling wine slowly, for it costs $6 a glass (1994 prices), though this also includes a plate of hors d'oeuvres.

Generally of melon and green peach, it is enhanced by a combination of new French and American oak.

Exports take about five to ten per cent of production and include red and white blends that are served at half time in the chain of UK theatres owned by Heytesbury.

A high point for Vasse Felix was the best exhibitor award at the 1993 Sheraton awards, thanks to outstanding results for the 1990 cabernet, 1992 hermitage and 1990 noble riesling. This latter wine was also runner up in the Sydney International Winemakers Exhibition.

Developments in 1994 provide for further vineyard plantings to a total of 20 hectares, the capacity of the winery property.

VIRAGE WINES

Bussell Highway via Cowaramup
Cellar door sales: By appointment

*Virage principals Pascale and Bernard
Abbott amid their vines*

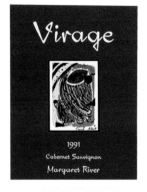

1993
Cabernet Shiraz
Zinfandel
Margaret River

1993
Semillon Sauvignon Blanc
Margaret River

1993
Figaro
Margaret River

A SOUTH Australian and a French-woman who met in California are the principals of South West producer Virage Wines. Bernard and Pascale Abbott lease the vineyard on the former Bramley Department of Agriculture research station six kilometres north of Margaret River and east of Bussell Highway.

The son of wheat and sheep farming parents from Farrell Flat, Bernard can claim a close geographic location with wine in his upbringing. For the Farrell Flat property is just 12 kilometres east of the Clare Valley, one of South Australia's fine wine producing areas.

But it was economics that he first studied, in Adelaide. Playing football with Stanley Leasingham winemaker Chris Proud, however, led to an invitation to work a vintage. It ended up being three before Bernard turned to fishing, poling tuna out of Port Lincoln. Europe then beckoned and for four years he wandered the great capitals and their countries, fitting work for two vintages in Germany's famous Rhinegau.

Back in Australia, the vintage trail continued with another season at Stanley and then one in California's Napa Valley. By this time Bernard was certain about winemaking and enrolled in the Roseworthy Agricultural College's oenology course, graduating in 1986. Work in the industry during this period led to appointment as winemaker at Vasse Felix in 1987 and the couple, by this time married, decided they wanted to settle in Margaret River. After three years they took up the research station lease for six years, with an option, planting a further two hectares to the 2.5 hectares previously established.

There are eight main varieties now flourishing at Bramley with four wines made. They are the flagship cabernet sauvignon, with additions of merlot, the dearest at $15 (1994 prices), a semillon-sauvignon blanc blend, a cabernet-shiraz-zinfandel, and Figaro, named because it represents the marriage of so many wines, the cheapest at $10.

The first commercial vintage realised 15 tonnes. By 1996 some 40 tonnes is expected. With the cabernets Bernard is looking for a style of elegance — fine tannins and good length. Early, the wine, with about 25 per cent new oak, shows more cassis and then mint with bottle development. The full and flavoursome 1991 vintage, with its spicy berry fruit and excellent vanilla-like oak, certainly reflected his aims and was twice named wine of the month by different Perth liquor retailers. The semillon-sauvignon is a 50-50 blend with a small amount of barrel fermentation for a dash of early complexity. A fruit-driven wine, it is crisp and dry with a touch of grassiness and gooseberry.

Cabernet also dominates the soft red blend which includes shiraz and zinfandel. It is picked a bit earlier than full ripeness, when Bernard says it generates lighter cherry-like flavours. For extra colour and body on the mid-palate, the shiraz and zinfandel are picked very ripe, adding spice and cracked pepper flavours as well.

Figaro is a slightly sweet, aromatic 'tutti frutti' blend of four white varieties. Clean and fresh, it has been given some nutty character from time on lees. It has proved ideal for people who do not like dry wines.

The Abbotts buy in fruit as needed and do their own marketing, which requires constant trips to Perth and the Eastern States by Pascale. She has also designed the brightly coloured labels.

'And the origins of the name?' I asked Bernard. 'It is used on road signs in France to indicate turn or bend and that is what we are doing, turning grapes into wine', he replied.

VOYAGER ESTATE

Stevens Road, Margaret River
Cellar door sales: Early 1996

*Overtones of Stellenbosch . . . the distinctive
Cape Dutch architecture looks equally at
home at Margaret River*

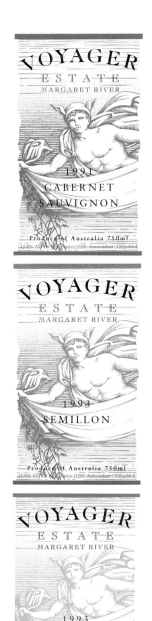

IN THE cool, green environment of Margaret River it is difficult to imagine a link with the harsh, red West Australian outback. But at Voyager Estate, it exists through principal Michael Wright, son of Peter who was a partner with Lang Hancock in major North West mining discoveries.

Formerly Freycinet, established by Peter and Jennifer Gherardi, it has been transformed since the purchase in 1991. The old cellar door sales area has been converted to guest bedrooms, the vineyard improved and expanded, and a major Cape Dutch facility constructed to provide for winemaking and storage, and visitors and functions, well into the next century.

I asked Michael why he opted for such a style, so much in contrast to others, especially those of rustic construction. 'I wanted something different', he explained. 'Something to stand out, that people would always remember.'

Michael Wright has long been impressed by such buildings in South Africa, their gracious elegance dignified in the midst of manicured garden surrounds. And he argues it fits well into the Australian bush. 'It is something that will not date, fits into the atmosphere, suits the purpose and is designed for people.'

Retaining early explorer Louis de Freycinet's name was fraught with difficulty. A legal challenge over its use had come from Spanish wine interests and there was confusion with Freycinet Wines of Tasmania, a small producer on the east

coast of the island. So Voyager was born, taken from the name of the Wright family farm.

But Freycinet has not been forgotten. In drawing his maps the Frenchman used many Australian features, including a garland of flowers he developed as a cartouche. This has been adopted by Voyager as its trademark and logo and it tops a giant entrance gate which leads up to the new cellar door centre.

A great deal of money has been invested in the rebirth of Voyager, though Michael Wright will not say how much. But he insists it is a commercial venture, with the first profits projected for 1997-98 and a comfortable return on investment by the year 2005.

By the end of 1994 Voyager will have 26 hectares planted on soils which vary from gravelly to loam. All are trickle-irrigated. The main varieties include cabernet sauvignon, chardonnay, chenin blanc, semillon and sauvignon blanc. To help the young vines become established, 7000 trees were planted as a wind break. By 1998 a crush of 300 tonnes a year is expected.

The grapes provide for five main styles, including a chardonnay, made as complex as possible. Barrel-fermented with lees stirring every fortnight for a year, it is generally a nutty, buttery wine of considerable life, perhaps up to ten years.

In the varietal semillon, a wine for the more serious consumers, the variety's fresh, grassy characters are given a lift and

Visitors to Voyager Estate sample fine wines in the peaceful atmosphere of the elegant winery, the stark whiteness flattered by frequent blue skies

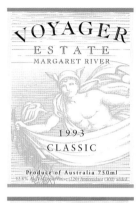

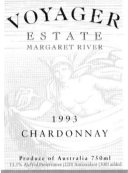

palate length with the addition of ten per cent sauvignon blanc. In addition, a third is barrel-fermented to add softness, complexity and roundness for another wine with good cellaring potential. The Classic, however, an unwooded, fruit-driven blend of semillon (65 per cent) and sauvignon blanc (35 per cent) is more approachable as a youngster, given its touch of residual sugar.

The biggest-selling Voyager white is the unheralded, uncomplicated chenin blanc, made for immediate drinking. A slightly sweet, soft, fruit salad wine, it finishes clean and fresh as a result of good balancing acid.

My preference, however, has been the cabernet, enhanced by the addition of 15 per cent merlot and five per cent of the aromatic cabernet franc. An elegant wine of complexity and structure, with 21 months oak ageing, its berry characters have been a delight.

Curiously, Michael Wright may never know the flavours of his own wine, as a drinker anyway. He is a teetotaller. 'It is nothing moralistic', he said. 'I just do not like the taste of alcohol.'

But he is comfortable in his new venture, speaking readily of blending wines, grape varieties, retrellising, new plant and equipment as if he had been in the business all his life. But then agriculture has been a core part of the family since the arrival in Victoria of pioneering settler Frederick Thomas Wright from Scotland in 1858. When he died 27 years later, the family moved to Western Australia where greater opportunities were seen.

WILDWOOD

Caves Road, Yallingup
Cellar door sales: Daily from 9 a.m.
Restaurant facilities and accommodation available

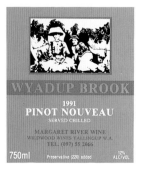

OVER THE years the Margaret River wine industry has attracted people from vastly different backgrounds. Initially, it was men of medicine who set out to prove the new region could match the best wines of the world, serious thought-provoking styles to stand the test of time.

In subsequent waves, others have had different ideas. Geoff Eastough, for example, a flamboyant, often controversial and brash up-front individual, has a different approach. As a result, he quickly found himself in conflict with the more conservative elements of the industry. Even now, there are mutterings about his temerity in bringing in wine from South Australia to sell, a consignment of one pallet of 1988 Clare Valley semillon. His aim was to dispute criticism that Margaret River wines of similar quality were much more expensive, and to supplement his

own stocks while his vineyard was in the development stages. In the early days he also purchased fruit for winemaking from the pioneering Forest Hill vineyard at Mount Barker.

I had come to know him well, in another arena, reporting for *The West Australian* on his activities when he was prominent in the fiercely competitive meat wholesaling and export business. As a result I knew he would not be phased by pressure, even if isolated by the rest of the industry. Indeed, Geoff argues strongly that his approach to wine will benefit all producers in the future. Included in the Wildwood range are a number of fun wines that he believes will be the vehicle to transport enthusiasts of today to serious wines tomorrow. 'That is what happened in the 1950s and 1960s with wines like Barossa Pearl, Barossa Rosé and Woodley's Est', he said.

Geoff and wife Lyn moved to Yallingup following the 1978 purchase of their 70-hectare property, fattening sheep for five years for live export. Combined with summer surfing, the initial aim was semi-retirement but Geoff realised the opportunities opening up in the wine industry. Initial experience was gained by working at Pierro and then contracting at a number of vineyards. An experimental two-hectare Wildwood planting was made in 1980 with the main vineyard begun in 1985. The 1994 crush of 30 tonnes was expected to reach 120 tonnes by the year 2000 with subsequent areas coming to maturity.

Varieties include chenin blanc, semillon, chardonnay, pinot noir, cabernet sauvignon, merlot and cabernet franc — flourishing on protected valley slopes that result in ripening much earlier than many others in the district. This leads to a problem, however, as birds damage the grapes because they mature before their main food source, the flowering of native trees.

The wines are made at Redgate, ten in all. Among them are Honeydew, a sweet white style made from chenin blanc and semillon, Cabaret cabernet, a light red style served chilled, and Wild Roses, a slightly sweet white wine made from red grapes. Generally, Wildwood wines are made to be soft, flavoursome, early drinking styles that appeal to the many younger visitors to the estate. 'To me, wine is fun', said Geoff.

But those who like to sniff and consider have not been ignored. Included are an unwooded herbaceous semillon, a big, ripe (1993) unwooded chardonnay — higher in alcohol than normally aimed for — a chenin blanc, pinot noir and a full-bodied cabernet sauvignon. Of the range tasted, my preference was the 1991 pinot noir, slightly spicy with hints of cherry, soft and round with good oak integration. In the long term, though, Geoff believes cabernets will be the vineyard red strength.

The wines are marketed under the Wyadup Brook label taken from a local feature, and all are sold direct, including through a family-run restaurant in Busselton. Geoff says marketing is his strength, with wines made for people, not judges. As well, Wildwood aims to service visitors. Given the location and the tremendous attraction of the South West, there will never be any shortage of potential customers.

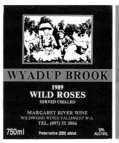 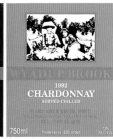 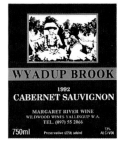

IT IS HARD to imagine a happier and broader smile than that on the face of Margaret River producer Kevin Squance at the 1989 Sheraton Perth annual wine awards. For at the event his 1987 Willespie cabernet sauvignon struck gold in the full-bodied dry red class. It was a significant moment in the short history of a winery whose name (adapted in part from the French *espérer*) means the hope of Willyabrup.

But while the award was a great thrill, it came as no real surprise to the former schoolteacher, principal of the property with wife Marian (also a teacher). For, he says, the cabernet grows on a 'happy block' in the vineyard, surrounded by protective bush so that the strong winds do not penetrate as they do elsewhere. At the same time the cooling southerly winds keep temperatures down in summer, and the vines face east, basking in the morning sun. The result — wines with strong cassis-like flavours, often distinctive in a line-up.

Though Marian had always enjoyed wine, Kevin's story goes back to a 1962 visit to the Barossa Valley which fired his enthusiasm, for there had been no family involvement of any kind in the industry. His grandfathers were colourful characters from Collie — one a bookie and the other a staunch miner unionist in the town, and as Kevin points out, that's pretty distant from the grape.

The couple eventually bought 40 hectares of land in 1976, some 24 kilometres from Margaret River, and set about planting the following year, inspired by the success of Dr Bill Pannell at Moss Wood. The varieties they chose initially included verdelho, semillon, rhine riesling and cabernet sauvignon. In 1989 merlot and sauvignon blanc were added to make 12 hectares in all, producing 80 tonnes in 1994.

The soil varies from gravelly (where the cabernet grows) to mostly loam, mixed with small, shotgun pellet-sized gravel with a clay base, which sees it hold its moisture.

'We have a permanent water level of about four metres at the base of the block so that we could pump water till the cows come home', Kevin said. 'But I can see no reason to irrigate with the natural moisture.' Certainly, the growth of the vines indicates a healthy vineyard, the sauvignon blanc reaching some four metres in height in 1994, well above the two-metre-plus trellis which includes a jarrah extension and movable wires.

Such construction has allowed for im-

WILLESPIE

Harmans Mill Road, Willyabrup
Cellar door sales: Daily 10 a.m. — 5 p.m.
Light food bar. Catering for groups by appointment

For Kevin and Marian Squance, the path from teaching to successful winemaking has offered constant challenge

proved sunlight penetration despite the growth, to give more fruit character in the wines.

A tasting of the trophy-winning 1993 vintage, for example, proved the point. Its clean, fresh, delicious grassy and tropical fruit flavours were opulent but refined and beautifully balanced. For me the style began to emerge with the 1991 vintage and has continued to impress since. The fruit also contributed to the excellent 1993 semillon-sauvignon blanc blend, a delightful wine with seafood. Just 13 days after bottling, it won the Sheraton silver trophy for its class, narrowly missing out on gold.

Such wines challenge the Willespie verdelho, initially regarded as the white wine flagship following the first commercial vintage in 1982. A big style but with good balance, the wine shows tropical fruit flavours early. After about three years, however, it develops complexity, becomes fuller and rounder, more like a chardonnay.

Vineyard maturity has seen a moderation of the semillon's grassy and herbaceous characters, and the wine is given a kiss of wood. The balance must have struck the right note, for it won a silver medal at a wine summit in Atlanta, Georgia, in 1993 along with the 1990 cabernet. Such results boosted Willespie export plans which are based on a 25 per cent of production target.

The rhine rieslings generally are slightly higher in alcohol than those of the Great Southern, with broader palates. Given time, however, they have the quality to age gracefully. So do the cabernets. Kevin believes the 1987 vintage, for example, will be at its best in the year 2000. I enjoyed the 1990 vintage for its overall structure and fruit quality and was not surprised it was in the final line-up of a major tasting of outstanding export wines.

A series of winemakers have been involved at Willespie — David Hohnen, Erland Happ, Mike and Jan Davies, John Smith and Kevin Squance himself. In 1991 Mike Lemmes joined Willespie and was appointed winemaker two years later, producing the additional Harmans Mill range. Designed to sell at $10 or just under (1994 prices), it includes a medium dry white made from verdelho, rhine riesling and semillon, and an unwooded, soft, early drinking red from cabernet.

The name is taken from the road on which Willespie has been established, in turn from a timber mill opposite, long since gone. The Willespie vineyard was once the mill's horse paddock.

Kevin has enjoyed the industry challenge, though admitting to initial naivety about the money needed to set up such a venture. 'Every dollar has gone into the place', he said. 'I did not realise that equipment would cost an arm and a leg.'

He considers strong winds at flowering times to be Margaret River's curse, with some extensive damage resulting. Of the birds, it is the little red wattle bird that does the mischief at Willespie. 'They are an aggressive bird and will ignore you even when you have a shotgun in your hands', says Kevin. 'They fly out of the vineyard with beaks full of berries, and when they finish their pecking, the bees move in. In 1988 I could have cried at the damage; you work all year, and then that happens.'

Once a young vineyard worker had the task of riding an old motor cycle up and down the rows, revving the machine and making it backfire to try to frighten the feeders away.

Despite setbacks, the many successes have made Kevin glad he made the career change, though he and Marian are grateful to teaching for providing the income that made it all possible.

But he could have been excused for having had second thoughts a few days after the 1989 Sheraton triumph. While working in the vineyard he cut off a large part of his right thumb with pneumatic secateurs. Hasty surgery reduced the damage which has not, says Marian, affected his golden touch.

WISE WINES

Eagle Bay Road, Cape Naturaliste Peninsula
Cellar door sales: daily 11 a.m. — 5 p.m.
(summer); Wed — Sun (winter); à la carte
restaurant lunch and snacks; dinners
Friday and Saturday evenings; chalet
accommodation

*With a view like this, and top-class wines
from Ron Wise's estates, visitors to the
restaurant could be excused for lingering on*

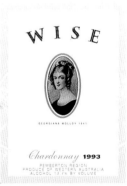

F ROM THE lofty restaurant and tasting area at Wise Wines, visitors can sometimes watch whales at play while they enjoy a sauvignon blanc. And the beautiful vistas over Geographe Bay are matched in other directions by the peaceful West Australian bush — a vineyard setting that Perth businessman Ron Wise and wife Sandra believe must be the most beautiful in the State.

Established in the Meelup Valley as Geographe Estate, the estate was purchased in 1992. Later the couple added further vineyard interests by buying adjoining Eagle Bay estate and then, as part of a syndicate with Californian lawyer Graham Taylor and local investor Gerry Lawrance, added Newlands at Donnybrook to their interests.

But the Wise way to wine was unconventional, to say the least. A science graduate from the University of Western Australia, Ron later completed a PhD in biochemistry to undertake four years research at the Florida and Stanford universities, before returning home to lecture for two years at the medical school. But business beckoned and in the early 1970s he ventured into stock exchange investment and real estate.

All along his interest in wine was growing, from the student days of cheap basic wine to browsing through cellars, seeking out old wines, like Penfolds Grange for $6.10 a bottle!

The initial foray into the industry was a small planting of chardonnay amid bracken and wild blackberries on a four-hectare property at Willyabrup, later sold. At least, he learnt, it was not just a question of putting sticks in the ground, and was able to call on old university mate and industry stalwart Dorham Mann to help him when he ultimately made his major investments.

Geographe and Eagle Bay have 12 hectares of vines and Newlands a further ten. In addition, pinot noir and chardonnay are bought from Pemberton's Phoenicia vineyard, for a total annual projected production of about 100,000 bottles from all areas.

Wine styles include a sauvignon blanc, a sauvignon blanc-semillon blend, a wooded and unwooded chardonnay (the latter identified by the word *aquercus* on the label, Latin for no oak), a light soft red and a cabernet, with merlot, pinot noir and shiraz in the future. 'We will be putting an emphasis on cabernet sauvignon-merlot as our flagship red', Ron said. 'I like it for its fruit intensity, its softness and drinkability, and because it is a bit different.'

The various vineyard strengths have been rated as sauvignon blanc and semillon at the peninsula properties, cabernet, cabernet franc and merlot at Newlands, and chardonnay and pinot noir from Pemberton, though it will be some years before all wine styles will be resolved.

Ron Wise contemplates the ultimate target — 100,000 bottles a year

The peninsula white blend has plenty of flavour from ripe fruit in the Mann mould, and a soft, refined finish. But it was the reds I enjoyed most, especially the silky merlot with its rich, full berry flavours while the cabernet and shiraz barrel samples were not far behind. As I sipped and reflected with pleasure at the satisfying mouth feel, I recalled Dorham's comment: 'You have to grow flavour'. He was excited about the prospects of producing wines from the three different areas, each distinctly different, affected by location and climate. Of the peninsula area, he noted the extent of cooling breezes coming across water, unless they were southerlies, and these were inherently cool anyway.

Ron Wise says his vineyard investments are not a commodity for trading, like other interests he has. 'This has got me in', he admitted. 'I am not a patient man, but wine is teaching me to be so.'

A late harvest classic white blend provides for the sweeter palates while the vines themselves at the peninsula gain from the Meelup spring, a supply of fresh water at the top of the valley hillside. A gravity-fed resource, the water is also used for drinking, as it was by American whalers last century.

Other less welcome visitors include

silvereyes and kangaroos. In 1993 the hopping marsupial got all the white fruit, two hectares in all. Now an electric fence guards the grapes.

The Wise label carries the picture of pioneer Georgiana Molloy, who lauded the beauty of the area when referring to 'nature's choicest flowers and fruit, the land of all others for vines . . .'

WOODLANDS

Caves Road, Willyabrup
Cellar door sales: Weekends by appointment

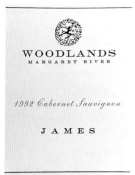

THERE WAS a time in David Watson's life when milk and beef were four letter words of the worst kind. I hasten to say that I have never heard David swear, but imagine how he felt when told wandering cows had broken through fences to feast on his newly planted Margaret River vineyard. 'They stripped everything and pulled out the young vines by wrapping their tongues around the plants', he said ruefully. 'There was not a leaf left.'

The incident set back the vineyard development but not the aspirations of David, a Perth consulting engineer, and his wife Heather, a lawyer, from establishing their venture, named Woodlands. This determination was sparked initially by Jack Mann and then, of all things, a broken nose.

The Mann connection came about when the Watson family moved from Greenmount to Redcliffe. Through new neighbours Len and Bebe Ives they met the Mann family socially, and David as a teenager was introduced to Houghton chablis and iced water. This was to lead to an invitation to see how this wine, and others, were made, the start of many such

visits in the search for knowledge of the industry. It was during one that Jack explained the addition of white acorn tannin from Switzerland to the famous white burgundy, to give the ripe grapes more backbone. Then came another surprise, when Jack offered David a bottle to take home to his father. When asked for his best, Jack produced a bottle of verdelho.

It was an amateur football match in which David suffered the nose injury. Taken to Royal Perth Hospital, he met Dr Bill Pannell, pioneer of Moss Wood, who became a valuable ally in establishing Woodlands on similar red-brown loamy country, over gravel and clay, a few hundred metres closer to the coast. The Watsons had bought the eight-hectare property for $5000 following a Busselton holiday, having seen a 'for sale' notice in a real estate office on the last morning of their visit. An unusual condition was that the owner's mother had to approve of the purchaser.

Then came the pick and shovel days, for they had no tractor. In preparing for their vineyard, David and Heather dug out the roots of 13 big trees which had

Woodlands' awards that reflect the stature of its Cabernet Sauvignon include best small vineyard (dry red), National Wine Show in Canberra, 1982; TAA gold medal trophy for best dry red, 1983 Mount Barker Wine Show; and best West Australian dry red, 1982 Perth Wine Show

been bulldozed. By 1994 they estimated that weekend and other trips to work their vineyard involved the equivalent of driving round the equator seven times.

Planting began in August 1974 with cabernet cuttings from Moss Wood. These were rooted in a nursery made available on the Pannell property. Cabernet today makes up more than half the vineyard with other varieties including malbec, merlot, cabernet franc and pinot noir. Chardonnay was planted in 1986, surprising some in the industry for David has been very much a red wine fanatic.

The first vintage, a modest 50 litres, was produced in 1978 from what the birds had left behind. David recalls he and Heather using scissors to clip off unpecked berries and his feet to tread the fruit with the must coming up to his ankles. 'It was a ceremonial stomp for us', he said. 'The wine had a lot of body!' Subsequently, he used more modern technology with experience at Vasse Felix for two vintages.

A small winery was built in 1979, and the first real crop of 2250 litres came in 1981. The following year Woodlands' cabernet created a sensation, winning the best West Australian dry red at the Perth Show, two trophies at Mount Barker and then the trophy for the best small vineyard dry red in Canberra.

Yet it had special challenges. Heather was pregnant at the time, giving David a real test of loyalty — his first significant crop, and a baby due. 'I was uptight, I can tell you', he said.

He was at the vineyard with the wine fermenting when Heather called to say she had to go into hospital. David rushed back to Perth for the birth of son Andrew, leaving instructions for a young neighbour to look after things. Fittingly, the wine was named Andrew, part of a policy of using family members to mark vintages.

I recall it well, a huge wine, big in everything, with 12 months in new French barriques. David remembered opening a bottle the night before the show, and becoming extremely depressed. 'I thought it was awful', he said. 'It was acid, tannic and tarry, and I felt I could not show my face at the show. I went to work and sulked.' Then Anne Gregg telephoned and urged him to get down to the Claremont Showgrounds as quickly as possible, for the wine had scored a gold medal with points indicating it might win a trophy. Heather also rushed to the show, but became frustrated when she got stuck behind a Rolls Royce which appeared to be heading in the same direction. It was the Governor, who a few minutes later presented them with their first-ever trophy, at their first-ever showing of a wine, a fairytale indeed. 'People raved about it, calling it an international wine and state-of-the-art for Australian red winemaking', David said with great pride. 'We sold the lot to a Sydney wholesaler. It saved our bacon. Had that not happened, we might have had to sell the place.'

The 1982 vintage followed part of the way by winning a gold medal in Perth in 1983, scoring 19 points out of 20 along with two others. But it missed out on the trophy.

However, it was judged the best

cabernet and best dry red at Mount Barker and won gold in Canberra. The medal was only one of four awarded in the open classes where the wine had been entered because the small winemakers' section had been dropped. It narrowly missed winning the trophy.

It was totally different in style, a lighter, more elegant wine from fruit that was not as ripe. Since 1980 the Watsons' cabernets have included five to 20 per cent of malbec in the blend, adding spiciness to the mid-palate in a plan for the wines to take five to six years to reach their peak, maintaining it for several years.

But family and business pressures saw the Watsons enter into an arrangement with Capel Vale to take the first ten tonnes of fruit in the late 1980s. The first year, however, proved disastrous when only 5.3 tonnes of the expected 15-tonne crop was picked from the vineyard. The disappointing result was due to two hailstorms during flowering and, ironically, drought conditions which meant the berries did not fill out as required. 'Selling fruit generates an earlier cash flow and allows us more time to concentrate on the wines we wanted to make', David said. 'It also helped fund expanded plantings.'

Further hail storms decimated crop hopes in 1992 and 1993, but the Watsons persisted, making their first chardonnay in 1990, the mouth-filling, lightly oaked wine extending the range, while an unwooded ripe-style sauvignon blanc, first made in 1993 and given a dash of verdelho for extra tropical fruit lift, has provided valuable cash flow. Its stablemate is a soft, flavoursome pinot, one of five wines in a marketing strategy aimed at year-round sales, as opposed to the tenuous economic tight-rope of dependence on full-bodied reds. To accommodate the changes, five further hectares are to be planted and a 100-tonne capacity winery established, with trellising modifications and vineyard improvements to lift the low-yielding vine production.

A cabernet-merlot early release restaurant wine is a pleasant, soft style with plenty of refined berry characters, ideal with pasta or lamb. But my preference of the wines has always been the flagship cabernet. Given the pick of the fruit and the attention, the wine is once again of the bigger style of earlier days, though more streamlined, more refined, after a period of lighter vintages.

In the battle against birds which abound in the surrounding attractive native bushland, nets are used. A more substantial barrier, an electric fence, confronts the sweet-toothed kangaroos.

WOODY NOOK

Metricup Road, Metricup
Cellar door sales: Daily 10 a.m. — 4 p.m.
Restaurant facilities available for lunches

HALFWAY between the Bussell Highway and Caves Road, tucked among the trees, is the aptly named Woody Nook, another of the small-scale developments in the Margaret River district. It is owned and run by the Gallagher family — Jeff and his wife Wynn, their son Neil, and his wife Linda — who with limited resources have had the task of gaining recognition against the better-known pacesetters of the area.

Certainly a crystal rose bowl holding pride of place on the cellar door bar has done much to symbolise that.

This was the trophy for the best West Australian dry red at the 1991 Perth Wine Show — won with the 1990 vintage — a memorable achievement indeed considering the high quality of such wines now produced in the State. It was especially pleasing for Neil as it was his first solo effort as a winemaker. 'I have told people the bowl is definitely not for sale and to my knowledge, never will be', said Linda.

Other quality cabernets produced by Woody Nook were the 1991 and 1992 vintages, both medal winners with the latter rated top of the cabernet classes in a 1994 national small vignerons award judging.

Originally from Perth, and the floor-covering business, the Gallaghers purchased the 24-hectare property in 1978. The first planting occurred in 1984, and the vineyard now is of six hectares comprising semillon, sauvignon blanc, chenin blanc, cabernet sauvignon and merlot. The first crush was in 1987 with the annual production about 40 tonnes, more than enough to supply their small restaurant which is part of the cellar door sales and winery complex.

The Woody Nook philosophy is simple — clean, crisp, fruity white wines and softer, early drinking red styles with sound cellaring potential for the full-bodied cabernet based on ripe fruit.

Wines made vary and depend on consumer demands. But a lot depends on how much fruit the birds leave for winemaking. In 1989, for example, they feasted on about half the crop, swooping in from the surrounding bush, once home to sleeper cutters. Hand-cut tree stumps on the property tell the story of the past,

Linda and Neil Gallagher with a sample of that clean, crisp, fruity Woody Nook white

while an old sawmill operated by the original owner provided timber for his cottage, taken from trees on the block.

The Woody Nook winery was built in 1989. Neil has learnt viticulture and winemaking in a 'hands-on' manner as the project has developed.

For something different the Gallaghers bought in a full-bodied fortified wine produced from shiraz. Called Nooky Delight, visitors can have it served in the family's Nookery restaurant.

WHEN Margaret River wine producers complain about attacks by birds, they should spare a thought for Cowaramup couple Henry and Maureen Wright. Far from just trying to preserve their grapes, they were busy trying to protect their lives from Somali guerillas in Africa before the call of a new home brought them to Western Australia.

All of that was more than a quarter of a century ago, when Henry was a District Commissioner in the British Colonial Service, operating in the remote and barren border country of northern Kenya. Guerillas from neighbouring Somalia were at the time extremely active in the fight for secession of some disputed territory, and attacks built up against British outposts.

'In the last house we had, on the Tana River, we used to sleep on the roof because of the heat', Henry recalled. 'As a warning, on the outside stairs we would put four beer bottles tied with string on each step, with four armed guards sleeping at the bottom.' On the roof Henry was equipped with a submachine gun, point 303 rifle and a hand gun, and when an

attack did come with bullets thudding into the walls Maureen, a former air hostess, remembered her legs shaking so much she could hardly get out of bed.

The couple, who had met in Nairobi, decided they did not want to settle in England or in Maureen's native South Africa, so they chose Western Australia. They knew nobody when they arrived by ship in 1964; their only contact was local radio personality John Harper Nelson who met them at Fremantle.

Henry's first job was as a farm manager at Katanning, and that's when the 'dishwasher money' came into play. In Kenya Maureen had saved £200 specifically to buy a dishwasher when they arrived in Australia. Henry suggested instead she should buy a property they saw advertised in Dwellingup for that same amount. The Dwellingup block, however, fell by the wayside, and so did the dishwasher for as a result of their inquiries they were told of other properties, eventually purchasing a pig farm at Cowaramup.

Later they bought their present 14-hectare property on Willyabrup Brook

WRIGHTS

Harmans Road South, Cowaramup
Cellar door sales: Daily 10 a.m. — 4.30 p.m.

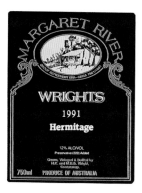

Self-taught producers Henry and Maureen Wright in their vineyard

opposite Vasse Felix, and turned to wine. 'We liked the idea very much', Maureen said. 'It was very exciting and other agriculture in the district was a bit flat at the time.'

The couple began planting in 1973 with 10.5 hectares now under vines made up of rhine riesling, cabernet sauvignon, hermitage, semillon and chardonnay.

Six years later the first commercial wines were produced under the Wrights label, with Maureen quitting a job at a dental clinic in Busselton to look after quality control and cellar door sales. Later she went on to complete a marketing

Besides the dry red, the Wrights also make a vintage port from the hermitage, and a white wine.

A measure of the quality quickly reached by the couple was shown in the selection of the 1980 and '82 hermitages for an International Wine and Food Society dinner in Sydney, along with the 1981 cabernet. It was a stunning achievement for the Wrights because they had submitted only the three wines for consideration, and the competition for selection was fierce. Another triumph was at the 1986 SGIO Winemakers Exhibition when the 1984 hermitage won the award for the best

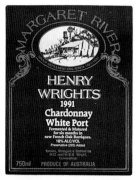

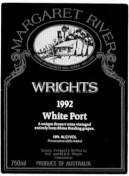

course with the Roseworthy Agricultural College.

The couple are self-taught producers and have achieved a great deal in their relatively short history, even though at times it has been a struggle for recognition against some of the district 'big guns'.

Depending on the season the Wrights crush 50 to 70 tonnes a year and make a range of wines that has appealed to a constant flow of visitors, estimated at 150,000 in the decade of the 1980s.

For me the early reds were memorable, such as the excellent full-bodied first vintage 1980 cabernet, and the 1980 and 1982 hermitage — full, soft, round wines of such palate pleasantness one could only wonder why more Margaret River producers did not embrace the variety, rather than shunning it. Some people have even suggested the Wrights were lowering the tone of the district by growing the variety!

The 1991 vintage also impressed for its fruit qualities and balance, as did the cabernet of that year.

full-bodied dry red from Margaret River.

Originally, a rhine riesling was made by the couple, with fermentation on lees in a bid to get more body into the wine. Production ceased, however, in 1986 for the fruit was needed for the amazingly successful white port, easily their best seller today. It is a style that will never be described as classic, but it is sweet and different, and loved by an enthusiastic band of supporters.

In 1982 it began as a fun wine, but it has become an important part of the Wrights' range. 'We have had a Melbourne restaurant seek exclusive rights for the wine and letters from overseas about supplies', Henry said.

With such success, it is no surprise then that another fortified innovation, Henry Wright white port made from chardonnay, has been introduced. First made in 1990, it is given six months' oak ageing with a similar level of sweetness to the riesling style.

An unusual blend of rhine riesling and

semillon (30-70) is the basis of Premium Estate. The aromatic riesling is more evident on the bouquet and the herbaceousness of the semillon on the palate. Henry believes the respective fruit qualities of the varieties and the high acid of the riesling with the low acid of the semillon, make the blend an ideal combination.

The couple have used nets to protect the chardonnay and semillon from bird damage. They have invested gradually in the business over the years, improving the winery and cellar door sales area, where about half the production is sold. Meeting so many people has convinced Maureen that more should take responsibility for their own appreciation of wines, and not just be swayed by the awards given by show judges.

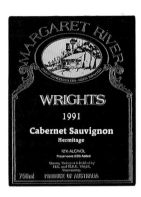

THERE WOULD be few vineyards in the world where one can view the sun rise over the sea and see it set upon it as well. Such a lucky location, however, is Yungarra Estate's at Dunsborough, where the outlook in one direction is over the sparkling waters of Geographe Bay, and in the other, across the blue Indian Ocean towards South Africa. Hence the name, a combination of two Aboriginal words meaning high up dwelling place.

In this environment, it is no wonder owners Wendy and Gerry Atherden are content working among the vines, able to look out across sturdy bush to the sea, to reflect on their development.

Planting began in 1988, a total of 7.6 hectares over three years. It includes eight varieties, semillon, verdelho, chenin blanc and sauvignon blanc in the whites, and cabernet franc, merlot, pinot noir and cabernet sauvignon in the reds. The wines are made at Happs, and it was not long before the wine world was introduced to the label when the 1992 cabernet was awarded a Sheraton silver trophy in the light-bodied classes. It was their first show, and the Atherdens, while happy with their wine, did not believe they should forgo a planned holiday at Kalbarri to attend the gala award presentation night. And when they received an urgent message to contact Happs, their immediate reaction was 'goodness, what could be wrong?'

YUNGARRA ESTATE

Yungarra Drive, Dunsborough
Cellar door sales: Daily 10 a.m. — 4.30 p.m. Restaurant facilities for lunches, morning and afternoon teas. Chalet accommodation. Private functions by arrangement

Above: The brilliant blue waters of the Indian Ocean are just a few minutes' drive from Yungarra Estate

It must be remembered that when the couple began the new vineyard, Gerry, then aged 58, was at a stage of life when many men are contemplating, or busy with retirement. Indeed, he headed south in 1984 after a busy city business life (including seven years as general manager of the Claremont Football Club) to take life easy. However, with Wendy's expertise in home science, they decided to take the wine plunge!

Knowledge was achieved by reading, attending industry events, asking questions and working on nearby properties. The couple have a policy of minimum chemical use and for three years they handweeded the property. Now the soils of gravel over clay and granite are mulched. The vines are trickle-irrigated to avoid stress from a spring-fed dam, benefiting even from the hot easterly. As it blows across Geographe Bay, it cools down to such an extent that temperatures on the property are some six degrees Celsius cooler than in nearby Busselton.

There are six wines in the range, five whites and a red with a 100-tonne crush expected at peak production in 1997-98, though some of the fruit is sold. Included in 1994 for the first time is a slightly oaked herbaceous semillon in the drier style. One definitely for the sweeter palate is the unusual combination of chenin blanc and verdelho. Its dominant flavours are of tropical fruit salad and it has the acid to balance the sweetness. The Pink Opal, made from cabernet with a slight touch of skin contact, has a little residual sugar but is not nearly as sweet. The fermentation was stopped early so it is lower in alcohol. Served chilled and carrying a slight spritzig character, it is an ideal summertime luncheon wine. Quartet is an unwooded blend of four whites with semillon prominent, while another Yungarra sweet style is Springtime in which ripe sauvignon blanc is combined with the aromatic verdelho.

The award-winning cabernet was unoaked and included a dash of ripe pinot noir grapes, adding to the berry flavours. A full-bodied red based on cabernet and a touch of merlot was made in 1993, for the first time. The Atherdens should not have any problems with family involvement in their project. Between them, their seven children had 13 grandsons before a granddaughter was born.

Warren Valley & environs

BLACKWOOD CREST

Chambers Road, Boyup Brook
Cellar door sales: Daily 10 a.m. — 5 p.m.

THERE WAS a surprise for me at the 1985 Perth Wine Show when a name I had never heard of was announced among the trophy winners. Blackwood who? I asked a wineman at my side. Equally mystified, he shrugged his shoulders. 'Never heard of them', he replied.

The winery, Blackwood Crest, had won the award for the best West Australian port, and was obviously worth investigating. So I checked around and soon came to learn of farmers Max and Roslynne Fairbrass, and of their vineyard and winery situated on a property half way between Boyup Brook and Kojonup. I knew this area well, and had a healthy respect for the quality of its wool and grain production, but I had never once thought of it as a place to grow grapes, and to make trophy winning wines.

in South Australia and claims freedom from climatic setbacks like frost because of the property's elevation, some 300 metres above sea level. But drought has proved another matter, with 1987 and 1988 the two worst years on record for the district. Now the vineyard is trickle-fed with no further moisture problems expected.

Max's grandfather William took up the 800-hectare block in 1906, working on the establishment of the Katanning-Donnybrook railway line to earn vital income necessary to develop the land. Some of the early settlers, including his grandfather, planted grapevine cuttings, and many still survive, despite the odd white ant attack. Max took a sample of table grapes from the Fairbrass property to the Department of Agriculture and was impressed with

Max Fairbrass, winemaker among woolmen, displays some earlier results from Blackwood Crest. The vineyard is on a property founded in 1906

Soon a visit was arranged, and as I approached the homestead and the new winery built from bricks and timber from the property, I found myself speculating that it must surely be one of the most isolated vineyards in Australia. Its nearest neighbour was another Boyup Brook pioneer 20 kilometres away and the next at Frankland River, about 100 kilometres away.

But I found a very relaxed couple, unconcerned about their remoteness and proud to show off the healthy green vineyard, an oasis in the dry, brown summertime surrounds where some 3000 sheep searched for feed. The vines grew in redgum loam, still home to many big trees, reflecting the depth of soil.

Max likens the area to the Clare Valley

the sugar-acid balance. So he decided to plant wine grapes, beginning operations in 1978 with the first vintage four years later.

The three hectares consisted of rhine riesling, semillon and sauvignon blanc, cabernet and shiraz. Subsequent plantings, including 2.5 hectares in 1994, have increased the area to more than seven hectares with a 50-tonne production expected at capacity.

The main wines are riesling, a semillon-sauvignon blanc blend, cabernet sauvignon and shiraz, the variety also used for the Blackwood Crest port.

A feature of the two whites is that Max has never had to add any acid, satisfied with natural levels achieved. He rates the 1993 riesling as good as he has made, being especially pleased with its length of palate.

The blend, made up of two-thirds semillon and a third sauvignon blanc, is given a touch of oak. It is light and crisp with fruit salad flavours.

Max believes Blackwood Crest fruit is as good as can be produced and with more finesse, the wines can match those of the high profile cooler southern areas.

'The vines show a will to live here', he said, recalling initial experimental plantings. His viticulture and winemaking knowledge has been developed from extensive reading, with help from Department of Agriculture advisers and noted winemaker Rob Bowen.

The trophy wine, a ruby port made from shiraz, was a worthy winner as a tasting revealed. I have also enjoyed an early silver medal winning rosé, an excellent, light, elegant style with surprising length.

Curiously, pepper characters began to develop in the shiraz (labelled hermitage) in the more recent wines. Max recalled that in 1993, the aromas were so distinct they were evident to pickers as they moved into the vineyard to begin harvesting.

I enjoyed the 1989 vintage, a huge mouthful of flavour from ripe fruit, with soft tannins. I was surprised when the age was revealed, for it was drinking as a much younger wine, such was its freshness. I rated the 1990 cabernet from the property almost as highly, again for the joy of its intense fruit quality and firm (but not aggressive) tannin structure, which will ensure cellaring potential.

A sweet white made from riesling and semillon and given a touch of muscat — labelled White Cascade — has proved its worth at cellar door.

Visitors to Blackwood Crest meet a man who, like many resourceful Australian farmers, seeks to adapt wherever possible, gathering equipment that can be put to good use. For example, we found a freezer unit that once cooled food and drink in a Perth nightclub.

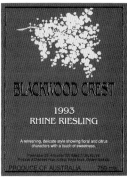

WHEN Vic Kordic retired in 1981 to tend stock on his 100-hectare Manjimup property, the lifelong enjoyment of wine led to the planting of a vineyard, to overcome boredom. Soon the vines were flourishing and the first harvest was upon him, so that any concerns about inactivity were quickly put aside.

The Kordic journey to WA's South West has been long and colourful. As a young man during World War II, he was taken to Germany as forced labour, to work on farms. Later, when the war ended, he felt there was nothing for him in his former Serbian home, and he joined the French occupation army in Austria. When in 1949 the opportunity came to migrate to Australia, he jumped at the chance to work as a mechanic, setting up business in Manjimup before involvement with brickmaking and real estate.

During this period, the land was purchased and, besides cattle and vines, it is home to olive and chestnut trees, and a two-hectare stand of Australian native bush.

Planting of the 11-hectare vineyard began in 1988 and is made up of chardonnay, verdelho, pinot noir, cabernet sauvignon and merlot. The first vintage in 1991 realised 35 tonnes while at full production in 1995, 100 tonnes is expected.

Although his father grew grapes in the backyard of his village home to make wine for the family, Vic himself confessed to ignorance about tending vines. But the horticultural instincts were keen, and backed by grandson Darren Crook and casual labour the vines have thrived, given water from a 60 million litre dam when required. Indeed, the property is something of a water wonderland, with its nine stock dams all fed by natural springs.

The area's climate for grapes is likened to that of Mount Barker, with the soils and location thought especially to enhance the flavour development of chardonnay and pinot noir, the first Chestnut Grove wines released, in April 1993.

Vic's daughter-in-law Gail, marketing manager for the label, recalled that the pinot 'smelt like freshly crushed strawberries' when processed in March 1991 at Alkoomi, Frankland, where the wines are made. 'It was a wonderful smell. We intend to let the grapes go the way they want and not try to make a French style.' A 1994 sparkling wine scheduled for release in 1997 will use half the pinot.

It is, of course, early days for the young development and it will take time for wine styles to evolve. The initial chardonnay is lightly wooded and pleasantly flavoured, supporting the belief in its potential. The 50-50 cabernet merlot blend was my choice of the range. The bouquet spoke of quality fruit, with hints of eucalypt amid good palate depth of flavour, though a touch more ripeness may have made a good wine *very* good indeed. It is soft and easy

CHESTNUT GROVE

Perup Road, Manjimup
Cellar door sales: By appointment

*The vigneron's life came late to Vic Kordic,
and gone are the thoughts of a quiet
retirement!*

drinking, with the first release in October 1993 modestly priced at $12, 1994 prices.

Perhaps the surprise packet in the initial wines has been the verdelho, a slightly sweet wine. Extremely abundant in tropical, banana flavours, it can be smelt across a room. It sold out quickly, with a particularly strong response from Melbourne consumers.

Rye grass and cover crops are grown between the rows, providing an excellent mulch, an ideal environment for the earthworms which abound.

Like any South West vineyard, birds pose problems, as can the occasional frost. Once the wind-protecting olive trees had to be pruned to allow for better air circulation, as a counter.

CONSTABLES

Graphite Road, West Manjimup
Cellar door sales most days 9 a.m. — 5 p.m.

DEVELOPING a vineyard from Perth at weekends is a tough assignment. It is even tougher when the accommodation is a three-metre square garden shed in a gravel pit and where the mice need to be shaken from the mattresses.

But the Constable family were undaunted, working for four years on weekends before they could settle on the property eight kilometres west of Manjimup. Despite their city background, they always had a yen for rural production, tending to overlook the long and at times arduous journey to the South West in pursuit of the glorious vine.

When the construction game got tough, as it did at various times, carpenter-builder

John Constable tried his luck on the land with sheep, cows, poultry and vegetables, while son Michael took up the challenge of landscape gardening.

A stint in the Eastern States led to visits to the Barossa and Hunter Valleys, convincing John and wife Bernice of the direction they should take, to get out of suburbia and take on viticulture. But this was business, and not simply a romantic notion of having the family name on a label. So the Constables decided to become contract growers for Houghton, retaining some wine to sell themselves.

Planting of the 40-hectare property, on one of the most elevated blocks in the area, began in the spring of 1987. It was com-

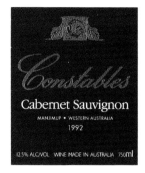

For the Constable clan, the move from city bustle to southern vines has proved rewarding

pleted in two seasons, the new vineyard covering 11.5 hectares. Located on deep loamy gravel with trickle irrigation from a 25 million-litre dam, the varieties include cabernet sauvignon (the biggest), cabernet franc, pinot noir, chardonnay, sauvignon blanc and riesling.

Manjimup and plummeting temperatures are synonymous, but according to John the vineyard has not suffered any frost problems.

The vines run north and south on the former vegetable and flower property which sees the odd gladioli still pop up. The grape harvest of eight tonnes in 1990 expanded to 94 tonnes in 1993, and is expected to rise to 150 tonnes at full production.

The Constables were guided by respected Great Southern vigneron Ted Holland in their new industry. All fruit except the pinot noir is machine-harvested with the Houghton contract long term.

The Constables market a chardonnay, sauvignon blanc, riesling and cabernet sauvignon under their own label.

Though it will take some years yet for regional wine characteristics to emerge, a reflection of the fruit quality from the vineyard is that the pinot noir grapes go to South Australia for inclusion in the base blend for Hardy's prestigious Sir James sparkling wine.

'We are happy with the situation', John said. 'It has given us the assurance and confidence we needed to progress. But it has been a huge learning curve for us all.'

'Friends and relatives said we were mad to get involved with something like this at our mature age. But we have proved them wrong. They enjoy coming down now to help us', said Bernice.

IN 1924, when Cynthia Rudd was brought by her husband George to a bush block in beautiful karri rainforest country 15 kilometres east of Northcliffe as part of a Group Settlement farm scheme, according to grandson Alan (Rudd) she cried for three months. From an English middle-class family who could afford domestic help, she found herself in remote and primitive circumstances, a far cry indeed from her previous position.

'Imagine her despair when she found mice and rats had eaten holes in her clothes', Alan said.

But the couple somehow stuck it out, managing to hold on to the land. Despite the collapse of the farm scheme, it remains in the family today. While one grandson tends cattle, prisons officer Alan and wife Judy are developing their D'Entrecasteaux vineyard.

They have taken the label from the French Admiral Bruni D'Entrecasteaux who visited the south coast of Western Australia 200 years ago. A seaside point

D'ENTRECASTEAUX

Boorara Road, Northcliffe
Cellar door sales planned for 1995

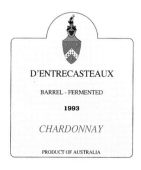

Above: Healthy young vines offer a strong colour contrast to the surrounding farmland Below: Estate produce against a nautical backdrop, reflecting the influence of the late 18th century D'Entrecasteaux voyage

about 20 kilometres from the new Rudd vineyard is named after him.

Despite warnings about the possible difficulty of grape ripening in the property's locality, the couple began planting on their karri loam block in 1988, stimulated by vineyard developments in Mount Barker where they live. The fruit from the four hectares under vines has proved more than satisfactory. Varieties include chardonnay, the biggest and set to make up half the vineyard with expansion planned, pinot noir, cabernet sauvignon and sauvignon blanc.

The first wines, made at Alkoomi, were produced in 1992, coincidentally the bicentenary of Admiral D'Entrecasteaux's visit to Western Australia. Naturally enough, the Rudds released a commemorative issue of 1000 numbered bottles of wine. It sold out quickly, some to be taken to France by members of a French delegation which had visited WA to mark the occasion. In 1993 some 7000 bottles were made and at full production 60,000 are expected.

The Rudds learnt viticulture by trial and error, trickle irrigating as required. The property is protected from strong winds by surrounding karri forest, part of the Boorara Nature Reserve. As with other vineyards in the Pemberton region birds, especially silvereyes, can be a problem depending on the local marri flowering, their preferred source of food.

Almost each weekend, the couple and their two children can be found travelling the 140 kilometres from Mount Barker to work the vineyard. It is a busy programme, leaving no time to admire the area's natural beauty spots like the Bibbulmun track, the nearby Canterbury River and Lane Pool falls, two kilometres away.

Whites from the property generally will be lighter in style, meaning that the chardonnay, for example, will only get a kiss of wood, with the reds fruity, soft and smooth. 'Our philosophy is good quality for a reasonable price', said Alan, who occasionally dresses up in a colourful French Admiral's uniform to promote their wine.

WHEN the Oldfield family began planting their vineyard 35 kilometres south of Pemberton, the signs from the heavens were hardly encouraging. It was a dismal day, of thunder and lightning and heavy rain, so intense they were forced to stop. But the conditions did not dampen their enthusiasm for the project in an industry totally new to them all. Indeed, their commitment was typical of the true pioneer, for they ended up establishing the new region's first winery.

Patriach George Oldfield, a former tradesman shopfitter, wooden toy maker and award-winning builder, had retirement in mind when he purchased the picturesque property fronting the Donnelly River for nearly two kilometres and straddling the Vasse Highway. He envisaged running a few cattle to produce baby beef, catching a trout or two, and snaring the odd marron.

But there was more to the operation than first thought, with son Kim and son-in-law Blair Meiklejohn helping out. Blair,

a teacher in Perth, was keen to get back to rural WA where he had spent a lot of his early years. The family began considering other alternatives for the land, and this led them to visit the Agriculture Department's Manjimup Research Station to investigate the wine grape trials. They were impressed but George's wife Coral said: 'We knew nothing, absolutely nothing'.

The area in which they were advised to plant the first vines had been a hay paddock for more than 100 years. Its heavy loamy soils over clay were thought to be ideal. Work began on 1 October 1986 — four hectares in all of chardonnay, semillon, sauvignon blanc, cabernet sauvignon, pinot noir and merlot.

'Knowing nothing meant we did not know the problems we would face', Blair said. It was a case of hard labour, but 95 per cent of the vines struck, helped by the rain. They are now supported by trickle irrigation. The first commercial vintage of 8.5 tonnes was in 1990 with well-known South West winemaker John Smith acting

DONNELLY RIVER WINES

Vasse Highway, Beedelup
Cellar door sales: Daily 9.30 a.m. — 4.30 p.m.

George Oldfield with son Kim; the family enterprise generates six wine styles

Donnelly River winemaker Blair Meiklejohn pictured at work in the winery

as consultant to Blair, who has since graduated in wine science from the Charles Sturt University.

Now the crush is about 50 tonnes, with a further two-hectare planting in 1992 of pinot and chardonnay set to boost this total.

In all, six wine styles are made at Donnelly River, a chardonnay, medium sweet semillon and sauvignon blanc, pinot, cabernet and a light red sweet blend, made up of semillon, of all things, and cabernet.

Blair seeks a melony style in the chardonnay with light wood, depending on the intensity of the fruit; earthy, dusty, mushroom, sometimes smoky bacon characters in the pinots; with minty eucalypt, sometimes blackberry, cassis or chocolate in the cabernets.

About 60 per cent of the wines are sold at the cellar door with a prized award in 1992 boosting interest, and making it a time of joyous celebrations for the family. This occurred when the 1991 chardonnay from only the second vintage won the silver trophy at the Sheraton Perth wine awards, the first estate-grown product from the region to do so. Suddenly, all the work and problems like regularly losing tonnes to birds from the surrounding State forest, seemed worth while.

Sometimes the cabernet is picked earlier than Blair would like, to beat the birds. 'Down the track, we will have to do something to protect the fruit', he said.

Fortuitously, it took local doctor Jeff Riley to bring the new young vignerons of

Pemberton together. Through his medical practice the good doctor, a keen wine man, heard about the various plantings and was one jump ahead of individual vignerons who did not know what their rivals were doing. This was to lead to a dinner party meeting and the formation of a local association to promote the district's wines.

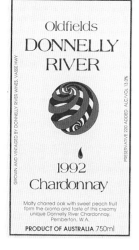

Oldfields
DONNELLY
RIVER

1992
Chardonnay

Malty charred oak with sweet peach fruit form the aroma and taste of this creamy unique Donnelly River Chardonnay, Pemberton. W.A.

PRODUCT OF AUSTRALIA 750ml

GROWN AND VINTAGED BY DONNELLY RIVER WINES, VASSE HWY
PRESERVATIVE 220 ADDED ALC/VOL 13.0%

EASTBROOK WINES

Vasse Highway, Pemberton
Cellar door sales operational late 1994

Eastbrook's Kim Skipworth — seeking quality fruit, not volume

WHEN Kim Skipworth takes up a challenge he gives it his all, and there is no better example than the Eastbrook vineyard and winery development.

It is one of four on Vasse Highway about 10 kilometres from Pemberton, established on a former grazing, orchard and potato property. Made up of a number of locations, this original property includes the vineyard of Dr Bill Pannell, plus Phoenicia and Salitage, on a strip of deep gravelly soils.

As a real estate agent formerly based in the Perth suburb of Nedlands, Kim Skipworth was never going to let a complete lack of knowledge about viticulture or oenology deter him, once he had made up his mind to get into the wine industry.

He came from sound West Australian farming stock, he had confidence, and he never hesitated once he felt he had the right piece of land (the result of a favourable report on the area by scientist Dr John Gladstones, and the enthusiasm of others.

Planting the 20-hectare property began in 1990, a total of 5.8 hectares of pinot noir and chardonnay. Hail damaged the small crop expected in 1993, a disappointment brushed aside by Kim as he worked on the unique jarrah pole, limestone and cedar weatherboard winery, its red roof clearly visible to people travelling to Pemberton. It was used for the first time for the 1994 vintage and its role will expand, especially with another two hec-

tares of shiraz planned for the vineyard.

At full production Kim Skipworth expects about 80 tonnes, non-irrigated. 'I want quality fruit, not volume', he said. 'I am learning by the seat of the pants but I reckon the best wines to come out of Western Australia are from non-irrigated vines.' Others may disagree, however.

Kim Skipworth's business interests include being a major shareholder of a Margaret River cheese making factory, source of an extremely popular brie, no doubt to have its place in the new winery, especially to go with an Eastbrook wine or meal.

Three wine styles are to be produced, a barrel-fermented chardonnay, an intense pinot and a soft shiraz.

The Eastbrook pinot grows on the harshest, meanest part of the property which Kim believes will yield the best fruit. 'The vines will have to work pretty hard', he said.

To get the right shiraz clone to plant, Kim studied the results of the top ten shows in Australia, looking for wines that consistently won gold meals. It whittled down to two, from South Australia, which he plans to graft to rootstock in 1994.

Wine prices will be in the $10-12 range (1994 prices), modest given the pioneering of a new area where Kim says every bug and every menace has to be contended with. 'Look sideways for a minute and something will get you', he said.

WHEN a wine producer has 250,000 tourists a year passing the gate, twice, it's a rare marketing opportunity matched by few others in the business. The constant flow of traffic visiting the world famous Gloucester Tree at Pemberton was one of the reasons Sue and Don Hancock decided to enter the wine business, establishing Gloucester Ridge, almost in the shadows of the giant karri tree 100 metres away.

Slowly at first, some of the visitors began to stop by, to sip and sample, and to buy. By 1993 the couple estimated that 10 per cent of the region's tourists were calling in — a figure likely to increase in the future with a new cellar sales outlet and bistro planned.

Another unusual feature about Gloucester Ridge is that it falls entirely within the Pemberton town boundary, making it a pleasant walk from most holiday accommodation.

Initially, the Hancocks owned a farm at Yelverton, near Willyabrup, where they

were almost surrounded by vineyards. Instead of developing that, they chose to lease a family property at Northcliffe, travelling to it each weekend to work, with cattle. But the vine seed had been sown, no doubt Don's Uncle Mick Knappstein, a well-respected, long-serving South Australian winemaker, being an influence. But the sandy Northcliffe soils were unsuitable for viticulture, and after searching elsewhere the Hancocks purchased Gloucester Ridge in 1981. Four years later the first vines, pinot noir and chardonnay from Moss Wood stock at Margaret River, were planted on the karri loam soils. But it was only a small area, just over a hectare, because of the uncertainty as to how vines would fare in the area. Meanwhile, the Hancocks had bought a school bus business to fund themselves and their new project.

'It really was only an experiment', Sue said. Three years later, excitedly picking the first fruit, 1.5 tonnes in all, they were convinced enough to expand. Subsequent

GLOUCESTER RIDGE VINEYARD

Burma Road, Pemberton
Open daily 10 a.m. — 5 p.m.

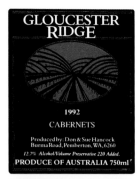

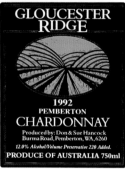

Vineyard manager Michael Hancock engaged in summer leaf plucking by hand

plantings of cabernet franc, sauvignon blanc, cabernet sauvignon and merlot has increased the vineyard to six hectares, which will be almost doubled in time. With fruit purchased from contract growers, the family (including son Michael as vineyard manager) aims for a

100 tonne-a-year crush.

'Basically, we see ourselves as a small niche vineyard with cellar sales being the mainstay', Sue said.

Wine styles include a barrel-fermented reserve chardonnay—a lighter unwooded wine from the variety which came about by chance when they ran out of barrels — an unwooded sauvignon blanc with tropical fruit overtones, riesling, including a late harvest, pinot noir, Aurora, a light dry red blend, Cabernets, a 50-50 blend of cabernet sauvignon and cabernet franc, and a port. It is a big range for a small organisation, but it has to cater for a vast range of tastes, especially the sweet palates of Asian visitors to the 'big tree'. It is proposed to add a sparkling wine to the portfolio in 1995.

Tastings over the years have revealed Gloucester Ridge wines to be of a consistent, good overall quality, without any being trophy winners.

'We believe we have done our apprenticeship and will now be looking to step up a notch now', Sue said. 'We have come a long way since the beginning when there was a total lack of knowledge in the area. We sort of made up the plot as we went. It is different now with a good core of trained talent attracted to the area.'

Now with visitors being strategically directed to the Gloucester Tree (just past 'that vineyard') the Hancocks can rightly claim to have made their mark.

LEFROY BROOK

Glauders Road, Pemberton
No cellar door sales

The healthy pinot noir berries shown here have not had to contend with birds, thanks to the protective netting pictured opposite

IT IS a remarkable place to have a vineyard, a small square deep in the South West State forest. But for Pemberton pioneers, Perth-based Pat and Barbara Holt, it is their bit of Burgundy in Western Australia.

For it was visits to the outstanding French vineyard and wine-producing area which inspired them to launch into a venture of their own, despite it being 'foreign' working territory. Pat, a University of Western Australia graduate in biochemistry and microbiology, works in medical research (specialising in child health) and knew nothing about vineyard establishment and management. But he was not fazed: 'I was obsessed with the idea of making Burgundy style wines outside of France', he said.

The couple chose Pemberton because of a passion for the area, from years of holidaying and trout fishing. Following another visit to Burgundy in 1981 they decided the time had come, purchasing 5.5 hectares, an old tobacco farm ten kilo-

metres south of the town. Planting began in the spring of 1982 and was completed two years later, a total of 1.5 hectares of pinot and chardonnay. The first significant vintage was in 1989, and in the intervening years, the Holts learned a lot about birds and kangaroos.

'The silvereyes were horrendous', he recalled. 'In those early years we were losing more than 75 per cent of the crop.'

Now a huge permanent net covers 80 per cent of the vines. The remainder and other future plantings will receive similar protection.

In turn, steel mesh protects the sides of the nets from 'low flying' kangaroos. 'Animals of 70 kilograms travelling at high speeds do an extraordinary amount of damage', he went on. 'They tear a hole the size of a ute on the way in, and the size of a truck on the way out. Before the steel mesh, we probably became the most expert net repairers in the Southern Hemisphere.'

But the nets and steel did not help in 1993 when about half the crop was lost to the South African garden weevil.

The Lefroy Brook fruit, from close-planted vines on karri loam and only irrigated for establishment, is carted for wine-making to Hainault at Bickley Valley where principal Peter Fimmel is an old mate.

The Holt aim is for a bottle of wine per vine, a crush of about 20 tonnes at full development which will always see it a small, specialised operation.

Pat says he does not show his wines because he does not believe Australian judges would understand them. The chardonnay is picked fully ripe and barrel-fermented to dryness, with lees maturation for at least 12 months. Deliberately, only a maximum of 20 per cent new oak is used, to make sure the final product is not over-wooded. The wines are big, buttery and nutty, with a steely finish, drinkable after about 18 months to two years in the bottle. Definitely food wines, Pat expects them to reach a peak after three to five years.

No doubt any sipper would liken the pinot flavours to forest floor, more gamey from my tasting.

The closer plantings of the vines and pruning provides for smaller bunches and berries, to generate flavour intensity. The fruit is lightly crushed and left on skins for 30-60 days, depending on the season, before being pressed. After 18 months on oak, the wine is kept for one to two years in bottles before release, as about a three-year-old. Pat says the pinot, with its complexity, length and depth, has been likened to a Volnay when taken to France for a Burgundian assessment. 'When young, they have a tight heart and silken finish which becomes more pronounced as they get older', he said.

The vineyard is a serious commercial business for the Holts and they expect to break even on operating costs in 1994, and ultimately in retirement are looking to a healthy profit.

ANDREW Mountford decided he wanted to live in the country, but not to grow cabbages. When an Australian he met at the Cannington Horticultural College in Somerset, England, helped cement a growing interest in wine, he decided to try his luck in the industry.

With wife Sue and their two children, he migrated in 1983 to establish a vineyard at Mudgee in New South Wales. But when this did not work out, they headed west, at the urging of a brother in Denmark. For three years, while Andrew worked as a landscape gardener in Perth, the couple explored the WA wine scene, finally settling on Pemberton which impressed with well-drained, deep karri loam soils and rolling hills. They eventually bought a 30-hectare former vegetable property on Five Mile Brook, 20 kilometres west of the town, in 1986. 'Then', says Andrew, 'the hard work began'.

Planting of pinot noir, chardonnay, sauvignon blanc, merlot, cabernet sauvignon and cabernet franc began in 1988 using the best 15,000 cuttings from 20,000 previously established in the Mountford nursery, for an area of six hectares.

Andrew says he does not irrigate the north and south running vines to achieve a greater intensity of fruit flavour. In 1992 they picked 22 tonnes of fruit and 28 tonnes in 1993. At full production, in 1995, they expect their harvest to be 45 tonnes.

Included in the wine range is a sauvignon blanc blended with 15 per cent semillon purchased from Margaret River;

MOUNTFORD WINES

Bamess Road, Pemberton
Cellar door sales: Daily 10 a.m. — 5 p.m.

A rough-hewn timber arch frames Sue Mountford at the cellar door sales outlet Below: Husband Andrew casts a critical eye over one of the Mountford reds

a full round style with a soft acid finish, Blanc De Noir, made from pinot; Melange, a fruity but dry rosé with a crisp clean finish made from cabernet and merlot with a dash of cabernet franc; a medium-bodied

lightly wooded chardonnay of considerable palate length; and a sweet berry fruit pinot, bigger, fuller, more extracted, made to last. Andrew says he wants his wines to be a signature of the vintage, and not be made to a formula, or to be consistently the same year in, year out.

An early highlight for the Mountfords was the winning of the 1992 SGIO award for the best Pemberton white wine, their first trophy. 'It was very exciting, the first time we had been in the competition', Andrew said. 'Having a vineyard and producing wine is not some overnight infatuation. It is the culmination of a dream we have harboured for 12 years. A vineyard is much more than a business. It is a lifestyle, action with an old tradition and a challenging future.'

There was more of that in 1994 when Andrew made the reds for the first time, in a winery, food and cellar door sales centre he has built himself, using the gravel based property dirt to make the bricks. The whites are being made at Frankland Estate.

While half the wines are sold at the cellar door, Sydney has proved an important market. A feature about the bottles is that they can be instantly recognised, having been sealed with bees wax. This was the Mountford alternative when lead seals were banned by the World Health Organisation.

A disappointing botrytis infection in 1992 was a blow to the Mountfords with half the chardonnay being lost, but another vineyard problem, snails, has been solved by the use of ducks. Foxes from the nearby forest, however, made a meal of some of the birds, as well as grapes, for dessert!

IN THE midst of the well-manicured Phoenicia vineyard just off Vasse Highway, about ten kilometres from Pemberton, is a superb stand of jarrah and marri trees. Even though they represent an important refuge for birds to attack and damage prime ripening grapes, they are not going to be cleared, protected by State Government regulations and the wishes of property owners, Perth doctors Graham Raad and Tony Samaha.

'We just have to grin and bear it', said vigneron manager John Rowe.

The move into the industry by the medicos, who have had a long involvement with agriculture, follows a well-established pioneering pattern of Australian doctors investing in vines and wine projects.

A start was made to the vineyard in 1989 with major plantings of the deep, gravelly soils the following year and again in 1991, to make up 15.38 hectares. The rows, which run mainly north and south on the 66-hectare property, are trickle-fed from a 100 million litre three-hectare dam, home as well to that succulent crustacean, the prized marron.

Chardonnay makes up about a quarter of the vineyard, with other varieties including shiraz, merlot, pinot noir, cabernet franc and sauvignon blanc. The first harvest of 29 tonnes was picked in 1993 with the fruit sold to Geographe Estate. Further plantings are to be made in 1994, with an ultimate production target of about 200 tonnes.

A tasting of early wines with consultant winemaker Dorham Mann revealed some real class, despite the tender years of the vineyard. Said Dorham: 'Pemberton and Manjimup seem to have a measure of special distinction. While there may be some problems with fruit ripeness where vines grow vigorously in the rich karri soils, the area will produce wines of elegance and distinctive varietal character.'

Two unwooded samples justified the comment. The 1993 pinot was a mouthful of sweet, ripe cherry fruit with good structural support, unlike some produced around the nation, while a chardonnay of the same vintage surprised for its tremendous fruit and length. Curiously, the ripe fruit generated the impression of some wood contact.

The 1993 shiraz was soft and refined, pleasant pepper overtones adding to a long, deep, satisfying palate. But said Dorham: 'We are going to have to watch crop levels, otherwise it will not ripen sufficiently'.

PHOENICIA WINES

East Brook Road, Pemberton
Cellar door sale planned for 1995

I was intrigued about the estate's unusual name, and asked how it came about. 'Early Lebanese are acknowledged as having bought the vine to Europe from the Middle East', Dorham replied, 'so the owners have linked the name with their forebears.'

Above: The ironstone entrance to Phoenicia Wines. Below: Some of the thriving young vines on gravelly soil

PIANO GULLY VINEYARD

Piano Gully Road, Manjimup
Cellar door sales: Weekends, public and school holidays 10 a.m. — 5 p.m.

Haydon White, at right, and above with wife Dianne, daughter Julie and son-in-law Ian

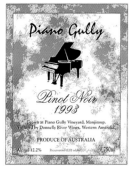

THERE was never much doubt that Haydon White would settle on Piano Gully for the name of his vineyard. The picturesque hill property 12 kilometres south of Manjimup is on Piano Gully Road, key access from South Western Highway to undulating Middlesex, a growing area of interest for vineyards.

Haydon White, however, would not want the same ending for his vineyard that led to the colourful name of Piano Gully. About the turn of the century, pioneering group settler Charles Young, a keen music lover, decided to import a piano from England for his wife. Many months later, after a long and arduous sea journey, the piano arrived at Fremantle and was sent by train to the then railhead at Bridgetown. By horse and cart it continued its mammoth journey, until almost within site of the Young cottage, the cart slipped on the dirt road and the piano fell into the gully and was ruined.

Farm machinery dealer Haydon White came from Busselton to Manjimup in 1972 to set up business, purchasing the 19-hectare Piano Gully block in 1986, in the search 'for a bit of space', possibly to run a few cattle. Later he looked at ways of making money from the land and was advised by a contract grape grower in Busselton to put in some vines. With the help of Jeff Moss, of Moss Brothers at Margaret River, Haydon and wife Dianne began planting in 1987, the rows running north and south. Initially, chardonnay and pinot noir were selected, considered ideal

for the deep, well-drained karri loam soils and the micro climate, with cabernet sauvignon added the following year, giving a total area of four hectares.

The first vintage was in 1991, with a harvest of 30 tonnes in 1994. The wines are made by Donnelly River Wines and excess fruit is sold.

The vines are trickle-irrigated with the

vineyard philosophy aimed at quality, not quantity.

The Whites have since been joined in the project on a partnership basis by daughter Julie Bremner, an accountant, and her husband Ian, an English high school teacher, as well as boxer pup Woody, in charge of stick removal and customer service.

Chardonnays from the vineyard are in the lighter, fruit-driven style, while the pinots display sound berry flavours with the best to come, especially in depth, as the vines mature. The first cabernet was due for release in the first half of 1994. Besides the three varietal wines (from chardonnay, pinot and cabernet), Piano Gully also produces a Concerto, a rosé made from pinot that is fruity and slightly sweet but with a clean, firm finish, an ideal summer drink served chilled.

The property is enhanced by an impressive stand of karri trees, and there are plans to provide a new cellar door facility from the temporary machinery shed set up for the initial service. 'The important thing is that we are getting recognition for our wines, though we have not won many medals yet', Haydon said. 'But I believe they will come. I am a fussy man and at this stage of the development, I am well satisfied.'

SALITAGE

Vasse Highway, Pemberton
Cellar door sales: Daily 9 a.m.— 4 p.m

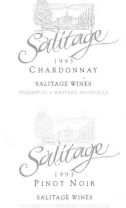

John and Jenny Horgan lend a willing hand at vintage time

DOODLING on a pad produced the name Salitage, a major Pemberton development. It was derived from the christian names of John and Jenny Horgan's four children, Sarah, Lisa, Tamara and Gerard.

But there is nothing doodling about the venture, a showpiece for the West Australian industry. The $4 million project is a bold commitment to a new producing area, helping cement its early credibility.

So far as the Horgans are concerned, there can be no compromise, no shortcuts. Salitage is all or nothing.

Situated on the Vasse Highway about 10 kilometres from the historic mill town, its winery dominates the hillside horizon, while the vineyard, snuggled beyond, can hardly be seen. For John Horgan, a prominent West Australian businessman with strong international connections, its flourishing growth is a matter of particular pride. Having been managing director of Leeuwin Estate at Margaret River from 1973 to 1980, key years in its establishment, he has now been able to apply this valuable development experience to his own property.

While at Leeuwin, and on trips to the United States, John Horgan became close friends with Californian industry guru Robert Mondavi, a regular visitor to Western Australia on behalf of American investors originally in the project, and then as a winemaking consultant. Mondavi's passion for wine, and particularly his unerring zeal for quality, proved a major influence on John Horgan who has set similar standards for Salitage.

However, prior to the Pemberton development John, using funds from the sale of his share in Leeuwin, organised an Australian syndicate of seven to buy a half share in the prized Burgundy premier cru producer, Domaine de la Pousse D'Or.

Subsequently, the group turned its attention to Pemberton to begin the Smithbrook Estate vineyard.

John, who saw the potential of the area, wanted to be involved with his own project. Salitage, a former grazing property, was purchased in 1988 after significant research. Now 50,000 trickle-irrigated vines cover just over 20 hectares on well-drained jarrah/redgum soils, over gravel. While the vineyard emphasis is based solidly on pinot noir and chardonnay, other varieties include merlot, cabernet franc, petit verdot and sauvignon blanc. As well as the aim of producing the classic pinot noir and chardonnay, Salitage will have a Bordeaux red blend and an unwooded sauvignon blanc in its range.

In 1993 the first meaningful harvest realised 25 tonnes, and was processed at Plantagenet Wines. In 1996 full production is expected to total 200-250 tonnes.

John Horgan has since taken in a half share partner in Salitage, Australian resident Shozo Kawasaki, while son-in-law Michael Bewsher is vineyard manager.

Early pinots have shown cherry-like flavours and a finely structured palate while the chardonnay is elegant but with surprising depth of flavour for such young vines. 'Our wines will be totally fruit driven', John said. 'It's our philosophy.'

The gleaming interior of the Salitage winery endorses the total commitment made by the Horgans to the new enterprise

FROM THE highest point of Scotts Brook vineyard, views extend ten to 15 kilometres, not across other rows of vines, but grain and grazing country. For the development is in the heart of some of Western Australia's best mixed farming land, prized for its valued production for decades. Initially, scepticism and even some downright annoyance were reactions to the intrusions of horticulture in such country, but strawberries and vines are now a reality.

Behind the label are Boyup Brook district high school deputy head Brian Walker and his English teaching wife Kerry. Their initial teaching appointments were to the town in 1969, and they sought to return, after ten years in Perth and two years in Dalwallinu. When friends Ian and Lorraine Robinson wanted to diversify on their sheep farm, the Walkers suggested grapes and wine, for which they had developed a strong interest.

A subdivision was arranged and the first vines planted in 1987 — 5.5 hectares flourishing today on the hilly location 20 kilometres south east of Boyup Brook, in the locality of Mayanup. The varieties include cabernet sauvignon, chardonnay, pinot noir, rhine riesling and semillon, with the first small harvest in 1990 a joyful occasion for the Walkers and Robinsons, who used old ten-gallon beer kegs to make the first Scotts Brook wine.

The business got serious the following vintage as the harvest increased with the fruit transported to Alkoomi at Frankland for winemaking. At capacity the vineyard, planted on gravelly soils with the rows running north-east, are expected to produce an annual crush of 50 tonnes, depending on nature's charm. Five wine styles are produced, cabernet sauvignon, chardonnay, rhine riesling, a soft red, and a late harvest for the sweet palate.

The cabernets, my pick of the range, can be very big and fruity — like the 1992. Deep and intense in colour, it showed pleasant peppermint characters, was relatively high in acid with a tannin structure to provide a good cellaring base, five to ten years predict the Walkers. Considering the young vines, the 1992 chardonnay surprised with its big, buttery, melony characters, reflecting ripe fruit and the skilful use of oak, 75 per cent new French and the rest American. A wine to go well with duck or turkey, for example, it has been a great marketing success for the youthful operation. The 1993 is more subtle, the fruit not as ripe. Rhine riesling reflects plenty of strong varietal character, the different vintages so far showing a

variety of citrus and limey flavours.

While the Walkers are now confident of their grape-growing ability after extensive self-education, they admit their biggest challenge is to market their 40,000 bottle crop, from an unrecognised wine growing area, and way off the main wine tasting track. Imagine their joy then, when their 1992 chardonnay was sold for $4.50 — $5 a glass in some of Perth's trendy wine bars.

Much of their confidence in the isolated vineyard is its base resource — cuttings from premium producers Wrights and Moss Wood who gave them plenty of help and encouragement as well.

SCOTTS BROOK

Scotts Brook Road, Boyup Brook
Cellar door sales: Weekends or by appointment

Above: Brian and Kerry Walker — educators who became self-taught vignerons

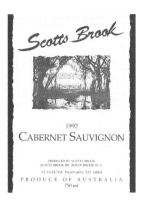

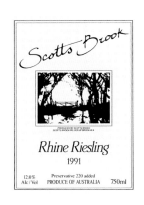

SMITHBROOK

Smith Brook Road, Middlesex
Cellar door sales: By appointment

Above: Young vines thrive in this lush, rolling farmland in a fertile pocket of the Middlesex region

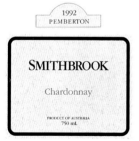

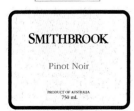

SURELY one of the most beautiful entrances into any WA vineyard must be that of Smithbrook Wines. It passes through a majestic 50-hectare karri forest, part of the Smithbrook nature reserve from which the label was taken, to burst suddenly into cleared vineyard country. Planted on a hillside, it commands panoramic vistas that could only stimulate any vineyard worker.

The major development had its origins in a visit by the French partners of the Australian syndicate in the Burgundy premier cru Domaine de la Pousse D'Or. They enthused over the flavours in fruit from the then unkempt experimental plantings at the former Agriculture Department Manjimup research station, rating them outstanding.

Dr Bill Pannell, who founded Moss Wood at Margaret River, was the original driving force behind the project, but he then left to develop his own vineyard on Vasse Highway, about ten kilometres from Pemberton.

In 1994 the main shareholders and directors, also partners in the Domaine de la Pousse D'Or project, included David Clarke, chairman of the Macquarie Bank, chairman of McGuigan Wines Ltd, chairman of the Sydney Wine Show for four years and principal of the Poole's Rock vineyard at Broke in the lower Hunter region of NSW; Ross Grant, merchant banker and a partner in Brokenwood Wines; and John Horgan, managing director of Leeuwin Estate between 1973-1980 and principal of Salitage vineyard at Pemberton. Burgundian vignerons Gerard Potel and Michel Juillot,

the partners at Domaine de la Pousse D'Or, are minor shareholders.

Phil May, the first professionally trained viticulturist to work in the region, was recruited to Smithbrook from Victoria. For his relative youth, his experience was considerable, his qualifications impeccable.

As a boy on school holidays, he worked with his uncle, Jesuit Brother John May (and winemaker at Seven Hills in the Clare Valley), subsequently graduating in agricultural science at Roseworthy Agricultural College in South Australia. There he majored in viticulture in 1983, winning the coveted Gramp, Hardy Smith memorial trophy for being the pick of the 500 students of the year from all courses. Before taking up the pioneering West Australian challenge at Smithbrook, he gained industry experience in South Australia, where he worked for a time under Penfolds Grange founder Max Schubert, and in Victoria's Yarra Valley specialising in growing pinot noir and chardonnay for some of Australia's best known premium winemakers.

The first vines were planted at Smithbrook in 1988 with the initial ten hectares being expanded to twenty-eight. It is estimated the 107-hectare property has the potential for another 30 hectares of vineyard in the future.

Nearly half the vines are chardonnay, almost a third pinot noir with the rest made up of cabernet sauvignon, cabernet franc, merlot, shiraz and petit verdot. They grow on well-drained soils, karri loam and redgum gravel, the rows facing north, east and west. Trickle irrigation is supplied from a 90 million-litre dam, but only to the redgum soil types because of a lower water holding capacity. And within these areas, the water is provided only strategically, on the basis of precise needs, as a result of detailed soil moisture mapping and monitoring studies. An area as small as two hectares, for example, has six valves controlling accurate water replacement according to soil type variations.

'We are seeking to fine-tune grape growing to the *nth* degree, minimising the risk', Phil said. 'Our aim is a desired fruit concentration rather than vines taking up water to grow water melons.'

In 1992 Smithbrook harvested 38 tonnes of fruit and in 1993, 95 tonnes. At full production, in 1996, 350 tonnes is expected to be picked.

Moss Wood made the 1991 pinot noir from the vineyard's first harvest and in December 1991 John Wade was appointed to make wines for Smithbrook, initially at Plantagenet and then from his new Denmark facility.

Recognition for early wines was swift. In March 1993 a party of 18 British Masters of Wine, on the organisation's first official visit to Western Australia labelled Tour of Discovery, lauded the 1991 pinot from the

first fruit, and the 1992 chardonnay. Said one, at a lunch in their honour: 'If they can produce that quality from young vines, what will they do when they mature.' Sniffing at the cherry-like aromas of the pinot, he went on: 'It's classic'.

The chardonnay was regarded as very French in style, its concentrated flavours true to the variety, more so than a lot of burgundies.

Then later in the year, elation came as Smithbrook won its first trophies. The 1992 chardonnay won gold at the Sheraton Perth wine awards, and then, at the annual SGIO wine awards, the chardonnay and 1992 pinot were judged best white and red wine from the region.

Phil May says pinots from Smithbrook in the future will be complex with great depth and tightness in structure as youngsters — wines that will last. He says the chardonnay's refined fruit aromas will be enhanced by the fermentation bouquets derivatives such as grapefruit, ensuring complexity with the balance for long life.

About 10 per cent of production goes into the Smithbrook label, the rest being sold to a keen demand from Eastern States producers as well as those in Western Australia. Investment in the project to the end of 1993 was estimated at $2.5 million.

Viticulturist Phil May and wife Elizabeth relax in the vineyard

TANTEMAGGIE VINEYARD

Kemp Road, Pemberton
Cellar door sales: Saturday, Sunday 9 a.m. — 5 p.m. and by appointment

**CABERNET
SAUVIGNON 1992**

Grown by The Pottingers
Pemberton
Vintaged by Donnelly River Wines

12.5% Alcohol/Volume
Preservative 223 added
750mls
PRODUCE OF AUSTRALIA

*Previous page: Neat rows of young vines
typify the way in which this emerging region
has branched out from traditional farming
Below: The Pottingers, David junior and
senior and Elma, have plenty of reasons to
look to a rosy future*

CERTAINLY the label Tantemaggie must be one of the most unusual in Australia. So its origin was the first question I put to principals David Pottinger and his son, also David. They explained it was in recognition of a late relative, an Aunt Margaret whose legacy helped fund the vineyard development. 'Tante', said David, 'means Aunt in French'.

Their journey to Pemberton and the wine industry has been a lengthy and diverse one, to say the least. It began in the cold windy Orkney Islands north of mainland Scotland where the Pottingers have been livestock farmers for 400 years. The family moved to Scotland in 1944 with David senior and wife Elma going to Canada in 1956 to try their luck on the land. But it was too cold, and they returned to Scotland, completing the cycle by returning to Orkney for seven years, where young David was born. But again they were bothered by the cold, and decided to try their luck in a warmer climate, migrating to WA in 1968.

While the family lived in a caravan in Perth for three weeks, David senior began a search for a farm, eventually buying a property in Cowaramup. But it did not suit, and soon they found themselves in Wyalkatchem growing wheat.

David senior, who described the next 13 years battling to survive as 'hard labour', decided to move again, choosing Pemberton as third time lucky. That was in 1982 and grapevines were not part of the plans for the 72-hectare property. Indeed, it was cashmere goats that the family pinned its hopes on, and then cauli-

flowers and pumpkins. Eventually, both men took off-farm jobs with David junior working on district vineyards.

Then the two attended a seminar at Manjimup run by Houghton Wines, which was seeking growers in the area. It was a turning point even though the remaining goats on the property decimated the pinot noir twice!

Planting began in 1987 with rows running east and west on a north facing slope. Initially, an area of 11 hectares of cabernet sauvignon was involved, under contract to Houghton. The Pottingers have since planted chardonnay, sauvignon blanc and semillon as small experimental areas, and more recently, again for Houghton, eight hectares of verdelho. The vines are trickle-irrigated from a property dam with the well-drained soils made up of deep karri loam.

The men have divided the vineyard which David senior says is good sound Scottish commonsense. 'Father and son doesn't work', he said. 'We have our own patches.' But they do share machinery and income from sales.

The Tantemaggie first vintage was in 1991 with a small parcel allowed under the contract to be made by Donnelly River wines for the Tantemaggie label. 'It was drunk very quickly', David senior said.

Their share of the 1992 harvest was 2400 bottles, a lighter style that 'does not put your throat out when you drink it', quipped David. Naturally enough, he likens the flavour to something Scottish — heather berry which grows wild in the hills of his native country. 'It is distinctive, a bit like blackcurrant', he said.

On a visit to Scotland in 1993, David senior included six bottles of the wine. When a hotelier in the Orkney Islands tasted it, he thrust £500 into David Pottinger's hand and said: 'That is the best wine I have had in my life. Send me what you can for the money.'

Friends and relatives were impressed as well, if puzzled, at a journey half way round the world to grow grapes. Production in 1993 was 75 tonnes with 200 expected at full development in 1997. The vineyard is mechanically harvested at night, and the grapes processed in mobile field crushers for transport to Houghton in refrigerated trucks

The picturesque sloping vineyard only three kilometres north of Pemberton, and with a three-kilometre frontage on Lefroy Brook as it loops around the block, is well worth a visit. But it is tricky to find, being at the end of a dead end dirt road which runs alongside the local golf links.

THE WARREN VINEYARD

224 Dickenson Street, Pemberton
Cellar door sales: Daily by appointment

Unusual sloping doors mark the entrance to The Warren Vineyard cellar

THE Warren Vineyard on the very edge of Pemberton has its origins in some of Western Australia's older liquor stores. There electrician Warren Wandless spent a lot of his spare time, scrounging around shelves, browsing for bargains among the dusty bottles. So successful was his searching that he collected a cellar of about 2000 bottles, and a yen eventually to produce his own label.

Warren and wife Anne, a primary school teacher, grew up in Fremantle and often visited Pemberton on holidays, considering it a place to retire. But when the opportunity arose much earlier than planned, they headed south, buying their small block in 1985.

Planting on the sloping karri loam soils over clay began in the spring of 1985, the 1.5 hectares of vines, all red varieties, facing north and south. Initially, the vineyard was an experiment to see how the vines, half cabernet sauvignon and half merlot, would go. But now that any doubts are fully set aside, the family plans further expansion, and a winery, hopefully involving son Glen, a graduate in wine science from the Roseworthy Agricultural College.

The Wandless philosophy is based on natural fertiliser like sheep manure and seaweed, and non-irrigated vines. 'I believe the only place quality and quantity come together is in a dictionary', Warren quipped, explaining his stand. 'I believe you get flavour from the stinginess of the grape and vine.'

Red wine is their speciality, but the couple have broadened their horizons to buy in some locally produced chardonnay and riesling grapes to add to their range.

'I believe reds are more solid in the market place while whites go up and down a bit', Warren said.

In 1989 the couple had their first bottling of 40 dozen. Since then average production has been about ten tonnes, with a further five to ten tonnes purchased.

The wines have been made at Redgate in Margaret River, with picking usually in April. The range includes a merlot, the softest style, a more complex cabernet merlot, and a big berry fruit cabernet. A common theme is a distinct perfumed floral bouquet in all the reds. Said Anne: 'We have been told at the SGIO tastings that you can smell our wines from six to seven metres away.' The couple's 1991 cabernet won the Pemberton region best dry red at the 1992 SGIO awards, securing for them their first trophy.

They are self taught, confident in the unique almost tropical rain forest conditions of their vineyard. 'The signs indicate that we have something special here', Warren said. 'I believe people will come to recognise and look for that perfumed character in the reds.'

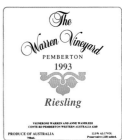

YANMAH ESTATE

Yanmah Road, Yanmah
Cellar door sales: By appointment

Above: Light mist enhances the beauty of the picturesque countryside surrounding Yanmah Estate

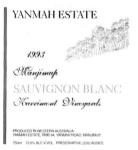

FINDING the Nicholas family vineyard in the Yanmah area of West Manjimup seemed like a compass and cut lunch affair. Sound directions are needed to find the 50-hectare property, a former grazing, orchard and berry farm situated 15 kilometres from the town.

But the effort is worth while. From the top of the sloping block, taken up in the early part of the century when it was named Karrimont, are 360-degree views, extending many kilometres over picturesque rolling hillsides of forests, livestock and horticultural country. It is one of the highest vineyards in the area, rising from an estimated 280 metres above sea level at the bottom to 325 metres at the peak.

Retired Commonwealth public servant and investor Tony Nicholas with wife Betty and son Peter, an Agriculture Department fruit research officer, are developing the vineyard, a ten-hectare planting of seven varieties. They include two hectares each of pinot noir, cabernet sauvignon and chardonnay with the rest semillon, sauvignon blanc, merlot and some cabernet franc.

Peter, a Roseworthy Agricultural College graduate with experience in the industry in France, urged his parents to take up the vineyard challenge, with the first commercial wines made in 1993. They included 150 cases of a sauvignon blanc-semillon blend and 200 cases of cabernet-

merlot, with the balance of the fruit sold to winemakers at Margaret River and Mount Barker. The family intention is to progress to complete winemaking by the year 2000, with plantings doubled. By this time, fruit production should be at capacity, 200-240 tonnes.

The vines, which run east-west, are trickle-irrigated. Peter says the intensity of fruit flavour is the strength of the vineyard, a reflection of the micro-climate and the well-drained karri loam soils interspersed with jarrah/redgum gravel.

The 1994 production of 80 tonnes saw 30 tonnes made into wine by John Wade at his new Denmark facility, and the surplus sold. A premium range is to be marketed under the Karrimont label. This will provide for the pick of the fruit and new oak treatment such as for a chardonnay and the best red.

Fruit has also been processed for a sparkling wine, the first due for release in 1995.

The first wine (1993 sauvignon blanc) may not be a world beater, but it is a credible effort, a sound basis on which to build. It shows more than enough to confirm Peter's belief in the project.

And while he spends weekends tending the vines, keeping them free of weeds and disease, guinea fowls are on the job every day, successfully controlling garden weevils.

Great Southern

ALKOOMI

Wingebellup Road, Frankland
Cellar door sales: Daily 10.30 a.m. — 5.30
p.m. including Lower Stirling Terrace,
Albany facility

*Judy Lange of Alkoomi, an estate that has
enjoyed considerable success since an initial
trial planting of a single hectare*

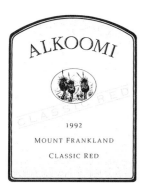

IT SOUNDS hard to believe but when Merv and Judy Lange of Alkoomi Wines at Frankland River decided to enter the industry, they had never drunk a bottle of wine between them. Yet 18 years down the winemaking road their production has burgeoned to about 220,000 bottles, and is targeted to become 360,000 by 1998.

The Langes had previously been in mixed farming (wheat, sheep and pigs) before disenchantment with wool caused them to look hard at their future. For in the late 1960s prices had tumbled to such an extent that some were calling sheep vermin. At the time Merv and his two brothers Kevin and Don were running 16,000 on the 2500-hectare family farm taken up in the 1920s.

As an alternative Merv and his wife planted about a hectare of cabernet sauvignon, encouraged by the develop-

ment of the nearby large Roche vineyard and the positive progress of the Department of Agriculture experimental plantings on the Pearse family farm at Forest Hill, Mount Barker. The move was taken in the face of scoffing conservative farmers in the region, scepticism that made the Langes even more determined to succeed.

And succeed they have in spite of some savage setbacks, like devastating frosts. For example, their initial plantings in 1970 were wiped out, and ploughed back into the ground. Then spring frosts in the early 1980s cut crops by two thirds. But Merv was undaunted and philosophical; he knew that frost, like drought with grain crops, was all part of agriculture.

Curiously, though, nature was to provide some compensation with the resulting cabernet wine of such quality that it won a gold medal in the Sheraton Perth wine awards the following year. That certainly did not seem possible at the time of harvest, for the fruit that survived was high in acid and seemed to lack flavour.

Since then Merv has systematically made changes to minimise the problems of frost by removing vines from susceptible areas to higher ground and a southerly aspect, as well as changing trellising design.

Merv's brothers subsequently went their separate ways, and he and Judy have completely concentrated on vines and wine. Total plantings include 32 hectares with a further 12 planned for 1994.

Initially, Merv confesses, they were naive about the whole business and he looked to seminars, courses and books to acquire the new skills needed. For her part Judy turned to the Roche vineyard, working with viticulturist Ted Holland to gain experience.

The couple had no capital and there were some fairly ordinary wines made following the first commercial vintage in 1976. But they had some significant advantages — enough basic farming knowhow to get them by, and machinery from the mixed farm to do a lot of the early establishment work.

For the label they chose the property name Alkoomi, an Aboriginal word for watering place, and 1989 saw their biggest early planting year, four hectares. This, they thought, would provide for a consolidation period, but consumer demand dictated further expansion. Five-year market projections budget for the sale of 10,000 cases a year in WA, with similar quantities in the Eastern States and overseas. Two-thirds of the production will be white wines with rhine riesling, a delicate style having heaps of flavour, the vineyard's backbone. A good 'bread and butter line', it is cheap to make and has a lot going for it. The 1992, for example, was judged the best wine of the inaugural Great Southern Festival in 1993, beating some outstanding reds and whites.

Extolling the virtues of the Great Southern for rieslings, Merv says they are blessed with lovely natural acid, and are crisp and elegant with attractive citrus flavours.

Cabernet leads the red production. These are wines of good balance that age gracefully with blackcurrant flavours coming through from time to time. 'Everything seems to go right for us with the variety', Merv says proudly, and results certainly support his claim.

Every cabernet made in the 1980s and shown, except the 1989 vintage, has won a gold medal in a wine show somewhere, achieving a hattrick of golds at the Sheraton awards in the years 1982-83-84.

Another red from the winery to receive wide acclaim has been the much lower profile specialty malbec. With the sparkling red made from shiraz, it is Alkoomi's dearest wine.

Malbec from the vineyard, ideal with blue cheese, has been hailed as among the best in the country. The wines are densely coloured soft styles, massive in flavour, and complete even though the variety does not get the best oak — that goes to the cabernets. 'It is a variety that seems to be at home in our vineyard', Merv said. 'It is very happy there.'

The first chardonnay was produced at Alkoomi in 1989 and has become an important part of the range. Four or five different styles are made and blended. The final wine is lightly oaked and more in the flinty chablis style with later wines. 'I believe big, heavily oaked, buttery chardonnays are on the way out', Merv said.

But it was a sauvignon blanc that gave the Alkoomis their greatest industry thrill. This occurred when the 1989 vintage was judged the best wine at that year's SGIO Winemakers' Exhibition, winning for the couple a rich prize — $5000 towards a trip to any winegrowing area of the world.

It is hardly likely the classic white and red could achieve such success but their popularity with consumers is ample reward for the Langes. The fresh, fruity and friendly wines are a blend of top varieties, semillon, chardonnay and sauvignon blanc with the white, and shiraz, merlot, malbec and cabernet with the red. 'They are unpretentious wines that people really like', Merv said. Production of 5500 cases of the two classics in 1994 is set to become about 13,000 in 1998.

The initial 14 hectares planted at Alkoomi were on strong gravelly country and the remainder on weaker stony soils, quality being assured with three dams providing the necessary water. Generally, the vines are low in vigour and do not produce large crops, resulting in a concentration of flavours, tannins and colours in the reds. Later plantings, however, are based on higher-yielding varieties.

The vineyard's relative isolation, located about 75 kilometres north-west of Mount Barker, has been a problem, especially for cellar door sales. But the Langes' decision in 1983 to open a facility in Albany was a timely move, giving the wines much more public exposure.

CASTLE ROCK
ESTATE

Porongurup Road, Porongurup
Cellar Door Sales: Wed — Fri 10 a.m. — 4
p.m. Weekends and public holidays 10
a.m. — 5 p.m.

*Visitors to Castle Rock would agree with
Wendy Diletti that with a view like that above
(the Stirling Range is in the distance)
producing grapes is anything but a chore*

I ONCE dubbed Angelo Diletti Western
Australia's singing wineman. This was
because of his tendency to break into song
when leaving his former desk job as Director of Nursing at the Albany Regional
Hospital to head for the vineyard he and
wife Wendy have developed in the lofty,
rugged Porongurups, 40 kilometres to the
north-east.

Now he lives on the block, their home
providing sweeping views across the
vineyard to the Stirling Ranges, surely
some of the most magnificent of any in the
wine world.

The couple named their property Castle Rock after a prominent nearby landmark in the Porongurup National Park. It
is made up of eight hectares of vines
yielding about 60 tonnes of fruit with the
emphasis on riesling, chardonnay, pinot
noir and cabernet.

But their wine odyssey did not begin
in Western Australia's Great Southern.
Curiously, it had its origins in the Perth
suburb of Inglewood where their backyard
had become too small for their vegetable
and flower garden. They wanted more
space to spread their wings, and so headed
south. Soon afterwards Angelo and Wendy
began to search for their dream block,
taking water and soil samples all over the
countryside in their spare time, and generally driving agents mad. Finally, in December 1981, they took possession of a 55-
hectare block on the eastern slopes of the
Porongurup Range and set about planting
their first vines in 1983.

The Dilettis were soon to find, however, that the sheer beauty of the area
contained a hidden, darker side — prob-

lems that made Angelo, the son of an
Osborne Park market gardener, realise
that establishing a vineyard was not going
to be easy, even with Wendy's willingness
to tackle any job.

For example, he was to learn that kangaroos from the park loved a grapey meal
or three, vegetable weevils chewed everything from the ground up and had to be
sprayed at night when they were active,
grasshoppers were ever ready to sweep
in, birds, especially silvereyes, posed a
constant threat, and strong winds could
hammer young vines and crops. (Castle
Rock Estate faces south and into the teeth
of stiff southerlies.) But Angelo reckons
the vineyard location provides protection
from the more damaging north-westerly
winds, and at 300 metres above sea level
provides for one of the coolest spots in the
State.

Long periods of protracted heat are
certainly rare, and two small dams provide enough water in most years. There is
further advantage in the climate: picking
times are usually late April, which means
the fruit is subject to a long, slow ripening
period. This results in the estate flagship,
riesling, for example, retaining maximum
flavour with excellent natural acid, generating a delicate Germanic floral style with
a long palate. While later wines were higher
in acid and better drinking as one-year-olds,
early releases were extremely fresh and floral
with attractive citrus-lime characters. A
vertical tasting in 1993 showed how well the
wines age, with the first vintage (1986) still
having plenty of life.

So it was no surprise when, at the 1989
Mount Barker Show, the Castle Rock ries-

ling of that vintage was awarded a gold medal. It was the Dilettis' first, after several silver and bronze awards indicated that the ultimate accolade was soon to come.

Since 1990 cabernet from the vineyard has included ten per cent merlot. The wines generally have plenty of bouquet, are bigger, long living and have had plenty of skin contact, and, with vine maturity, a more definite berry character. They are given two years in oak and released as three-year-old wines.

Pinot noir, first vintaged in 1992, provides a lighter red to the range, while the chardonnays are more medium-bodied in style, enhanced by subtle, soft new French wood treatment, ideal with pasta,

according to Angelo.

There are no plans for a winery at Castle Rock with Frankland River producer Alkoomi responsible from the start for making the wines. Trellis changes in the vineyard in the early 1990s to the Scott Henry system have helped improve crop levels and provide riper fruit with greater exposure to sunlight. Now consolidation is the aim, for the Dilettis are realistic in acknowledging that the wine business is one where profits are going to take time.

'Going into wine has opened a new world for us', Angelo said. 'It is a most friendly and interesting industry with the social and business side extremely satisfying, despite the problems and fierce market competition.'

CASTLE ROCK
ESTATE
Porongurup Rhine Riesling
MOUNT BARKER
750 ml WINE MADE IN WESTERN AUSTRALIA

CHATSFIELD WINES

O'Neill Road, Mount Barker
Cellar door sales: Tues — Sun 10 a.m. — 5 p.m.

I F THERE is to be any good advice at all on wine, surely it should emerge from the French, who certainly have not lagged when it comes to per capita consumption of their national beverage. But it was not in France itself that Dr Ken Lynch stumbled across the earnest counsel of a Gallic doctor-cum-author. Ken happened to be in Nassau Street, Dublin, visiting Fred Hanna's secondhand bookshop, much favoured by medical students who traded books there as they advanced along their studies.

Dr Lynch unearthed a small wine book in which a French doctor claimed that people who drank up to a litre of good wine a day did not suffer like others from heart or liver disease. Since then Ken has been sharing a bottle of wine a day, and has been directly responsible for a lot of good wine being made.

Indeed, talking to Ken Lynch about wine is a bit like experiencing a travelogue — he began drinking wine, mostly German, while on a two-year working stint as a medico in the former West African territory of Cameroon. Three years later, in 1963, he got some further 'education' on wine in an unlikely spot, the wheatbelt town of Dalwallinu. Ken, who had migrated to Western Australia, called in to the local pub seeking a bottle of wine. 'Jeez, doc, are you a plonko?' was the response. When that idiom was explained, he was asked whether he wanted sweet or very sweet, for all that was available was medium dry and sweet sherry.

Much has transpired since these early, and rather unusual, initiations into wine, and the Dublin bookshop browser is now the outright owner of Chatsfield Wines.

Originally, Chatsfield (named after a

small bird called a chat that nests in the vineyard) was established in 1976 by Ron Waterman and his wife Jan, and called Waterman's Wines. Dr Lynch, who had moved to Albany in 1966, invested in the business with others in 1984, taking complete control in February 1989 by buying out former partners, including the Watermans.

Daughter Siobhan Lynch now runs the operation, including sales, promotion and vineyard management

The property, of 75 hectares, is seven kilometres east of Mount Barker. Of the 8.5 hectares planted to vines, rhine riesling makes up 2.5 hectares and there is just over a hectare each of traminer, cabernet franc, shiraz, chardonnay and cabernet sauvignon. The soils are mostly ironstone gravel with the balance medium density clay on slopes facing generally north-east. The crush of 35 tonnes in 1994 will rise significantly — to an estimated 150 tonnes — with proposed plantings of some 12 hectares in the next ten years. Then a winery is on the drawing boards.

Six wines are made for Chatsfield, four whites and two reds. Among them is a rhine riesling which brought great family joy in 1993 when the excellent, delicate vintage won two trophies at the Mount Barker Show for the best young wine exhibited and for the best of its variety. Yet intense rain two weeks before harvest — 200mm in 24 hours — resulted in extensive fruit damage and much heartache. 'We lost about half and had to go through and pick out the quality bunches and even the berries that were left', Siobhan said. But finally, with a record two golds, two silver and two bronze medals from the show, the unhappy memories vanished.

Chatsfield

1 9 9 3
Mount Barker
RIESLING

12.0%
Mount Barker, Western AUSTRALIA Alc.v/v

Chatsfield

1 9 9 1
Mount Barker
SHIRAZ

13.0%
Mount Barker, Western AUSTRALIA Alc.v/v

Curiosity in a Dublin bookshop prompted Ken Lynch's interest in wine, one that has burgeoned since

And what a tonic after the disastrous 1991 season when a devastating two-day heatwave hit Great Southern vineyards, cooking fruit on the vines. As a result, Chatsfield made no whites in that year. Fortunately, however, the reds were not affected and in 1994 a lovely, smooth, easy-drinking mulberry shiraz enhanced by American oak for the first time — very different to the traditional firm claret style — was marketed.

Chatsfield also produce a cabernet franc, the 1992 vintage a plummy, spicy, rich wine of considerable class.

Siobhan says general vine maturity is adding richness to fruit character and wine depth. Regular rainfall at the property, mostly light showers in summer, usually results in botrytis affecting the rieslings, adding aroma complexity and enhancing palate fullness and richness. There are often hints of apricot and tropical fruit, different to the region's more traditional and sometimes austere citrus characters.

The 1990 chardonnay recorded a major triumph for Chatsfield when it was named chardonnay-of-the-year at a national magazine's judging of wines from producers under 100 tonnes, rocketing the vineyard's image in the Eastern States. When it is realised that the first chardonnay vintage was only in 1988, it was a remarkable result.

The variety is barrel-fermented but the oak is limited in its influence. With the 1993 vintage, for example, fruit flavours at the tropical end of the spectrum jump out of the glass and follow through strongly on the palate.

But it was shiraz that initially enthused Ken Lynch, endorsed by the full flavour and softness of the first from the property, the 1988 vintage. His belief in the variety was based on wines made by Plantagenet and Alkoomi, showing that Mount Barker-Frankland was indeed a magnificent region for the variety.

Others must feel the same, for the 1988 Chatsfield wine won silver medals at the 1989 and 1990 Sheraton Perth wine awards. The 1989 shiraz won the best red of the region in the 1990 SGIO Winemakers Exhibition. Five years earlier in the Sheraton competition, Chatsfield won its first gold medal with a 1985 traminer. The 1993 traminer brought more joy when it won the aromatic category in the national Small Winemakers' Top 100 competition. Further, it was the highest scoring Australian white wine entered.

Previously, the vineyard had given an early indication of its promise when the first vintage, a 1979 riesling, won a gold medal.

A special friend for the family is the Albany 'doctor', the summer sea breeze that cools down the ripening grapes on most days. But the South African vegetable weevil and snails certainly do not come into that category, nor does the odd freak hail storm, of the kind that cost Chatsfield half its chardonnay in 1989.

The family will be looking to consolidate in the 1990s, with a strong push to get Chatsfield wines on as many Perth restaurant lists as possible. That reflects the commitment to quality, and the need to provide the finance for all the necessary equipment. 'If you are going to make top wines, you have to put the money into it', Dr Lynch said. 'You cannot have good fruit and bad gear.'

DALYUP RIVER WINES

Murray Road, Esperance
Cellar door sales: Weekends and public
holidays 10 a.m. — 4 p.m. between
September and Easter

What began as a hobby is now very much a business for Dalyup River's Tom Murray

TOM MURRAY, Western Australia's most isolated wineman, had an unusual visitor on one of my trips to the property, 40 kilometres west of Esperance and 700 kilometres south-east of Perth. It was a tiger snake, enmeshed in a net over the vines to protect the fruit from birds which abound in the prolific bush surrounding the Dalyup River a short distance away. It was a delicate operation releasing the unhappy snake without harm to it or to the rescuer. Once free, it slithered quickly away, leaving Tom to prepare for another vintage.

That involves tending a three-hectare vineyard established on a 2500-hectare coastal grazing and grain property purchased by the family in 1949. One of the early farming locations in the district, it was taken up in the 1890s by the Stewart family who built a solid stone homestead that Tom and wife Jenny still use today. Among the pioneering pursuits of the Stewarts was the production of fruit and vegetables to be sent to Norseman for miners in the fledgling goldmining industry of the area. Grapes from a nearby property were sent to Albany at about the same time.

Tom, a graduate in farm management from the Marcus Oldham Agricultural College in Victoria, took over the property in 1970 to run some 8500 sheep and 350 cattle. An interest in vines was sparked when members of an Esperance wine club considered planting a vineyard, inspired by exciting new developments at Margaret River and Mount Barker. Former State Government Viticulturist Bill Jamieson was invited to the district to advise on its potential and enthused over the Dalyup

River area. 'So we decided to give it a go', Tom said.

In 1976 an experimental hectare of shiraz and riesling was planted but it was to be longer than usual before the first vintage due to hungry sheep — about 600 in all — who gorged themselves on the succulent growth after a gate was left open.

In 1983 the first fruit was processed in the family bath on the back verandah, tasting authentic if not memorable, according to Tom. So plantings were expanded to include sauvignon blanc and cabernet sauvignon for an annual production of about 25 tonnes, processed at Plantagenet Wines in Mount Barker.

Depending on seasons, wine styles include a dry and sweet white from riesling, a wooded dry white from sauvignon blanc, dry red shiraz, and a port. I especially enjoyed the 1993 riesling, a well-made, floral, elegant style that sells particularly well in the town after which it is named, as are the other dry table wines. Featured on the label is the ship sailed by French Admiral D'Entrecasteaux who visited the area in 1792. The sweet wine is called Recherche after another of his ships and the Dalyup port, Le Grand, after a member of the fleet and from whom a local national park takes its name. With such significant local history, it is not surprising that most wine sold off the property is in Esperance.

Another enjoyable wine from the vineyard was the 1991 shiraz, a medium-bodied soft and smooth style with pleasant peppery characters, though not as intense as most wines from Mount Barker made of the variety.

The first vintage sauvignon blanc

(1992) of tropical fruit salad flavours also showed some early class by winning a silver medal at the Mount Barker Show of that year.

Now the vineyard is no longer a hobby but a business. Tom says the wines do not suffer because the fruit has to be carted 450 kilometres to Mount Barker for vinification. It is picked early in the morning and backloaded on a refrigerated truck which brings milk from Albany to Esperance.

While it can be very hot on some days

in summer in the area, Tom regards the climate as mild because the closeness to the sea means that the nights are cool. He says winds are his biggest problem and the isolation makes it difficult to compare notes with others in the industry. The nearest vineyard is in the Porongurup Ranges, 420 kilometres away!

Now a winery is seen as the next step, by the year 2000, Tom having completed a Bachelor of Applied Science in winemaking by correspondence with the Charles Sturt University.

FOREST HILL

Muirs Highway, Mount Barker
Cellar door sales: By appointment

Above: Co-owners Ron McGrath and Andrew Morton inspect ripening grapes at their newly purchased Forest Hill vineyard

W HEN BETTY Pearse was helping establish the Forest Hill vineyard at Mount Barker, she banned her small children from crying among the vines. The idea was to keep the vines happy, and she added to the scenario by playing radio music to the small cuttings, inspired by a report of a tomato grower who claimed that his plants produced more with the encouragement of a gentle symphony or two.

Betty took a strong personal interest in the vineyard as soon as arrangements were finalised for the Agriculture Department to conduct experiments there. Even though the first plantings failed dismally, she took to walking among the vines (addressed personally as 'you little darlings'), urging them to 'produce something great'.

Betty and Tony Pearse had agreed to the vineyard move at the time because of

the decline of the apple industry on which their 300-hectare property was based. They saw it as a golden opportunity to diversify into something new — and they had nothing to lose. Normally, contract work would have been sought off the farm to make ends meet — for this was the mid-1960s and wool, their other main farming pursuit, was in the doldrums. Instead, the Department of Agriculture was paying them to develop their own vineyard. Under the terms of the ten-year lease, in which just over two hectares of vines were planted, half rhine riesling and half cabernet, the vineyard was left to the family to do what they wished. 'If it was a flop we could have used the posts and wires to develop other areas of the farm', Betty recalled.

But such action proved totally unnecessary. For despite the disastrous start to the experiment, when virtually the whole vineyard had to be replanted, the vines flourished and some outstanding wines resulted. For example, the 1975 rhine riesling, made by Dorham Mann at Sandalford, went on to win a stunning 12 gold medals and nine trophies. It was after that vintage that the vineyard reverted to the Pearse family and expansion began immediately. This involved a steady programme of planting with the emphasis on cabernet sauvignon (about 65 per cent) and rhine riesling the rest. Unfortunately though, the red wine boom began to give way to a strong market surge to white wine, setting back family hopes.

But they were philosophical. They had seen other farming cycles and felt they had to stick at it.

The Department of Agriculture took the early fruit to Houghton for processing, and when Dorham Mann left the department in 1972 to take over at Sandalford, he made the wines. The next move involved Paul Conti at Wanneroo, who became the winemaker on a share farmer basis, believed to be a unique development for the local wine industry. 'We grew the grapes, Paul made the wine, and we shared it on a 50-50 basis', Betty said. It must be remembered, however, that this was still a time of tight finance so some short cuts had to be taken. Said Betty: 'The grapes went to Perth in banana boxes, leaving a trail of juice along the highways'. In 1983 fruit was sold to Michelton in Victoria as well, leading jokingly to the claim that they were the most travelled whole bunches of grapes in the world. Fruit was also sold to Houghton. In 1984 Plantagenet took over winemaking duties.

Today there are 24 hectares of vines planted with other varieties including chardonnay, sauvignon blanc, colombard, shiraz and traminer. The peak crush totalled 110 tonnes in 1986, but the tonnage has fluctuated dramatically with seasonal crises like the damaging cyclone Alby, and birds. In 1978, for example, silvereyes nearly took the lot. 'We saved about ten per cent of the fruit by driving a tractor and a car along the rows, 12 hours a day, for a fortnight', Betty said. 'It really was a desperate bid to drive them out. We went through two car horns.'

An unfortunate sequel was the damage to the soil from the tyre pounding, turning it into a powder that covered everything. Fire fighting equipment was used in an attempt to rid the fruit of the dust, and the family felt sure the grapes would have to be dumped on the tip. Amazingly, the resulting rhine riesling won a gold medal, even though the fruit looked terrible.

Wind and rain at the wrong time have also caused problems, severely affecting fruit set, while at the minute berry stages shedding has occurred with temperature changes. In addition, cellar door sales proved a waste of time. While Forest Hill is only 18 kilometres west of Mount Barker, off the Muirs Highway, it was on the wrong side of town to attract tourists.

But there were plenty of industry visitors, people from all over the world, keen to see the new experimental vineyard, the beginnings of a new industry.

So the family were never disheartened, with Betty forging a reputation as the area's 'first lady of wine'. They were always confident the property's micro-climate, its white clay soils and a generous supply of water providing underground moisture to the vines even at the highest points, would produce flavoursome and balanced fruit.

Subsequently, she and former husband Tony went their own ways with the property sold to Perth magnate (the late) Robert Holmes à Court's family company, Heytesbury Holdings Pty Ltd, for $1.3 million in 1989. In 1994 it was sold again, this time to a duo from the oil industry, Ron McGrath, a marine officer from Perth, and Andrew Marton, an electrical engineer from the Northern Territory. 'We were looking for a property to grow trees', Ron said. 'The vineyard was a bonus.'

Bruce Pearse, however, carries on the family involvement, being retained as vineyard consultant along with vineyard management of Vasse Felix which retains long-term contracts for the fruit.

Under the Vasse Felix ownership, two wines were made carrying the Forest Hill label, a riesling and cabernet. The policy is to be continued with plantings to be increased by some six hectares to cater for expanded Vasse Felix production and for some wines under the new ownership.

Rieslings from the property generally have been typical of the area, of lime citrus characters with plenty of acid. The 1993 carried seven grams per litre of residual sugar in a package that certainly pleased the consumer. The 1500 cases sold out in six weeks.

Cabernets have been generally medium bodied and earthy rather than herbaceous.

The balance of the fruit from the low-yielding vineyard, ensuring intensity of fruit flavours, goes towards various Vasse Felix styles, including its Noble Riesling in years of botrytis infection.

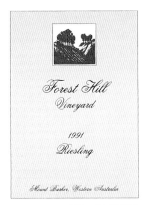

Forest Hill
Vineyard

1991
Riesling

Mount Barker, Western Australia

Forest Hill
Vineyard

1991
Cabernet Sauvignon

Mount Barker, Western Australia

FRANKLAND ESTATE

Frankland Road, Frankland
Cellar door sales: By appointment

Barrie Smith and Judi Cullam celebrate their first release of Frankland Estate wine

SELDOM is there a vineyard planted just to red varieties, especially at a time when the national emphasis firmly favours whites. At Frankland Estate in the Great Southern, however, Judi Cullam and husband Barrie Smith set out with a 'Bordeaux blend vision', to produce exciting reds. The initial vineyard was planted to 40 per cent each of merlot and cabernet franc, and the rest cabernet sauvignon. But in the interests of cash flow and economic balance, whites were added, resulting in another impressive development for the region.

The couple bought their property in 1974 as an investment and to run sheep, like their families before them. Judi, a radiotherapist, and Barrie, a realtor, wanted to bring up their children in a rural environment. In 1985 a holiday trip to France with former Houghton winemaker Bill Hardy was to turn on the 'wine tap'. 'We saw the best in winemaking, visited beautiful vineyards and chateaux, ate beautiful food and tasted beautiful wines', Judi said. 'It inspired us, building strongly on our keen interest in wine.'

Barrie Smith had been brought up on a vineyard in the Riverland area of South Australia where his family at the time were contract grape growers. So after a couple of good years in wool and real estate, the couple decided to take the plunge.

Planting began in 1988 and now totals 20 hectares. Besides the red varieties of shiraz, cabernet sauvignon, cabernet franc, merlot, malbec and petit verdot, there is rhine riesling, chardonnay and sauvignon blanc. The first winemaking crop was in 1991, with 150 tonnes picked in 1994. The first two vintages were made at Alkoomi, but 1993 saw Frankland Estate complete its own winery, a 300-tonne facility and the fifth in the region, bringing their commitment to the industry to more than $1 million.

The Frankland vineyard is established on an undulating ridge, part of the Frankland River valley system, five kilometres north of Rocky Gully. It is trickle-fed from a 25,000 cubic metre dam to avoid vine stress while rose bushes at the end of rows enhance the beauty of an impressive vineyard.

The main wine styles include rhine riesling, sauvignon blanc, chardonnay, a shiraz-based blend called Isolation Ridge, cabernet sauvignon and the Bordeaux blend, released for the first time in 1994. Called Olmo's Reward, the estate flagship acknowledges the role played by University of California Professor Harold Olmo in the development of the WA industry.

The rieslings so far have been typical of the region — floral aromatics, lime characters and fresh, crisp acidity. With later vintages, fruit intensity has increased. The 1992 sauvignon blanc, the first from the estate, is an elegant wine. Unwooded, it revealed distinct passionfruit aromas and fresh tropical fruit flavours on the palate. The chardonnay is expected to be the white flagship. A barrel-fermented wine, the 1992 is a fine example.

It showed classic aromas and light

melon flavours, enhanced by nutty oak complexity, a refined and restrained style compared to many Australian up-front wines.

The Frankland aim for the Isolation Ridge is a spicy bouquet and a rich, ripe berry fruit palate with soft tannins, the depth of flavour enhanced by the inclusion of cabernet franc, malbec and merlot.

The relative richness in the initial release cabernet impressed. A smooth wine with blackberry flavours balanced by subtle oak, it was a very good first-up effort indeed.

Olmo's Reward, however, should make the other reds seem almost insipid in comparison. Big, rich, velvety and complex, the first was due for release in late 1994 when it would be regarded as very approachable for a three-year-old wine, yet with years of cellaring potential ahead.

Under the Frankland ten-year-plan, the couple are budgeting for their first profits by 1998, with the main markets Perth, Sydney and Melbourne. To help reduce vineyard risks, they have joined other West Australian vineyards to employ internationally respected viticulturist Dr Richard Smart as a consultant.

Frankland does not show its wines. 'We would rather they speak for themselves, for consumers to decide, not judges', Judi said.

GREAT SOUTHERN producers Ian and Linda Tyrer, of Galafrey Wines, reckon they 'dug holes all over Western Australia' before choosing a Mount Barker property for their vineyard. Recalling the period, in the mid 1970s, jovial Ian quipped, 'It's a wonder the place doesn't leak'. They were, of course, sampling the soil in the search for a place to grow grapes for premium wine production.

But it might well have been marron, for the couple had identified the tasty crustaceans as a possible future direction, along with the wine industry, while working in computers in Melbourne. Ian always wanted to return to his home state and felt the slower pace of rural life was the place to bring up a family.

When the final decision was made in favour of wine, following extensive research suggesting it had a better future, the couple headed west to target properties at Margaret River and Mount Barker before making their final choice. In August 1976 they purchased a 60-hectare block ten kilometres west of Mount Barker, then headed back to Melbourne. For they had used annual holidays for their search and the income from computer work was considered essential, at least for another year. The first four hectares of vines were planted in 1977, with additional plantings the following year and again later to a total of 11 hectares. But great commitment was needed for Ian had taken a position in Perth to generate a cash flow and thousands of kilometres were travelled between city and property over succeeding weekends so the couple could nurture the young vines.

Their efforts resulted in a flourishing vineyard comprising a third rhine riesling, a third cabernet, and the rest chardonnay, merlot, shiraz, cabernet franc and a variety grown by few vignerons in Australia, müller thurgau. The first vintage, in 1982, was processed at Plantagenet Wines. Subsequently, shearing and machinery sheds were converted on their property for a winery.

But though ten kilometres is only a few minutes by car on a bitumen road, the winery and cellar door sales facility location was just too far from the major traffic flow to attract economic cellar doors sales. An important decision was made to transfer to Albany. 'We decided it was easier to cart 100 tonnes of grapes to town than to attract 100,000 tourists to our winery', Ian said.

So the Tyrers purchased an old wool store at the foot of York Street, selling all their land but the vineyard area, and set about a re-establishment period. The move with cellar door sales to the centre of a major West Australian tourist town saved them, said Ian, though in late 1991, in the interests of efficiency, he moved the winemaking sector back to the vineyard to a new 100-tonne facility.

Ian continued to supplement income with a variety of local jobs outside the industry, but he also worked vintages at Plantagenet, Houghton and at Hay River, in the Mount Barker area. Such effort has been essential, especially when nature plays wild cards like a cool spring, even snow, seriously affecting the 1993 crop and, a hailstorm in November 1988 which cut the 1989 crush to 26 tonnes, less than half expected. The damage to the vines also affected the 1990 crop. However, if the label has anything to do with it, such tribulations will be taken in their stride — Ian is quick to point out that Galafrey comes from 'gala', French for festivities

GALAFREY WINES

145 Lower Stirling Terrace, Albany
Cellar door sales: 10 a.m. — 5 p.m. Mon — Sat, and Sundays in school holidays and long weekends

Bare vines, but not for long. Ian Tyrer looks ahead to Galafrey's ultimate crush of 100 tonnes

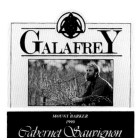

while 'frey' derives from a Nordic god of happiness.

Usually seven styles are made at the winery, depending on production and demand. Three wines were to provide major highlights, the 1985 cabernet which won the best open dry red trophy at the 1987 Mount Barker Show, the 1983 rhine riesling which was a trophy winner in the museum classes at the 1988 show, and the 1991 rhine riesling, trophy winner in the aromatics section of the 1993 Sydney International Top 100 Wine Competition. The latter was the first Great Southern riesling to win a trophy against international competition, other entries being from New Zealand, California and Chile, as well as all Australian mainland states. The success of the two rhines especially generated great satisfaction while the museum classes award for the 1983 cemented Ian's original belief that Mount Barker could grow quality fruit to be used successfully in making aged wines. It also underscored the Galafrey philosophy — to make traditional classic wine styles that can live long periods.

Ian chose rhine riesling and cabernet as his flagship wines because earlier styles produced in the area had shown great strength of varietal character. With time in the bottle, rhines like the successful 1983 and 1991 generate sweet, honeyed, floral flavours while in the cabernet, chocolate and tobacco flavours emerge. Blending plans for the variety in the future will include merlot and cabernet franc to add fullness. This will increase the palate length and help the wine age well, though

it may be 'a bit hard to drink early' according to Ian.

But while the buffs may applaud such wines, many consumers prefer the less pedigreed medium dry wine made from müller thurgau. (This variety is important in Germany and comes from a cross of riesling and sylvaner made at Geisenheim in 1882 by Dr Müller, a Swiss from Thurgau.) To Ian this light, fruity style is ideal when watching tennis on a Sunday afternoon, and eating cucumber sandwiches. To fill out the palate a dash of rhine riesling is added. It sells extremely well at cellar door and the Japanese have taken a liking to the wine, with a 1993 order of 1000 cases.

Ian rated year three as his low point when such development is at its economic worst, and so is morale. 'You have done so much work and spent so much money, and still there is no real return', he said. Overall the development has been a financial battle with labour substituted for dollars. 'If we could not afford something we had to go out and build or make it', he commented.

The winery target is for a crush of 100 tonnes, looking into the present decade and given a kind smile from nature. During this time Ian predicts the Galafrey wine quality level will continue its strong improvement. 'We have needed time to gain experience', he said. 'This has been a new world for us, a totally new life. I am confident of the future and believe there is a sound place for us. We are selling what we make, and have developed a firm reputation for value-for-money.'

SUPPORT for wine comes from strange places at times — like the Antarctic for the Gilberts of Kendenup, 18 kilometres north of Mount Barker. Their 1991 shiraz has been enjoyed in the ice and snow, with a bottle photographed at the Taylor Glacier, 100 kilometres west of the Mawson base.

The wine was sent to electrician Glen Scherell of Mount Barker by his mother as a taste of a local product during a working stint at the base.

The Gilberts have also had a call from Beijing seeking a wine after a Chinese diplomat had paid them a call during a visit to Western Australia.

Jim and Bev Gilbert are third-generation horticulturists, the family having established a solid reputation for apple and stone fruit production for more than half a century. But they chose vines, inspired by the success of the local Mount Barker industry.

Establishment began in 1985 on gravelly loam, about a metre deep over clay — old redgum country previously used for grazing. Initially rhine riesling and chardonnay were planted, and then shiraz for a total of four hectares. Further plantings in 1994, including cabernet sauvignon and merlot, doubled the trickle-fed vineyard area.

The wines are made at Plantagenet with about a third of the fruit sold to other winemakers to offset costs. At full production the Gilberts expect to market about 3000 cases.

The main wine styles are riesling, chardonnay and shiraz, with a cabernet blend to come, and perhaps a straight merlot. The aromatic, lemony riesling (some spoke of appley flavours in the first vintage) is the best yielder so far, and has had most pats on the bottle. Each vintage has gained four stars out of five in the annual tasting of West Australian wines by the national magazine *Winestate*. It has twice been recommended in the best new releases from the State. Clean and fresh, the 1992 chardonnay was fuller than I expected, with early trellis changes seeking to open up the canopy, exposing the fruit more to the sunlight. Initially, it was well and truly hidden, inclined to produce more herbaceous characters. "We are looking for a little bigger, more generous wine in the buttery style', Bev said. The 1992 Gilbert shiraz, released in 1994, has intense colour and flavour with soft tannins and the spicy, peppery characters usually associated with Mount Barker wines of the variety. The shiraz and chardonnay were priced at $13 a bottle, with the riesling $11 (1994 prices).

Well may Jim Gilbert marvel at the wonders of wine. His shiraz below, quaffed at the Antarctic's Taylor Glacier, was vintaged in the heat of a Kendenup summer

They can be sipped in an appropriate historical environment, for the cellar door sales facility is the restored original farm cottage, made of hand-cut bush poles and weatherboard, and believed to have been moved to the property from a block opposite in the 1930s.

GILBERTS WINES

Albany Highway, Kendenup
Cellar door sales: Wed — Sun and public holidays, 10 a.m. — 5 p.m.

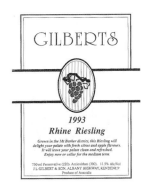

GILBERTS

1993
Rhine Riesling

GOUNDREY WINES

Cellar door sales: North Street, Denmark
(old butter factory) Mon — Sat 10 a.m. —
4.30 p.m. Sun 11 a.m. — 4.30 p.m.
Langton homestead, Muirs Highway,
Mount Barker, same opening times.
Tearooms available

Above: Autumn leaves, soon to fall. Mike and
Alison Goundrey savour the results of
another successful vintage

I T WAS a humble beginning, just a small
vineyard in the Hay River valley about
15 kilometres south-west of Mount Barker,
and surely one of the State's most unusual
wineries, an old butter factory at Denmark. But that was the start in the grape
and wine industry for former shearer
Michael Goundrey and his schoolteacher
wife Alison, an enthusiastic and energetic
couple whose extensive expansion has
seen them emerge as one of the strengths
in the Great Southern.

The original planting of cabernet
sauvignon was on a modest two hectares
of land; as the total size of the block they
had bought was only 30 hectares, the couple realised that whatever they went in for
would have to be intensive — even if it
was pigs or passionfruit.

The butter factory was taken over in
November 1978 as a place to make and sell
their wines.

Having opted for wine, they realised
they could not look after their little vineyard with hand tools. Machinery was
needed, and to justify the cost they decided to double the area.

Today the butter factory, which operated for about 50 years from the 1920s and

is a tourist attraction in itself, is a cellar
door sales centre and bottling facility while
a massive winery has been built on the
historic Langton property on the Muirs
Highway, ten kilometres west of Mount
Barker. The vineyard established on its
picturesque slopes is one of four owned
by a company structure which is also responsible for the care and management of
others, some belonging to Perth professional people.

The Goundreys put up their premium
vineyard Windy Hill and the butter factory for a major share of a new company
which includes local investors.

More than $3.5 million has been in-
vested, including the purchase of Chateau
Barker, one of the pioneering properties
established by the Cooper family, six kilometres north of Mount Barker on the
Albany Highway. It has been renamed
Williams' Rest, in honour of the original
owners, the Williams family. One of their
children was killed by a stage coach accident last century, and a tomb on the road-
side marks his grave.

The Goundrey masterplan envisages
1500 tonnes of processed fruit by 1995
from its associated vineyards, and 2000

tonnes by the turn of the century. Langton is the biggest planting with 68 hectares of the 106.5 hectare total.

The company had its eyes on the Langton land for three years before effecting the purchase. Michael had carted hay there as a boy and realised its potential. His grandmother also knew the property from visits in the early days.

Not far away is another reminder of the past, a crumbling wooden bridge over the Hay River, once used by horse and wagon teams to cart wool to Albany.

In 1839, only ten years after the founding of the Swan River Colony, the property was granted to two privates in an infantry regiment. However, only a few days later a deed of sale was drawn up to Sir Richard Spencer, the government resident at the time and Western Australia's first farmer, who had taken up land at Strawberry Hill Farm, Albany. The 'coastal disease' (in fact, a mineral deficiency) had attacked his sheep and caused heavy losses, so he moved his flock inland to rich river pastures on the banks of the Hay River at St Werburghs. Langton passed to his son, Edward Spencer, whose executors sold it to enable his estate to be settled. The new owner, Sir Alexander Cockburn Campbell, MLC for Albany and later editor of *The West Australian*, was a Scottish baronet whose family seat was Cockburn Castle.

The property acquired the name Langton after the Marquis of Berwickshire, the founder of the family title. In 1883 the Mitchell family became part of the Langton story when William Wallace Mitchell built the first homestead, although his purchase of the land from the Cockburn Campbell family was not formalised until 1890. W.W. Mitchell was a grandson of William Mitchell, who in 1842 became chaplain of the Church of England in the Swan River Colony and the first rector of the parish, which included the Guildford, Midland and Upper Swan churches.

William Mitchell was also responsible for the building in 1839 of Western Australia's first church, All Saints Church in Upper Swan. It was constructed on the site that Captain James Stirling had visited only 12 years earlier and pronounced suitable for settlement.

In 1928 Clayton Mitchell, nephew of W.W. Mitchell and great-grandson of Reverend Mitchell, took over the property. Clayton Mitchell was MLA for Stirling for nine years and the first president of the Plantagenet Shire Council. During the years of Clayton's tenure, the property became one of the district's foremost ap-

ple producers. Now young vines grace its slopes as Langton moves into a new form of agriculture.

The property is certain to be an increasing tourist attraction in its own right with visitors able to undertake a comprehensive self-guided tour. Photographs, diagrams and text will explain the picturesque outlook — including young cherry trees — and features of the winery below. Another treat will be tastings in the restored 1920s Langton homestead.

No doubt they will also be told as they sip a sample how the vineyard workers turned their hand to roofing the huge winery, fixing 170,000 sheoak shingles and combining the work with their hobby interest, abseiling up and down the lofty roof that reaches 18 metres at its highest point.

The landmark also includes rammed earth walls and timber from an old road bridge replaced by concrete. The winery's modern facilities are a far cry from 1981 when the Goundreys — faced with cold weather and a yeast problem that had prolonged fermentation — wrapped a fermenting tank of rhine riesling in three electric blankets. Fortunately, Alison recalled, friends had gone north so they were able to strip their beds. They kept the blankets in place for a month, raising the temperature by about five or six degrees to complete the fermentation process.

Another problem the group would like to have behind them is birds, which took a massive 60 per cent of their crops in 1978. But two years earlier the 1976 vintage was to produce a cabernet sauvignon that won the Goundrey's their first medal. It was only a bronze, but it was a start.

Since then they have gone on to win 14 trophies and 82 medals as well as being named in the national Sydney top hundred competition on four occasions, with the 1985 cabernet sauvignon judged the outstanding wine in 1988. The Goundrey 1989 cabernet from the company's Windy Hill vineyard gained further honours when it became the first WA wine to be awarded a Certificate of Excellence by the Institute of Masters of Wine. The successes reflected the continued improvement with the variety over the years flowing from viticultural changes, especially in trellising, based on the Lyre or U-system.

This provides for more light penetration and results in more depth of flavour in the fruit. Michael says that even in the driest seasons the vines are not stressed using the system. In addition low pH and high acid levels combine to give the wines long life.

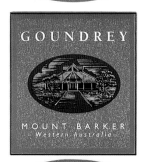

No fewer than 170,000 sheoak shingles make up Goundrey's Langton winery roof. The walls are of rammed earth

variety was certainly supported when the 1992 vintage from the winery was judged top- of- the- month by a German national magazine. Such successes are enormously important to exports, which represented about 40 per cent of production in 1993-94 and were worth $750,000 to the UK alone.

There are eight main wines in the Goundrey range, including three reserve styles, riesling, cabernet and chardonnay. Others are a cabernet-merlot, chardonnay, classic red and white and chenin blanc, the latter from purchased fruit grown at Bindoon.

I have always enjoyed the cabernets from Windy Hill, especially for their berry flavour intensity, usually of blackcurrant and cassis. In more recent years a combination of American and French cask maturation has provided sweet oak flavours to young wines and an underlying structure for long ageing. Big fruit, of melon and figs, is the feature of the top chardonnay with oak from three different French coopers adding early subtle vanilla flavours to youthful touches of spiciness, and butterscotch with development.

For me, the 1992 vintage from the Windy Hill vineyard has been most memorable and it was no surprise that it went on to win two trophies, three gold and three silver medals in 1993.

To overcome confusion, a major marketing change in 1994 saw all wines come under the Goundrey label, with only the Langton and Windy Hill vineyards identified on back labels.

Other important factors for grape growing in the region, according to Michael, are deep red loam soils and the cold night breezes, which also help prolong the ripening period and retain flavour. This has been especially significant for the rhine rieslings, resulting in aromatic, powerfully flavoured styles that are fresh and crisp as youngsters, high in acid for cellaring, and usually showing strong citrus characters, often with a botrytis influence. Michael's claim that the Mount Barker region would produce the best wines in Australia this decade from the

HOWARD PARK

South Coast Highway, Denmark
Cellar door sales: By appointment

THE establishment of Howard Park as a label was the culmination of a dream for Great Southern winemaker John Wade. Since joining Wynns in South Australia's Coonawarra in 1978, where the production was greater than that of the total West Australian crush, he looked forward to his own wine. Not just any wine, mind you, but wines that enthusiasts could cellar for long periods, even 20 or 30 years. That represents a significant change from the norm, where tight economics and high interest rates make cash flow from early selling wines absolutely vital for many producers, while on the consumer side most look to drink their wines within 36 hours of purchase.

But John's main target is very much those people who appreciate aged wines, and he is committed to ensuring they have the flavour and structure to go the distance, in obviously what must be a good cellar.

John's path into the business was unconventional, to say the least. An electrician by trade, he served in the army and then worked in a nursery before becoming a trainee supermarket manager, moving on to a Melbourne licensed grocery. This was to spark an interest in wine, stimulated by courses that saw him return to school to establish a career in winemaking, urged along by eminent makers like Ian Hickenbotham and Pam Dunsford. Lecturers, top Australian industry men like Brian Croser, Tony Jordan and Don Lester, further stimulated the interest. Vintage experience included Hollydene and Arrowfield in the New South Wales upper Hunter area, and Boroka in Victoria. In addition he helped establish a winery in two converted old sheds at the Riverina College of Advanced Education, now the Charles Sturt University.

Another budding winemaker involved in the project was Rob Bowen, whose position at Plantagenet Wines, Mount Barker, John Wade was later to take. The duo had kept in touch throughout, for Rob Bowen was to be something of a weather forecaster for John. 'I would ring him regularly, because generally the weather Rob was having in Mount Barker would get to us two or three days later at Coonawarra', he said.

When he came to Western Australia in January 1986, John was appointed to two wineries 140 kilometres apart, Alkoomi at Frankland River and Goundrey Wines at Denmark. Part of the deal involved providing fruit for his Howard Park label, an arrangement which carried on at Plantagenet.

There are three wines in the range, initially a riesling and cabernet to which merlot is added, and then, in 1994, the first chardonnay was released. Two years earlier, a dry white and dry red was made and introduced under Madfish Bay, a label taken from a local seaside beauty spot, so called because of often seen desperately jumping fish, seeking to escape hungry feeding dolphins. The wines are made to be clearly identified as Australian with an Aboriginal-designed label. They are soft, early drinking styles, definitely classier than most on the market and modestly priced. A ready market was quickly established to the UK with John predicting sales of 10,000 cases by the turn of the century. By that time, he expects to be crushing 500 tonnes a year at a new winery established at Denmark. In 1993 John left Plantagenet to venture out on his own, the move a half share between himself and wife Wendy, and the family company of Perth businessman Jeff Burch and his wife Amy. It is based on Great Southern fruit purchases and contract winemaking for vineyards from a wide area including Mount Barker, Pemberton, Denmark, Margaret River and the Porongurups.

Since his arrival in WA John has produced many trophy winning wines for Plantagenet and for other producers whose wines he has made. None have been sweeter, however, than the best wine at the 1993 SGIO Winemakers Exhibition; this went to the 1991 Howard Park cabernet-merlot, and with the accolade came a prized overseas trip for two. The chief judge, Sydney Master of Wine Nick Bulleid, praised the wine for its combination of full, lush rich flavours, fine grain tannins, excellent balance and long life potential. It revealed a combination of flavours, blackcurrant, cassis and mocha

characters from well seasoned oak and quality fruit. It reminded me of John's hatstand theory for reds in which the various components — acid, tannin, flavour, oak and so on — are distributed in such a way that the stand does not fall over.

He regards the time fruit is picked for winemaking as critical, so that the flavour and balance is at its peak. Over-ripe fruit to him produces wines that are 'jammy and liquorice-like'. He ferments reds in open vats because the oxygen helps stabilise the colour and tannin, with ageing in new French Troncais barriques which he believes are suited best to Mount Barker wines.

'A combination of fine grain tannin and tight wood has the effect of pulling the wine together', he says. 'It gives the impression of leanness, but it is not.'

John Wade's aim is to tap a market where people appreciate good aged wines

However, John argues strongly that aged rieslings are Australia's greatest wines and supports a view shared by many that Mount Barker is one of Australia's best areas for the variety.

John's skills could probably see him in a senior position anywhere in the country, so his decision to go to Mount Barker is fortunate for the region. And while he feels the area has done particularly well in its short history, he sees a major need for more professional winemakers if it is really to have its natural potential exploited. For him, such development would see some of the small growers taking the next step and making their own wine, rather than contracting it out.

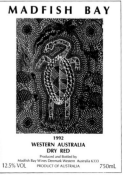

JINGALLA WINES

Adjacent Porongurup National Park
Cellar door sales 10.30 a.m. — 5 p.m.

S HEEP love grapevines, as some un-
lucky vignerons have found, especially
when a gate has been left open to a neighbouring paddock of stock. They are also
fond of grapes as well, no matter how green.
Geoff Clarke, of Jingalla Wines on the
northern slopes of the Porongurup Ranges,
16 kilometres east of Mount Barker, has
first-hand experience that proves sheep will
devour everything they can reach. 'All they
will leave is the trunk and arms of the vines,
and nothing else', he says.

Geoff, a former shearer, originally began the venture with wife Nita, and were
later joined by Nita's brother Barry Coad
and his wife Shelley. The vineyard has
been established on part of the former 95-
hectare Coad family property and is the
end product of a search for 'something
different' in agriculture.

The first vines were planted in 1979 on
the steep slopes of the block which is
adjacent to the popular Porongurup National Park and, like other estates in the
tiny producing area, commands panoramic views. For Barry these are always a
tonic, providing a lift whenever vineyard
work takes its toll.

Now a teacher at Mount Barker Senior
High School, he was based at Busselton
when he and his wife became involved in
Jingalla. As a result many hours were

*Jingalla's vines give a different hue to the
olive green slopes of the Porongurups. Geoff
Clarke checks the berries with Shelley Coad*

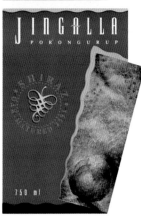

spent behind the wheel as the couple commuted between the two areas to help with the workload.

There are eight hectares planted at Jingalla, comprising cabernet, rhine riesling, shiraz, semillon and verdelho. At capacity in 1995, a production of 50 tonnes is envisaged. The original plan had been to sell the grapes and not bother with wine. But, said Geoff, 'when the crop came along, it looked pretty good — why let somebody else have all the fun?'

And it was not long before there was a great deal of rejoicing. At the 1988 Mount Barker Wine Show, an event that attracts wineries from all over the State, the 1986 Jingalla cabernet sauvignon won the trophy for the best open dry red, creating a niche in the history of the fledgling Porongurup industry. For in beating the best from Western Australia, it registered the first trophy to go to a local wine.

More accolades followed such as trophies in 1991 for most successful exhibitor in red wine classes, and for the best West Australian shiraz (with the 1989 vintage) at the Perth Wine Show.

No wonder that by 1994 Geoff was phasing himself out of the commercial sheep industry.

The wines have been made at Goundrey's under a label that has the same name as the family farm — an Aboriginal word meaning half moon shape (which is roughly the way the block looks).

Its soils vary from pea-size gravelly loams to red granite loam that Geoff describes as particularly strong country, generating in the red wines earthy flavours and long life. The highest point of the property is 350 metres above sea level which, while exposing the leaves and shoots to damage from south-westerlies, provides cool conditions. This makes for late picking; the 1989 rhine riesling, for example, was picked from 22 April, while the 1991 was still being harvested in May. Sometimes the season has broken by this time. 'We do not have any problems getting the grapes ripe in our conditions', Geoff said, 'but we will never get the sugar levels up unless it is an exceptional year'. Even so, the whites, left to age in the bottle, have developed honey characters helped by vine maturity, though as youngsters they were lighter, more elegant styles. Cabernet and rhine riesling proved the early Jingalla flagships, but a lot of family faith rests on a floral, sometimes tropical fruit, lightly oaked verdelho. For my palate, however, give me the reds, like the 1989 cabernet and shiraz, and 1991 shiraz. Delicious berry characters of the

cabernet swamped the mouth with flavour, while the lighter, fresh, spicy, peppery fruit of the shiraz wines and their soft, smooth and generous finish, seemed more French Rhone-like than Porongurup. There are four reds and four whites in the Jingalla range, including two specialty fortifieds, based on Swan Valley material.

Although a farmer all his life, Geoff acknowledges there has been a lot to learn in a totally new enterprise, and applauds Department of Agriculture adviser John Elliott for his help. The work involved in running a vineyard far exceeded his expectations, whether it was netting to counter the bird problem or trying to unravel the mystery of what was devouring their vines. Inspection after inspection found no cause, and only when they followed advice to look at night by torchlight was the answer revealed. Hordes of vegetable weevils proved the culprits, resulting in a lot of nocturnal spraying to counter the invaders. Then there was the hail storm of November 1992 which devastated the vineyard, jagged triangles of ice like tiny swords, cutting off shoots as swiftly as razors. The fruit that remained however, produced some very good wine, but Jingalla had to buy in supplies to meet consumer demand. It has done so regularly from the nearby Bolganup vineyard, another pioneering planting of the area.

The good fortune for the Porongurup industry is that they border the national park — an important local tourist attraction — ensuring a constant flow of visitors, many of whom take time off from sightseeing to try some of the wines, creating a genuine developing interest in the area.

Geoff Clarke, with Shelley and Barry Coad, make a toast on the occasion of their tenth winemaking anniversary

KARRIVALE

Woodlands Road, Porongurup
Cellar door sales: Wed — Sun and public
holidays 10 a.m. — 5 p.m. and other days
by appointment. BBQ facilities. Group
catering by arrangement

C AMPBELL McGREADY is one of the
few industry people I know to drive
from home to vineyard via a scenic tourist
route. Karrivale is adjacent to the
Porongurup National Park and almost
directly under Gibraltar Rock, a rugged
outcrop towering above the landscape. A
big, solid man like the ranges above his
vines, Campbell took over the 200-hectare

grazing property on the death of his
Scottish-born dairy farmer father in 1956.
    But it was not until about a quarter of
a century later, in 1979, that he and his
wife Annette planted their first vines, rhine
riesling. For like others in the district they
had been inspired by Mount Barker pioneer Tony Smith of Plantagenet Wines, a
close friend, who convinced them that

*Above: 'Solid as the Rock of Gibraltar' goes
the saying. That's the local namesake of the
famous Mediterranean landmark in the
distance, and before it, Campbell McGready
Right: Earthy tones of timber and stone create
a welcoming environment in Karrivale's
cellar sales and gallery*

winemaking was interesting and exciting, and a future industry of the region.

Originally, they marketed their wine as Narang, but a lawyer's letter was to see a change. They were instructed to remove all their wines from retailing shelves wherever they may be. The major national producer Lindemans evidently considered the name clashed with one of its labels, Nyrang Hermitage.

The Karrivale vines grace a sloping block, 360 metres above sea level at the top end. They grow on gravelly karri loam eroded from the ranges over clay to varying depths, and next to tall, majestic karri trees regenerated from the 1930s. For in a bizarre move at the turn of the century, a local parliamentarian had the area ringbarked. He planned to set up a sanitarium for Welsh coalminers suffering from silicosis, and a deer park. Deer eventually were run on the property, ultimately to be shot out, but the plan for the miners did not proceed.

The McGreadys have added further riesling to their original plantings, along

with chardonnay, shiraz and cabernet sauvignon, providing for wooded white and red wine in an annual crush of 65 tonnes by the turn of the century.

Campbell enjoys shiraz for the pepperiness of the wines produced in the area, and the intensity of the fruit. The rieslings so far have been dry, floral wines with a lime citrus character found in such wines from Porongurup vineyards. They reflect good quality fruit, and I especially enjoyed the 1991 and 1993 vintages, the latter light and clean with apple and lemon sorbet-like freshness and excellent vari-

etal fruit. The earlier vintage surprised for its youthful qualities but not for its extremely positive riesling characteristics. While all shown have been medal winners, the 1990 labelled Premium Dry surpassed all by being runner-up in a 1992 national competition for small winemakers held in Canberra.

The prime crops from the property are enjoyed by the birds as well, particularly parrots. Their invading beaks certainly keep Campbell on his toes, trying to protect the precious fruit.

At other times he is busy working in support of the district's wine industry, or building (a passion). That includes the family house and the culmination of a dream, a stone wine sale and storage facility with materials from the property, an attraction in itself.

The Albany sea breeze plays its part in keeping the vineyard cool while the average rainfall of 750mm received a hefty boost in 1988 when 1100mm was recorded and 959mm in 1993. 'Even the ducks had to wear gumboots', Campbell quipped.

Eventually four varieties will be marketed by Karrivale, with cabernet added. The McGreadys will look to tourists visiting the scenic, popular area as a major market. No doubt some of the visitors will picnic by adjacent Mindyegilup Creek, a small stream that provides permanent water for the vines, essential in the early establishment stages.

D EEP IN the heart of South West karri country a family group has established Karriview, a tiny vineyard amid the giant trees. But this is a case of small being beautiful. For not only is this one of the State's most attractive settings in a popular tourist area, its wines have done remarkably well in its short history, winning important show awards. For example, there was the best chardonnay and best white wine trophies at consecutive Mount Barker shows with the 1990 chardonnay, their first produced, gold medal in Melbourne for the 1990 pinot noir, gold again for the 1991 and 1992 vintages at Mount Barker, and a silver trophy at the Sheraton wine awards for the 1991 pinot noir.

So Bruce and Mary Day, who took a five-year lease of the property in 1993 from relatives Robin, Cathy and Frances Day, and Richard Manser, were a contented couple as they recounted their change of direction in life on my first visit.

Originally, they purchased the 47-hec-

KARRIVIEW WINES

Cnr Scottsdale Road and Roberts Road, Denmark
Cellar door sales and tearooms: Daily 10 a.m. — 5 p.m. in summer and school holidays. From Feb — May, Fri — Mon. Winter, weekends only, tearooms closed

Spirits are high, and so are the trees, as Bruce and Mary Day reflect on the joys of winemaking

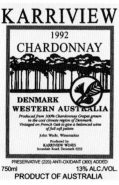

tare property as a weekend escape from their lives in Perth, forming a partnership in 1982. Half is covered by karri and redgum forests and cannot be cleared under remnant vegetation protection enforced by the Department of Conservation and Land Management.

In the search for some form of intensive agriculture for the rest of the land, the group turned to vines, inspired by other vineyard developments in the area. They began planting in 1986, two hectares of chardonnay and pinot noir, considered best suited to the cool Denmark environment. When Bruce (a woolclasser) and Mary (a nurse) decided to settle on the property, the others followed.

Nearly 8000 closely planted vines now flourish with production expected to reach 15 tonnes in optimum conditions.

But in the idyllic setting nature sometimes plays a wild card, such as with hail storms at the wrong time, and that bad day in the summer of 1991 when searing temperatures which hit Western Australia cooked most of the chardonnay. Curiously, however, the pinot noir — at an early stage of maturity — did not suffer, with the vintage going on to be a trophy winner.

For their part the towering karri trees act as windbreaks and prevent the vineyard becoming too wet in this traditional high rainfall area. They also happen to be home to many birds, necessitating protective netting around the vines. No pesticides are used on the property; bugs are kept under control by guinea fowl which are partial to some of the fruit as well.

John Wade has made the wines for Karriview, forecasting a five to seven-year life for the chardonnays. These are barrel-fermented, lovely clean wines with melon and light citrus characters. They are complex and yet uncomplicated with good weight and texture. A feature of the outstanding 1990 was its balance and generous palate depth, surprising for fruit from such young vines.

The 1992 pinot noir is another stunning wine, one of the best of the many tried for this publication. Elegant and refined with a gamey bouquet, it is soft and round with a finish that exploded like the fanned tail feathers of a peacock! It should still be drinking well in 1997.

With such quality, the future looks bright for Karriview. Vine maturity can only enhance fruit intensity and quality.

MATILDA'S MEADOW

Hamilton Road, Denmark
Cellar door sales and restaurant, morning
and afternoon teas and lunches: Daily 10
a.m. — 4 p.m.

*Don Turnbull and Pamela Meldrum on
their semillon block with tall young karris in
the background*

TWO PEOPLE with diverse back-grounds are behind the Matilda's Meadow development situated in a pictur-esque tourist drive area four kilometres east of Denmark. Pamela Meldrum and Don Turnbull had by 1994 spent $500,000 creat-ing their vineyard Eden.

Queenslander Pamela, a former oil industry executive of 21 years' standing, and Don, a New South Wales hotelier like his father before, joined forces in 1989 after deciding to settle in Western Aus-tralia. In July 1990, besotted with Den-mark, they purchased a former major apple and pear orchard surrounded by karri and redgum trees. Spurred on by a love of wine, they began planting two months later. Today six hectares of pinot noir, cabernet sauvignon, cabernet franc, chardonnay and semillon flourish in the karri loam soils, watched by the proud owners from their renovated Group Set-tlement scheme cottage.

But as they reflected on their first seri-ous vintage in 1994, the admission came that it was not all sweetness and light. Kangaroos, foxes and silvereyes took an early toll, such that Pamela had to resort to some unusual tactics to say the least, to counter the birds. Watermelons were cut and left on a table under their main roost-ing trees, along with a bowl of sugar and water. 'It worked and saved us some of our valuable fruit', Pamela said.

The first wines, made by John Wade, include an unwooded chardonnay, a pinot noir and a blend of semillon and pur-chased sauvignon blanc.

'We like our whites young and cheeky', Pamela said. 'We will be looking to clean, dry styles like the sauvignon blanc-semillon which goes down so well in our climate. I will encourage visitors to try our pinots slightly chilled while the fuller-bodied style reds will be aged for two years before release.'

By 1998 the couple expect a produc-tion of 70 tonnes, some 4500-5000 cases. The aim is to export half, mainly to the UK, with the rest sold to liquor stores and restaurants, and at cellar door.

Despite his life time in the hospitality business, Don, who attended agricultural college as a young man, has taken to the new life. As an extension of his activities, he has set up Great Southern Vineyard Services to establish, manage and main-tain other properties.

MILLINUP ESTATE WINES

Porongurup Road, Porongurup
Cellar door sales: Weekends and holidays
10 a.m. — 5 p.m., and most other days

BY ANY standards, Peter Thorn's Millinup Estate is postage stamp in size. Located on a hill in the foothills of the majestic Porongurup Range, it is less than half a hectare, planted to rhine riesling. Such is its cool climate situation, located 350 metres above sea level, that Peter likens it to the German homeland of the variety.

But it is in reality vastly different. The vines flourish in karri loam soils, next to a national park of Australian bush that could never be part of Europe.

To me it is not surprising that Peter Thorn (pictured above) has ended up among vines and wines. The former real estate agent who specialised in the hills of Perth and Midland area, lived his early life among the vines of the Swan Valley. His late father Lindsay, originally a vigneron, represented the area as part of the seat of Toodyay and for six years was Minister for Lands. 'When my father was away in World War I, my mother would travel out from Fremantle by horse and sulky to water the vines', Peter said. 'They established the property in 1913.'

Peter and his late wife Lesley bought the 64-hectare Porongurup property in 1988, naming it after the Millinup Pass in the adjacent ranges. Included were vines that had been planted some 15-16 years earlier, producing wines for a season or two under the Point Creek label. By 1996 the vineyard is to be expanded to two hectares. As well, fruit is purchased to extend the wine range. Besides the elegant, crisp, citrusy riesling, it includes a sweeter, fruity, late harvest riesling, an attractive, medium-bodied, slightly spicy cabernet franc, and a fuller cabernet sauvignon based on the Bordeaux style, of blackcurrant and vanilla oak flavours.

The wines are attractive and well made, but Millinup is worth a visit regardless. From the verandah of the cellar door sales centre are sweeping views across to the Stirlings and Green Range. Lesley Thorn's paintings hang on the walls, an added bonus to the visitor. Some have been used for the wine labels.

Millinup also has cottage accommodation, ideal for people who might like to walk the bush trails, climb the rugged nearby peaks, or walk up to the vineyard, pausing to take in the view which improves with every step.

N O ONE could blame Mark and Debbie Noack of Rocky Gully for believing they had something special in their new vineyard, after they were asked to fly a case of their second release wine, the 1992 pinot, to London, for a rich Arab sultan who has since been put on their mailing list. Then followed the purchase of their fruit by Domaine Chandon, a noted Victorian sparkling winemaker.

The sale of ten tonnes of pinot noir, netting $8152.80, saved their 460-hectare farm, where income had been savagely hit by a depressed wool market.

But it was the wool industry which provided the vineyard start, and a taste of life Mark would not care to repeat. He was shearing in the United States with a West Australian friend in 1980, when a story appeared in a local newspaper about their record-breaking efforts. This was to lead to their arrest for working illegally (or too hard, as Mark put it!) and a week in a Denver, Colorado gaol before being escorted from the county at gunpoint.

In the early 1950s under a land settlement scheme, Mark's father took up the block, right where the karri trees end eight

kilometres south of Rocky Gully. For two years he and his wife lived in a tent as they sought to establish a sheep and cattle grazing property.

Mark and Debbie, who married on the farm in 1983, took over the property two years later, Mark doing contract shearing to raise the deposit.

Debbie, meanwhile, had been working on the Westfield vineyard at Frankland when they decided to plant their own vines on light, silty loam soils, the intent being to replace shearing with income from the vineyard,

They knew little, however. 'We planted chardonnay and pinot noir [in 1985] without knowing they were the base wines for champagne', Mark said. 'We picked them out of a book because theoretically, it was felt, they would do well down here.'

They have five hectares in all, with Debbie taking an active role. During quiet spells, like winter, Mark often handles the domestic chores, including looking after their two daughters, while his wife is busy with vineyard maintenance.

The first crop of about two tonnes was picked in 1989, and sold to Houghton. By

OLD KENT RIVER

Turpin Road, Rocky Gully
Cellar door sales: By appointment

Above: Sheep still play a part in ex-shearer Mark Noack's life, but for him and wife Debbie the future is very much in wine

1994 it had risen to 50 tonnes. About 10-15 per cent is retained and made at Alkoomi for the Old Kent River label. 'We aim to be in the top ten pinot makers in Australia', Mark said, 'and we will get there.'

The trickle-fed, hand-picked vines flourish under conditions described by Mark as 'true Mediterranean'. The property is about 45 kilometres inland and the 'Albany doctor' (sea breeze) usually reaches it by 4.30 p.m. There might be the odd hot day in summer, but it cools down at night and sometimes gets quite cold.

Botrytis caused heavy chardonnay losses in 1993, neighbour's sheep have twice feasted on the young vines, and bird damage has been as high as 50 per cent, depending on the native marri flowering.

To help overcome salt problems and to create a healthier environment on their property, the Noacks plant a tree for every bottle sold. 'This is not a marketing gimmick but to involve city people in land care', Mark says. 'It costs them no extra and we do the work, but they can feel involved. Our target here is 100,000 trees and shrubs and then we will move off farm, to the Frankland and Kent River water catchments.'

A special treat for cellar door enthusiasts who visit the property will be a taste of marron from the farm. Later they will be able to sip a sparkling wine as well as the pinot and chardonnay. To be called Diamontina, it will be made in association with Plantagenet winemaker Gavin Berry who is developing a vineyard in the Porongurups.

PATTERSONS

St Werburgh's Road, Mount Barker
Cellar door sales: School holidays and most weekends 11 a.m. — 4 p.m. Other times by appointment

THERE WERE no trumpets, no fanfare when the new label Pattersons slipped quietly on to the West Australian market in the late 1980s. There was only a limited quantity available, but for vineyard principals Arthur and Sue Patterson it marked the start of what they hope would be a significant toehold in the local industry.

Their property, situated on St Werburgh's road some ten kilometres south west of Mount Barker, represents a solid commitment in a lifestyle filled with interest and diversity. The couple are teachers at the Mount Barker Senior High School, Arthur in physics and chemistry, and Sue in mathematics, so considerable time before and after school, plus holidays, is spent among the vines. Busy though this sounds, Arthur still finds time for his hobby, gliding, and his passion, trout fishing, while Sue also looks after their cattle which she prefers to vines because 'cows will do what they are told'.

For various reasons, including a lot of encouragement by Plantagenet's Tony Smith, the Pattersons decided to move into the wine business, beginning planting in August 1982 even though they had no tractor and had to borrow equipment. Half the four-hectare area is now taken up with chardonnay and the rest divided between pinot noir and shiraz, producing about 30 tonnes of fruit. But a plague of wingless grasshoppers set back early hopes when they devastated the young vines. 'They moved through eating everything that was green', Arthur recalls ruefully. The couple were forced to replant 1300 of the first 2200 vines which had begun their venture. Then, in December

1992, more disappointment came when a freak hail storm wiped out 75 per cent of the expected crop.

The previous year, with other vignerons in the area, they were hit by some blazing heat which cooked fruit on the vines and cost about a third of the vintage. However, the surviving fruit was to bring great joy when, in the following year, the 1991 chardonnay won the couple their inaugural trophy, for the best dry white wine at the Mount Barker Show.

'It was an emotional moment', Arthur said. 'We were hanging from the ceiling for months.'

Yet the development all seemed wrong in conventional terms. 'We are tucked in a valley, the vineyard faces south, rows are planted east-west instead of north-south and grey sand takes over half way down the slope', Arthur said.

However, there is a keen demand for the fruit, some of which is sold. The rest is made into wine at Plantagenet and includes a pinot noir and shiraz as well as the chardonnay with experiments continuing for a sparkling burgundy, hopefully for release in about 1996-97.

I enjoyed the 1991 chardonnay tasted three years after it was vintaged, indicating its capacity for graceful ageing. An elegant and refined wine, much lighter than the 1990, it surprised with its weight and flavour depth that lingered and lingered.

As the shiraz vines mature, more pepper characters are being reflected in the wine, typical of the Mount Barker area. The 1990 had a pleasant touch, enhancing a soft, rich, smooth mid-palate, a promising indicator of some fine wines to come.

The chardonnay has been given the

Teacher-cum-vigneron Arthur Patterson with a variety that gets particularly pampered — chardonnay

preferred treatment in the vineyard, being planted on the highest part of the red loamy soils. The other two varieties are partly on the same soils and partly on the sand section, as the vines follow the slope down the hillside. Growth is vigorous, aided by some supplementary watering, with trellising changes opening up the canopy for improved sunlight penetration. This, Arthur believes, has helped in improving fruit set in the chardonnay which has been disappointing at times with the formation of many 'chicken' (match-head sized) berries.

The Pattersons say they make the sort of wine they like, so they believe in what they sell. And despite their short history, the couple confirm what many other West Australian vignerons have found: a direct link between redgum flowering and the damage caused by silvereyes. 'There was a massive flowering of the trees in 1988 and we never saw a bird in the vineyard', Arthur noted. 'We could see and hear them in the trees, and that is where they stayed.'

The couple's aim is to become full-time primary producers as income and experience expands. Initial knowledge was gained from extensive reading and word of mouth. 'We have made a lot of mistakes but never the same ones twice', Sue said.

PLANTAGENET

Albany Highway, Mount Barker
Cellar door sales: Mon — Fri 9 a.m. — 5 p.m. Sat — Sun 10 a.m. — 4.p.m.

Part of the Wyjup vineyard, where plantings date back to 1971

IN THE early days of pioneering Plantagenet Wines at Mount Barker, the local rubbish tip was to run red, the blood of a disappointing vintage that saw about 9000 litres dumped. It was a costly sacrifice, perhaps worth $60,000 to $70,000 at the time, but made with steadfast resolve. For the wine was unable to meet the firmly set policy of not marketing an inferior product. 'So we had no choice', said managing partner Tony Smith, 'but to dump it'.

It was, however, to prove only a hiccup in the steady path of progress for the Great Southern producer which has seen it achieve great heights, not only in the West Australian industry, but nationally as well. For example, in its first ten years it recorded a remarkable 26 show trophies, 235 medals and seven Sheraton Perth wine awards. Then in 1989 its wines scored four places in the Australian Smallmakers Top 100, with two it made for Wignalls of Albany included as well. Since then many other accolades have followed.

I first met Tony Smith at his Denbarker farm in 1970 where he was putting on a brave face, inspecting the first (1968) Bouverie plantings that a mob of sheep had managed to invade to enjoy a succulent feast on the shoots and leaves. It was a hard lesson in a totally new world for the former English agriculturist turned New South Wales jackaroo and then station overseer, who had come to Western Australia in the search for cheaper farming land. Certainly then no one would have ever dreamed that this quietly spoken man would become such a force in helping and urging others into the industry. His participation at district, state and national level includes membership of the industry's guiding body, the Australian Wine and Brandy Corporation.

It must be remembered that in those early days there were a lot of local sceptics ready to pick at something so radically different as winemaking. The cynicism heightened with the first-year failure of the Department of Agriculture experimental plantings at the Pearse family's Forest Hill farm. Tony was warned the vines would not grow at Denbarker, they would not produce fruit, the fruit would not ripen, he would not be able to make wine, and the wines would not win medals!

He had been attracted to the business by the success (after the initial disappointment) of the experimental plantings. In addition friend and local shire councillor Ernie Mead supported him enthusiastically, and both took up the cudgels.

In 1971 plantings were extended to Wyjup, one of three farms owned by a partnership that by then included the Smiths and English relatives, the Meredith-Hardy families (who sold out in 1994). Four years later Plantagenet Wines was formed and included Perth accountant Rob Devenish and his family. This was a year after the first vintage, which was processed at Sandalford by Dorham Mann.

But such an arrangement never had long-term prospects, and the decline of the apple industry was to give a new agricultural pursuit its opportunity as Plantagenet took over an old run-down apple shed on Albany Highway, at the entrance to Mount Barker. While it was no showpiece, it provided the group with a low-cost headquarters that has developed

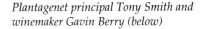

Plantagenet principal Tony Smith and winemaker Gavin Berry (below)

and prospered over the years. It was the district's first winery, and has meant valuable contract winemaking facilities for growers not having their own.

By 1994 the Mount Barker-Frankland area had established new records for grape production with the Plantagenet share 230 tonnes. This was a significant increase indeed from the humble five tonnes harvested in 1974. The first winemaker was David McNamara who had worked at Houghton, and then Victorian Rob Bowen joined the fledgling operation in time for

the 1979 vintage. It was to prove a vital appointment, not just for Plantagenet, but the area and State as a whole, with the shy, bearded young man producing wines of a quality and style not seen from the district before.

He was to be followed by John Wade whose six vintages at the winery built strongly on the solid quality foundation that had been established. In 1994 his deputy, Gavin Berry, was appointed to the position of chief winemaker when John decided to move on.

An enthusiastic young man, he will not, however, have to rely on innovation for winemaking gear as Rob Bowen once did.

He turned to the defunct Albany whaling station for refrigeration equipment that once cooled brine in the production of whale oil. This unique cool fermentation process using a 20-tonne am-

contract for other labels, has been necessary to service a keen local, Eastern States and overseas market, mainly to the United Kingdom and Japan. By 1994 annual sales were worth $1.2 million.

In all, ten table wines are made in the range as well as three fortifieds and a brut for which there is an ambitious aim. Plantagenet wants to emulate the great French producer Bollinger, whose wines are noted for their richness, complexity, body and length. A winery newsletter claims heritage of the great French maker and quotes Madame Lily Bollinger on champagne: 'I drink it when I am happy, and when I am sad. Sometimes I drink it when I am alone. When I have company, I consider it obligatory. I trifle with it when I am not hungry, and drink it when I am. Otherwise, I never try it — unless I am thirsty.'

Of the white wine range, the rhine

With Plantagenet's many wine awards adorning the cellar wall, the sign on Gill Graham's left says it all — 'Hurry before the judges drink it all'

monia unit did the job, and at the right price too — $2000 as opposed to $25,000 for a new refrigeration unit doing the same work.

But despite Plantagenet's success, Tony confessed that for much of the 1980s he felt frustrated that Mount Barker wines did not get the media recognition enjoyed by Margaret River producers. Now he believes the situation is more balanced with Mount Barker wines regarded as longer living and better remembered. And new plantings, with 45 growers in the Great Southern tending more than 600 hectares of vines, strengthen the position of the district.

Plantagenet's steady expansion, including significant tonnages made under

rieslings over the years have helped the district back its claim that it is one of the top areas in Australia for the variety. Its chardonnays are often tighter than those of Margaret River as youngsters, with melon and nutty flavours underlying the floral characters. A marketing coup was achieved with the variety in 1990 when an unwooded style was produced. This was a result of so many consumers at cellar door saying they did not want wines with so much wood.

By 1993 production represented an amazing 25 per cent of the total output and amounted to 5000 cases in 1994.

The 1992 was an excellent wine, aromatic and herbaceous as a youngster, a fresh, crisp, delicious drink, ideal for consumption with food or without. Later it developed grapefruit and melon-like flavours and it was no surprise that it went on to win four gold medals and a trophy, such was its class. But it proved controversial. Judges subsequently disqualified it from the chardonnay classes, believing it to be a sauvignon blanc! Curiously, many tasters, including a prominent Eastern States critic, considered it to be oaked, as it developed in the bottle, such was its flavour and body.

But when it comes to talking trophies, then the amazing record of the 1990 Plantagenet shiraz must surely be hard to beat. For it has won six, four at the 1993 Perth Wine Show, including the WA Wine Press Club award for best of all from the State, making it the estate's most successful red win in nearly 20 years of shows.

A style of pepper and violets from low-yielding vines, it appealed immediately for its lush bouquet, and rich, velvety palate. A complete wine, it retained subtlety and delicacy while still being full flavoured and complex.

For me it was almost matched in quality by the following vintage, another outstanding Plantagenet wine, though perhaps more of pepper and raspberry flavours. Initially, however, the fruit arriving at the winery had a distinctive smoky character for there were several days of bushfires near the Wyjup vineyard where they were produced. The wine just pipped the 1990 at the 1993 Mount Barker Show for the best dry red.

Certainly, the use of the variety in such (generally) cooler climate areas, has given shiraz the chance to shine, and at times even to outdo 'King' cabernet in whose shadow it has languished so often. Such wines from the estate, which initially included a dash of malbec, and more recently merlot and cabernet franc, show strong blackcurrant flavours, soft tannins and lovely length. As young wines, the cabernets are not as opulent, more lean and hungry than, for example, the earlier generosity of Margaret River wines.

But usually it is only a matter of time before they come together, when the fine-grained tannins and the often cassis-like flavours combine, such as in the very fine 1986 wine. Others I have enjoyed for their fruit integration and balance include the 1988, 1990 and 1992, wines that will live long into the present decade.

Given the chance, rieslings also age well. Indeed, Gavin says the 1992 and 1993 vintages, back to the crisp limey styles of the past, will cellar well till the year 2000.

A FEATURE of the West Australian wine industry is that so many of the vineyards are in picturesque peaceful rural settings, worth the drive just for the scenery. Scotsdale Brook, seven kilometres north-west of Denmark, is certainly one of them. Situated in rolling karri and marri country, the vines (pictured here) run up a steep slope to the peak of a hill some 200 metres above the brook from which it was named. Today about four hectares of close-planted vines flourish on former prime apple, stone fruit and potato growing land, irrigated from a freshwater spring.

The 28-hectare property was first identified and purchased by prominent local wine folk Michael and Alison Goundrey, a bold move given that Denmark did not rate at the time as a vine and wine area.

In 1984 the Goundreys formed a partnership to develop a vineyard that would grow the fruit for premium wines to compete with the increasing range being produced in the Mount Barker-Frankland area. Subsequently, they were to sell their share but are still involved in winemaking and vineyard management.

SCOTSDALE BROOK

Cnr Scotsdale and Mount Lindsay Roads, Denmark
No cellar door sales

harvest of 22 tonnes in 1990. It led to joyous celebrations, not just because the crop represented the fruition of effort, but because of what was achieved. The riesling was judged best at the Mount Barker Show of the year, winning a gold medal and a trophy, justification of investment and toil indeed. This was especially so with near neighbour Karriview and another Denmark vineyard, Tingle-Wood, winning major awards in the year as well. Other medals have since been won by Scotsdale with the sauvignon blanc and the soft, medium-bodied pinot noir-shiraz.

An excellent example of what the vineyard can achieve was shown in the 1992 Scotsdale Brook chardonnay, This is a wine with strong ripe varietal aromas and strong fruit flavours on the palate. With excellent oak integration and balance, it is a style that could cope comfortably with game meats, veal or pork.

More vines have been planted at the vineyard in 1994 with a production target of 100 tonnes by the turn of the century.

But says Terry: 'We will not release any wine that I would not have in my cellar. Our aim is premium quality, selling fruit surplus to our winemaking needs.'

All partners are involved in marketing, seeking a niche for their wines to build upon as production increases. There will also be demands in the vineyard as vine vigour is a problem. Improved canopy management aims to overcome this, and provide for greater sun penetration to improve grape flavours.

Sloping vines thrive on fertile soil with abundant water nearby

BankWest executive Terry Wynne and wife Pat, of Fremantle, who had joined a wine and food club while on transfer to Mount Barker, are among the shareholders. Others include Gooseberry Hill residents Dr Andrew Glover and Ian and Laurie McEwen.

On weekend journeys from Perth they helped establish a nursery, planting the first vines in 1986. The varieties include chardonnay, sauvignon blanc, rhine riesling, pinot noir and shiraz with the first

TINGLE-WOOD

Glenrowan Road, Denmark
Cellar door sales: Mon — Sun 9 a.m. — 5 p.m.

A SMALL vineyard at Denmark produces wine styles going by the unusual name of Yellow Tingle and Red Tingle. It is no surprise then that the name of the business is Tingle-Wood.

Abutting state forest about eight kilometres north-west of Denmark, the property has been developed by Bob and Judy Wood, whose other interests include the grazing of cattle and the making of sheepskin products. Yellow and red tingle, Bob explains to visitors, are the names of eucalypts found in the area. Perhaps the best known (until its untimely collapse a few years ago) was a red tingle in the Valley of the Giants which featured prominently for many years in tourist brochures, newspapers and magazines, often with vehicles backed up into its huge trunk.

The first vines were planted at Tingle-Wood in 1976 on two hectares of newly cleared land, part of an 80-hectare property. Bob said he looked to an intensive

form of primary production because of the clearing costs involved, about $2500 per hectare. 'We carted away about 50 tonnes of rock and you could hardly notice the difference', he said.

The block is on a high ridge which makes it particularly wind-prone. As well, hail and birds have combined to dash vintage hopes in some years.

The initial 1.9-hectare planting of rhine riesling, cabernet sauvignon and shiraz has been doubled for a 15-tonne crop at full production — more than 10,000 bottles — depending of course on the bird menace.

Such a serious problem did not exist in the Swan Valley where Bob had his first taste of the industry in the 1950s. A Perth workmate, Bill Pervan, invited him to give a hand with the picking on their Herne Hill property on weekends, and this proved to be an experience Bob thoroughly enjoyed.

But it was a nervous man who called

me in 1990, asking if he could accompany us to the Sheraton awards presentation. He knew he had won an award because he was asked to provide some wines for the event, but what? It turned out to be a trophy for their 1990 rhine riesling, a heady occasion indeed for the quiet, gentle man. Other awards have included a gold medal at Mount Barker for the 1991 riesling, the best in its class, and a bronze for the 1990 cabernet sauvignon-shiraz at the 1993 Mount Barker Show.

Tingle-Wood wines are made by John Wade. The rieslings are elegant, limey styles with excellent acids and quality varietal fruit. The red blend generally has fragrant blackberry and mulberry fruit flavours with a long, clean, firm finish, a style enhanced by bottle ageing. 'Regular tastings of wines back to 1981 show that the older, the better', Bob said. Plans for the 1994 crop of red fruit were for the making of a port, to complete the small Tingle-Wood range.

The label also carries the words Southern Dales. This is because the vineyard is located at Scotsdale, which adjoins Kent Dales (in turn abutting the Tingle Dales).

Native forest and introduced vines share common ground at Tingle-Wood estate. Below: Bob and Judy Wood at the wine and craft sales door

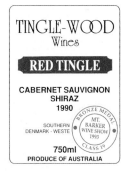

WIGNALLS

Chester Pass Road, Albany
Cellar door sales: Daily noon — 4 p.m. or
by appointment

*The Lyre trellis system used at Wignalls is
ideal for achieving optimum exposure to
leaves and fruit*

B ILL WIGNALL has earned the title of Prince of Pinots. For in the relatively short time the family operation has been involved in the WA wine industry, they have achieved a great deal with the contrary variety, winning national recognition for their wines.

Bill, wife Pat and son Robert run their King River property five kilometres from the centre of Albany, an area greeted initially with derision.

Because backyard grapes in the town tended often not to ripen, the Wignalls, when their plans were made known, became the target of jibes: 'Look at those idiots planting vines. They will never grow grapes here.'

Pat Wignall still remembers what a 'lot of flak' was flying around. 'When our vines produced grapes and they did ripen, people said — imagine what they will taste like.' Today former critics speak of Wignalls as 'Albany's vineyard' with pride and justification, for the wines stamp their authority on all who taste them.

While in 1994 space is running out on the walls of their cellar door facilities to show off trophies and medal awards, imagine the elation of the family when their 1985 pinot noir, the first from the property, won a gold medal, as did the 1986. Imagine too their sheer joy when their 1985 chardonnay was judged the top wine at the 1987 SGIO Winemakers Exhibition.

When the couple came down to earth, they realised they had won a trip to France where they learnt a great deal about viticulture — and the success was to be repeated in 1991 with the pinot noir of the previous year.

The French visit confirmed earlier research when they were considering going into the business on their King River farm, encouraged by Great Southern industry pioneer and principal of Plantagenet Wines Tony Smith. This had led them to conclude that the area had similarities to the great French producing region of Burgundy and in particular, the Côte de Nuits, where pinot noir thrives.

But the couple's path to the grape and the glass was far from traditional. Indeed, it could probably best be described as a fluke. Bill Wignall, a third-generation Fijian and a veterinary graduate from Sydney, took former Adelaide girl Pat off to New Zealand after their marriage. Later they went to South Australia. But fate took a hand when a client asked Bill to go to Western Australia to consider prospects there. He took one look at Albany and decided it was the place in which to settle. That was in 1963, and it led to the newcomer pioneering a veterinary practice in the district as well as developing farming alternatives with stud cattle and a huge production of seed. Subsequently, the Wignalls moved to their present property and looked to some form of intensive ag-

Bill and Pat Wignall proudly display some of their many awards at the cellar sales area

riculture to go with their charolais stud.

At the time, Bill said, local knowledge on growing grapes and making wine was akin to voodoo. But he would not contemplate failure, and pushed ahead.

The vineyard is the most southerly in Western Australia, with summer temperatures moderated through the influence of the nearby ocean. In the vineyard sandy gravel covers a layer of coffee rock that has been broken up by bulldozer deep ripping, allowing for root penetration of the friable clay and the retention of warmth at night. 'Our vines', Bill says, 'go to sleep earlier than those in Mount Barker and wake up earlier. We have a very long, cool and constant ripening and growing period, harvesting generally two weeks before Mount Barker for the same varieties.'

The combination of soil and climate at King River generates the qualities that attract many consumers. The pinots, for example, have tremendous depth of flavour and colour, are velvety in texture, and have long, rich finishes. So many have been very good, it is difficult to distinguish. But the 1993 will live long in my memory, ironically from a judging in which it failed to win a prize (a rare occasion indeed!) It was at the 1993 SGIO Winemakers Exhibition and it was stunning, for the joy of its freshness, superb fruit qualities, palate feel and depth. For me, it was just pipped, along with the 1990 Plantagenet shiraz, by the Howard Park

cabernet merlot, the ultimate overall exhibition winner, and all made by the same man, John Wade. At the 1991 and 1992 Sheraton awards, however, the 1990 and 1991 vintages were the chairman's selection as best wines shown. Bill likens his main pinot flavour as being of stewed strawberries, like the juice at the bottom of a bowl of the fruit eaten with cream, and sometimes black cherry, gamey and tobacco.

The chardonnays, another stylish range, also reflect intense fruit on the nose and palate. I especially enjoyed the 1990, a complex, subtle combination of toasty peach and melon characters packaged in elegance with a long, lingering finish. The Wignalls cabernets are also elegant wines with soft tannins but possessing the underlying structure for long cellaring. A pleasant, fruity sauvignon blanc is also part of the range of seven wines.

The nine-hectare Wignall vineyard was extended by two in 1993 and another 3.5 in 1994, all based on the Lyre trellising system to increase sun and light penetration to the fruit. By the year 2000, the family is aiming for a crush of 100-150 tonnes with a significant export component.

The vineyard has also sustained a significant amount of bird damage over the years, with losses in wine value terms estimated at $40,000 in 1989. Special plantings of native flower and bush patches provide a feeding distraction to the ripening fruit.

YANWIRRA

Redman Road, Denmark
Cellar door sales: By appointment

Perth to Denmark commuters Ian and Liz McGlew relax with a Yanwirra red

I N THE early years of vintage at Yanwirra, it would not surprise to find principals Ian and Liz McGlew staring at the skies rather than their ripening fruit. From the surrounding bush, crows especially have swooped in on the attack, inflicting heavy and disappointing losses, putting crops well down on expectations. For example, no sauvignon blanc at all was picked in 1994, a particularly bitter blow with the style expected to be the Yanwirra white flagship. The 1993 vintage, for example, the first release from the property, appealed for its delicious passionfruit and peach flavours, enhanced by the inclusion of a dash of semillon and a touch of wood from barrel fermentation.

Ian, a Perth anaesthetist, and Liz purchased their 12-hectare property amid picturesque rolling hills and karri trees four minutes from Denmark, in 1988. A few months later planting was under way, ultimately reaching four hectares made up of rhine riesling, semillon, sauvignon blanc, chardonnay, cabernet sauvignon, merlot and cabernet franc. At full production, about the year 1999, the couple expect the trickle-fed vineyard to produce about 40 tonnes of fruit.

Ian's love of wine and his desire to nurture an eventual retirement interest were the motivating forces in his acquisition of the land. The rural urge, he says, came from his grandparents. In the 1930s grandfather Aubrey McGlew exported live sheep to Indonesia and Singapore from Derby in the Kimberley region of Western Australia. For a period he ran a sheep station in the Gascoyne before moving south to farm Seaton Ross near Beverley, where Ian grew up. The property on the banks of the Avon River was named after a small village in Yorkshire. On his mother's side, grandfather Jim Mahood came from South Australia to set up the stock firm Elder Smith in Western Australia. With him and wife Lily came the name Yanwirra which the couple used for their house in Adelaide. 'As they always enjoyed excellent wine, it seemed appropriate we use the name for our label', Ian said.

On most weekends he and Liz can be found on the road south from Perth, keen to delight in their vineyard, despite the crows. Its establishment has been based on the Lyre trellising system to enhance sunlight penetration of the fruit. The vineyard is professionally managed with the wines made by John Wade. Like others in the new southern areas of the State, it has been subject to hail. In addition, the vines at the top of the block, exposed to occasional strong winds, are not quite as forward as those on the protected slopes.

Nonetheless, the couple are happy about their move and confident of the wines of the future, based on initial releases. The first red was the 1992 cabernet sauvignon, a plummy, smooth, medium-bodied wine, a very credible initial effort given the youth of the vines. Ian says in future vintages he will look to include some cabernet franc and merlot for extra flavour intensity to provide for increased oak maturation, an all-round fuller style.

The Taste Test

OVER THE years of wine writing, many people have asked how to taste a wine properly. Mostly they were consumers who just wanted to get more pleasure out of a good wine, without necessarily getting too involved. Those who did ask I directed further, especially to the courses run by the Wine Education Centre at Claremont.

For the others, however, I came up with my own easy-to-remember judging checklist to take as far as they wished. I am referring to BLF, RD and WC.*

Let's start with BLF. It stands for balance, life and flavour, three of the most important features of a wine. Balance is the term used to describe the harmony with which the wine's various components come together — some sweet, like flavour, sugar and alcohol, and others dry, like acid and tannin. For instance, if the tannin is too aggressive, leaving a furry coating on the gums especially behind the front teeth, or the acid dominates the aftertaste, leaving a hardness or bitterness in the back palate, the wine is said to be out of balance. Once at a tasting with Dorham Mann the balance of a wine being assessed was in such harmony that he said: 'This wine really smiles at you'.

An easy way to explain the life in a wine is when it is the opposite, flat and dull. This usually means the wine lacks acid, or it is oxidised, or perhaps it has reached the end of its life and should have already been drunk. The term flabbiness is often given to wines with insufficient acid so that freshness and life is lacking.

Flavour is self explanatory and usually relates to the expression of the fruit character of the grape, and other tastes developed during the winemaking process. For people who get bitten by the wine-interest bug, I recommend they organise an invitation to a vineyard at picking time, and taste berries direct from the vine. The trick then is to remember the flavour of the fruit, to see how well it is retained in the ensuing wine.

The R in my list is for refinement which is often used to describe a wine of fine quality and breeding. The D is for depth of character and aftertaste, the combination of rich interlocking flavours and the length of time they stay on the palate after swallowing. A British Master of Wine once told me that some tasters in the United Kingdom use stopwatches to time the aftertaste. The longer it lasts, the better the wine.

The W and C apply to wood flavours affecting a wine, and the wine's overriding characters. The latter includes basic features like dry or sweet, light-bodied or full, firm, aggressive or soft, simple or complex. Usually experienced consumers prefer complexity in a wine, considering such a style more interesting, with many more responses being generated from smelling and sipping.

All senses are employed when evaluating a wine — even hearing (some people find joy in the bursting bubbles of a sparkling wine) and feeling (such as the sensation in the mouth of the intensity of certain fortified or sweet wines).

Some tasters often refer to the weight of a wine, how it feels on the palate and its texture, whether it is smooth, silky or even velvety.

But it is sight, smell and taste that are the most important. In Australian shows judges give 3, 7 and 10 points for appearance, bouquet and palate respectively, with the total out of 20 deciding whether a wine receives a medal or not.

I recall once being at a tasting in Coonawarra with Dr Bryce Rankine, former head of the School of Oenology and Viticulture at Roseworthy Agriculture College, when he addressed the question of a wine's appearance being an important guide to its condition — an aspect of the assessment often neglected.

Assuming good light conditions, the wine should be examined for its limpidity (brilliance or dullness), and colour (density or hue). Hue is the actual shade, be it red, straw-green or golden and so on, while density is the concentration in which the hue manifests itself. For the more technically astute, appearance also indicates other basic information such as viscosity, the visible presence of carbon dioxide, and the level of alcohol revealed by the capillary action on the side of the glass.

While the depth of colour is not necessarily a criterion of quality, Dr Rankine explained that it can be a guide to the wine's structure. This was followed by a tasting of cabernets where the deep colours resulted in wines that were full bodied, tannic and abundant in flavour, though this may not always be so. The hue relates to age and shows the wine's state of development. Young red wines, for example, have a lively purple or ruby-red hue which becomes brick-red and brown with development. These are best

---

* The initials BLF, possibly unfamiliar to international readers, have been commonly used in Australia for many years for the trade union, the Builders' Labourers' Federation. While WC should be familiar to all, RD may not. These letters are taken from the sparkling winemaking term 'recently disgorged', which refers to the removal of the sediment arising from the second fermentation that occurs in the bottle.

Picture preceding page: Great Cabernet tasting at Cape Mentelle winery, Margaret River

The annual Sheraton Perth wine awards are a glittering affair in more ways than one — a generous supply of glasses is a prerequisite for efficient and effective judging

Left: After many years as State Government Viticulturist, Bill Jamieson was hardly likely to be far from the world of wine, and involvement in competitive events like the Sheraton Perth awards. He is pictured here pouring a sample for judging

appreciated by tilting the glass over a light source or a piece of white paper, closely examining the area just at the edge of the wine (the meniscus). If a wine looks dull, it is an indication that there may be something wrong. If a red wine is excessively brown, it usually means that it is past its best.

While it is true that appearance can be deceptive, it has been said that a wine's colour is its face, in which age and character can be read. A French experiment revealed that under blindfolds, some tasters could not tell the difference between red or white wines.

White wines usually vary from straw to light golden with tinges of green (young rhine riesling) to yellow and deep gold (aged semillon) indicating variety, and age or development.

To gain a better understanding of response to the bouquet and palate structure, I turned to wine enthusiast and show judge Dr Lou Papaelias. He explained that smell and taste are known as chemical senses, reacting to the molecules in vapour signals like sight does to light waves.

The nose is not the real organ of smell, but a channel for the chemicals in the gaseous state to get to the sensitive olfactory mucosa, a yellowish mucous membrane of approximately 1.5 square centimetres located at the back of the nasal cavities. Its surface is covered with some 50 million olfactory hairs which are bathed in fluid. Odour-laden molecules dissolve in the mucous fluid and react with the hairs, which send nerve

Prominent Perth show judge John Hanley — the first Western Australian to judge internationally — examines the clarity of a Sheraton Perth wine awards' entry, then the bouquet, before finally making the ultimate test by sipping the wine

impulses through the olfactory nerve to the part of the brain which analyses smell, the olfactory bulb.

A second path to the olfactory mucosa is through the mouth, the retronasal route where air is drawn up the internal passage connecting the back of the mouth to the nasal channels. When a wine is sipped there is an increased release of aromas with the warming and spreading by the tongue and cheeks. The retronasal passage also explains why informed winetasters draw air across the wine when it is in the mouth, sometimes with such intensity that they cause the liquid to bubble, to increase the bouquet response. By the time the wine is swallowed, tongue and olfactory senses have been stimulated to the maximum. But before taking a sip they rotate the glass to swirl the wine, releasing its vapours for the important first sniff, which often tells the most about a wine.

Of course, due to genetic variation people have different threshold sensitivities to smell and taste. Dr Papaelias recalled how a bitterness taste test at medical school resulted in a third of the students reacting extremely positively, and two-thirds not at all. 'The sense of smell is very important', he said. 'It can be ten thousand times more sensitive than taste. We can smell things in such small concentrations that they cannot even be measured.'

But regardless of the mechanics, it is tasting that brings the real enjoyment of wine, and the tongue is the key. It responds to the four primary tastes, sweetness at the tip, bitterness at the back, acidity at the sides and just underneath, and saltiness by the edges. As well, the tongue responds to the touch of the wine. For example, a rich, velvety muscat generates a totally different feeling in the mouth to, say, a sparkling wine.

It should be noted that the responses to the four different tastes do not occur at the same time, and that sweetness is a short-lived sensation because of rapid fatigue. Bitterness, however, is slow to develop and persists with the intensity developing and lingering on the palate after a wine is swallowed or spat out. So an initial pleasant impression can be very different from the finish of a wine, giving way to a hard acidity or an excessive bitterness.

The initial contact of a wine with the palate is referred to by the French as the attack, the mid-palate as the evolution, and the finish, the farewell. In a good wine it means that the initial agreeable impression is prolonged, and enhanced by a long aftertaste. Such a wine holds up on the palate without breaking down, to develop well. These wines are said to be long. Quite often, though, an initially favourable beginning gives way to an increased acidity, cutting out the flavour and reducing the appeal, in which case the wine is said to be short.

In his book *Scents and Sensuality* Max Lake refers to 'umami' as the fifth important component of taste. Defined around 1909 by Professor Kikunae Ikeda, it is the Japanese

word for a delicious or savoury quality, something the Western palate still finds difficult to distinguish from other elements of taste.

I always try in tastings to look for the positive features first, having been disappointed on occasions with immediate reactions that criticise or downgrade a product. By this I am not suggesting that faults should be overlooked. They should not, but a wine can still be very enjoyable, especially with a meal, even if it is not a gold medal winner.

That brings me to the point of letting a wine speak for itself, with the taster the best judge for his or her own palate, regardless of the claims of the labels or the show judges.

Generally white wines, especially those with the fruity characters of youth, are drunk cool to enhance their fresh aromatic characters. Reds are served at room temperature* to bring out their bouquet and supple texture. An experiment worth trying is to serve a wine chilled for assessment, with a second glass warmed. The differences are marked. Indeed, many might regard them as totally different products. Wines that are too cold or too warm are difficult to judge.

I have often been surprised at tastings at the ability of some people to see a vast range of odours, aromas and flavours in wines. For example, I have heard gamey, musky,

---

* Room temperature means about 20-22 degrees Celsius which, under Australian summer conditions, may require red wines to be cooled.

catty, vanilla, smoked, toasted bread, dough, almond, hay, straw, coffee, leather, tarry, chocolate, nail varnish, acetic, phenolic, rubbery, sulphur and its derivatives, oxidized, yeast and ferment, clove, pepper, cinnamon, nutmeg, rosemary, truffle, liquorice, mint, cassis, violet, citronella, jasmine, iris, lime, blackcurrant, raspberry, cherry, gooseberry, plum, mulberry, strawberry, apricot, mushroom, damp straw, damp moss, cowshed, earthy, sweaty saddle, and greenleaves, just to mention a few.

One of the most eloquent tasters I have ever met is Gunther Brozel, recruited to South Africa from Germany where he reached a pinnacle in gaining international wineman-of-the-year status. He spoke of a rosé being friendly and romantic, a sweet white behaving like an orchestra, of the valleys and hills and hay in the meadow. He referred to the pinot noir variety as being like an Eskimo, in adjusting to relatively few sunshine areas, and acidity like a protecting police force, or steel in concrete. Of older wines lacking freshness, he said: 'We would all like to buy back our youth'.

To help appreciate good wines, here are some faults to watch out for:

— Excessive sulphur dioxide (SO2). Small quantities of this chemical are used by winemakers around the world as a preservative to prevent oxidation and spoilage from yeast or bacterial infection. Too much SO2 will bleach the colour from a wine. Flavour is also reduced, making the wine flat and dull and leaving a hardness on the late palate.

— Oxidation is the chemical action of oxygen on a substance. A good example can be seen when a bite is taken from an apple and it is left. It soon goes brown, losing its fresh, fruity flavour. The immediate indication of oxidation in a wine is also the brownness and the lack of fruity aroma when the wine is sniffed.

— Then there is a vinegary wine which smells like nail polish remover. It is the smell of the ester of acetic acid. A wine affected in this way is often called volatile. The ester known as ethyl acetate is usually a by-product of bacterial spoilage. Bacteria infect the wine and multiply rapidly, particularly in the presence of air. This mainly happens after fermentation, but it can also occur during the fermentation process when wild yeasts are not controlled by the winemaker. The microbes metabolise various chemicals, including sugars and alcohol, with one of the by-products being acetic acid. If you are game enough to try such a wine, you will find the vinegary characteristics leave a sharp, bitter aftertaste.

— Hydrogen sulphide (H2S) or rotten egg character can be caused in a number of ways, but generally results from microbial action on sulphur in a wine. There are simple techniques to remove the problem, the most usual by adding minute quantities of copper. Where such action has not been taken, the rotten egg character carries through on the palate, making the taste most unpleasant. An offshoot, mercaptan, is said to smell like burnt rubber or rotten onions. Thankfully, the standard of winemaking is such today in Western Australia that such faults are rare.

The Department of Agriculture supports the industry in a variety of ways, and problems encountered by winemakers frequently end up in its well-equipped laboratory. The equipment includes one of Australia's few high pressure liquid chromatography analysers (below), a sophisticated device that does breakdowns to determine factors such as acid and alkalinity levels, and sugar component

It is not the fault of a winemaker, however, if a wine is corked. This results from a diseased cork which makes the wine dank and 'wet bag'-like, distinctly disagreeable.

People often ask me about tannin, and I can find no better immediate description than one that a winemaking friend once proffered: 'That is what puts the muscle into a good red. Without it, wines would taste flat and insipid.'

All wines contain tannin, a naturally astringent compound present in grape seeds, stalks and skins, and in oak casks. It occurs more in red wines than whites because the skins and pips are part of the fermentation process and there is generally longer cask ageing, especially so for the premium wines. Tannin is an important component in increasing cellaring life, but too much spoils the flavour. Some wines are excessively tannic from over-extraction (usually due to excessive pressing of skins and pips during

processing) which makes the wines hard or astringent, leaving the mouth dry, with a furry feeling on the gums.

In white wines the juice is usually separated from the skins and pips immediately after crushing and so do not have the same level of tannin as red wines. Some white wines, however, like chardonnay, semillon and sauvignon blanc, can be fermented in oak casks and matured in them as well — usually for a much shorter period than red wines.

An Eastern States colleague once described tannin as having a mouth-puckering effect, like sucking a teabag or the end of a freshly sawn piece of timber. I have not tried either, but there is never any doubt when a wine is high in tannin, for it grips at the mouth. Such levels are often found in young red wines, released before they have softened and mellowed. Most will improve with cellaring until they are more in harmony. In recent years many winemakers have tended to 'lighten off' some of their reds to get away from the big, gutsy wines that need long ageing. This makes them more attractive for earlier drinking, and able to be sold sooner. Under food regulations, tannin can be added to wine during processing because it is a natural component of the grape. It can be purchased as a brown powder.

A firm tannin finish is the hallmark of a good Bordeaux style. As a red wine matures, one of the major changes that occurs is in the nature of the tannins. They turn to a brown colour and soften. Often tannin drops out of the wine to be a deposit on the side or bottom of the bottle. Careful decanting will enable the wine drinker to enjoy a softer, more mature wine.

In Australia acid can be added to a wine, but it is illegal to add sugar at any stage of the winemaking process before fermentation. Adding sugar is allowed in Europe. It is called chaptalisation and is necessary when there is not enough sunshine for the desired sugar levels to occur naturally in the fruit.

A German winemaker once told me how proud growers were of the warmth in their vineyards. He related a story of a grower returning to his village who remarked to a neighbouring vigneron: 'It was so hot in my vineyard, I had to go into yours to cool off!'.

Occasionally, consumers have queried the development of crystals in wine, concerned that something had gone wrong. Their fears are generally groundless. These are potassium bitartrate deposits which can be found in red and white wines that have not been adequately stabilised (refrigerated) during manufacture. The crystals form from the natural components of wine and are often labelled as 'wine diamonds'.

But diamonds or disaster, consumers who feel a wine they have purchased from a West Australian producer is unsound can take it back confident the bottle will be replaced if there is a problem.

The Grape Varieties

MORE THAN 80 varieties of grapes are grown in Australia for winemaking. In many cases their history goes back to cuttings brought from the Cape of Good Hope, Germany, Spain, France and England. Gradually, the industry is sorting out which does best and where, with respect to quality and yield. In the long-established wine growing areas of the world, such selection has taken place over centuries.

The West Australian industry has benefited from such knowledge so that in a few short years producers have come to realise the advantages of a number of varieties around the State. For example, rhine riesling, cabernet sauvignon and shiraz have done very well at Mount Barker-Frankland, pinot noir at Albany and Pemberton, semillon, chardonnay, sauvignon blanc and cabernet sauvignon at Margaret River, chenin blanc and shiraz on the coastal plain, and chenin blanc, verdelho and shiraz in the Swan Valley, Gingin and Bindoon.

Other varieties have also produced some sound wines, such as malbec, merlot, frontignan and traminer. For some winemakers, no one variety produces exactly what they are looking for, resulting in blending. Under Australian labelling regulations up to 15 per cent of a wine in a bottle (previously 20 per cent) can be other than the variety stated on the label.

The trend to premium wines in the last 30 years has seen the marketing emphasis swing to wines named after the variety of grape used, as opposed to established generic names such as claret, hock, chablis and white burgundy. Such wines in Australia are usually a blend of different varieties used to develop a style, as distinct from some cases in Europe where, for example, a white burgundy in France must be made only from chardonnay. Many people applaud the trend away from broad-brush names, while at the same time respecting the tremendous success of wines like the famous Houghton white burgundy.

The main varieties grown in Western Australia include:

RIESLING. Commonly called rhine riesling, a tendency which developed to avoid confusion with Hunter River riesling (semillon) and Clare riesling (crouchen). It is the noble grape variety of Germany. In Australia it has suffered in recent years with the consumer swing to wooded white wines such as chardonnay, sauvignon blanc, semillon and blends. This in some ways has been disappointing for the variety can produce some stunning wines. The rieslings of Mount Barker, for example, have been compared with the best in the country. The bunches are small and compact with small berries and tough skins. The wines usually have a distinct varietal flavour that shows up well in dry or slightly sweet wines. As well, it can be extremely attractive in luscious sweet wines where the fruit has been affected by noble rot (Botrytis cinerea), a prized mould which causes the berries to dehydrate, concentrating the sugar and flavours.

CHARDONNAY. If cabernet sauvignon is 'king' of the reds then chardonnay is 'queen' of the whites. This magnificent ancient variety, which the Lebanese and Syrians claim to have originally nurtured, is used exclusively in the great wines of Chablis and Burgundy including Montrachet, Meursault and Pouilly-Fuisse. It is also important along with pinot noir in champagne-making.

Of all the white varieties chardonnay perhaps has the greatest affinity to oak fermentation and maturation, adding complexity and depth, and often giving years of cellaring life.

Although yields in the Margaret River area have been disappointing at times, some outstanding wines have been produced in the area, gaining recognition in the annual

RIESLING

CHARDONNAY

SEMILLON

SAUVIGNON BLANC

CHENIN BLANC

CABERNET SAUVIGNON

'great chardonnay tasting' event run by the Cullen family. Pitched against the world's best, they have often been the top wines when the final points from a wide range of tasters have been compiled.

In the Swan Valley, the class of John Kosovich's wines (Westfield) have seen them picked in masked tastings as products from so-called superior cooler regions of the nation.

The wines of this variety are usually the highest-priced of the whites with winemakers providing the best oak they can afford, often inspired by the wines of France, regarded by many as the finest, most subtle and complex dry whites made in the world despite challenges from newer areas like Australia and California.

SEMILLON. This is the main white wine variety of Bordeaux with the biggest planting outside France in Chile, where it accounts for about 75 per cent of all white wine produced. In South Africa it goes by the unusual name of greengrape. In her book *Vines, Grapes and Wines* Jancis Robinson says: 'In most of the world's vineyards where it is planted, it sits around sullenly, like an overweight schoolgirl, showing awkward fatness or just plain dullness in the wine it produces. In odd places though, as if under the spell of a fairy godmother, it can be transformed into a raving beauty.'

The variety certainly seems to have found a happy home in Margaret River, where Evans and Tate, Chateau Xanadu, Ashbrook and Moss Wood, for example, have produced some very fine wines.

At tastings people often refer to the variety as being grassy and herbaceous. More producers are now tending to blend it with sauvignon blanc. In France the combination provides the base for the great luscious sweet wines of Sauternes and Barsac, where the fruit has been affected by botrytis.

SAUVIGNON BLANC. This is a vigorous variety which growers try to curb in favour of fruit production. It usually produces wines of strong varietal character, ranging from green grass herbaceousness to melon and tropical fruit where the grapes have been left to ripen a little more. Often the pungent aroma can be too much for some consumers. Like chardonnay and semillon, the variety can be oaked to advantage. Margaret River producer Cape Mentelle has done much to forward the cause of the variety with its New Zealand production of Cloudy Bay. In the Margaret River district, notable wines have been produced at Leeuwin Estate and in 1993, at Ribbon Vale. Alkoomi at Frankland River produced a very fine wine in 1989.

CHENIN BLANC. This is the main variety of the Loire Valley in France. Cultivated in that country in the ninth century, it can now be found in the remotest growing regions of the world, producing table and sparkling wines and the base for sherries and brandy.

In Western Australia it was formerly, and incorrectly, known as semillon. Another vigorous variety, it has done well in the Swan Valley, Bindoon and the coastal plain especially. The Peel Estate wood-aged chenin has long been a favourite.

Other good wines have been produced from Moondah Brook fruit, especially the 1992, and by Amberley Estate at Margaret River. The variety has good acidity with the wines generally found in the mid-range of quality, at modest prices compared with the more favoured white wines. It is used very successfully for well-balanced dry table wines in South Africa and California.

VERDELHO. This is a Portuguese variety, the most planted white vine on the Island of Madeira, and in the Douro Valley.

It has probably adapted better to West Australian conditions than anywhere else in Australia, especially in the Swan Valley, Gingin and Margaret River. The variety has shown that it copes well with heat, maintaining acid levels and producing dry white table wines of strong varietal character.

I have long been an admirer of wines produced by Houghton from grapes grown at Moondah Brook, and by Westfield especially. The wines do have the capacity for long life. A 1976 Sandalford made by Dorham Mann, for example, was drunk with friends in March 1990. It was excellent.

CABERNET SAUVIGNON. This is the aristocrat of red wines, the major variety in some of the best wines of the Medoc, Bordeaux. Its influence has spread around the vine growing globe with Western Australia no exception.

The variety does well in all areas of the State, producing some excellent wines. The pronounced varietal character can be very intense, especially where the vines are grown under cooler conditions. Tasters often use terms like minty, eucalyptus, cigar box, cassis, cedar wood and blackcurrant to describe flavours.

Like chardonnay, cabernet also has a special affinity to oak while plenty of tannin makes the wines ideal for ageing. Pips are an important source of tannin in red wines, and cabernet has one of the highest proportions of pip-to-pulp of any grape.

Many West Australian producers like to add shiraz, cabernet franc, merlot and sometimes malbec and petit verdot to help fill out their cabernets and give complexity. Often the mid-palate is referred to as being doughnut-like in structure (a hole in the middle) in wines made just from the variety.

SHIRAZ. This variety is tremendously important throughout Australia. It produces thousands of tonnes a year for dry red table wine and for ports.

The other major producing area of the world is in the Hermitage region of the Rhone Valley in France, where it is known as Syrah. One tradition suggests it was brought to Hermitage from Shiraz in Iran by the hermits, and another that it was brought from Syracuse by the Roman legions.

Some West Australian producers label their wines shiraz and others hermitage, in the quest for marketing advantage. However, under agreements with the European Community, the use of hermitage has to be phased out.

The vigorous variety is extremely versatile, growing well in all viticultural areas, quite happy in warm temperatures. Because of its 'workhorse' status it is often underrated in favour of the more fashionable cabernet, undeserved on quality and value terms. At Mount Barker wines like those produced by Plantagenet can be appealingly spicy and peppery. In the Swan Valley they are usually big, soft and flavoursome, a real mouthful of wine.

SHIRAZ

PINOT NOIR is the bastion of the great red wines of Burgundy while providing the power and the long life in wines of Champagne. In Australia the variety has probably done more to develop grey hairs on winemakers than any other. It is a difficult variety, tantalising for its feats in France, but frustrating to growers, makers and consumers alike due to the variable results achieved.

While some very good wines have been made in Western Australia, including Wignalls, Leeuwin, Karriview and Moss Wood, the reality is that the industry is still struggling to come to terms with the variety. Sometimes the wines are more dry red, sometimes thin and hard, lacking flavour, and sometimes attractive strawberry, cherry or raspberry characters are over-ripe, a taste at times likened to boiled lollies.

While plantings in the State are still generally small, they have increased in recent years with interest keen despite the problems. For many producers, however, the fruit is more likely to be part of their sparkling winemaking than for a dry red table wine.

The cooler areas seem best suited to the variety with high hopes for the young vineyards of the Pemberton-Manjimup district. The colours of wines from such areas may not be intense, but the distinctive characters and flavours of the best wines will be keenly appreciated. Generally fruit from hot areas makes uninteresting wines, lacking in colour and flavour.

PINOT NOIR

MERLOT. For many people in Australia this important Bordeaux variety is best suited to blending, especially to soften and fill out the more austere cabernet for earlier drinking. Yet it is a variety of class on its own as wines of Evans and Tate, Westfield and Happs would indicate. Its problem, however, is the battle for acceptance. The wines are fruity and forward, not always meant for ageing. Devotees find its sweet fruit character distinctive and appealing, and seek it out. Despite its potential for top quality wines, it seems destined in Western Australia to remain very much the underdog to cabernet.

MALBEC. Like merlot this variety produces soft, mouth-filling wines, again not always meant for ageing. They too are usually thought of as best suited to blending but some very good individual wines have been made in the country. Perhaps the most notable in Western Australia is that produced by Alkoomi, where the wines are dense in colour and massive in flavour. Local expert John Hanley has rated the fruit from the vineyard as the best in Australia.

MERLOT

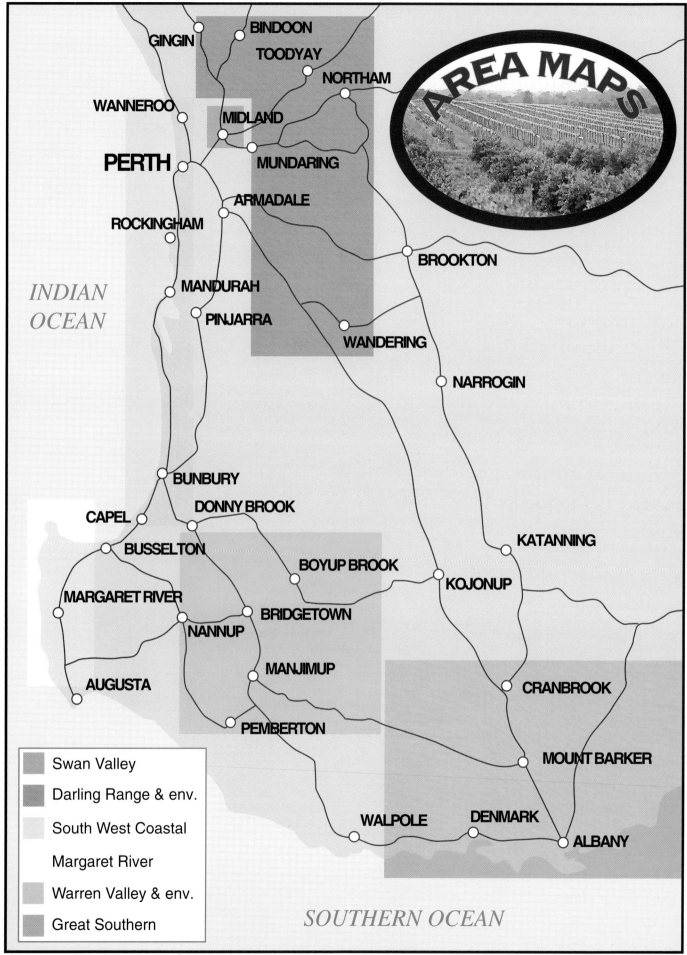

AREA MAPS

GINGIN
BINDOON
TOODYAY
NORTHAM
WANNEROO
MIDLAND
PERTH
MUNDARING
ARMADALE
ROCKINGHAM
BROOKTON

INDIAN
OCEAN

MANDURAH
PINJARRA
WANDERING
NARROGIN

BUNBURY
DONNY BROOK
CAPEL
BUSSELTON
KATANNING
BOYUP BROOK
KOJONUP
MARGARET RIVER
BRIDGETOWN
NANNUP
MANJIMUP
CRANBROOK
AUGUSTA
PEMBERTON
MOUNT BARKER
WALPOLE
DENMARK
ALBANY

SOUTHERN OCEAN

Swan Valley

Darling Range & env.

South West Coastal

Margaret River

Warren Valley & env.

Great Southern

Adapted maps courtesy Wine Industry Assoc. of WA

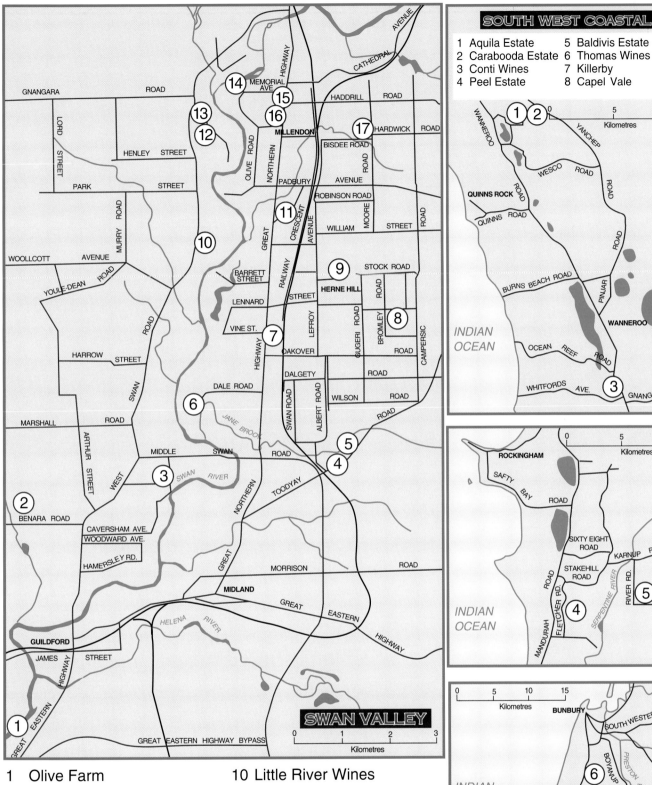

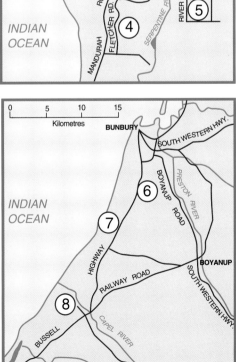

SOUTH WEST COASTAL

1 Aquila Estate
2 Carabooda Estate
3 Conti Wines
4 Peel Estate
5 Baldivis Estate
6 Thomas Wines
7 Killerby
8 Capel Vale

SWAN VALLEY

1 Olive Farm
2 Pinelli Wines
3 Sandalford Wines
4 Garbin Wines
5 Jane Brook Estate
6 Houghton Wines
7 Highway Wines
8 Valley Wines
9 Cobanov Wines
10 Little River Wines
11 Talijancich Wines
12 Evans & Tate
13 Henley Park Wines
14 Mann
15 Westfield Wines
16 Twin Hill Wines
17 Lamont Wines

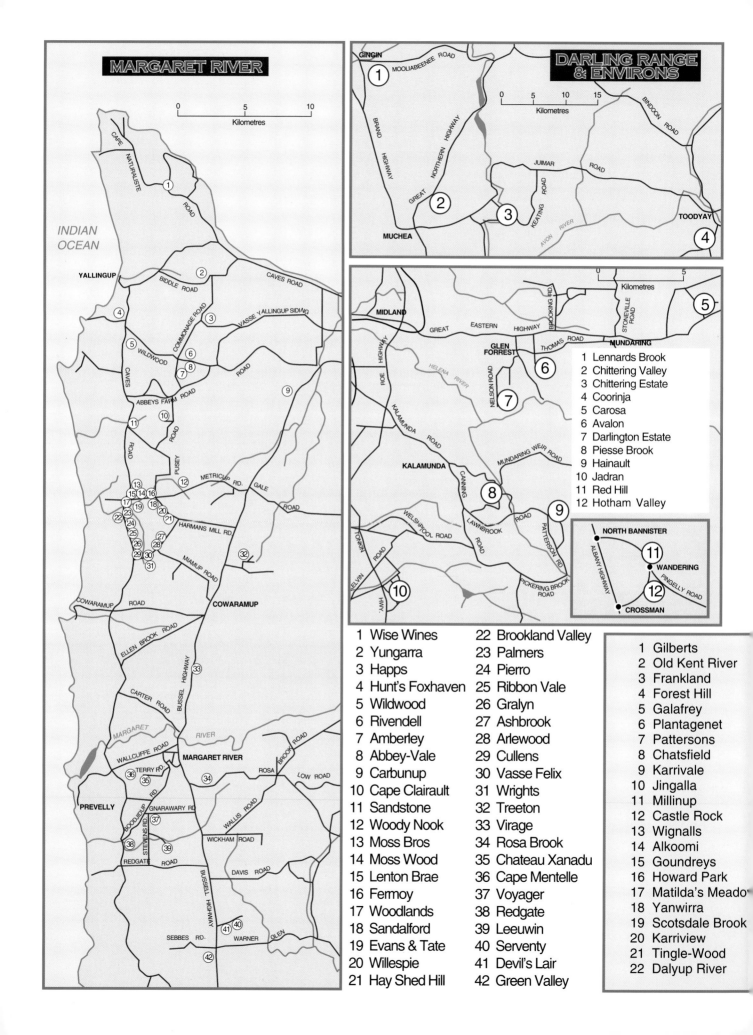

MARGARET RIVER

0   5   10
Kilometres

INDIAN OCEAN

DARLING RANGE & ENVIRONS

0   5   10   15
Kilometres

1 Lennards Brook
2 Chittering Valley
3 Chittering Estate
4 Coorinja
5 Carosa
6 Avalon
7 Darlington Estate
8 Piesse Brook
9 Hainault
10 Jadran
11 Red Hill
12 Hotham Valley

1 Wise Wines	22 Brookland Valley
2 Yungarra	23 Palmers
3 Happs	24 Pierro
4 Hunt's Foxhaven	25 Ribbon Vale
5 Wildwood	26 Gralyn
6 Rivendell	27 Ashbrook
7 Amberley	28 Arlewood
8 Abbey-Vale	29 Cullens
9 Carbunup	30 Vasse Felix
10 Cape Clairault	31 Wrights
11 Sandstone	32 Treeton
12 Woody Nook	33 Virage
13 Moss Bros	34 Rosa Brook
14 Moss Wood	35 Chateau Xanadu
15 Lenton Brae	36 Cape Mentelle
16 Fermoy	37 Voyager
17 Woodlands	38 Redgate
18 Sandalford	39 Leeuwin
19 Evans & Tate	40 Serventy
20 Willespie	41 Devil's Lair
21 Hay Shed Hill	42 Green Valley

1 Gilberts
2 Old Kent River
3 Frankland
4 Forest Hill
5 Galafrey
6 Plantagenet
7 Pattersons
8 Chatsfield
9 Karrivale
10 Jingalla
11 Millinup
12 Castle Rock
13 Wignalls
14 Alkoomi
15 Goundreys
16 Howard Park
17 Matilda's Meadow
18 Yanwirra
19 Scotsdale Brook
20 Karriview
21 Tingle-Wood
22 Dalyup River

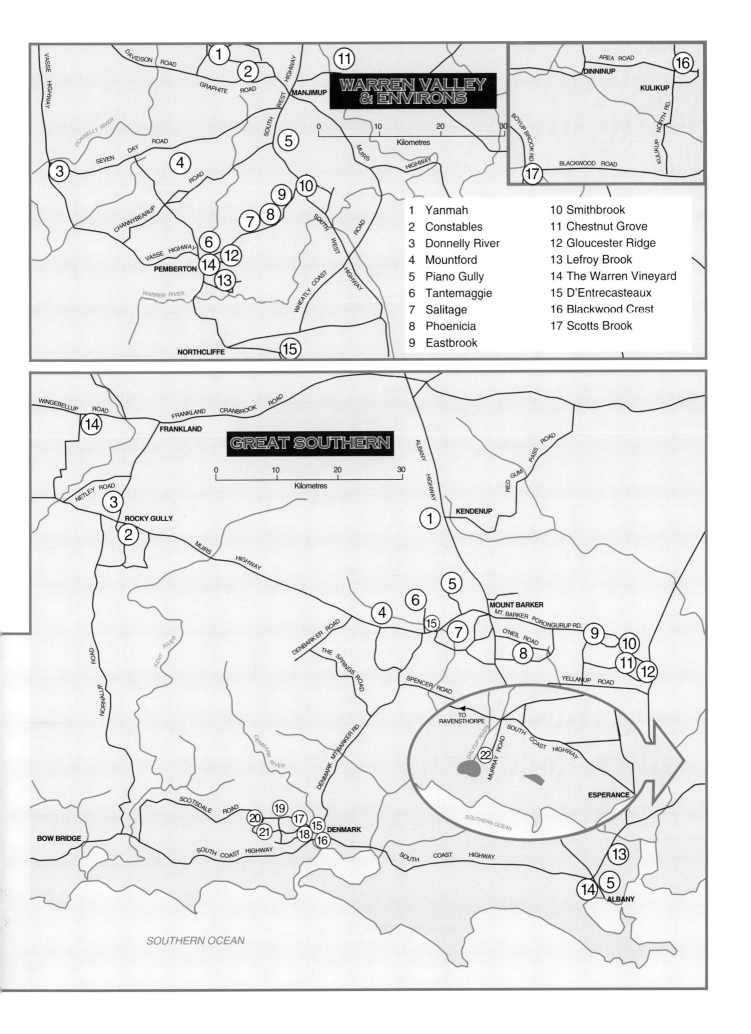

WARREN VALLEY & ENVIRONS

1 Yanmah	10 Smithbrook
2 Constables	11 Chestnut Grove
3 Donnelly River	12 Gloucester Ridge
4 Mountford	13 Lefroy Brook
5 Piano Gully	14 The Warren Vineyard
6 Tantemaggie	15 D'Entrecasteaux
7 Salitage	16 Blackwood Crest
8 Phoenicia	17 Scotts Brook
9 Eastbrook	

GREAT SOUTHERN

Index

Bibliography

Anderson, Ross (ed.).*Katanning, A Century of Stories.* Katanning Shire Council, 1988

Antcliff, A. J. *Some Wine Grape Varieties for Australia.* CSIRO, 1976

Battye, J. S. (ed.) *The Cyclopedia of Western Australia, An Historical and Commercial Review* (facsimile edition). Hesperian Press, Perth, 1985

Bonser, Philip. *The Houghton Vineyard 1836-1980.* Houghton Wines, 1987

Brockman, Allen. *Baker's Hill, A Brief History*

Burvill, George H. *Agriculture in Western Australia 1829-1979.* University of Western Australia Press, Perth, 1979

Despeissis, Adrian. *The Handbook of Horticulture and Viticulture of Western Australia,* 1921

Elliot, Ian. *Mundaring, A History of the Shire.* Mundaring Shire Council, 1983

Erickson, Rica. *Old Toodyay and Newcastle.* Toodyay Shire Council, 1974

Jackson, Janice. *Not An Idle Man, A Biography of John Septimus Roe.* M. B. Roe, 1982

Lake, Max. *Scents and Sensuality, The Essence of Excitement.* John Murray, London, 1989

Robinson, Jancis. *Vine Grapes and Wines: The Wine Drinker's Guide to Grape Varieties.* Knopf, 1986

Acknowledgements

WINE IS a colourful subject, and this book owes much to the talents of many photographers whose work is represented here. In particular I would like to thank colleagues from the photographic department of West Australian Newspapers Limited for their enthusiastic assistance: Barry Baker, Kerry Edwards, Nic Ellis, Mal Fairclough, Mogens Johansen, Guy Magowan, John Mokrzycki, Don Palmer, Bill Plowman, Sharon Smith and Joe Wheeler. In dozens of instances, wineries themselves provided their own photographic material, and I express my sincere appreciation to them and their respective photographers for their support. Without this, the compilation of pictures would have been considerably more difficult. Some photographs too were provided by the Department of Agriculture, and I thank them for this gesture.